Land Licences

Land Licences

John Sharples

Published by
Jordan Publishing Limited
21 St Thomas Street
Bristol BS1 6JS

Whilst the publishers and the author have taken every care in preparing the material included in this work, any statements made as to the legal or other implications of particular transactions are made in good faith purely for general guidance and cannot be regarded as a substitute for professional advice. Consequently, no liability can be accepted for loss or expense incurred as a result of relying in particular circumstances on statements made in this work.

© Jordan Publishing Ltd 2011

All rights reserved. No part of this publication may be reproduced, stored in a retrieval system, or transmitted in any way or by any means, including photocopying or recording, without the written permission of the copyright holder, application for which should be addressed to the publisher.

Crown Copyright material is reproduced with kind permission of the Controller of Her Majesty's Stationery Office.

British Library Cataloguing-in-Publication Data

A catalogue record for this book is available from the British Library.

ISBN 978 1 84661 098 1

Typeset by Letterpart Ltd, Reigate, Surrey

Printed in Great Britain by CPI Antony Rowe, Chippenham, Wiltshire

For my daughter, Grace

FOREWORD

The topic of land licences is one which, 100 years ago, would hardly have merited more than a couple of paragraphs in a book – even one about land law or contract law – and yet now it clearly justifies a whole book. The point is well made by considering how few of the cases in the Table of Cases in this book were decided before 1900; indeed, a remarkable proportion of the cases were decided within the past twenty-five years. Land licences represent a fast-growing topic.

It is also an interesting, difficult, and important topic. It is interesting because it covers an area which involves an overlap of various different areas of law, most notably two fundamental areas of law, land law and contract law, whose principles do not always easily lie together. This leads to fascinating problems, such as the relationship of licences with easements and profits, the extent to which rights and obligations can bind successors, licences in the context of construction contracts, and the effect of licences when entered into by members of the same family are but four familiar examples. Also, there is often the impact of a statutory provision to consider – eg sections of the Law of Property Act 1925, the Agricultural Holdings Act 1986, the Limitation Act 1980, the Mobile Homes legislation, and some of the Housing Acts.

The topic is often difficult, not only for the same sort of reasons, but also because it represents a subject which often embraces other areas of law, which are themselves in a state of development: examples that spring to mind include proprietary estoppel and human rights (particularly article 8 of the European Convention on Human Rights). There are a number of problems in relation to licences where there has been a sharp difference of judicial opinion – in addition to some of the topics already mentioned, there is the distinction between a licence and a tenancy, the effect of a lawful, or an unlawful, termination, equitable rights arising from licences, and the interrelationship of licences and the acquiring of limitation rights.

Land licences comprise an important topic, because land plays a more and more important role in society, as is demonstrated by the ever-growing volume of litigation and legislation relating to the topic. Further, because of their traditionally essentially simple contractual nature, and because of the volume of legislation relating to tenancies, licences have been used over the past fifty years or so by landowners.

There is no doubt that a modern, authoritative, well-structured, comprehensive and readable book on land licences is required, and I am pleased to be able to say that John Sharples has written such a book. And the fact that it contains useful appendices shows that it is directed at practitioners, as well as to non-practising lawyers.

Lord Neuberger of Abbotsbury
Master of the Rolls

ACKNOWLEDGMENTS

The appearance of the name of a single author is often, as in this case, deceptive. I should wish to acknowledge my thanks to Jordan Publishing for their kindness and consideration, in particular to Tony Hawitt for his gentle encouragement and patience.

I must also extend my thanks to fellow members of St John's Chambers in Bristol who made comments on early versions of the text, especially Matthew White for his input to Chapter 11 (**11.1–11.29**) and Leslie Blohm QC who had the kindness and stamina to read the majority of the book. Any remaining errors are, of course, my sole responsibility. I should also thank my family, who were forced to put up without me for long periods of time during the research and writing of this book.

Finally, I wish to extend my profound gratitude to Lord Neuberger, Master of the Rolls, for his opening remarks.

The law is stated as at 18 November 2010.

CONTENTS

Foreword	vii
Acknowledgments	ix
Table of Cases	xxi
Table of Statutes	xlvii
Table of Statutory Instruments	liii

Chapter 1
Introduction 1

Chapter 2
The Nature and Types of Licences 5
The nature of the licence 5
  The concept of the licence 5
  Distinguishing licences from other private rights/interests 6
  Distinguishing licences and public rights 7
Types of licences 7
  Bare licences 8
    Bare licence granted on terms 8
  Contractual licences 8
    Family arrangements and contractual intent 9
    The imputation of contractual intent 9
    Consideration 10
  Licences coupled with an interest 11
  Estoppel licences 12
Licences and possession 13
  The relevance of possession 13
  Factual possession 15
  The right to possession 16

Chapter 3
Licences Distinguished from Other Rights/Interests 19
Licences and leases 20
  The concept of exclusive possession 23
  The nature of the right 23
  Joint possession, licensees and sharing agreements 24
  Terms negativing/indicating exclusive possession 25
  Terms: shams 27
  Terms: the parties' expressed intentions 28

Occupation pending negotiations	29
Licences and bailment	30
Licences and easements/profits	30
Licences and trusts	32
Customary rights	33
Town and village greens	33
Highways	34
Wayleaves	34
Matrimonial homes rights	35

Chapter 4
Creation of Licences

Creation of Licences	**37**
The licensor's status	37
Co-owners	37
Bare licences	38
Express licences	38
Unilateral licences	38
Sufficient manifestation of consent	39
The user's position	39
Express disclaimer	40
Implied disclaimer	40
Unauthorised/part-unauthorised user	41
Implied licences	41
Overt conduct justifying the inference of consent	42
Encouragement etc as overt conduct	45
Circumstances justifying the inference of consent	46
Contractual licences	47
Implied contractual licences	48
Contractual licences arising by conduct	48
Licences coupled with an interest	49
Estoppel licences	50
The expectation	50
The nature of the reliance	52
The nature of the detriment	52
Unconscionability	52
Relief granted	53

Chapter 5
Licences and Adverse Rights

Licences and Adverse Rights	**55**
General	55
The nature of consent	58
The quality of consent necessary to prevent the acquisition of adverse rights	58
User in excess of the licence	61
Limited duration	61
Limited scope	62
Permission to limited persons	63

Licences and limitation	63
General	63
Limitation by licensee against licensor	64
Possession during the subsistence of the licence	64
Continued use after licence expires	64
Effect of grant/renewal of licence after limitation period expires	65
Limitation against true owner	65
Limitation in favour of third parties	66
Licences and prescription	67
Licensees and prescription	67
Meaning of consent	67
Form of consent	68
Licensors and prescription	68
Prescription by third parties	68
Licences and public rights of way	69
Licences and town or village greens	70
Custom	71

Chapter 6
Occupation Licences

	73
Introduction	73
Business licences	74
General	74
Distinguishing leases and licences	75
Nature of the right	76
Typical business licences	77
Partnership	77
Shared or serviced office accommodation	77
Shops, market stalls and concession stands	77
Advertising hoardings	78
Front-of-house rights	78
Mineral rights	78
Building licences	78
Agricultural licences	79
Licences subject to conversion	79
Exceptions	81
The effect of the application of the Agricultural Holdings Act 1986	82
Residential licences	83
Lodgers	83
Holiday accommodation	84
Mobile structures	84
Occupation referable to some other relationship	84
Service occupiers	85
Test for service occupier	85
Date for applying test	86
Occupation in anticipation of performing duties	87
Post-employment occupation	87
Effect of service occupation	87

Residential licensees with security of tenure	88
Public authority accommodation	88
Licences treated as secure tenancies	88
Licences treated as introductory tenancies	91
Restricted contracts	91
Agricultural workers	92
Occupation under the Rent (Agriculture) Act 1976	93
Assured agricultural occupancies under the Housing Act 1988	94
Mobile Homes Act licensees	95
Caravan Sites Act 1968	97
Matrimonial home rights	99

Chapter 7
User Licences

	103
Introduction	103
User licences and easements/profits	104
General	104
Licences and the ouster principle	105
Types of user rights	107
Access	107
Limited activities	108
Rights to place/erect something on the land	108
Parking/storage rights	108
Licences to place structures on land	110
Licences to remove things from land	110

Chapter 8
The Licence Terms

	113
Bare licences	113
Contractual licences	114
Ascertaining the terms	114
Incorporation of terms	114
Construction of terms	115
Express terms	116
Implied terms	116
Particular terms	117
Scope of the licence	117
Exclusivity	118
Assignment and sub-licences	119
Termination	119
Right to terminate	119
Termination for breach	122
Manner of termination	122
The licensor's obligations	122
Title	122
Quiet enjoyment, not to interfere etc	123
Non-derogation from grant	125
Fitness for purpose	126

Repair and maintenance	128
Security	129
The licensee's obligations	130
Payment of licence fee	130
Licensee estopped from denying licensor's title	130
Responsibility for the condition of the premises	130
Statutory control of terms	131
Unfair Contract Terms Act 1977 and Unfair Terms in Consumer Contracts Regulations 1999	131
Supply of Goods and Services Act 1982	132
Licences with security of tenure	132
Housing Act 1985 licences	132
Restricted contracts under the Rent Act 1977, s 19	133
Agricultural workers	133
Agricultural holdings	134
Mobile homes occupiers	134
Estoppel licences	135
The basic equitable right	135
The relief	135
Licences coupled with an interest	136

Chapter 9
The Burden of the Licence — 137

The licensor's successors in title	138
General	138
The need to register – registered land	138
The need to register – unregistered land	139
Bare licences	139
Contractual licences	140
The general rule	140
The licence as a proprietary interest	140
The current position	140
Exceptions to the general rule	141
Constructive trust	141
New licences	144
Licences with statutory security of tenure	145
Tort	145
Licences coupled with an interest	146
Licences and the mutual benefit and burden principle	146
Estoppel licences	148
Inchoate equity – unregistered land	148
Inchoate equity – registered land	149
Effect after judgment	149
Licences converted by the Law of Property Act 1925, s 62	150
Matrimonial home rights	150
Licences together with other interests	151
Licensee's interest	151
Licensor's interest	152

Persons with a superior interest to the licensor	152
Persons deriving title through the licensor	155
Persons with no right to use the land	155
Trespass	155
Claim by the licensor	155
Claim by the licensee	156
Nuisance	157

Chapter 10
The Benefit of the Licence — **159**

Assignment of the licence	159
Bare licences	159
Contractual licences	160
Assignment	160
Are the benefits assignable?	161
Express prohibitions/limitations on assignment	161
Implied prohibitions on assignment	163
Manner of assignment	164
Effect of prohibited assignment	165
Between the licensee/assignee and licensor	165
Between the licensee and assignee	166
Effect of valid assignment	167
Between licensee/assignee and licensor	167
Novation	168
Licences and the mutual benefit and burden principle	169
Licences coupled with an interest	169
Estoppel licences	170
Inchoate equity	170
Assignment of the equity	170
Independent equity of stranger	171
Post judgment	171
Sub-licences	171
Bare licences	171
Contractual licences	172
Right to create sub-licences	172
Sub-licences created in compliance with licence	173
Sub-licences created in breach of term	174
Licences and the mutual benefit and burden principle	174
Licences coupled with an interest	174
Estoppel licences	174
Bruton tenancies	175

Chapter 11
The Parties' Non-contractual Rights and Obligations — **177**

Liability arising from the condition or use of the premises	178
Occupiers' Liability Act 1957	178
The scope of the duty	178
The nature of the duty	179

The person who owes the duty	181
One/both parties in occupation	181
The persons to whom the duty is owed	184
Exclusion or restriction of the duty	185
Occupiers' Liability Act 1984	185
Defective Premises Act 1972	187
Works in connection with provision of dwelling	187
Licensor's obligation to repair/maintain (s 4(1))	187
Licensor's right to repair/maintain (s 4(4))	188
Negligence	188
Liability for escape of dangerous things	190
Private nuisance	191
Causation	191
Authorisation	191
Adoption	192
Continuation	192
Non-domestic rates	193
Council tax	194
Tax implications of granting the licence	195
Value added tax	195
Stamp duty land tax	199
Statutory compensation on compulsory acquisition	200
General	200
Disturbance payments	200
Home loss payments	201
Planning and environmental liabilities	201
Planning control	201
Environmental Protection Act 1990	202

Chapter 12
Termination of Licences

	205
Bare licences	205
Effluxion of time	205
Automatic determination	206
Notice/demand	207
Notice by licensor	208
Notice by occupier	209
Notice by licensee	209
Contractual licences	210
Effluxion of time	210
Automatic determination	210
Exercise of option	211
Termination on notice	211
Manner of exercise – express term	212
Manner of exercise – implied term	213
(Non-)compliant notices	214
What constitutes reasonable notice?	217
Form and contents of notice	219

Service on recipient	222
Termination for breach	223
Repudiation	224
Agreement, abandonment	224
Frustration	224
Disclaimer	226
Miscellaneous non-contractual limitations on termination	226
Wrongful purported termination	227
Specifically performable licences	227
Licences that are not specifically performable	229
Licences coupled with an interest	229
Estoppel licences	230
The inchoate equity	230
The relief	230
The grace period	231
When the period applies	231
The length and purpose of the period	232

Chapter 13
Post Termination   235

The licensee's obligations on termination	237
Obligation to quit	237
Sub-licences and *Bruton* tenants	237
Removal of chattels	237
Things incorporated into the land	239
Obligation to remove/reinstate	239
Right to remove	239
Land, fixtures and chattels	239
Enforcing the licensee's obligations	240
Self-help	240
Injunction	244
Possession	244
Remedy	244
Procedure	245
Damages for continued use of land after expiry of licence	246

Appendix 1
Sample Licences   249

Informal gratuitous licence	249
Contractual licence to share house	250
Licence to use structure on licensor's land	254
Contractual licence to use serviced office accommodation	257
Licence of part of commercial premises including provision of services by licensee	263
Novation agreement regarding shared occupation by licensees	267

Appendix 2
Notices **271**
Licensor's consent to assignment 271
Notice of assignment of benefit of licence 272
Notice to terminate bare licence (non-dated) 272
Notice to terminate licence (terminable forthwith) 273
Notice to terminate periodic licence terminable at end of period
    (non-dwelling) 273
Notice to terminate periodic licence at end of period (dwelling) 273
Notice to terminate periodic licence terminable on reasonable notice
    (non-dwelling) or indefinite licence 274
Notice to terminate periodic licence terminable on reasonable notice
    (dwelling) 274
Agent's notice to terminate licence requiring dated notice 275
Licensee's notice to terminate indefinite or periodic licence terminable
    on reasonable notice (non-dwelling) 276
Letter in response agreeing to accept short service 276
Acknowledgement of title preventing running of limitation period 276
Acknowledgement of title preventing acquisition of prescriptive rights 277

Appendix 3
Statements of Case **279**
Claim Form – injunction/possession 279
Particulars of Claim – licence fee arrears 280
Particulars of Claim for injunction/damages to restrain trespass after
    termination of contractual licence 280
Particulars of Claim for possession (adapting Form N.121) 282
Defence – licence not expired 284
Defence – estoppel 285

Index **287**

TABLE OF CASES

References are to paragraph numbers.

A-G of Belize v Belize Telecom Ltd [2009] UKPC 10, [2009] 1 WLR 1988, [2009] Bus LR 1316, [2009] 2 All ER 1127, [2009] 2 All ER (Comm) 1, [2009] BCC 433, [2009] 2 BCLC 148	4.27, 8.11
A-G of Southern Nigeria v John Holt & Co (Liverpool) Ltd [1915] AC 599	7.6
A-G v Blake (Jonathan Cape Ltd third party) [1998] Ch 439, [1998] 1 All ER 833, [1998] 2 WLR 805, [1998] 04 LS Gaz R 33, [1998] NLJR 15, 142 Sol Jo LB 35, [1998] EMLR 309, CA, [2001] 1 AC 268, [2000] 4 All ER 385, [2000] 2 All ER (Comm) 487, [2000] 3 WLR 625, [2000] NLJR 1230, [2000] 32 LS Gaz R 37, 144 Sol Jo LB 242, [2000] EMLR 949, [2001] 1 LRC 260, [2000] All ER (D) 1074, [2000] IP & T 1261, HL	13.26
A-G v Corke [1933] Ch 89	11.31
A-G v Tod-Heatley [1897] 1 Ch 560	11.31
Abbey National Building Society v Cann [1991] 1 AC 56, [1990] 2 WLR 832, [1990] 1 All ER 1085, [1990] 2 FLR 122, (1990) 22 HLR 360, (1990) 60 P & CR 278, (1990) 87(17) LSG 32, (1990) 140 NLJ 477, (1990) *Times*, 30 March	6.1, 9.40
AC Billings & Sons Ltd v Riden [1958] AC 240, [1957] 3 WLR 496, [1957] 3 All ER 1, (1957) 101 Sol Jo 645	11.26
Addiscombe Garden Estates v Crabbe [1957] 2 QB 615, [1957] 2 WLR 964, [1957] 2 All ER 205, 101 Sol Jo 410, QBD; [1958] 1 QB 513, [1957] 3 WLR 980, [1957] 3 All ER 563, 101 Sol Jo 959; [1958] 1 QB 513, [1957] 3 WLR 980, [1957] 3 All ER 563, [2008] BTC 7020, (1957) 101 Sol Jo 959, CA	3.13, 3.16, 8.29, 8.47
Admiral Taverns (Cygnet) Ltd v Daniel [2008] EWCA Civ 1501, [2009] 1 WLR 2192, [2009] 4 All ER 71, [2009] CP Rep 17, [2009] L & TR 19, [2009] 1 EGLR 35, [2009] 10 EG 112, [2008] 48 EG 100 (CS), (2009) *Times*, 12 January	13.22
AG Securities v Vaughan, Antoniades v Villiers 1990 1 AC 417, [1988] 3 WLR 1205, [1988] 3 All ER 1058, (1989) 21 HLR 79, (1989) 57 P & CR 17, [1988] 47 EG 193, [1988] EG 153 (CS), (1989) 86(1) LSG 39, (1988) 138 NLJ Rep 325, (1988) 132 Sol Jo 1638, (1988) *Times*, 11 November	3.8, 3.9, 3.15
Akici v LR Butlin Ltd [2005] EWCA Civ 1296, [2006] 1 WLR 201, [2006] 2 All ER 872, [2006] 1 P & CR 21, [2006] L & TR 1, [2006] 1 EGLR 34, [2006] 07 EG 136, [2005] 45 EG 168 (CS), (2005) 149 SJLB 1352, [2005] NPC 126	9.44
Albany Construction Ltd v Cunningham [2004] EWHC 3392	9.6
Aldin v Latimer Clark Muirhead & Co [1894] 2 Ch 437, 63 LJ Ch 601	12.8, 12.40
Alfred F Beckett Ltd v Lyons [1967] Ch 449, [1967] 2 WLR 421, [1967] 1 All ER 833, 65 LGR 73, (1966) 110 Sol Jo 925, (1966) *Times*, 30 November	4.18, 4.23
Allam & Co v Europa Poster Services [1968] 1 WLR 638, [1968] 1 All ER 826, (1968) 112 Sol Jo 86	12.19, 12.25
Allan v Liverpool Overseers (1874) LR 9 QB 180	9.53

Allen v Matthews [2007] EWCA Civ 216, [2007] BPIR 281, [2007] 2 P & CR
    21, [2007] NPC 30   4.14
Alston & Sons Ltd v BOCM Pauls Ltd [2008] EWHC 3310 (Ch), [2009] 1
    EGLR 93   2.34
Altman v Royal Aquarium Society (1876) LR 3 Ch D 228   8.15
American Cyanamid v Ethicon [1975] AC 396, [1975] 2 WLR 316, [1975] 1
    All ER 504, [1975] FSR 101, [1975] RPC 513, (1975) 119 Sol Jo 136   13.19
AMF International v Magnet Bowling [1968] 1 WLR 1028, [1968] 2 All ER
    789, 66 LGR 706, (1968) 112 Sol Jo 522   8.39, 11.4, 11.12
Andrews v Cunningham [2007] EWCA Civ 762, [2008] HLR 13, [2008] L &
    TR 1, [2007] NPC 93   12.25
Annen v Rattee [1985] 1 EGLR 136   4.3
Anthony v Coal Authority [2005] EWHC 1654 (QB), [2006] Env LR 17   11.37
Appah v Parncliffe Investments Ltd [1964] 1 WLR 1064, [1964] 1 All ER
    838, (1964) 108 Sol Jo 155   3.21, 8.43, 11.26
Armstrong v Sheppard & Short Ltd [1959] 2 QB 384, [199] 2 All ER 651,
    [1959] 3 WLR 84, 123 JP 401, 103 Sol Jo 508, CA   13.10
Arscott v Coal Authority [2004] EWCA Civ 892, [2005] Env LR 6, (2004)
    148 SJLB 880, [2004] NPC 114   11.27
Arthur v Anker [1997] QB 564, [1996] 2 WLR 602, [1996] 3 All ER 783,
    [1996] RTR 308, (1996) 72 P & CR 309, (1996) 146 NLJ 86, [1995]
    NPC 187, (1996) 71 P & CR D28, (1995) *Times*, 1 December, (1995)
    Independent, 7 December   13.8, 13.9
Ashburn Anstalt Ltd v Arnold [1989] Ch 1, [1988] 2 WLR 706, [1988] 2 All
    ER 147, (1988) 55 P & CR 137, (1987) 284 EG 1375, (1988) 132 Sol
    Jo 416, (1987) *Times*, 9 November   1.8, 2.17, 2.25, 9.3, 9.9, 9.12–9.15, 9.17
Ashby v Tolhurst [1937] 2 KB 242, [1937] 2 All ER 837, 53 TLR 770, CA   2.37, 3.21, 7.13, 8.43
Ashdale Land Property Co v Mannus [1992] 2 EGLR 5   6.17
Asher v Whitlock (1865) LR 1 QB 1   2.32, 9.53
Aslan v Murphy (No 1) and (No 2), Duke v Wynne [1990] 1 WLR 766,
    [1989] 3 All ER 130, (1989) 21 HLR 532, (1990) 59 P & CR 407,
    [1989] 38 EG 109, [1989] EG 98 (CS), (1989) 139 NLJ 936, (1989)
    Independent, 28June   3.13
Aspden v Seddon, No 2 (1876) 1 Ex D 496   10.22
Attorney-General v Antrobus [1905] 2 Ch 188   5.32
Attorney-General v Teddington UDC [1989] 1 Ch 66   5.2
Australian Blue Metal Ltd v Hughes and others [1963] AC 74, [1962] 3
    WLR 802, [1962] 3 All ER 335, 106 Sol Jo 628, PC   8.19, 12.3, 12.10, 12.17, 12.18,
                                                      12.22–12.24, 12.47, 12.52, 12.53

Bahamas International Trust Co Ltd v Threadgold [1974] 1 WLR 1514,
    [1974] 3 All ER 881, (1974) 118 Sol Jo 832   6.18
Balfour v Balfour [1919] 2 KB 521   2.15, 2.16
Balthasar v Mullane (1985) 17 HLR 561, 84 LGR 55, (1986) 51 P & CR
    107, [1985] 2 EGLR 260, [1986] JPL 751   6.56, 6.60
BANES v Nicholson [2002] All ER (D) 327 (Feb)   4.16, 4.17, 8.18, 12.3
Bannister v Bannister [1948] 2 All ER 133, [1948] WN 261, (1948) 92 Sol Jo
    377   9.14
Barbados Trust Co Ltd v Bank of Zambia [2007] EWCA Civ 148, [2007] 2
    All ER (Comm) 445, [2007] 1 Lloyd's Rep 495, [2007] 1 CLC 434,
    (2006-07) 9 ITELR 689   10.11, 10.18, 10.20
Barnes v Barratt [1970] 2 QB 657, [1970] 2 WLR 1085, [1970] 2 All ER 483,
    (1970) 21 P & CR 347, (1970) 114 Sol Jo 265   3.3
Barraclough v Johnson 112 ER 773, (1838) 8 Ad & El 99   5.32
Batchelor v Marlow [2001] EWCA Civ 1051, [2003] 1 WLR 764, [2003] 4 All
    ER 78, [2003] RTR 16, (2001) 82 P & CR 36, (2001) 98(28) LSG 45,
    [2001] NPC 111, (2001) 82 P & CR DG17   3.24, 7.6–7.9, 7.13
Batsford Estates (1983) Ltd v Taylor [2005] EWCA Civ 489, [2006] 2 P &
    CR 5, [2005] 2 EGLR 12, [2005] 33 EG 68, [2005] 19 EG 174 (CS)   4.16, 4.17
Baybut v Eccle Riggs Country Park Ltd (2006) *Times*, 13 November   8.18, 8.20, 8.52, 9.9, 9.18,
                                                            9.19, 9.28, 9.31, 10.23

Table of Cases

Belvedere Court Mgmt Ltd v Frogmore Dvpts Ltd [1997] QB 858, [1996] 3 WLR 1008, [1996] 1 All ER 312, (1996) 28 HLR 398, [1996] 1 EGLR 59, [1996] 05 EG 131, [1995] EG 159 (CS), [1995] NPC 158	3.15
Berkley v Poulett [1977] 1 EGLR 86, (1977) 241 EG 911, (1976) 120 Sol Jo 836, (1976) *Times*, 4 November	13.14
Berrisford v Mexfield Housing Co-Operative Ltd [2010] EWCA Civ 811, [2010] HLR 44, [2010] 2 EGLR 137, [2010] 29 EG 87 (CS)	3.1, 3.4, 7.4, 12.29
Bettison v Langton 2001 UKHL 24, [2002] 1 AC 27, [2001] 2 WLR 1605, [2001] 3 All ER 417, (2001) 82 P & CR 37, [2001] 21 EG 166 (CS), (2001) 98(26) LSG 44, (2001) 145 SJLB 141, [2001] NPC 92, (2001) *Times*, 30 May	3.24
Beverley Corpn v Richard Hodgson & Sons Ltd (1972) 225 EG 799	8.19, 8.20
Binions v Evans [1972] Ch 359, [1972] 2 WLR 729, [1972] 2 All ER 70, (1972) 23 P & CR 192, (1972) 116 Sol Jo 122	9.8, 9.9, 9.14, 9.15, 10.32
Bird v Great Eastern Rly Co (1865) 19 CBNS 268	11.51
Birmingham DC v Kelly (1985) 17 HLR 572	11.60
Birmingham Dudley & District Banking Co v Ross (1888) 38 ChD 295	9.36
Birmingham Midshires Mortgage Services Ltd v Sabherwal (2000) 80 P & CR 256	9.29, 9.32
Blewett v Blewett [1936] 2 All ER 188	12.27
BMTA v Salvadori [1949] Ch 556, [1949] 1 All ER 208, 65 TLR 44, [1949] LJR 1304	9.21
Bolch v Smith 158 ER 666, (1862) 7 Hurl & N 736	2.36, 8.1
Bomford v South Worcestershire Assessment Committee [1947] KB 575, [1947] 1 All ER 299, 63 TLR 141, (1947) 111 JP 202, [1947] LJR 660, (1947) 91 Sol Jo 192	8.37
Bone v Bone [1992] EGCS 81	12.32
Booker v Palmer [1942] 2 All ER 674	2.15, 2.36, 3.4
Bostock v Bryant (1990) 22 HLR 449, (1991) 61 P & CR 23, [1990] 39 EG 64, [1990] EG 89 (CS), (1990) *Times*, 29 June	2.19
Bottomley v Todmorden Cricket Club [2004] PIQR 277	11.26
Bower v Peate [1876] 1 QBD 321	11.31
BP Properties Ltd v Buckler (1988) 55 P & CR 337, (1987) 284 EG 375, (1987) 137 NLJ 899	4.9–4.11, 4.16, 4.28, 5.4, 12.10
Bracewell v Appleby [1975] Ch 408, [1975] 2 WLR 282, [1975] 1 All ER 993, (1975) 29 P & CR 204, (1974) 119 Sol Jo 114	13.27
Braithwaite v South Durham Steel Co Ltd and another [1958] 3 All ER 161, [1958] 1 WLR 986, 102 Sol Jo 655	11.7
Bramley v Chesterton (1857) 2 CBNS 592	13.23
Bretherton v Paton (1986) 18 HLR 257, [1986] 1 EGLR 172, (1986) 278 EG 615	3.18, 13.3
Brew Bros v Snax (Ross) [1970] 1 QB 612, [1969] 3 WLR 657, [1970] 1 All ER 587, (1969) 20 P & CR 829, (1969) 113 Sol Jo 795	11.36
Bridle v Ruby [1989] 1 QB 169	5.2
Bright v Walker 150 ER 1057, (1834) 1 Cr M & R 211	5.4
Brikom Investments Ltd v Carr [1979] QB 467, [1979] 2 WLR 737, [1979] 2 All ER 753, (1979) 38 P & CR 326, (1978) 251 EG 359	10.30
Brillouet v Landless (1995) 28 HLR 836	13.16
British Anzani (Felixstowe) Ltd v International Marine Management (UK) Ltd [1980] QB 137, [1979] 3 WLR 451, [1979] 2 All ER 1063, (1980) 39 P & CR 189, (1978) 250 EG 1183, (1979) 123 Sol Jo 64	8.45
British Waggon Co v Lea & Co (1880) 5 QBD 149	10.4
Brocklebank v Thompson [1903] 2 Ch 344	5.37
Brown v Brash [1948] 2 KB 247, [1948] 1 All ER 922, 64 TLR 266, [1948] LJR 1544, (1948) 92 Sol Jo 376	9.47
Brown v Draper [1944] KB 309, [1944] 1 All ER 246	3.38
Bruton v London & Quadrant Housing Trust [2000] 1 AC 406, [1999] 3 WLR 150, [1999] 3 All ER 481, (1999) 31 HLR 902, [1999] L & TR 469, [1999] 2 EGLR 59, [1999] 30 EG 91, [1999] EG 90 (CS), (1999)	

Bruton v London & Quadrant Housing Trust [2000] 1 AC 406, [1999] 3 WLR 150, [1999] 3 All ER 481, (1999) 31 HLR 902, [1999] L & TR 469, [1999] 2 EGLR 59, [1999] 30 EG 91, [1999] EG 90 (CS), (1999) —*continued*
96(28) LSG 26, (1999) 149 NLJ 1001, (1999) 143 SJLB 195, [1999] NPC 73, (1999) 78 P & CR D21, (1999) *Times*, 25 June ... 1.9, 2.30, 3.1, 3.3, 3.13, 3.16, 9.46, 10.48, 13.5

Brynowen Estates Ltd v Bourne (1981) 131 NLJ 1212 ... 8.62, 12.49

Buckinghamshire CC v Moran [1990] Ch 623, [1989] 3 WLR 152, [1989] 2 All ER 225, 88 LGR 145, (1989) 58 P & CR 236, [1989] EG 21 (CS), (1989) 139 NLJ 257, (1989) 133 Sol Jo 849 ... 4.22, 5.16, 5.17

Bulstrode v Lambert [1953] 1 WLR 1064, [1953] 2 All ER 728, (1953) 97 Sol Jo 652, (1953) 97 Sol Jo 557 ... 8.13

Burns v Anthony (1997) 74 P & CR D41 ... 2.34

Burrows v Brent LBC [1996] 1 WLR 1448, [1996] 4 All ER 577, [1997] 1 FLR 178, HL ... 5.2

Burton v Winters [1993] 1 WLR 1077, [1993] 3 All ER 847 ... 13.15

Byrne v Kinematograph Renters Society Ltd [1958] 1 WLR 762, [1958] 2 All ER 579, (1958) 102 Sol Jo 509 ... 5.10, 11.7

C&P Haulage v Middleton [1983] 1 WLR 1461, [1983] 3 All ER 94, (1983) 127 Sol Jo 730 ... 12.40, 13.12

Cal Brown Ltd v Van Wagner UK Ltd [2005] EWHC 1901 ... 13.7, 13.21

Cambridge CC v Douglas [2000] All ER (D) 2424 ... 11.60

Cambridge Water Co v Eastern Counties Leather plc [1994] 2 AC 264, [1994] 2 WLR 53, [1994] 1 All ER 53, [1994] 1 Lloyd's Rep 261, [1994] Env LR 105, [1993] EG 211 (CS), (1994) 144 NLJ 15, (1994) 138 SJLB 24, (1993) *Times*, 10 December, (1993) *Independent*, 10 December ... 11.27

Camden LBC v McBride [1999] CL 3737 ... 8.53

Camden LBC v Shortlife Community Housing Ltd (1993) 25 HLR 330, 90 LGR 358, [1992] EG 31 (CS), [1992] NPC 52, (1992) *Times*, 12 March ... 3.16, 4.24

Cameron Ltd v Rolls-Royce plc [2007] EWHC 546 (Ch), [2008] L & TR 22 ... 3.3, 3.18, 3.20

Canadian Imperial Bank of Commerce v Bello (1992) 24 HLR 155, (1992) 64 P & CR 48, [1991] EG 126 (CS), (1992) 89(3) LSG 32, (1992) 136 SJLB 9, [1991] NPC 123, (1991) *Times*, 18 November ... 6.15, 9.5, 9.9

Canadian Pacific Railway Co v The King [1931] AC 414 ... 4.17, 4.18, 12.6, 12.7, 12.21, 12.23, 12.24

Canter v Gardner & Co [1940] 1 All ER 325 ... 11.26

Capital Prime Properties Ltd v Worthgate Ltd [2000] BCC 525, [2000] 1 BCLC 647, [1999] EG 112 (CS) ... 12.36

Cardiothoracic Institute v Shrewdcrest Ltd [1986] 1 WLR 368, [1986] 3 All ER 633, [1986] 2 EGLR 57, (1986) 279 EG 69, (1986) 83 LSG 1063, (1986) 130 Sol Jo 244 ... 3.18, 13.3

Carmichael v National Power plc [1999] 1 WLR 2042, [1999] 4 All ER 897, [1999] ICR 1226, [2000] IRLR 43, (1999) 96(46) LSG 38, (1999) 143 SJLB 281, (1999) *Times*, 23 November, (1999) *Independent*, 25 November ... 8.8

Carr v Benson (1867-68) LR 3 Ch App 524 ... 8.16

Cartwright v Merthyr Tydfil BC (unreported), CA, 22 May 2000 ... 8.8, 8.13, 8.16, 8.25, 8.30, 9.53

Cavalier v Pope [1906] AC 428, [1904-7] All ER Rep Ext 1221, 75 LJKB 609, 95 LT 65, 22 TLR 648, 50 Sol Jo 575 ... 8.11, 10.48

Central Midland Estates Ltd v Leicester Dyers Ltd (2003) 100(11) LSG 33, [2003] 2 P & CR DG1, (2003) *Times*, 18 February, (2003) *Independent*, 3 March ... 7.6

Chamberlain v Farr [1942] 2 All ER 567 ... 3.19

Chandler v Kerley [1978] 1 WLR 693, [1978] 2 All ER 942, (1978) 8 Fam Law 108, (1978) 122 Sol Jo 332 ... 1.8, 2.17, 2.18, 9.14, 12.24

Charing Cross Electricity Supply Co v Hydraulic Power Co [1914] 3 KB 772 ... 11.27

Chartered Trust Plc v Davies (1998) 76 P & CR 396, [1997] 2 EGLR 83, [1997] 49 EG 135, [1997] NPC 125, (1998) 75 P & CR D6 ... 8.30, 8.34

Table of Cases

Chattey v Farndale Holdings Inc (1998) 75 P & CR 298, [1997] 1 EGLR 153, [1997] 06 EG 152, [1996] NPC 136, (1996) *Times*, 17 October — 9.17
Chelsea Yacht & Boat Co Ltd v Pope [2000] 1 WLR 1941, [2001] 2 All ER 409, (2001) 33 HLR 25, [2000] L & TR 401, [2000] 2 EGLR 23, [2000] 22 EG 139, (2000) 80 P & CR D36, (2000) *Times*, 7 June — 3.7, 13.14
Clarence House Ltd v Nat West Bank [2009] EWCA Civ 1311, [2010] 1 WLR 1216, [2010] Bus LR 1066, [2010] 2 All ER 201, [2010] 2 All ER (Comm) 1065, [2010] 2 P & CR 9, [2010] L & TR 1, [2010] 1 EGLR 43, [2010] 8 EG 106, [2009] 50 EG 66 (CS), [2009] NPC 141 — 9.44
Clark v Adie, No 2 (1876-77) LR 2 App Cas 423 — 8.25
Clarke v Grant [1950] 1 KB 104, [1949] 1 All ER 768, 65 TLR 241, [1949] LJR 1450, (1949) 93 Sol Jo 249 — 13.3
Clayton v Sale UDC [1926] 1 KB 415 — 11.59
Cleadon Trust Ltd v Davis [1940] Ch 940 — 9.13
Clear Channel UK Ltd v Manchester City Council [2005] EWCA Civ 1304, [2006] L & TR 7, [2006] 1 EGLR 27, [2006] 04 EG 168, [2006] 1 P & CR DG17 — 3.4, 3.16, 6.3, 6.12, 7.14
Clevedon Trust Ltd v Davis [1990] Ch 940 — 13.5
Clore v Theatrical Properties Ltd [1936] 3 All ER 483 — 3.6, 6.6, 9.8, 9.14, 10.14
Clowes Developments (UK) Ltd v Walters [2005] EWHC 669 (Ch), [2006] 1 P & CR 1, [2005] 17 EG 123 (CS) — 4.18, 5.17, 9.7, 9.18
Cobb v Lane [1952] 1 All ER 1199, [1952] 1 TLR 1037, [1952] WN 196, (1952) 96 Sol Jo 295 — 1.8, 2.15, 2.30, 3.5
Cobbe v Yeoman's Row Management Ltd [2008] UKHL 55, [2008] 1 WLR 1752, [2008] 4 All ER 713, [2009] 1 All ER (Comm) 205, [2008] 3 EGLR 31, [2008] 35 EG 142, [2008] 36 EG 142, [2008] WTLR 1461, (2008-09) 11 ITELR 530, [2008] 31 EG 88 (CS), (2008) 152(31) SJLB 31, [2008] NPC 95, (2008) *Times*, 8 September — 1.12, 4.33, 4.35, 4.36
Colchester & East Essex Co-op Ltd v Kelvedon Labour Club & Institute Ltd [2003] EWCA Civ 1671 — 8.19, 12.12
Colchester & East Sussex Co-op Ltd v Kelvedon Labour Club & Institute Ltd [2003] EWCA Civ 1671 — 8.20
Colchester BC v Smith [1991] Ch 448, [1991] 2 WLR 540, [1991] 2 All ER 29, (1991) 62 P & CR 242, [1990] EG 83 (CS) — 2.36, 3.4, 3.16, 3.18, 5.18, 6.17, 8.48
Colin Dawson Windows Ltd v King's Lynn BC [2005] EWCA Civ 9, [2005] 2 P & CR 19, [2005] NPC 8 — 12.3, 4.16, 4.17
Colin Smith Music v Ridge [1975] 1 WLR 463, [1975] 1 All ER 290, (1975) 29 P & CR 97, (1974) 5 Fam Law 128, (1974) 119 Sol Jo 83 — 9.47
Collier v Hollinshead [1984] 2 EGLR 14 — 2.15, 6.18
Commissioners of Customs & Excise v Sinclair Collis Ltd [2001] UKHL 30, [2001] STC 989, [2001] 3 CMLR 6, [2001] BTC 5284, [2001] BVC 378, [2001] STI 893, [2001] 27 EG 131 (CS) — 11.45
Coombes v Smith [1986] 1 WLR 808, [1987] 1 FLR 352, [1987] Fam Law 123, (1986) 130 Sol Jo 482 — 4.33, 4.37
Cooper v Crabtree (1882) 20 ChD 589 — 9.52
Copeland v Greenhalf [1952] Ch 488, [1952] 1 All ER 809, [1952] 1 TLR 786, (1952) 96Sol Jo 261 — 7.6, 7.7
Corby v Hill (1858) 4 CB(NS) 556 — 11.26
Cornish v Stubbs (1870) LR 5 CP 334 — 9.19, 10.23, 12.52, 12.53
Costagliola v English (1969) 210 EG 1425 — 5.26
Countryside Residential (North Thames) Ltd v Tugwell (2001) 81 P & CR 2, [2000] 3 PLR 55, [2000] 2 EGLR 59, [2000] 34 EG 87, [2000] JPL 1251, (2000) 97(17) LSG 34, (2000) 144 SJLB 198, [2000] Env LR D31, (2000) *Times*, 4 April — 2.30, 7.12, 9.53
Cowell v Rosehill Racecourse Co Ltd (1937) 56 CLR 605 — 2.22
Crabb v Arun DC [1976] Ch 179, [1975] 3 WLR 847, [1975] 3 All ER 865, (1976) 32 P & CR 70, (1975) 119 Sol Jo 711 — 8.63, 10.32
Crancour v De Silvaesa (1986) 18 HLR 265, (1986) 52 P & CR 204, [1986] 1 EGLR 80, (1986) 278 EG 618 — 3.13, 6.21
Crane v Morris [1965] 1 WLR 1104, [1965] 3 All ER 77, (1965) 109 Sol Jo 456 — 12.5, 12.13

Crawford v Elliott [1991] 1 EGLR 13	6.18
Crawley BC v Ure [1996] QB 13, [1995] 3 WLR 95, [1996] 1 All ER 724, [1995] 1 FLR 806, [1996] 1 FCR 6, (1995) 27 HLR 524, 93 LGR 307, (1996) 71 P & CR 12, [1995] Fam Law 411, [1995] NPC 24, (1995) 69 P & CR D33, (1995) *Times*, 23 February, (1995) *Independent*, 18 April	12.26
Creed v McGeoch & Sons Ltd [1955] 1 WLR 1005, [1955] 3 All ER 123, (1955) 99 Sol Jo 563	11.9
Crestfort Ltd v Tesco Stores Ltd [2005] EWHC 805 (Ch), [2005] L & TR 20, [2005] 3 EGLR 25, [2005] 37 EG 148, [2005] NPC 74	8.16, 9.21
Cullen v Cullen [1962] IR 268	5.4
Cumbernauld & Kilsyth DC v Dollar Land (Cumbernauld) Ltd 1992 SC 357, 1992 SLT 1035, 1992 SCLR 668	5.25
Cyma Petroleum Ltd v CAS Business Services [2000] All ER (D) 1214	12.28
Daly v Edwardes (1900) 83 LT 548	6.6
Davies v Davies [2002] EWCA Civ 1791, [2003] 1 EG 65 (CS), (2002) 146 SJLB 281	6.18
Davies v Jones [2010] 1 P&CR 423	9.27, 9.28, 10.27
Davis v Lisle [1936] 2 KB 434	4.23, 12.6, 12.8
De Falbe, Re, Ward v Taylor [1901] 1 Ch 523, 70 LJ Ch 286, 84 LT 273, CA, affd *sub nom* Leigh v Taylor [1902] AC 157, [1900–3] All ER Rep 520, 71 LJ Ch 272, HL	13.14
Dean and Chapter of Canterbury Cathedral v Whitbread plc (1996) 72 P & CR 9, [1995] 1 EGLR 82, [1995] 24 EG 148, [1995] EG 13 (CS), [1995] NPC 15, (1995) 69 P & CR D34, (1995) *Times*, 7 February, (1995) *Independent*, 20 March	13.28
Decco Wall International v Practitioners in Marketing Ltd [1971] 1 WLR 361, [1971] 2 All ER 216, (1970) 115 Sol Jo 171	12.20
Dellneed Ltd v Chin (1987) 53 P & CR 172, (1987) 281 EG 531	2.34, 3.14, 3.16, 6.3
Demeuren v Seal Estates (1978) 7 HLR 83	3.9
Desnousse v Newham LBC [2006] EWCA Civ 547, [2006] QB 831, [2006] 3 WLR 349, [2007] 2 All ER 547, [2006] HLR 38, [2007] BLGR 368, [2006] NPC 58, (2006) *Times*, 28 June, (2006) *Independent*, 19 May	13.16
Devefi Pty Ltd v Mateffy Pearl Nagy Pty Ltd [1993] FCA 152	10.19, 10.20, 12.29
DHN Food Distributors Ltd v Tower Hamlets LBC [1976] 1 WLR 852, [1976] 3 All ER 462, 74 LGR 506, (1976) 32 P & CR 240, [1976] JPL 363, (1976) 120 Sol Jo 215	9.8, 11.51
Dilwyn v Llewelyn (1862) 4 De GF & J 517	10.32
Divall v Harrison [1992] 38 EG 147, [1991] 14 EG 108, [1992] NPC 25	12.25
Doe d Dayman v Moore 115 ER 1387, (1846) 9 QB 555	4.10
Doe d Johnson v Baytup 111 ER 384, (1835) 3 Ad & El 188	8.27, 8.28
Doe d Knight v Smythe 105 ER 862, (1815) 4 M & S 347	8.28
Doe d Robertson v Gardiner 138 ER 927, (1852) 12 CB 319	3.4
Don King Productions Ltd v Warren [2000] Ch 291, [1999] 3 WLR 276, [1999] 2 All ER 218, [1999] 1 Lloyd's Rep 588, [2000] 1 BCLC 607, [1999] EMLR 402, (1999) *Times*, 9 February, (1999) *Independent*, 25 January	10.5, 10.7
Donington Park Leisure Ltd v Wheatcroft & Sons Ltd [2006] EWHC 904 (Ch), [2006] All ER (D) 94	8.10, 8.12, 8.13, 8.23, 8.33, 9.4, 9.39, 10.5, 10.14, 10.39, 12.28
Dorling v Honnor Marine Ltd [1964] Ch 560, [1963] 3 WLR 397, [1963] 2 All ER 495, [1963] 1 Lloyd's Rep 377, [1963] RPC 205, (1963) 107 Sol Jo 738	10.5, 10.14, 12.20
Dresden Estates v Collinson (1988) 55 P & CR 47, [1987] 1 EGLR 45, (1987) 281 EG 1321	3.13, 6.3, 8.30
Dudley Port Warehousing Co Ltd v Gardner Transport & Distribution Ltd [1995] EGCS 5	12.28, 8.9, 8.23, 8.36
Duke of Sutherland v Heathcote [1892] 1 Ch 475	8.15
Duke of Westminster v Guild [1985] QB 688, [1984] 3 WLR 630, [1984] 3 All ER 144, (1984) 128 Sol Jo 581, CA	8.41, 10.48

Table of Cases xxvii

Dunn v Bradford MDC [2002] EWCA Civ 1137, [2003] HLR 15, [2003] L &
    TR 11, [2002] 3 EGLR 104, [2002] 32 EG 87 (CS), (2002) 99(35)
    LSG 39, [2002] NPC 110, (2002) *Times*, 5 September   8.52, 8.53

E&L Berg Homes Ltd v Grey [1980] 1 EGLR 103   4.37
East Sussex CC v Miller (1991) June *Legal Action* 13   4.17
Edler v Auerbach [1950] 1 KB 359, [1949] 2 All ER 692, 65 TLR 645,
    (1949-51) 1 P & CR 10, (1949) 93 Sol Jo 727   8.39
Edwards v Railway Executive [1952] AC 737, [1952] 2 All ER 430, 98 Sol Jo
    493, [1952] 2 TLR 237, HL   4.18, 11.14
Edwin Hill & Partners v First National Finance Corp [1989] 1 WLR 225,
    [1988] 3 All ER 801, [1989] BCLC 89, [1988] 48 EG 83, [1988] EG
    116 (CS), (1988) 85(32) LSG 44, (1988) 138 NLJ Rep 268, (1988) 122
    Sol Jo 1389   9.22
Elitestone v Morris [1997] 1 WLR 687, [1997] 2 All ER 513, (1998) 30 HLR
    266, [1997] 2 EGLR 115, [1997] 27 EG 116, [1997] EG 62 (CS),
    (1997) 94(19) LSG 25, (1997) 147 NLJ 721, (1997) 141 SJLB 113,
    [1997] NPC 66, (1997) *Times*, 7 May   13.14
Ellenborough Park, Re [1956] Ch 131, [1955] 3 WLR 892, [1955] 3 All ER
    667, (1955) 99 Sol Jo 870   3.24, 7.4
Ellis v Lambeth LBC (1999) 32 HLR 596   4.7
Elsden v Pick [1980] 1 WLR 898, [1980] 3 All ER 235, (1980) 40 P & CR
    550, (1980) 254 EG 503, (1980) 124 Sol Jo 312   6.20, 12.19
Elvidge v Coventry CC [1994] QB 241, [1993] 3 WLR 976, [1993] 4 All ER
    903, [1994] ICR 68, (1994) 26 HLR 281, 92 LGR 237, [1993] EG 140
    (CS), [1993] NPC 110   6.36
Elwes v Brigg Gas Co (1886) 33 ChD 562   8.14
Elwood v Bullock 115 ER 147, (1844) 6 QB 383   5.38
Endstaff Ltd v Anglo Overseas Group Properties Ltd [2008] EWCA Civ 243   8.21
Environment Agency v Hillridge Ltd [2003] EWHC 3023 (Ch), [2004] 2
    BCLC 358, [2004] Env LR 32, [2004] JPL 1258, [2003] NPC 155   12.37
ER Ives Investments Ltd v High [1967] 2 QB 379, [1967] 2 WLR 789, [1967]
    1 All ER 504, (1966) 110 Sol Jo 963   9.6, 9.29, 10.2, 10.5, 10.31
Errington v Errington and Woods [1952] 1 KB 290, [1952] 1 All ER 149,
    [1952] 1 TLR 231, (1952) 96 Sol Jo 119   1.8, 2.17, 9.8, 9.9
Essex Plan Ltd v Broadminster (1988) 56 P & CR 353, [1988] 43 EG 84   3.3, 3.18, 3.20, 6.3
Esso Petroleum Co Ltd v Fumegrange Ltd [1994] 2 EGLR 90   2.34, 3.7, 3.13
Esso Petroleum Co Ltd v Kingswood Motor (Addlestone) Ltd [1974] QB
    142, [1973] 3 WLR 780, [1973] 3 All ER 1057, [1973] CMLR 665,
    (1973) 117 Sol Jo 852   9.21
Europa 2000 Ltd v Keles [2005] EWCA Civ 1748   8.13, 8.34, 8.64
Euston Centre Properties v H&J Wilson [1982] 1 EGLR 57   3.2, 3.20, 8.30, 8.45
Excelsior Wire Rope Co v Callan [1930] AC 404   11.26
Eyre v Hall (1986) 18 HLR 509, [1986] 2 EGLR 95, (1986) 280 EG 193   12.35

Facchini v Bryson 1952] 1 TLR 1386, (1952) 96 Sol Jo 395   3.16
Fairchild v Glenhaven Funeral Services Ltd, Fox v Spousal (Midlands) Ltd,
    Matthews v Associated Portland Cement Manufacturers (1978) Ltd
    [2002] UKHL 22, [2003] 1 AC 32, [2002] 3 All ER 305, [2002] ICR
    798, [2002] IRLR 533, 67 BMLR 90, [2002] NLJR 998, *Times*, 21
    June, [2003] 1 LRC 674, [2002] All ER (D) 139 (Jun), HL, Fairchild v
    Glenhaven Funeral Services Ltd and other appeals [2001] EWCA Civ
    1881, [2002] 1 WLR 1052, [2002] ICR 412, [2002] IRLR 129, *Times*,
    13 December, [2001] All ER (D) 125 (Dec), CA   11.26
Fairweather v St Marylebone Property Co Ltd [1963] AC 510, [1962] 2
    WLR 1020, [1962] 2 All ER 288, (1962) 106 Sol Jo 368   5.23
Family Housing Association v Jones [1990] 1 WLR 779, [1990] 1 All ER
    385, (1990) 22 HLR 45, (1990) 60 P & CR 27, [1990] 22 EG 118,
    [1989] EG 148 (CS), (1990) 87(7) LSG 33, (1989) 139 NLJ 1709,

Family Housing Association v Jones [1990] 1 WLR 779, [1990] 1 All ER 385, (1990) 22 HLR 45, (1990) 60 P & CR 27, [1990] 22 EG 118, [1989] EG 148 (CS), (1990) 87(7) LSG 33, (1989) 139 NLJ 1709, —*continued*
(1990) 134 Sol Jo 233, (1989) *Times*, 6 November, (1989) *Independent*, 3 November, (1989) Guardian, 28 November, (1989) *Daily Telegraph*, 15 December 3.13
Feltham v Cartwright 132 ER 1219, (1839) 5 Bing NC 569 .... 13.10
Ferguson v Welsh [1987] 1 WLR 1553, [1987] 3 All ER 777, 86 LGR 153, [1988] IRLR 112, 131 Sol Jo 1552, [1987] LS Gaz R 3581, [1987] NLJ Rep 1037, HL 4.3, 11.15, 11.20
Ferris v Weaven [1952] 2 All ER 233, [1952] WN 318, (1952) 96 Sol Jo 414 .... 9.11
Ferrishurst Ltd v Wallcite Ltd [1999] Ch 355, [1999] 2 WLR 667, [1999] 1 All ER 977, [1999] 1 EGLR 85, [1999] 05 EG 161, [1998] EG 175 (CS), (1998) 95(47) LSG 30, (1999) 96(4) LSG 39, (1999) 143 SJLB 54, [1998] NPC 157, (1999) 77 P & CR D20, (1998) *Times*, 8 Decembe 9.40
Field Common Ltd v Elmbridge BC [2008] EWHC 2079 (Ch), [2009] 1 P & CR 1, (2008) 105(34) LSG 21, [2008] NPC 101 .... 13.27, 13.28
Fifield v W&R Jack Ltd [2001] L & TR 4 .... 12.19
Finch v Underwood (1876) 2 ChD 310 .... 12.15
First Real Estates (UK) Ltd v Birmingham CC [2009] EWHC 817 .... 6.3
Fisher v CHT Ltd and others [1966] 2 QB 475, [1966] 1 All ER 88, [1966] 2 WLR 391, 196 EG 793, [1965] EGD 355 .... 11.12
Fletcher v Brent LBC [2006] EWCA Civ 960, [2007] HLR 12, (2006) 150 SJLB 920, [2006] NPC 81 .... 6.39, 12.26
Flood v Shand Construction Ltd [1996] EWCA Civ 1241 .... 10.7
Folkestone Corp v Brockman [1914] AC 338 .... 5.31, 5.33
Forster v Baker [1910] 2 KB 636, 79 LJKB 664, 102 LT 29, 26 TLR 243, CA 10.17
Forsyth-Grant v Allen [2008] 2 EGLR 18 .... 13.26, 13.28
Foster v Robinson [1951] 1 KB 149, [1950] 2 All ER 342, 66 TLR (Pt 2) 120, (1950) 94 Sol Jo 474 .... 3.4, 4.23
Foster v Warblington UDC [1906] 1 KB 648 .... 9.54
Francis v Cockrell (1870) LR 5 .... 8.38
Frank Warr & Co v London CC [1904] 1 KB 713 .... 2.23, 3.5, 3.6, 6.6, 9.8, 10.39, 11.51
Fryer v Brook [1998] BPIR 687, (1984) 81 LSG 2856, (1984) *Times*, 2 August 10.31

Gamerco SA v ICM/Fair Warning (Agency) Ltd [1995] 1 WLR 1226, [1995] CLC 536, [1995] EMLR 263, (1995) *Times*, 3 May 10.19
Gardner v Hodgson's Kingston Brewery Co Ltd [1903] AC 229 .... 4.17, 5.4, 5.25, 5.28, 5.37
Gentle v Faulkner [1900] 2 QB 267 .... 10.7
Gilham v Breidenbach [1982] RTR 328 .... 12.5
Gillett v Holt [1998] 3 All ER 917, [1998] 2 FLR 470, [1998] Fam Law 596, (1998) 95(26) LSG 31, (1998) *Times*, 18 June; [2001] Ch 210, [2000] 3 WLR 815, [2000] 2 All ER 289, [2000] 2 FLR 266, [2000] 1 FCR 705, [2000] WTLR 195, [2000] Fam Law 714, (2000) 97(12) LSG 40, (2000) 144 SJLB 141, [2000] NPC 25, (2000) 80 P & CR D3, (2000) *Times*, 17 March 4.32, 4.38
Gillmore v LCC [1938] 4 All ER 331 .... 8.38
Gladstone v Bower [1960] 2 QB 384, [1960] 3 WLR 575, [1960] 3 All ER 353, 58 LGR 313, (1960) 104 Sol Jo 763 .... 6.17
Glaister v Appleby-in-Westmoreland Town Council [2009] EWCA Civ 1325, [2010] PIQR P6, (2010) 107(1) LSG 14, [2009] NPC 143 .... 11.26
Glasgow Corp v Johnstone [1965] AC 609, [1965] 2 WLR 657, [1965] 1 All ER 730, 1965 SC (HL) 1, 1965 SLT 133, (1965) 129 JP 250, 63 LGR 171, [1965] RA 49, [1965] RVR 111, 11 RRC 127, (1965) 109 Sol Jo 196 .... 11.38
Glasgow Corp v Muir [1943] AC 448, [1943] 2 All ER 44, 1943 SC (HL) 3, 1944 SLT 60 .... 11.26
Glossop v Ashley [1921] 2 KB 451 .... 4.28

Goldberg v Edwards [1950] Ch 247, (1950) 94 Sol Jo 128	9.34
Goldsack v Shore [1950] 1 KB 708, [1950] 1 All ER 276, 66 TLR (Pt 1) 636, (1950) 94 Sol Jo 192	2.36, 6.18, 6.50, 8.1
Goldsmith v Burrow Construction Ltd (1987) *Times*, 31 July	5.27
Gonthier v Orange Contract Scaffolding Ltd [2003] EWCA Civ 873	8.62, 12.49
Gould v McAuliffe [1941] 2 All ER 527, 57 TLR 468, CA	8.13, 11.7
Governing Body of Henrietta Barnett School v Hampstead Garden Suburb Institute (1995) 93 LGR 470	12.6, 12.21–12.23
Graham v Northern Ireland Housing Executive (1986) 8 NIJB 93	8.11
Gray v Taylor [1998] 1 WLR 1093, [1998] 4 All ER 17, (1999) 31 HLR 262, [1998] L & TR 50, [1998] EG 62 (CS), (1998) 95(20) LSG 34, (1998) 142 SJLB 141, [1998] NPC 60, (1998) *Times*, 24 April	2.14, 3.3
Graysim Holdings Ltd v P&O Property Holdings Ltd [1996] AC 329, [1995] 3 WLR 854, [1995] 4 All ER 831, 94 LGR 553, [1996] 1 EGLR 109, [1996] 03 EG 124, [1995] EG 182 (CS), (1996) 93(2) LSG 28, (1995) 145 NLJ 1813, (1996) 140 SJLB 23, [1995] NPC 183, (1996) 71 P & CR D22, (1995) *Times*, 24 November	3.6, 6.11, 9.47
Great Central Ry Co v Bates [1921] 3 KB 581	4.23
Green v Ashco Horticulturalists Ltd [1966] 1 WLR 889, [1966] 2 All ER 232, (1966) 110 Sol Jo 271	3.24, 7.4
Greenfield v Berkshire CC (1996) 28 HLR 691, (1997) 73 P & CR 280, [1996] EG 38 (CS)	6.34
Greenhalgh v BRB [1969] 2 QB 286, [1969] 2 WLR 892, [1969] 2 All ER 114, (1969) 113 Sol Jo 108	11.14
Greenhalgh v Brindley [1901] 2 Ch 324	4.12
Grigsby v Melville [1972] 1 WLR 1355, [1973] 1 All ER 385, (1972) 24 P & CR 191, (1972) 116Sol Jo 784	7.6
Groveside Properties Ltd v Westminster Medical School [1983] 2 EGLR 68	9.47
Gwilliam v West Hertfordshire Hospitals NHS Trust [2002] EWCA Civ 1041, [2003] QB 443, [2003] 3 WLR 1425, [2003] PIQR P99, *Times*, 7 August, [2002] All ER (D) 345, Jul	11.13
Hackney LBC v Hackney African Organisation [1999] L & TR 117, [1998] EG 139 (CS), (1999) 77 P & CR D 18	12.26
Hair v Gillman (2000) 80 P & CR 108, [2000] 3 EGLR 74, [2000] 48 EG 117	7.3, 7.6, 9.36
Halbauer v Brighton Corpn [1954] 1 WLR 1161, [1954] 2 All ER 707, (1954) 118 JP 446, (1954) 98Sol Jo 572	7.13
Hale v Jennings Bros [1938] 1 All ER 579	11.28
Hall v Beckenham Corpn [1949] 1 KB 716, [1949] 1 All ER 423, 65 TLR 146, (1949) 113 JP 179, 47 LGR 291, 42 R & IT 247, [1949] LJR 965, (1949) 93 Sol Jo 219	11.32
Hall v Nottingham (1875-76) LR 1 Ex D 1	3.31
Halsall v Brizell [1957] Ch 169, [1957] 2 WLR 123, [1957] 1 All ER 371, (1957) 101 Sol Jo 88	9.28, 10.27
Hammersmith LBC v Monk [1992] 1 AC 478, [1991] 3 WLR 1144, [1992] 1 All ER 1, [1992] 1 FLR 465, (1992) 24 HLR 206, 90 LGR 38, (1992) 63 P & CR 373, [1992] 1 EGLR 65, [1992] 09 EG 135, [1992] Fam Law 292, (1992) 156 LG Rev 481, [1991] EG 130 (CS), (1992) 89(3) LSG 32, (1991) 141 NLJ 1697, (1992) 136 SJLB 10, [1991] NPC 132, (1991) *Times*, 6 December, (1991) *Independent*, 10 December	12.26
Handel v St Stephens Close Ltd [1994] 1 EGLR 70	7.6, 7.9, 8.13
Haniff v Robinson [1993] QB 419, [1992] 3 WLR 875, [1993] 1 All ER 185, (1994) 26 HLR 386, [1992] 45 EG 145, [1992] NPC 98	13.16
Hanina v Morland (2000) 97(47) LSG 41	7.6
Hanson (W) (Harrow) Ltd v Rapid Civil Engineering Ltd (1987) 38 BLR 106	13.7
Hardwick v Johnson [1978] 1 WLR 683, [1978] 2 All ER 935, (1978) 122 Sol Jo 162, (1977) *Times*, 10 December	1.8, 2.17, 2.18, 8.18, 10.32, 12.49
Harley Queen v Forsyte Kerman [1983] CLY 2077	7.13
Harrison-Broadley v Smith [1964] 1 WLR 456, [1964] 1 All ER 867, [2008] BTC 7085, (1964) 108 Sol Jo 136	6.8, 6.18, 8.20

Harrow LBC v Qazi [2003] UKHL 43, [2004] 1 AC 983, [2003] 3 WLR 792,
[2003] 4 All ER 461, [2003] 2 FLR 973, [2003] 3 FCR 43, [2003]
HRLR 40, [2003] UKHRR 974, [2003] HLR 75, [2004] 1 P & CR 19,
[2004] L & TR 9, [2003] 3 EGLR 109, [2003] Fam Law 875, (2003)
100(38) LSG 34, (2003) 147 SJLB 937, [2003] NPC 101, (2003)
Times, 1 August, (2003) *Independent*, 3 October ... 12.26
Hartwell v Grayson Rollo & Clover Docks Ltd [1947] KB 901, (1947) 80 Ll
L Rep 381, [1947] LJR 1038 ... 11.26
Harvey v Plymouth CC [2010] EWCA Civ 860, [2010] PIQR P18, (2010)
154(31) SJLB 30, [2010] NPC 89 ... 4.13, 5.9, 8.2, 11.7, 12.3
Haselmere Estates Ltd v Baker [1982] 1 WLR 1109, [1982] 3 All ER 525,
(1982) 126 Sol Jo 463 ... 9.6
Healey v Hawkins [1968] 1 WLR 1967, [1968] 3 All ER 836, (1969) 20 P &
CR 69, (1968) 112 Sol Jo 965 ... 5.6, 12.32
Hellawell v Eastwood 155 ER 554, (1851) 6 Ex 295 ... 13.14
Helstan Securities Ltd v Hertfordshire CC [1978] 3 All ER 262, 76 LGR 735 ... 10.7, 10.18, 10.19
Hemmings v Stoke Poges Golf Club [1920] 1 KB 720 ... 13.16
Henderson v Squire (1868-69) LR 4 QB 170 ... 13.4, 13.5, 13.25, 13.28
Hendry v Chartsearch Ltd [1998] CLC 1382, (2000) 2 TCLR 115, (1998)
Times, 16 September ... 10.6, 10.8, 10.11
Henry Boot & Sons (London) Ltd v Uttoxeter UDC (1924) 88 JP 118 ... 12.22
Herbert v Doyle [2010] EWCA Civ 1095, [2010] NPC 100 ... 4.35
Herrington v BRB [1972] AC 877, [1972] 2 WLR 537, [1972] 1 All ER 749,
(1972) 116 Sol Jo 178 ... 4.19
Heslop v Burns [1974] 1 WLR 1241, [1974] 3 All ER 406, (1974) 118 Sol Jo
581 ... 2.15, 2.30, 7.12, 9.53
Hicks Developments Ltd v Chaplin [2007] EWHC 141 (Ch), [2007] 1 EGLR
1, [2007] 16 EG 192 ... 4.16, 4.18
Hill v Harris [1965] 2 QB 601, [1965] 2 WLR 1331, [1965] 2 All ER 358,
(1965) 109 Sol Jo 333 ... 8.39
Hill v Tupper 159 ER 51, (1863) 2 Hurl & C 121 ... 3.1, 3.24, 6.5, 7.12, 9.53
Hillen and Pettigrew v ICI (Alkali) Ltd [1936] AC 65, 104 LJKB 473, 41
Com Cas 29, [1935] All ER Rep 555, 153 LT 403, 51 TLR 532, HL ... 11.7
Hilton v John Smith & Sons (Norwood) Ltd [1979] 2 EGLR 44, (1979) 257
EG 1063 ... 7.13
Hindcastle Ltd v Barbara Attenborough Associates Ltd [1997] AC 70,
[1996] 2 WLR 262, [1996] 1 All ER 737, [1996] 2 BCLC 234, HL ... 12.36
Hirji Mulji v Cheong Yue SS Co Ltd [1926] AC 497, [1926] 1 WWR 917,
[1926] WN 89 ... 12.34
Hodgson v Marks [1971] Ch 892, [1971] 2 WLR 1263, [1971] 2 All ER 684,
(1971) 22 P & CR 586, (1971) 115 Sol Jo 224 ... 9.40
Holaw (470) Ltd v Stockton Estates Ltd (2001) 81 P & CR 29, [2000] EG 89
(CS) ... 9.40
Holbeck Hall Hotel Ltd v Scarborough BC [2000] QB 836, [2000] 2 WLR
1396, [2000] 2 All ER 705, [2000] BLR 109, (2000) 2 TCLR 865, 69
Con LR 1, [2000] BLGR 412, [2000] EG 29 (CS), (2000) 97(9) LSG
44, (2000) 97(11) LSG 36, (2000) 150 NLJ 307, (2000) 144 SJLB 109,
[2000] NPC 17, (2000) *Times*, 2 March ... 11.37
Holland v Hodgson (1872) LR 7 CP 328, [1861-73] All ER Rep 237, 41
LJCP 146, Ex Ch ... 13.14
Hollins v Verney (1884) 13 QBD 304 ... 5.2
Holt v Heatherfield Trust Ltd [1942] 2 KB 1, [1942] 1 All ER 404, 111
LJKB 465 ... 10.17
Hooper v Eaglestone 76 LGR 308, (1977) 34 P & CR 311, (1977) 245 EG
572, [1978] JPL 307, [1978] Crim LR 161 ... 6.60, 13.16
Hopgood v Brown [1955] 1 WLR 213, [1955] 1 All ER 550, (1955) 99 Sol Jo
168 ... 9.29
Horkulak v Cantor Fitzgerald International [2004] EWCA Civ 1287, [2005]
ICR 402, [2004] IRLR 942, (2004) 148 SJLB 1218 ... 10.9
Horrocks v Forray [1976] 1 WLR 230, [1976] 1 All ER 737, (1975) 6 Fam
Law 15, (1975) 119 Sol Jo 866 ... 1.8, 2.17, 4.24, 4.27

Table of Cases xxxi

Hounslow LBC v Pilling [1993] 1 WLR 1242, [1994] 1 All ER 432, [1993] 2
  FLR 49, (1993) 25 HLR 305, 91 LGR 573, (1993) 66 P & CR 22,
  [1993] 26 EG 123, [1993] Fam Law 522, [1993] EG 36 (CS), (1993)
  137 SJLB 187, [1993] NPC 35, (1993) *Times*, 4 March   12.26
Hounslow LBC v Twickenham Garden Developments Ltd [1971] Ch 233,
  [1970] 3 WLR 538, [1970] 3 All ER 326, 7 BLR 81, 69 LGR 109,
  (1970) 114 Sol Jo 603   2.8, 2.13, 2.22, 2.36, 6.1, 12.42, 12.43, 12.45
Howard E Perry & Co Ltd v British Railways Board [1980] 1 WLR 1375,
  [1980] 2 All ER 579, [1980] ICR 743, (1980) 124 Sol Jo 591   13.7
Hughes v Greenwich LBC [1994] 1 AC 170, [1993] 3 WLR 821, [1993] 4 All
  ER 577, [1994] ICR 48, (1994) 26 HLR 99, 92 LGR 61, (1995) 69 P
  & CR 487, [1993] EG 166 (CS), (1993) 90(46) LSG 38, (1993) 137
  SJLB 244, [1993] NPC 137, (1993) *Times*, 26 October   6.31
Hughes v Griffin [1969] 1 WLR 23, [1969] 1 All ER 460, (1969) 20 P & CR
  113, (1968) 112 Sol Jo 907   5.16
Hunter v Canary Wharf Ltd [1997] AC 655, [1997] 2 WLR 684, [1997] 2 All
  ER 426, [1997] CLC 1045, 84 BLR 1, 54 Con LR 12, [1997] Env LR
  488, [1997] 2 FLR 342, (1998) 30 HLR 409, [1997] Fam Law 601,
  [1997] EG 59 (CS), (1997) 94(19) LSG 25, (1997) 147 NLJ 634,
  (1997) 141 SJLB 108, [1997] NPC 64, (1997) *Times*, 25 April, (1997)
  Independent, 2 May   2.30, 9.54
Hunts Refuse Disposal Ltd v Norfolk Environmental Waste Services Ltd
  [1997] 1 EGLR 16, [1997] 03 EG 139, [1996] NPC 88   3.7, 6.3, 6.6, 6.14
Hurst v Picture Theatres Ltd [1915] 1 KB 1   12.20, 12.42, 12.43, 2.22, 6.37, 8.32
Huwyler v Reddy (1996) 65 P & CR D3   6.21

IDC Group Ltd v Clark [1992] 1 EGLR 187, [1992] 08 EG 108, Ch D;
  (1992) 65 P & CR 179, [1992] 49 EG 103, [1992] EG 93 (CS), [1992]
  NPC 88, [1992] 2 EGLR 184, (1992) *Times*, 23 July, (1992)
  Independent, 20 July, CA   1.8, 3.26, 7.5, 9.9, 9.12, 9.17, 9.28, 10.14, 10.27
Industrial Properties (Barton Hill) Ltd v Associated Electrical Industries
  Ltd [1977] QB 580, [1977] 2 WLR 726, [1977] 2 All ER 293, (1977)
  34 P & CR 329, (1977) 242 EG 955, (1977) 121 Sol Jo 155   8.27
International Drilling Fluids Ltd v Louisville Investments (Uxbridge) Ltd
  [1986] Ch 513, [1986] 2 WLR 581, [1986] 1 All ER 321, (1986) 51 P
  & CR 187, [1986] 1 EGLR 39, (1985) 277 EG 62, (1986) 83 LSG 436,
  (1985) *Times*, 29 November   10.10
International Tea Stores Co v Hobbs [1903] 2 Ch 165   9.34
Inverugie Investments v Hackett [1995] 1 WLR 713, [1995] 3 All ER 841,
  [1996] 1 EGLR 149, [1996] 19 EG 124, [1995] EG 37 (CS), [1995]
  NPC 36, (1995) 69 P & CR D48   13.28
Investors Compensation Scheme Ltd v West Bromwich BS [1998] 1 WLR
  896, [1998] 1 All ER 98, [1998] 1 BCLC 531, [1997] CLC 1243, [1997]
  PNLR 541, (1997) 147 NLJ 989, (1997) *Times*, 24 June   8.8
Inwards v Baker [1965] 2 QB 29, [1965] 2 WLR 212, [1965] 1 All ER 446,
  (1965) 109 Sol Jo 75   2.25, 9.29
Isaac v Hotel de Paris [1960] 1 WLR 239, [1960] 1 All ER 348, (1960) 104
  Sol Jo 230   3.18, 6.13, 12.12
Islington LBC v Green [2005] EWCA Civ 56, [2005] HLR 35, [2005] L &
  TR 24, [2005] NPC 11   9.46
Iveagh (Earl) v Martin [1961] 1 QB 232, [1960] 3 WLR 210, [1960] 2 All ER
  668, [1960] 1 Lloyd's Rep 692, 58 LGR 356, (1960) 104 Sol Jo 567   12.24
Ivory v Palmer [1975] ICR 340, (1975) 119 Sol Jo 405   6.37, 12.13

J Alston & Sons Ltd v BOCM Pauls Ltd [2008] EWHC 3310 (Ch), [2009] 1
  EGLR 93   4.11, 4.15, 4.16, 4.23, 5.14, 5.17, 5.24
J Miller Ltd v Laurence & Bardsley [1966] 1 Lloyd's Rep 90   10.5, 10.13, 10.14
J Spurling Ltd v Bradshaw [1956] 1 WLR 461, [1956] 2 All ER 121, [1956] 1
  Lloyd's Rep 392, (1956) 100 Sol Jo 317   8.6

JA Pye (Oxford) Ltd v Graham [2002] UKHL 30, [2003] 1 AC 419, [2002] 3
    WLR 221, [2002] 3 All ER 865, [2002] HRLR 34, [2003] 1 P & CR
    10, [2002] 28 EG 129 (CS), [2002] NPC 92, [2002] 2 P & CR DG22,
    (2002) *Times*, 5 July, (2002) *Independent*, 9 July   2.29, 2.31, 2.34, 3.13, 3.14, 4.17, 4.18,
                                                                    4.22, 5.10, 5.16, 5.17
Jackson v Mulvaney [2002] EWCA Civ 1078, [2003] 1 WLR 360, [2003] 4
    All ER 83, [2003] 1 P & CR 16, [2002] 3 EGLR 72, [2002] 44 EG
    175, (2002) 99(38) LSG 34, [2002] NPC 102, [2003] 1 P & CR DG5,
    (2002) *Times*, 27 August, (2002) *Daily Telegraph*, 1 August   7.4
James Jones & Sons Ltd v Earl of Tankerville [1909] 2 Ch 440   2.23, 4.30, 8.64
James Maccara Ltd v Barclays [1945] KB 148   9.13
Jani-King (GB) Ltd v Pula Enterprises Ltd [2007] EWHC 2433 (QB), [2008]
    1 All ER (Comm) 451   8.20, 12.12
Javad v Aquil [1991] 1 WLR 100   3.18
Jennings v Rice [2002] EWCA Civ 159, [2003] 1 FCR 501, [2003] 1 P & CR
    8, [2002] WTLR 367, [2002] NPC 28, [2002] 2 P & CR DG2   4.40, 8.63
Joel v International Circus and Christmas Fair (1920) 124 LT 459   3.13
John Laing & Sons Ltd v Kingswood Area Assessors [1949] 1 KB 344,
    [1949] 1 All ER 224, 65 TLR 80, (1949) 113 JP 111, 47 LGR 64, 42
    R & IT 15, (1949) 93 Sol Jo 26   11.38
John Smith & Co (Edinburgh) Ltd v Hill [2010] EWHC 1016   9.52
Johnson v Rea [1962] 1 QB 373, [1961] 1 WLR 1400, [1961] 3 All ER 816,
    [1961] 2 Lloyd's Rep 243, (1961) 105 Sol Jo 867   11.26
Jolley v Carmel [2000] 2 EGLR 153, [2000] EG 72 (CS)   10.19
Jolliffe v Willmett & Co [1971] 1 All ER 478, (1970) 114 Sol Jo 619   4.3
Jones (Insurance Brokers) Ltd v Portsmouth CC [2002] EWCA Civ 1723,
    [2003] 1 WLR 427, [2003] BLR 67, 87 Con LR 169, [2003] 1 EGLR
    99, [2003] 15 EG 139, [2002] 47 EG 146 (CS), (2003) 100(2) LSG 32,
    (2002) 146 SJLB 255, (2002) *Times*, 21 November   11.33, 11.35
Jones and Jones v Lloyd [1981] Crim LR 340   10.36
Jones v Foley [1891] 1 QB 730   13.16
Jones v Jones [1977] 1 WLR 438, (1977) 33 P & CR 147, (1976) 242 EG 371,
    (1976) 120 Sol Jo 802, (1976) *Times*, 1 November   2.25, 8.63, 9.29, 10.31, 12.50
Jones v Llanwrst UDC [1911] 1 Ch 393   9.52
Jones v Pritchard [1908] 1 Ch 630   8.48

Kay v Lambeth LBC [2006] UKHL 10, [2006] 2 AC 465, [2006] 2 WLR 570,
    [2006] 4 All ER 128, [2006] 2 FCR 20, [2006] HRLR 17, [2006]
    UKHRR 640, 20 BHRC 33, [2006] HLR 22, [2006] BLGR 323,
    [2006] 2 P & CR 25, [2006] L & TR 8, [2006] 11 EG 194 (CS), (2006)
    150 SJLB 365, [2006] NPC 29, (2006) *Times*, 10 March, (2006)
    Independent, 14 March   2.30, 9.46, 10.48, 13.5
Keown v Coventry NHS Trust [2006] EWCA Civ 39, [2006] 1 WLR 953,
    [2006] PIQR P19, (2006) 103(8) LSG 23, (2006) 150 SJLB 164, [2006]
    NPC 18, (2006) *Independent*, 10 February   11.19
Kewal Investments Ltd v Arthur Maiden [1990] 1 EGLR 193   6.12
Kinch v Bullard [1999] 1 WLR 423, [1998] 4 All ER 650, [1999] 1 FLR 66,
    [1998] 3 EGLR 112, [1998] 47 EG 140, [1998] Fam Law 738, [1998]
    EG 126 (CS), [1998] NPC 137, (1999) 77 P & CR D1, (1998) *Times*,
    16 September, (1998) *Independent*, 12 October   12.16
King v David Allen & Sons Billposting Ltd [1916] 2 AC 54   3.6, 6.12, 7.14, 9.8, 9.14
King v Liverpool CC [1986] 1 WLR 890, [1986] 3 All ER 544, (1986) 18
    HLR 307, 84 LGR 871, [1986] 1 EGLR 181, (1986) 278 EG 278,
    (1986) 83 LSG 2492, (1986) 136 NLJ 334, (1986) 130 Sol Jo 505   8.30
Kirklees MBC v Yorkshire Woolen District Transport Ltd (1978) 77 LGR
    448   12.15
Koeller v Coleg Elidyr [2005] EWCA Civ 856, [2005] 2 BCLC 379, [2005]
    NPC 90   6.26
Krell v Henry [1903] 2 KB 740, 72 LJKB 794, [1900–3] All ER Rep 20, CA   7.12, 12.33

Kumar v Dunning [1989] QB 193, [1987] 3 WLR 1167, [1987] 2 All ER 801, (1988) 55 P & CR 64, (1987) 283 EG 59, (1987) 84 LSG 1812, (1987) 137 NLJ 522, (1987) 131 Sol Jo 974	10.29
L Meretz Investments v ACP Ltd	9.22
Lace v Chantler [1944] KB 368, [1944] 1 All ER 305, 113 LJKB 282, CA	3.1, 3.4, 3.25, 7.4, 12.14
Lakshmijjt v Sherani [1974] AC 605, [1974] 2 WLR 232, [1973] 3 All ER 737, (1973) 118 Sol Jo 35	5.11
Lambert v Roberts [1981] 2 All ER 15, (1981) 72 Cr App R 223, [1981] RTR 113, [1981] Crim LR 257	4.23, 12.5–12.7, 12.9
Lambeth LBC v Rumbelow [2001] All ER (D) 176	4.5, 4.12, 4.15–4.17, 4.23
Land v Sykes [1992] 1 EGLR 1, [1992] 03 EG 115, [1991] EG 98 (CS)	13.3
Langridge v Mansfield DC [2008] EWCA Civ 264, [2008] HLR 34, (2008) 105(8) LSG 25	6.41
Latchman v Pickard [2005] EWHC 1011	6.9
Law Debenture Trust Corp v Ural Caspian Oil Corp Ltd [1993] 1 WLR 138, [1993] 2 All ER 355, (1993) *Independent*, 12 March, (1993) *Financial Times*, 20 March	9.23
LCC v Wilkins (Valuation Officer) [1957] AC 362, [1956] 3 WLR 505, [1956] 3 All ER 38, (1956) 120 JP 481, 54 LGR 427, 1 RRC 88, 49 R & IT 495, (1956) 100 Sol Jo 567	11.38
Leadenhall Residential 2 Ltd v Stirling [2001] EWCA Civ 1011, [2002] 1 WLR 499, [2001] 3 All ER 645, [2002] HLR 3, [2002] L & TR 14, (2001) 98(35) LSG 35, (2001) 151 NLJ 1005, [2001] NPC 112, (2001) *Times*, 25 July	2.36, 3.3
Leakey v National Trust for Places of Historic Interest or Natural Beauty[1980] QB 485, [1980] 2 WLR 65, [1980] 1 All ER 17, 78 LGR 100, (1979) 123 Sol Jo 606	11.37
Lee v Berkeley Leisure Group Ltd (1997) 29 HLR 663, (1997) 73 P & CR 493, [1995] EG 162 (CS), [1995] NPC 159	10.10
Lee v Leeds CC [2002] EWCA Civ 6, [2002] 1 WLR 1488, [2002] HLR 17, [2002] BLGR 305, [2002] 2 P & CR 23, [2002] L & TR 35, [2002] 1 EGLR 103, (2002) 99(10) LSG 31, (2002) 146 SJLB 46, [2002] NPC 12, [2003] Env LR D3, (2002) *Times*, 29 January	8.37, 11.25
Legal & General Assurance Society Ltd v General Metal Agencies Ltd (1969) 20 P & CR 953, (1969) 113 Sol Jo 876	13.3
Leigh v Jack (1879) 5 Ex D 264	4.22
Lemmerbell Ltd v Britannia LAS Direct Ltd [1999] L & TR 102, [1998] 3 EGLR 67, [1998] 48 EG 188, [1998] EG 138 (CS), [1998] NPC 135	12.25
Lester v Woodgate [2010] EWCA Civ 199, [2010] 2 P & CR DG14	4.18, 11.14
LeStrange v Pettefar (1939) 161 LT 300	7.13
Liggins v Inge (1831) 7 Bing 682	13.10
Linden Gardens Trust Ltd v Lenesta Sludge Disposals Ltd, St Martin's Property Corp v Sir Robert McAlpine & Sons [1994] 1 AC 85, [1993] 3 WLR 408, [1993] 3 All ER 417, 63 BLR 1, 36 Con LR 1, [1993] EG 139 (CS), (1993) 143 NLJ 1152, (1993) 137 SJLB 183, (1993) *Times*, 23 July, (1993) *Independent*, 30 July	9.2, 10.1, 10.4, 10.6, 10.7, 10.13, 10.18, 10.19
Linden v DHSS [1986] 1 WLR 164, [1986] 1 All ER 691, (1986) 51 P & CR 317, (1985) 277 EG 543, (1986) 83 LSG 612, (1986) 130 Sol Jo 128, (1985) *Times*, 21 November	9.47
Lippiat v South Gloucestershire Council [2000] QB 51, [1999] 3 WLR 137, [1999] 4 All ER 149, (1999) 31 HLR 1114, (1999) 1 LGLR 865, [1999] BLGR 562, (1999) 96(15) LSG 31, (1999) *Times*, 9 April, (1999) *Independent*, 30 April	11.31
Liverpool City Council v Irwin [1977] AC 239, [1976] 2 WLR 562, [1976] 2 All ER 39, (1984) 13 HLR 38, 74 LGR 392, (1976) 32 P & CR 43, (1976) 238 EG 879, [1976] JPL 427, (1976) 120 Sol Jo 267	8.10, 8.42
Llanelly Ry & Dock Co v London & North Western Ry Co (1874–5) LR 7 HL 550	8.18, 8.19

Llanelly Ry & Dock Co v London & North Western Ry Co (1874-5) LR 7 HL 550 ..... 8.20
Lloyd v Dugdale [2001] EWCA Civ 1754, [2002] 2 P & CR 13, [2002] WTLR 863, [2001] 48 EG 129 (CS), (2001) 98(47) LSG 28, [2001] NPC 168 ..... 9.9, 9.13–9.15, 9.29, 9.32, 9.40, 9.41
Lombard Tricity Finance Ltd v Paton [1989] 1 All ER 918, (1989) 8 Tr LR 129, (1988) 138 NLJ Rep 333, (1988) *Times*, 31 Octobe3 ..... 10.9
London & Associated Investment Trust v Calow (1987) 53 P & CR 340, [1986] 2 EGLR 80, (1986) 280 EG 1252 ..... 3.16, 6.3
London & Blenheim Estates Ltd v Ladbroke Retail Parks Ltd [1992] 1 WLR 1278, [1993] 1 All ER 307; [1994] 1 WLR 31, [1993] 4 All ER 157, (1994) 67 P & CR 1, [1993] EG 100 (CS), [1993] NPC 86, (1993) *Times*, 1 June, CA 3.24, 7.4, 7.7, 7.9
London Development Agency v Nidai [2009] EWHC 1730 (Ch), [2009] 2 P & CR DG23 ..... 3.6, 6.5, 6.12, 7.14
Longrigg, Borough & Trounson v Smith [1979] 2 EGLR 42, (1979) 251 EG 847 ..... 13.3
Lord Advocate v Young (1887) 12 App Cas 544 ..... 2.34
Lowe v Adams [1901] 2 Ch 598 ..... 2.23
Lowery v Walker [1911] AC 10, 80 LJKB 138, [1908-10] All ER Rep 12, 55 Sol Jo 62, 103 LT 674, 27 TLR 83, HL 4.18, 11.14
Luganda v Services Hotels [1969] 2 Ch 209, [1969] 2 WLR 1056, [1969] 2 All ER 692, (1969) 20 P & CR 337, (1969) 113 Sol Jo 165 ..... 3.13, 6.47
Lyme Valley Squash Club Ltd v Newcastle under Lyme BC [1985] 2 All ER 405 ..... 9.35
Lymington Marina Ltd v Macnamara [2006] EWHC 704 (Ch), [2006] 2 All ER (Comm) 200, [2006] NPC 43; [2007] EWCA Civ 151, [2007] 2 All ER (Comm) 825, [2007] NPC 27, [2007] Bus LR D29 ..... 8.8, 8.10, 10.5, 10.8, 10.9, 10.40
Lynes v Snaith [1899] 1 QB 486 ..... 2.30
Lyus v Prowsa Developments Ltd [1982] 1 WLR 1044, [1982] 2 All ER 953, (1982) 44 P & CR 213, (1982) 126 Sol Jo 102 ..... 9.13–9.18, 9.29

Mackley v Nutting [1949] 2 KB 55, [1949] 1 All ER 413, 65 TLR 255, [1949] LJR 803, (1949) 93 Sol Jo 197, (1949) 93 Sol Jo 248 ..... 8.28
Maclenan v Segar [1917] 2 KB 235 ..... 8.38
Maddocks v Clifton [2001] EWCA Civ 1837 ..... 11.11
Madrassa Anjuman Islamia of Kholwad v Johannesburg Municipal Council [1922] 1 AC 500 ..... 6.1
MAFF v Matthews [1950] 1 KB 148, [1949] 2 All ER 724, 65 TLR 655 ..... 2.36, 3.1
Maguire v Sefton MBC [2006] EWCA Civ 316, [2006] 1 WLR 2550, [2006] PIQR P25, (2006) 103(11) LSG 27, (2006) *Times*, 16 March 8.37, 8.38
Maharaj v Chand [1986] AC 898, [1986] 3 WLR 440, [1986] 3 All ER 107, (1986) 83 LSG 2568, (1986) 130 Sol Jo 633 ..... 2.25, 9.30, 9.33, 9.48
Malone v Laskey [1907] 2 KB 141, CA 9.54
Manchester Airport plc v Dutton, *sub nom* Dutton v Manchester Airport plc [2000] QB 133, [1999] 3 WLR 524, [1999] 2 All ER 675, (2000) 79 P & CR 541, [1999] 1 EGLR 147, [1999] EG 31 (CS), (1999) 96(11) LSG 69, (1999) 96(9) LSG 34, (1999) 149 NLJ 333, (1999) 143 SJLB 89, [1999] Env LR D19, (1999) *Times*, 5 March, (1999) *Independent*, 2 March 1.3, 1.8, 2.29, 2.30, 2.36, 8.16, 9.52, 9.53, 13.15, 13.18
Manchester City Council v National Car Parks [1982] 1 EGLR 94 ..... 3.13, 6.6
Mander v Falcke [1891] 2 Ch 554, 65 LT 203, CA 9.48
Manfield & Sons Ltd v Botchin [1970] 2 QB 612, [1970] 3 WLR 120, [1970] 3 All ER 143, (1970) 21 P & CR 587, (1970) 114 Sol Jo 338 ..... 6.4
Mann v Brodie (1884-85) LR 10 App Cas 378 ..... 5.32, 5.33
Mannai Investment Co Ltd v Eagle Star Life Assurance Co Ltd [1997] AC 749, [1997] 3 All ER 352, [1997] 2 WLR 945, [1997] CLC 1124, [1997] 1 EGLR 57, [1997] 25 EG 138, [1997] 24 EG 122, (1997) 16 Tr LR 432, [1997] EGCS 82, (1997) 94(30) LSG 30, (1997) 147 NLJ 846, (1997) 141 SJLB 130, [1997] NPC 81, (1997) *Times*, 26 May, HL,

Table of Cases xxxv

Mannai Investment Co Ltd v Eagle Star Life Assurance Co Ltd [1997] AC 749, [1997] 3 All ER 352, [1997] 2 WLR 945, [1997] CLC 1124, [1997] 1 EGLR 57, [1997] 25 EG 138, [1997] 24 EG 122, (1997) 16 Tr LR 432, [1997] EGCS 82, (1997) 94(30) LSG 30, (1997) 147 NLJ 846, (1997) 141 SJLB 130, [1997] NPC 81, (1997) *Times*, 26 May, HL, —*continued* reversing [1996] 1 All ER 55, [1995] 1 WLR 1508, (1996) 71 P & CR 129, [1996] 1 EGLR 69, [1996] 6 EG 140, [1995] EGCS 124, [1995] NPC 117, (1995) 139 SJLB 179, (1995) *Times*, 19 July, CA	12.19
Marchant v Charters [1977] 1 WLR 1181, [1977] 3 All ER 918, (1977) 34 P & CR 291, (1976) 241 EG 23, (1976) 120 Sol Jo 509, (1976) *Times*, 9 July	6.22, 6.47
Marcroft Wagons Ltd v Smith [1951] 2 KB 496, [1951] 2 All ER 271, (1951) 95 Sol Jo 501	2.15, 2.19, 2.36, 3.4, 5.2, 9.53, 13.3
Markfield Investments Ltd v Evans [2001] 1 WLR 1321, [2001] 2 All ER 238, (2001) 81 P & CR 33, [2000] EG 127 (CS), [2000] NPC 121, (2001) 81 P & CR DG15	4.9, 5.14
Matharu v Matharu [1994] 2 FLR 597, [1994] 3 FCR 216, (1994) 26 HLR 648, (1994) 68 P & CR 93, [1994] Fam Law 624, [1994] EG 87 (CS), (1994) 91(25) LSG 31, (1994) 138 SJLB 111, [1994] NPC 63, (1994) *Times*, 13 May, (1994) *Independent*, 18 May	10.31
May v Borup [1915] 1 KB 830	12.16, 12.19, 12.25
McCall v Abelesz [1976] QB 585, [1976] 2 WLR 151, [1976] 1 All ER 727, (1976) 31 P & CR 256, (1975) 238 EG 335, (1975) 120 Sol Jo 81, (1975) *Times*, 24 December	13.16
McCarthy v Bence [1990] 1 EGLR 1	6.18
McGeown v Northern Ireland Housing Executive [1995] 1 AC 233, [1994] 3 All ER 53, [1994] 3 WLR 187, 70 P&CR 10, 26 HLR 711, 92 LGR 629, HL	11.16
McKinley v Montgomery [1993] NI 93	11.16
McPhail v Persons Unknown [1973] Ch 447, [1973] 3 WLR 71, [1973] 3 All ER 393, 72 LGR 93, (1973) 117 Sol Jo 448	13.16
Mehta v Royal Bank of Scotland (2000) 32 HLR 45, [1999] L & TR 340, [1999] 3 EGLR 153, (1999) 78 P & CR D11, (1999) *Times*, 25 January	9.53, 12.18, 12.24, 12.40
Melbury Road Properties 1995 Ltd v Kreidi [1999] 3 EGLR 108, [1999] 43 EG 157	9.13
Mellor v Watkins (1873-74) LR 9 QB 400	9.46, 10.2
Melluish v BMI (No 3) Ltd [1996] AC 454, [1995] 3 WLR 630, [1995] 4 All ER 453, [1995] STC 964, 68 TC 1, [1995] EG 150 (CS), (1995) 92(40) LSG 22, (1995) 139 SJLB 220, (1995) *Times*, 16 October, (1995) *Independent*, 6 November	13.13
Mendelsohn v Normand [1970] 1 QB 177, [1969] 3 WLR 139, [1969] 2 All ER 1215, (1969) 113 Sol Jo 263	7.13, 8.43
Mercer v Denne [1905] 2 Ch 538	3.31, 5.1
Midland Bank Trust Co v Green (No 3) [1982] 1 Ch 529	9.21
Mikeover Ltd v Brady [1989] 3 All ER 618, (1989) 21 HLR 513, (1990) 59 P & CR 218, [1989] 39 EG 92, [1989] EG 82 (CS), (1989) 139 NLJ 1194	3.8, 3.9
Miles v Bull (No 2) [1969] 3 All ER 1585, (1970) 21 P & CR 23	9.21
Millennium Productions Ltd v Winter Theatre (London) Ltd [1946] WN 151, (1946) 115 LJ Ch 297, [1946] 1 All ER 678, revsd [1948] AC 173, [1947] 2 All ER 331, 63 TLR 529, [1947] LJR 1422, 177 LT 349, (1947) 91 Sol Jo 504	2.13, 2.22
Mills v Colchester Corpn (1867) LR 2 CP 476	5.38
Mills v Silver [1991] Ch 271, [1991] Fam 271, [1991] 2 WLR 324, [1991] 1 All ER 449, (1991) 61 P & CR 366, [1990] EG 90 (CS), (1990) 134 Sol Jo 1402, (1990) *Independent*, 11 July	4.17, 4.18, 4.23, 5.4, 5.26
Milmo v Carreras [1946] KB 306	9.43, 10.42
Milton (Peterborough) Estates Co Ltd v Harris [1989] 2 EGLR 299	6.18
Minister of Health v Bellotti [1944] KB 298, [1944] 1 All ER 238	12.6, 12.20, 12.24
Ministry of Defence v Ashman (1993) 25 HLR 513, (1993) 66 P & CR 195, [1993] 40 EG 144, [1993] NPC 70	13.24, 13.28
Ministry of Defence v Thompson [1993] 2 EGLR 107	13.28

Mitton v Farrow [1980] 2 EGLR 1	6.18
Moncrieff v Jamieson [2007] UKHL 42, [2007] 1 WLR 2620, [2008] 4 All ER 752, 2008 SC (HL) 1, 2007 SLT 989, 2007 SCLR 790, [2008] 1 P & CR 21, [2007] 43 EG 200 (CS), (2007) 151 SJLB 1368, [2007] NPC 106, [2008] 1 P & CR DG6, 2007 GWD 33-564	3.24, 7.4, 7.7–7.9, 7.13
Morris Thomas v Petticoat Lane Rentals (1987) 53 P & CR 238, (1986) *Times*, 18 June	8.11, 8.39, 8.42
Morris v Pinches [1969] 212 EG 1141	4.23
Morris v Tarrant [1971] 2 QB 143, [1971] 2 WLR 630, [1971] 2 All ER 920, (1970) 115 Sol Jo 204	2.25, 4.18
Moses v Lovegrove [1952] 2 QB 533, [1952] 1 All ER 1279, [1952] 1 TLR 1324, (1952) 96 Sol Jo 344	5.16
Mount Carmel Investments Ltd v Peter Thurlow Ltd [1988] 1 WLR 1078, [1988] 3 All ER 129, (1989) 57 P & CR 396	5.21
Mountney v Smith [1904] HCA 7	10.36
Mulliner v Midland Railway (1879) LR 11 Ch D 611	3.24
Murphy v Hurley [1992] 1 AC 369	8.41
Muskett v Hill 132 ER 1267, (1839) 5 Bing NC 694	10.21, 10.28
Nat West Bank v Hart [1983] QB 773, [1983] 2 WLR 693, [1983] 2 All ER 177, (1983) 8 HLR 91, (1984) 47 P & CR 102, (1983) 267 EG 252	8.27
National By-Products Ltd v Brice 81 LGR 652, (1983) 46 P & CR 281, (1983) 127 Sol Jo 241	6.56
National Car Parks Ltd v Trinity Developments (Banbury) Co Ltd [2001] EWCA Civ 1686, [2002] 2 P & CR 18, [2002] L & TR 24, [2002] 1 P & CR DG19	6.6
National Carriers v Panalpina (Northern) Ltd [1981] AC 675, [1981] 2 WLR 45, [1981] 1 All ER 161, (1982) 43 P & CR 72, (1981) 125 Sol Jo 46, *Times*, December 17, 1980	12.33
National Provincial Bank Ltd v Ainsworth [1965] AC 1175, [1965] 3 WLR 1, [1965] 2 All ER 472, (1965) 109 Sol Jo 415	2.33, 3.38, 6.65, 9.2, 9.3, 9.5
National Provincial Bank Ltd v Hastings Car Mart Ltd [1965] AC 1175, [1965] 3 WLR 1, [1965] 2 All ER 472, (1965) 109 Sol Jo 415	9.11, 9.17
National Westminster Bank v Jones [2001] 1 BCLC 98, [2000] BPIR 1092, [2000] EG 82 (CS), (2000) 97(28) LSG 31, [2000] NPC 73, (2000) *Times*, 7 July	3.15
NCP Ltd v Trinity Development Co (Banbury) Ltd [2001] L & TR 33, [2001] 2 EGLR 43, [2001] 28 EG 144, [2000] EG 128 (CS), (2001) 81 P & CR DG21	2.34, 3.7, 3.13
Nesbitt v Mablethorpe UDC [1917] 2 KB 568	8.27
Never-Stop Railway (Wembley) Ltd v British Empire Exhibition (1924) Inc [1926] Ch 877	13.11
New Hart Builders Ltd v Brindley [1975] 1 Ch 342	12.27
Newman v Jones (22 March 1982, unreported)	7.6, 7.9
Newnham College Cambridge v HM Revenue & Customs [2008] UKHL 23, [2008] 1 WLR 888, [2008] 2 All ER 863, [2008] STC 1225, [2008] BTC 5330, [2008] BVC 452, [2008] STI 1231, [2008] 16 EG 152 (CS), (2008) 158 NLJ 592, (2008) 152(17) SJLB 29, [2008] NPC 45, (2008) *Times*, 17 April	11.45
Newnham v Willison (1988) 56 P & CR 8	5.26
Niblett v Confectioners Materials Co Ltd [1921] 3 KB 387	8.39
Nicolaou v Pitt (1989) 21 HLR 487, [1989] 21 EG 71, [1989] EG 10 (CS)	3.11
Norris v Checksfield [1991] 1 WLR 1241, [1991] 4 All ER 327, [1991] ICR 632, (1991) 23 HLR 425, (1992) 63 P & CR 38, [1992] 1 EGLR 159, [1992] 01 EG 97, [1991] EG 45 (CS), (1991) 141 NLJ 707, (1991) 135 SJLB 542, (1991) *Times*, 23 April, (1991) *Daily Telegraph*, 29 April	3.3, 6.29, 6.32, 6.35, 6.37, 8.18, 12.13
O'Leary v Islington LBC (1983) 9 HLR 86	8.30

Table of Cases xxxvii

OBG Ltd v Allan [2007] UKHL 21, [2008] 1 AC 1, [2007] 2 WLR 920, [2007] Bus LR 1600, [2007] 4 All ER 545, [2008] 1 All ER (Comm) 1, [2007] IRLR 608, [2007] EMLR 12, [2007] BPIR 746, (2007) 30(6) IPD 30037, [2007] 19 EG 165 (CS), (2007) 151 SJLB 674, [2007] NPC 54, (2007) *Times*, 3 May, (2007) *Times*, 4 May	9.21, 9.22
Odey v Barber [2006] EWHC 3109 (Ch), [2008] Ch 175, [2008] 2 WLR 618, [2007] 3 All ER 543	4.9, 4.10, 5.26, 12.10
Ofulue v Bossert [2009] UKHL 16, [2009] 1 AC 990, [2009] 2 WLR 749, [2009] 3 All ER 93, [2010] 1 FLR 475, [2009] 2 P & CR 17, [2009] Fam Law 1042, [2009] 11 EG 119 (CS), (2009) 106(12) LSG 15, (2009) 153(11) SJLB 29, [2009] NPC 40, *Times*, March 11, 2009	4.17, 5.17
Old Groverbury Manor Farm Ltd v W Seymour Plant Sales & Hire Ltd (No 2) [1979] 1 WLR 1397, [1979] 3 All ER 504, (1980) 39 P & CR 99, (1979) 252 EG 1103	2.3, 10.18, 10.28
Olley v Marlborough Court Ltd [1949] 1 KB 532, [1949] 1 All ER 127, 65 TLR 95, 9 ALR2d 806, [1949] LJR 360, (1949) 93 Sol Jo 40	8.6
On Demand Information plc v Michael Gerson (Finance) plc [2001] 1 WLR 155, [2000] 4 All ER 734, [2000] 2 All ER (Comm) 513, [2002] BCC 122, (2000) 150 NLJ 1300, (2000) *Times*, 19 September	12.29
Orion Finance Ltd v Crown Financial Management Ltd [1994] BCLC 607	10.18
P&S Platt v Crouch [2003] EWCA Civ 1110, [2004] 1 P & CR 18, [2003] 32 EG 67 (CS), (2003) 147 SJLB 934, [2003] NPC 97, [2003] 2 P & CR DG19, (2003) *Times*, 27 August	7.7
Page Motors Ltd v Epsom & Ewell BC (1981) 80 LGR 337	11.31
Parker v Clarke [1960] 1 WLR 286, [1960] 1 All ER 93, (1960) 104 Sol Jo 251	2.15, 2.19
Parker v Parker [2003] EWHC 1846 (Ch), [2003] NPC 94	3.18, 3.19, 12.6, 12.7, 12.18, 12.21, 12.22, 12.24, 12.53
Parker v South Eastern Ry (1877) 2 CPD 416	8.6
Parkins v Westminster CC (1998) 30 HLR 894, [1998] 1 EGLR 22, [1998] 13 EG 145, (1998) 75 P & CR D39	6.41
Parsons v Parsons [1983] 1 WLR 1390, (1984) 47 P & CR 494, (1984) 269 EG 634, (1984) 81 LSG 43, (1983) 127 Sol Jo 823	12.26
Pascoe v Turner [1979] 1 WLR 431, [1979] 2 All ER 945, (1978) 9 Fam Law 82, (1979) 123 Sol Jo 164	9.33, 10.32
Patel v WH Smith (Eziot) Ltd [1987] 1 WLR 853, [1987] 2 All ER 569, (1987) 84 LSG 2049, (1987) 131 Sol Jo 888	13.19
Pavledes v Ryesbridge Properties Ltd (1989) 58 P & CR 459	4.13, 4.17, 4.28
Pearson v Coleman Bros [1948] 2 KB 359, [1948] 2 All ER 274, [1948] LJR 1781, (1948) 92 Sol Jo 392	8.13, 11.7
Penarth Dock Engineering Co Ltd v Pounds [1963] 1 Lloyd's Rep 359	13.6, 13.26, 13.27
Perry v Clissold [1907] AC 73	9.53
Perry v Sharon Developments [1937] 4 All ER 390	8.37
Petra Investments Ltd v Rogers [2003] 2 EGLR 120	8.34
Phelps v Spon-Smith & Co [2001] BPIR 326	10.16
Phillips v Homfray (1870-71) LR 6 Ch App 770	13.27
Phipps & Co Ltd v Rogers [1925] 1 KB 14	12.19
Piper v Muggleton [1956] 2 QB 569, [1956] 2 WLR 1093, [1956] 2 All ER 249, (1956) 100 Sol Jo 360	6.11
Pirabakaran v Patel [2006] EWCA Civ 685, [2006] 1 WLR 3112, [2006] 4 All ER 506, [2006] HLR 39, [2006] 2 P & CR 26, [2006] L & TR 24, [2006] 3 EGLR 23, [2006] 36 EG 260, [2006] 23 EG 165 (CS), (2006) 103(24) LSG 28, (2006) 150 SJLB 743, [2006] NPC 63, (2006) *Times*, 19 July, (2006) *Independent*, 6 June	13.16
Platt v London Underground Ltd [2001] 2 EGLR 121, [2001] 20 EG 227 (CS), (2001) 98(17) LSG 37, (2001) *Times*, 13 March, (2001) *Independent*, 2 April	8.34
Plimmer v Wellington Corp (1883-84) LR 9 App Cas 699	2.25, 4.33, 8.22, 10.31, 12.38
Pocock v Carter [1912] 1 Ch 663	6.8

Polarpark Enterprises Inc v Allason [2007] EWHC 1088 (Ch), [2008] 1 P &
CR 4, [2008] L & TR 6, [2007] 2 EGLR 85, [2007] 33 EG 92, [2007]
WTLR 1829, (2007) *Times*, 26 June 2.20, 12.18, 13.16
Polo Woods Foundation v Shelton-Agar [2009] EWHC 1361 (Ch), [2010] 1
All ER 539, [2010] 1 P & CR 12, [2009] 2 P & CR DG20 .... 3.24, 7.7, 7.8
Port of London Authority v Ashmore [2009] EWHC 954 (Ch), [2009] 4 All
ER 665, [2009] 19 EG 111 (CS), (2009) 159 NLJ 712, [2009] NPC 69 .... 2.34, 3.7
Powell v McFarlane(1979) 38 P & CR 452 .... 13.15
Pratt v Richards [1951] 2 KB 208, [1951] 1 All ER 90 (Note), [1951] 1 TLR
515 .... 6.25
Price v Bouch (1987) 53 P & CR 257, [1986] 2 EGLR 179, (1986) 279 EG
1226 .... 10.9
Prudential Assurance Co Ltd v Excel UK Ltd [2010] L&TR 7 .... 12.25
Prudential Assurance Co Ltd v London Residuary Body [1992] 2 AC 386,
[1992] 3 WLR 279, [1992] 3 All ER 504, (1992) 64 P & CR 193,
[1992] 36 EG 129, [1992] EG 100 (CS), (1992) 142 NLJ 1087, [1992]
NPC 105, (1992) *Times*, 23 July, (1992) *Independent*, 14 August 1.8, 2.17, 2.36, 3.3, 3.4,
6.15, 9.3, 9.9, 12.14
Pulleyn v Hall Aggregates (Thames Valley) Ltd (1993) 65 P & CR 276,
[1992] EG 102 (CS), [1992] NPC 107 .... 4.17, 5.2
Pwllbach Colliery Co Ltd v Woodman [1915] AC 634 .... 3.24

QFS Scaffolding Ltd v Sable [2010] EWCA Civ 682, [2010] NPC 70, (2010)
Times, 20 July 10.23

R (Beresford) v Sunderland CC [2003] UKHL 60, [2004] 1 AC 889, [2003] 3
WLR 1306, [2004] 1 All ER 160, [2004] 2 P & CR 23, [2004] 1 PLR
85, [2004] 1 EGLR 94, [2004] JPL 1106, [2003] 47 EG 155 (CS),
(2003) 147 SJLB 1365, [2003] NPC 139, (2003) *Times*, 14 November 4.11, 4.15–4.20,
5.2–5.4, 5.27, 5.32, 5.33
R (First Real Estates (UK) Ltd) v Birmingham CC [2009] EWHC 817,
Admin 12.17
R (Fullard) v Woking Magistrates Court [2005] EWHC 2922 (Admin) 12.5, 12.8, 12.53
R (Godmanchester TC) v Secretary of State for the Environment [2007]
UKHL 28, [2008] 1 AC 221, [2007] 3 WLR 85, [2007] 4 All ER 273,
[2008] 1 P & CR 12, [2007] 3 EGLR 119, [2007] JPL 1691, [2007] 26
EG 163 (CS), (2007) 104(27) LSG 29, (2007) 151 SJLB 858, [2007]
NPC 74, (2007) *Times*, 22 June 5.4, 5.32, 5.33
R (Khatun) v Newham BC [2004] EWCA Civ 55, [2005] QB 37, [2004] 3
WLR 417, [2004] Eu LR 628, [2004] HLR 29, [2004] BLGR 696,
[2004] L & TR 18, (2004) 148 SJLB 268, [2004] NPC 28, (2004)
Times, 27 February, (2004) *Independent*, 4 March 8.52, 8.53
R (Lewis) v Redcar and Cleveland BC [2010] UKSC 11, [2010] 2 AC 70,
[2010] 2 WLR 653, [2010] 2 All ER 613, [2010] BLGR 295, [2010] 2 P
& CR 16, [2010] 1 EGLR 153, [2010] JPL 1135, [2010] 10 EG 116
(CS), (2010) 160 NLJ 390, (2010) 154(9) SJLB 30, [2010] NPC 27,
(2010) *Times*, 4 March 4.17, 4.20, 5.2, 5.4, 5.27
R v Ahmad (1987) 84 Cr App R 64, (1986) 18 HLR 416, (1986) 52 P & CR
346, [1986] Crim LR 739, (1986) 83 LSG 2569, (1986) 130 Sol Jo 554 .... 13.16
R v Broke (1859) 1 F&F 514 .... 3.34
R v Burke [1991] 1 AC 135, [1990] 2 WLR 1313, (1990) 91 Cr App R 384,
(1990) 154 JP 798, (1990) 22 HLR 433, [1990] Crim LR 877, (1990)
154 JPN 546, (1990) 154 LG Rev 637, (1990) 87(24) LSG 43, (1990)
140 NLJ 742, (1990) 134 Sol Jo 1106 .... 13.16
R v Green (1829) 9 B&C 203 .... 11.38
R v Oxfordshire CC ex parte Sunningwell PC [2000] 1 AC 335, [1999] 3
WLR 160, [1999] 3 All ER 385, [1999] BLGR 651, (2000) 79 P & CR
199, [1999] 2 EGLR 94, [1999] 31 EG 85, [2000] JPL 384, [1999] EG

R v Oxfordshire CC ex parte Sunningwell PC [2000] 1 AC 335, [1999] 3 WLR 160, [1999] 3 All ER 385, [1999] BLGR 651, (2000) 79 P & CR 199, [1999] 2 EGLR 94, [1999] 31 EG 85, [2000] JPL 384, [1999] EG —*continued*
    91 (CS), (1999) 96(29) LSG 29, (1999) 149 NLJ 1038, (1999) 143 SJLB 205, [1999] NPC 74, (1999) *Times*, 25 June, (1999) *Independent*, 29 June   5.1, 5.2, 5.4, 5.25, 5.33, 5.36, 5.37
R v Roberts (1978) 67 Cr App R 228   4.23
R v Wandsworth County Court ex parte Wandsworth LBC [1975] 1 WLR 1314, [1975] 3 All ER 390, 74 LGR 62, (1975) 119 Sol Jo 529   13.18
R v Wear Valley DC ex parte Birks [1985] 2 All ER 699   12.39
Radaitch v Smith [1959] 101 CLR 209   2.30
Radstock Co-Op v Norton Radstock [1967] Ch 1094, [1967] 3 WLR 588, [1967] 2 All ER 812, (1967) 131 JP 387, 65 LGR 518   10.22
Rafique v Walton Estate (1993) 65 P & CR 356, [1992] NPC 75   4.10
Rainham Chemical Works v Belvedere Fish Guano Co [1921] 2 AC 465   11.27, 11.28
Ramnarace v Lutchman [2001] UKPC 25, [2001] 1 WLR 1651, [2002] 1 P & CR 28   2.36, 3.18, 3.19
Ramsden v Dyson and Thornton (1866) LR 1 HL 129, 12 Jur NS 506, 14 WR 926   8.22, 12.38
Read v J Lyons & Co Ltd [1947] AC 156, [1946] 2 All ER 471, (1947) 80 Ll L Rep 1, (1946) 62 TLR 646, [1947] LJR 39, 175 LT 413   11.27
Red House Farms (Thorndon) Ltd v Catchpole [1977] 2 EGLR 125   2.34
Reid-Newfoundland Co v Anglo-American Telegraph Co [1910] AC 560   8.15
Reilly v Booth (1890) 44 Ch D 12   7.6
Revill v Newbury [1996] QB 567, [1996] 2 WLR 239, [1996] 1 All ER 291, (1995) 92(44) LSG 31, (1996) 146 NLJ 50, (1995) 139 SJLB 244, (1995) *Times*, 3 November, (1995) *Independent*, 10 November   13.15
Reynolds v Ashby & Son [1904] AC 466, [1904–7] All ER Rep 401, 73 LJKB 946, HL   6.24
RH Buckley & Sons v N Buckley & Sons [1898] 2 QB 608   8.48
Rhone v Stephens (Executrix) [1994] 2 AC 310, [1994] 2 WLR 429, [1994] 37 EG 151, [1994] EG 50 (CS), (1994) 138 SJLB 77, [1994] NPC 43, (1994) *Times*, 18 March, (1994) *Independent*, 23 March   9.2, 9.27
Rich v Basterfield 136 ER 715, (1847) 4 CB 783   11.32
Rickman v Brudenell-Bruce [2005] EWHC 3400   8.10, 10.9
Right v Cuthell (1804) East 491   12.26
Roads v Trumpington Overseers (1870) LR 6 QB 56   11.38
Roberts v Aylesbury Overseers (1853) 1 El &Bl 423   11.38
Roberts v Fellowes (1906) 94 LT 279   5.4
Roberts v Swangrove [2007] EWHC 513 (Ch), [2007] 2 P & CR 17, [2007] NPC 35   5.14, 5.19, 5.20
Robson Paul v Farrugia (1969) 20 P & CR 820, (1969) 113 Sol Jo 346   4.3
Robson v Hallett [1967] 2 QB 939, [1967] 3 WLR 28, [1967] 2 All ER 407, (1967) 51 Cr App R 307, (1967) 131 JP 333, (1967) 111 Sol Jo 254   4.23, 10.36, 12.6–12.8, 12.51, 12.53
Rokewood Nurseries v Burrell [1955] EGD 304   6.37
Romulus Trading Co Ltd v Comet Properties Ltd [1996] 2 EGLR 70, [1996] 48 EG 157, [1996] NPC 52   8.34
Rose v Krieser [2002] 212 DLR (4) 123   5.10
Ross Auto Wash Ltd v Herbert [1979] 1 EGLR 95   3.7
Rossvale Ltd v Green [1979] 1 EGLR 64   3.6, 3.7
Royal Bank of Canada v Secretary of State for Defence [2009] EWHC 1350 (Ch), [2010] 1 P & CR 7, [2010] L & TR 7   12.25
Rylands v Fletcher (1868) LR 3 HL 330, HL   11.1, 11.2, 11.27

Saed v Plustrade [2002] 2 EGLR 19   9.5
Sanders v McDonald & Pringle [1981] CLY 1534   4.3
Sandhu v Farooqui [2003] EWCA Civ 531, [2003] HLR 55, [2004] 1 P & CR 3   12.2, 12.3, 12.13, 4.17, 5.4, 8.18
Scarborough BC v Adams (1983) 147 JP 449, (1984) 47 P & CR 133, [1983] JPL 673   11.55
Scarborough v Cosgrove [1905] 2 KB 805   8.43, 11.26

Scene Estates Ltd v Amos [1957] 2 QB 205, [1957] 2 WLR 1017, [1957] 2 All
    ER 325, 56 LGR 14, (1957) 101 Sol Jo 445 — 6.19
Scottish Widows v Stewart [2006] EWCA Civ 999, [2007] 1 P & CR DG5 — 3.5, 3.13, 3.16, 6.3
Secretary of State for Social Services v Beavington [1982] 1 EGLR 13 — 6.18
Secretary of State v Meier [2009] UKSC 11, [2009] 1 WLR 2780, [2010]
    PTSR 321, [2010] 1 All ER 855, [2010] HLR 15, [2010] 2 P & CR 6,
    [2010] 1 EGLR 169, [2009] 49 EG 70 (CS), (2009) 153(46) SJLB 34,
    [2010] NPC 3, (2009) *Times*, 4 December — 13.16, 13.18, 13.19
Seddon v Smith (1877) 36 LT 168 — 2.35
Sedleigh-Denfield v O'Callaghan [1940] AC 880, [1940] 3 All ER 349 — 11.34, 11.36, 11.37
ServicePower Asia Pacific Pty Ltd v ServicePower Business Solutions Ltd
    [2009] EWHC 179 (Ch), [2010] 1 All ER (Comm) 238 — 8.20, 12.12
Sevenoaks Ry Co v London, Chatham & Dover Ry Co (1879) 11 ChD 625 — 3.4
Severn Trent Water Ltd v Barnes [2004] EWCA Civ 570, [2004] 2 EGLR 95,
    [2004] 26 EG 194, [2005] RVR 181, (2004) 148 SJLB 693, [2004] NPC
    76 — 13.28
Sharneyford Supplies Ltd v Edge [1986] Ch 128, [1985] 3 WLR 1, [1985] 1
    All ER 976, (1985) 50 P & CR 343, (1985) 82 LSG 2081, (1985) 35
    NLJ 288, (1985) 129 Sol Jo 316 — 12.20
Sharpe, Re, ex parte Trustee of the Bankrupt's Property [1980] 1 WLR 219,
    [1980] 1 All ER 198, (1980) 39 P & CR 459, (1980) 124 Sol Jo 147 — 1.8, 2.25, 9.8, 9.17, 9.29, 9.33
Shayler v Woolf [1946] Ch 320, [1946] 2 All ER 54, [1947] LJR 71, 175 LT
    170, (1946) 90 Sol Jo 357 — 10.12–10.14
Shell-Mex and BP Ltd v Manchester Garages [1971] 1 WLR 612, [1971] 1
    All ER 841, (1971) 115 Sol Jo 111 — 2.34, 3.13, 6.2, 6.3, 8.29
Shepherd's Bush Housing Association v HATS Co-Operative (1992) 24
    HLR 176, [1991] EG 134 (CS) — 13.5
Shiloh Spinners Ltd v Harding [1973] AC 691, [1973] 2 WLR 28, [1973] 1
    All ER 90, (1973) 25 P & CR 48, (1972) 117 Sol Jo 34 — 9.29, 12.29
Shore v Ministry of Works and others [1950] 2 All ER 228, CA — 8.38
Sifton v Sifton [1938] AC 656, [1938] 3 All ER 435, 82 Sol Jo 680 — 12.14
Simpson v Fergus (2000) 79 P & CR 398, (2000) 79 P & CR D16 — 7.13
Sims v Mahon [2005] 3 EGLR 67, [2005] 39 EG 138, (2005) *Times*, 16 June — 10.9
Sinclair Collis Ltd v Commissioners of Customs & Excise [2003] STC 898,
    [2003] ECR I-5965, [2003] 2 CMLR 36, [2003] CEC 452, [2003] BTC
    5318, [2003] BVC 374, [2003] STI 1070, (2003) *Times*, 30 June — 11.46
Singh v Sandhu (unreported), CA, 4 May 1995 — 9.5
Skipton BS v Clayton (1993) 25 HLR 596, (1993) 66 P & CR 223, [1993]
    NPC 52, (1993) *Times*, 25 March — 8.20
Sledmore v Dalby (1996) 72 P & CR 196, [1996] NPC 16 — 4.39
Smeaton v Ilford Corpn [1954] Ch 450, [1954] 2 WLR 668, [1954] 1 All ER
    923, (1954) 118 JP 290, 52 LGR 253, (1954) 98 Sol Jo 251 — 11.36
Smirk v Lyndale Developments Ltd [1975] Ch 317, [1975] 2 WLR 495,
    [1975] 1 All ER 690, (1975) 29 P & CR 407, (1974) 119 Sol Jo 220 — 5.9
Smith v Bridgend CC [2001] UKHL 58, [2002] 1 AC 336, [2001] 3 WLR
    1347, [2002] 1 All ER 292, [2001] BCC 740, [2002] 1 BCLC 77, [2002]
    BLR 160, [2002] TCLR 7, 80 Con LR 172, [2001] NPC 161 — 13.7
Smith v Brudenell-Bruce [2002] 2 P & CR 4, [2001] 28 EG 143 (CS) — 5.26
Smith v Colbourne [1914] 2 Ch 573 — 4.12
Smith v Marrable 152 ER 693, (1843) 11 M & W 5 — 8.37
Smith v Muscat [2003] EWCA Civ 962, [2003] 1 WLR 2853, [2004] HLR 6,
    [2004] L & TR 7, [2003] 3 EGLR 11, [2003] 40 EG 148, [2003] 30 EG
    144 (CS), (2003) 100(35) LSG 37, (2003) 147 SJLB 900, [2003] NPC
    88, (2003) *Times*, 12 August, (2003) *Independent*, 17 July — 8.45
Smith v Northside Developments (1988) 55 P & CR 164, (1987) 283 EG
    1211 — 3.6, 3.12, 6.11, 12.18
Smith v Nottinghamshire CC (1981) *Times*,13 November — 8.29
Smith v Scott [1973] Ch 314, [1972] 3 WLR 783, [1972] 3 All ER 645, (1972)
    116 Sol Jo 785 — 11.32
Smith v Titanate Ltd [2005] 3 EGLR 63 — 9.47

Table of Cases xli

Snook v Mannion [1982] RTR 321, [1982] Crim LR 601	12.5
Snook v West Riding Investments Ltd [1967] 2 QB 786, [1967] 2 WLR 1020, [1967] 1 All ER 518, (1967) 111 Sol Jo 71	3.15
Somma v Hazlehurst [1978] 1 WLR 1014, [1978] 2 All ER 1011, (1983) 7 HLR 30, (1979) 37 P & CR 391, [1978] JPL 554, (1978) 122 Sol Jo 280	3.9
South Glamorgan CC v Griffiths (1992) 24 HLR 334, [1992] 2 EGLR 232, [1992] NPC 13	6.29, 6.36
Southampton Cargo Handling Ltd v Lotus Cars Ltd [2000] 2 All ER (Comm) 705, [2000] 2 Lloyd's Rep 532, [2001] CLC 25	7.13, 8.44
Southern Foundaries (1926) Ltd v Shirlaw [1940] AC 701, [1940] 2 All ER 445	9.18
Southwark LBC v Mills [2001] 1 AC 1, [1999] 3 WLR 939, [1999] 4 All ER 449, [2000] Env LR 112, (2000) 32 HLR 148, [2000] BLGR 138, [2000] L & TR 159, [1999] 3 EGLR 35, [1999] 45 EG 179, [1999] EG 122 (CS), (1999) 96(42) LSG 41, (1999) 96(42) LSG 45, (1999) 149 NLJ 1618, (1999) 143 SJLB 249, [1999] NPC 123, (2000) 79 P & CR D13, (1999) *Times*, 22 October	8.37
Southwark LBC v Williams [1971] Ch 734, [1971] 2 WLR 467, [1971] 2 All ER 175, 69 LGR 145, *Times*, December 17, 1970	2.1
Spenborough UDC's Agreement, Re [1968] Ch 139, [1967] 2 WLR 1403, [1967] 1 All ER 959, 56 LGR 300, (1967) 111 Sol Jo 253	8.7, 8.19, 8.20
Sports International Bussum BV v Inter-Footwear Ltd [1984] 1 WLR 776, [1984] 2 All ER 321, (1984) 81 LSG 1992, (1984) 134 NLJ 568, (1984) 128 Sol Jo 383	12.29
Staffordshire AHA v South Staffordshire Waterworks Co [1978] 1 WLR 1387, [1978] 3 All ER 769, 77 LGR 17, (1978) 122 Sol Jo 331	8.7, 8.19, 10.39
Starside Properties Ltd v Mustapha [1974] 1 WLR 816, [1974] 2 All ER 567, (1974) 28 P & CR 95, (1974) 118 Sol Jo 388	12.30
Stening v Abraham [1931] 1 Ch 470	9.44
Stevens v Bromley LBC [1972] Ch 400, [1972] 2 WLR 605, [1972] 1 All ER 712, 70 LGR 170, (1972) 23 P & CR 142, (1971) 116 Sol Jo 123, (1971) *Times*, 15 December	11.55
Stirling v Maitland 122 ER 1043, (1864) 5 B & S 840	8.32, 9.10, 9.13, 9.17, 9.18
Stockport Waterworks Co v Potter (1864) 3 H&C 300	9.54
Stone v Taffe [1974] 1 WLR 1575, [1974] 3 All ER 1016, (1974) 118 Sol Jo 863	11.11
Strand Electric v Brisford [1952] 2 QB 246, [1952] 1 All ER 796, [1952] 1 TLR 939, (1952) 96 Sol Jo 260	13.6
Straudley Investments Ltd v Mount Eden Land Ltd (1997) 74 P & CR 306, [1996] EG 153 (CS), [1996] NPC 138, (1997) 73 P & CR D31	10.10
Street v Mountford [1985] AC 809, [1985] 2 WLR 877, [1985] 2 All ER 289, (1985) 17 HLR 402, (1985) 50 P & CR 258, [1985] 1 EGLR 128, (1985) 274 EG 821, [2008] BTC 7094, (1985) 82 LSG 2087, (1985) 135 NLJ 460, (1985) 129 Sol Jo 348	1.8, 2.19, 2.29, 2.30, 2.36, 3.3, 3.7, 3.9, 3.13, 3.16, 3.20, 6.3, 6.17, 6.18, 6.26, 6.28, 6.41, 7.10
Stribling v Wickham [1989] 2 EGLR 35	3.10, 3.11
Sutcliffe v Lloyd [2008] EWHC 1329 (Ch)	4.40, 9.29
Swainland Builders Ltd v Freehold Properties Ltd [2002] EWCA Civ 560, [2002] 2 EGLR 71, [2002] 23 EG 123, [2002] 17 EG 154 (CS)	8.8
Swordheath Properties Ltd v Tabet [1979] 1 WLR 285, [1979] 1 All ER 240, (1979) 37 P & CR 327, (1978) 249 EG 439, (1978) 122 Sol Jo 862	13.6, 13.26
Sze To Chun Keung v Kung Kwok Wai David [1997] 1 WLR 1232, (1997) 141 SJLB 171, [1997] NPC 107	5.19, 8.25
Tadman v Henman (1893) 2 QB 168	8.28, 8.45
Taff Vale Railway v Cardiff Railway [1917] 1 Ch 299	7.6
Tanham v Nicholson (1871) LR 5 HL 561	12.27
Tanner v Tanner [1975] 1 WLR 1346, [1975] 3 All ER 776, (1975) 5 Fam Law 193, (1975) 119 Sol Jo 391	1.8, 2.17
Taylor v Caldwell (1863) 3 B&S 826	12.33

Taylor v Pendleton Overseers (1887) 19 QBD 288	3.6, 6.12, 7.14
Teasdale v Walker [1958] 1 WLR 1076, [1958] 3 All ER 307, (1958) 102 Sol Jo 757	3.7
Tennero Ltd v Majorarch Ltd [2003] EWHC 2601 (Ch), [2003] 47 EG 154 (CS), [2004] 1 P & CR DG13	12.25
Terunnanse v Terunnanse [1968] AC 1086, [1968] 2 WLR 1125, [1968] 1 All ER 651, (1968) 112 Sol Jo 134	8.25, 9.7, 12.3
Tetley v Chitty [1986] 1 All ER 663, (1985) 135 NLJ 1009	11.32
Tharsis Sulphur & Copper Co v M'Elroy & Sons [1891] 2 QB 647	8.39
Thatcher v Douglas [1996] NPC 406	9.32
Thomas v DPP (2009) *Times*, 25 November	2.32, 9.53, 13.15
Thomas v Sorrell 124 ER 1098, (1673) Vaugh 330	2.3, 2.21, 8.13
Thomas W Ward Ltd v Alexander Bruce (Grays) Ltd [1959] 2 Lloyd's Rep 472	7.6
Thompson (Funeral Furnishers) v Phillips [1945] 2 All ER 49	6.32, 6.36
Thompson v McCullough [1947] 1 KB 447	12.25
Thompson v Park [1944] KB 408, CA	12.43, 12.45, 13.4
Thompson v Ward [1953] 2 QB 153, [1953] 2 WLR 1042, [1953] 1 All ER 1169, (1953) 97 Sol Jo 352	9.47
Thorgood v Robinson 115 ER 290, (1845) 6 QB 769	13.7
Thorn v London County Council (1876) 1 App Cas 120	8.39
Thorner v Major [2009] UKHL 18, [2009] 1 WLR 776, [2009] 3 All ER 945, [2009] 2 FLR 405, [2009] 3 FCR 123, [2009] 2 P & CR 24, [2009] WTLR 713, (2009-10) 12 ITELR 62, [2009] Fam Law 583, [2009] 13 EG 142 (CS), (2009) 159 NLJ 514, (2009) 153(12) SJLB 30, [2009] NPC 50, [2009] 2 P & CR DG2, (2009) *Times*, 26 March	2.16–2.18, 4.32, 4.33, 4.36, 4.38, 8.8
Thornton v Shoe Lane Parking Ltd [1971] 2 QB 163, [1971] 2 WLR 585, [1971] 1 All ER 686, [1971] 1 Lloyd's Rep 289, [1971] RTR 79, (1970) 115 Sol Jo 75, (1970) *Times*, 19 December	8.6
Thorogood v Robinson 115 ER 290, (1845) 6 QB 769	9.25
Thorpe v Brumfitt (1872-73) LR 8 Ch App 650	8.16
Tinsley v Dudley [1951] 2 KB 18, [1951] 1 All ER 252, [1951] 1 TLR 315, (1951) 95 Sol Jo 106	7.13, 8.43, 11.26
Tito v Waddell (No 2), Tito v Att-Gen [1977] Ch 106, [1977] 2 WLR 496, [1977] 3 All ER 129, (1976) 121 Sol Jo 10, (1976) *Times*, 6 December	10.22
Tolhurst v Associated Portland Cement Manufacturers (1900) Ltd [1903] AC 414, HL	10.5, 10.13, 10.14
Tomlinson v Congleton BC [2003] UKHL 47, [2004] 1 AC 46, [2003] 3 WLR 705, [2003] 3 All ER 1122, [2004] PIQR P8, [2003] 32 EG 68 (CS), (2003) 100(34) LSG 33, (2003) 153 NLJ 1238, (2003) 147 SJLB 937, [2003] NPC 102, (2003) *Times*, 1 August, (2003) *Independent*, 7 October	11.3
Totton and Eling Town Council v Caunter [2008] EWHC 3630 (Ch)	12.3
Tower Hamlets LBC v Barrett (2006) 1 P & CR 132	4.18
Transco v Stockport MBC [2003] UKHL 61, [2004] 2 AC 1, [2003] 3 WLR 1467, [2004] 1 All ER 589, 91 Con LR 28, [2004] Env LR 24, [2003] 48 EG 127 (CS), (2003) 153 NLJ 1791, (2003) 147 SJLB 1367, [2003] NPC 143, [2004] 1 P & CR DG12, (2003) *Times*, 20 November, (2003) *Independent*, 25 November	11.27
Treloar v Bigge (1873-74) LR 9 Ex 151, (1874) 22 WR 843	10.10
Trustees of Grantham Christian Fellowship v Scouts Association [2005] EWHC 209 (Ch)	12.3, 12.28
Trustees of the Grantham Christian Fellowship v Scouts Association Trust Corpn [2005] EWHC 209 (Ch)	4.14
Tungsten Electric Co Ltd v Tool Metal Manufacturing Co Ltd (No 3) [1954] 1 WLR 862, [1954] 2 All ER 28, (1954) 71 RPC 201, (1954) 98 Sol Jo 389; [1955] 1 WLR 761, [1955] 2 All ER 657, (1955) 72 RPC 209, (1955) 99 Sol Jo 470	12.18, 12.20, 12.22
Turcan, Re (1880) 40 Ch D 5	10.19
Tyler v Royal Borough of Kensington & Chelsea (1990) 23 HLR 380	6.41

Table of Cases xliii

Tyrone v Smith (1838) 9 Ad & El 406	5.38
Uglow v Uglow [2004] EWCA Civ 987, [2004] WTLR 1183	4.39, 12.48
Underground (Civil Engineering) Ltd v Croydon LBC [1990] EGCS 48	12.30
Valuation Commissioner (Northern Ireland) v Fermanagh Protestant Board of Education [1969] 1 WLR 1708, [1969] 3 All ER 352, (1969) 133 JP 637, [1969] RA 475, (1969) 113 Sol Jo 875	6.1, 6.29, 11.38
Vandepitte v Preferred Accident Insurance Corp [1933] AC 70, (1932) 44 Ll L Rep 41	10.20
Vandersteen (Executor of the Estate of McGinnes, Deceased) v Agius (1993) 65 P & CR 266, [1992] NPC 108; (1997) 94(41) LSG 28, (1997) 141 SJLB 218, (1997) *Times*, 14 November	3.13, 6.22
Vaughan v Hampson (1875) 33 LT 15	2.22
Vaughan v Vaughan [1953] 1 QB 762, [1953] 1 WLR 236, [1953] 1 All ER 209, (1953) 97 Sol Jo 65	12.40
Vaughan-Armatrading v Sarsah (1995) 27 HLR 631	9.19, 13.3
Venus Investments Ltd v Stocktop Ltd (1997) 74 P & CR D23, [1996] EGCS 173	3.13, 6.3
Verrall v Farnes [1966] 1 WLR 1254, [1966] 2 All ER 808, (1966) 110 Sol Jo 406	6.18
Verrall v Great Yarmouth BC [1981] QB 202, [1980] 3 WLR 258, [1980] 1 All ER 839	12.28, 12.43, 12.45
Vesely v Levy [2007] EWCA Civ 367, [2008] L & TR 9, [2007] NPC 52	2.19, 2.36, 3.4, 6.26
Vine v Waltham Forest LBC [2000] 1 WLR 2383, [2000] 4 All ER 169, [2000] RTR 270, [2000] BLGR 481, (2000) 97(18) LSG 37, (2000) *Times*, 12 April, (2000) *Independent*, 22 May	13.8
W Davies (Spitalfields) Ltd v Huntley [1947] 1 KB 246	12.17
Wallis v Harrison 150 ER 1543, (1838) 4 M & W 538	9.7, 12.3
Wallis's Cayton Bay Holiday Camp Ltd v Shell-Mex and BP Ltd [1975] QB 94, [1974] 3 WLR 387, [1974] 3 All ER 575, (1975) 29 P & CR 214, (1974) 118 Sol Jo 680	4.17, 4.21
Wallshire v Advertising Sites [1988] 33 EG 51, [1988] 2 ELGR 167	6.12, 7.14, 12.11, 12.17, 12.22
Walsh v Lonsdale (1882) LR 21	5.4
Walton Harvey Ltd v Walker and Homfrays Ltd [1931] 1 Ch 274	11.51
Wandsworth LBC v A [1999] All ER (D) 1498	12.39
Warborough Investments Ltd v Central Midland Estates Ltd [2006] EWHC 2622 (Ch), [2007] L & TR 10	12.17
Ward v Kirkland [1967] Ch 194, [1966] 1 WLR 601, [1966] 1 All ER 609, (1966) 110 Sol Jo 289	5.27, 9.29
Ward v Warnke (1990) 22 HLR 496, [1990] EG 103 (CS)	2.15
Warnford Investments Ltd v Duckworth [1979] Ch 127, [1978] 2 All ER 517, [1978] 2 WLR 741, (1977) 76 P&CR 295, (1977) 122 Sol Jo 63	12.36
Warren v Keen [1954] 1 QB 15, [1953] 3 WLR 702, [1953] 2 All ER 1118, (1953) 97 Sol Jo 742	8.48
Watts & Ready v Storey (1983) 134 NLJ 631	8.62, 12.49
Waverley BC v Fletcher [1996] QB 334, [1995] 3 WLR 772, [1995] 4 All ER 756, (1996) 71 P & CR 361, (1995) 159 LG Rev 789, (1995) 145 NLJ 1365, [1995] NPC 122, (1995) 70 P & CR D47, (1995) *Times*, 14 July, (1995) *Independent*, 14 July	8.14
Wayling v Jones [1995] 2 FLR 1029, [1996] 2 FCR 41, (1995) 69 P & CR 170, [1996] Fam Law 88, [1993] EG 153 (CS), (1993) *Independent*, 2 August	4.37
Webb v Paternoster 81 ER 713, (1619) 2 Rolle 143	9.7, 12.3
Webb v Pollmount [1966] Ch 584, [1966] 2 WLR 543, [1966] 1 All ER 481, (1965) 109 Sol Jo 1029	9.40
Well Barn Farming v Backhouse [2005] EWHC 1520 (Ch), [2005] 3 EGLR 109	12.12
Wells v Kingston upon Hull (1874-75) LR 10 CP 402	3.13, 4.25

Wessex Reserve Forces & Cadets Association v White [2005] EWCA Civ
1744, [2006] 2 P & CR 3, [2006] L & TR 15, [2006] 1 EGLR 55,
[2006] 13 EG 142, [2005] 49 EG 89 (CS) 13.14
West Wiltshire DC v Snelgrove (1998) 30 HLR 57, [1997] COD 452 2.19, 13.16
Western Australia v Ward (2002) 191 ALR 1 2.30
Westhoughton UDC v Wigan Coal & Iron Co Ltd [1919] 1 Ch 159 10.22
Westminster CC and Kent Valuation Committee v Southern Rly Co Ltd
[1936] AC 511, [1936] 2 All ER 322, 34 LGR 313 11.38
Westminster CC v Basson (1991) 23 HLR 225, (1991) 62 P & CR 57, [1991]
1 EGLR 277, [1990] EG 141 (CS), (1990) *Times*, 23 November 2.19, 4.17, 6.40, 9.19, 13.3
Westminster CC v Clarke [1992] 2 AC 288, [1992] 2 WLR 229, [1992] 1 All
ER 695, (1992) 24 HLR 360, 90 LGR 210, (1992) 156 LG Rev 681,
[1992] EG 13 (CS), (1992) 142 NLJ 196, (1992) 136 SJLB 82, [1992]
NPC 18, (1992) *Times*, 13 February, (1992) *Independent*, 7 February,
(1992) Guardian, 12 February 3.13, 6.41
Westminster City Council v Southern Railway Co [1936] AC 511, [1936] 2
All ER 322, 34 LGR 313 3.13
Wettern Electric Ltd v Welsh Development Agency [1983] QB 796, [1983] 2
WLR 897, [1983] 2 All ER 629, (1984) 47 P & CR 113 2.29, 3.13, 4.28, 8.37–8.39
Wheat v E Lacon & Co Ltd [1966] AC 552, [1966] 1 All ER 582, [1966] 2
WLR 581, [1966] RA 193, 110 Sol Jo 149, [1966] RVR 223, HL 6.28, 11.9, 11.11–11.13
Wheeler v Mercer [1956] 1 QB 274, [1955] 3 WLR 714, [1955] 3 All ER 455,
(1955) 99 Sol Jo 794; [1957] AC 416, [1956] 3 WLR 841, [1956] 3 All
ER 631, (1956) 100 Sol Jo 836 2.15, 2.19, 3.19
Whitbread West Pennines Ltd v Reedy [1988] ICR 807, (1988) 20 HLR 642 12.13, 13.21
White v Jameson (1874) LR 18 Eq 303 11.32
Whitmores Ltd v Stanford [1909] 1 Ch 427 11.28
Wigan BC v Green & Sons (Wigan) Ltd [1985] 2 EGLR 242 3.13
Wilkie v LPTB [1947] 1 All ER 258, 63 TLR 115, (1947) 111 JP 98, [1947]
LJR 864, 177 LT 71 8.2
William Brandt's Sons & Co v Dunlop Rubber Co [1905] AC 454 10.15, 10.28
Williams & Glyn's Bank Ltd v Boland [1981] AC 487, [1980] 3 WLR 138,
[1980] 2 All ER 408, (1980) 40 P & CR 451, (1980) 124 Sol Jo 443 9.40, 9.41
Williams v Jones [2002] EWCA Civ 1097, [2002] 3 EGLR 69, [2002] 40 EG
169 2.34
Williams v Sandy Lane (Chester) Ltd [2006] EWCA Civ 1738, [2007] 1 P &
CR 27, [2007] 1 EGLR 10, [2007] 7 EG 144, [2007] 2 EG 125 (CS),
(2007) *Times*, 5 January 5.30
Williams v Staite [1979] 1 WLR 291, [1979] 1 All ER 48, (1979) 68 Cr
App R 53, [1979] RTR 106, (1978) 130 NLJ 1109, (1978) 122 Sol Jo
680; [1979] Ch 291, [1978] 2 WLR 825, [1978] 2 All ER 928, (1978)
36 P & CR 103, (1978) 122 Sol Jo 333 2.25, 8.62, 8.63, 9.14, 9.33, 12.49, 12.50
Willis v Willis [1986] 1 EGLR 62, (1985) 277 EG 1133 8.62, 12.49
Wilson v Tavener [1901] 1 Ch 578 3.6, 6.12, 7.14, 12.24
Wiltshire CC v Frazer (No 2) [1986] 1 WLR 109, [1986] 1 All ER 65, (1986)
52 P & CR 46, (1985) 82 LSG 3448, (1985) 135 NLJ 1080, (1985)
Times, 27 September 13.22
Winch v Mid Bedfordshire DC [2002] All ER (D) 380 (Jul) 11.31, 11.33
Winter Garden Theatre (London) Ltd v Millennium Productions Ltd [1948]
AC 173, [1947] 2 All ER 331, 63 TLR 529, [1947] LJR 1422, 177 LT
349, (1947) 91 Sol Jo 504 6.37, 7.12, 8.18–8.20, 12.6, 12.7, 12.10, 12.12, 12.18, 12.22–12.24,
12.42, 12.43, 12.45, 12.51–12.54
Wood v Leadbitter 153 ER 351, (1845) 13 M & W 838 2.22, 8.64, 12.42, 12.45, 13.4, 13.15
Wood v Manley 113 ER 325, (1839) 11 Ad & El 34 4.29, 13.10
Wood v Waud (1849) 3 Exch 748 5.4
Wragg v Surrey CC [2008] EWCA Civ 19, [2008] HLR 30, [2008] NPC 12,
(2008) *Times*, 19 March 6.30
Wretham v Ross [2005] EWHC 1259 (Ch), [2005] NPC 87, [2006] 1 P & CR
DG2 5.17
Wrexham Maelor BC v MacDougall (1993) 66 P & CR 327 11.52

Wright v Macadam [1949] 2 KB 744, [1949] 2 All ER 565, (1949) 93 Sol Jo 646	7.6, 9.36
Wringe v Cohen [1939] 4 All ER 241	11.36
Wyld v Silver [1963] 1 QB 169, [1963] Ch 243, [1962] 3 WLR 841, [1962] 3 All ER 309, 60 LGR 461, (1962) 106 Sol Jo 875	5.1
Yarmouth Harbour Commissioners v Harold Hayles Ltd [2004] EWHC 3375	12.38

TABLE OF STATUTES

References are to paragraph numbers.

Access to Neighbouring Land Act 1992	2.1
Acquisition of Land Act 1981	11.51
Agricultural Holdings Act 1986	3.2, 6.1, 6.16, 6.17, 6.20, 8.58
s 1(1)	6.19
s 1(4)	6.18
s 2	6.18, 6.19, 8.58
s 2(1)	6.18, 9.20
s 2(1)(b)	9.20
s 2(3)	6.18, 6.19
s 2(3)(a)	6.19
s 12	6.20
s 13	6.20
s 25(2)	6.20
s 25(3)	6.20
s 27(2)	6.20
s 27(3)	6.20
ss 60–63	6.20
ss 64–69	6.20
ss 70	6.20
ss 71–73	6.20
s 96(1)	6.18
Sch 1	6.20
Sch 2	6.20
Sch 3	6.20
Schs 7–9	6.20
Agricultural Holdings (England) Act 1875	1.3
Agricultural Holdings (England) Act 1883	1.3
Agricultural Tenancies Act 1995	3.2
s 4(1)	6.16
s 38	6.16
Agriculture Act 1947	
s 109	6.18
Animals Act 1971	
s 7(1)	13.9
Caravan Sites Act 1968	6.1, 6.56, 6.60–6.64, 11.23, 13.16
Pt I	6.38, 6.60
s 1(2)	6.60
s 2	6.61
s 3(1)(a)	6.62
s 3(1)(b)	6.62
s 3(1)(c)	6.63, 13.16
s 3(1A)	6.63
s 3(2)	6.62
s 3(4)	6.62
Caravan Sites Act 1968—*continued*	
s 3(4A)	6.63
s 3(5)	6.63
s 4(1)	6.64
s 4(2)	6.64
s 4(3)	6.64
s 4(4)	6.64
s 4(5)	6.64
s 4(6)	6.64
s 5(3)	6.61
s 5(5)	6.62, 13.16
Caravan Sites and Control of Development Act 1960	
Pt I	6.60
s 1(1)	6.60
Civil Liability (Contribution) Act 1978	11.37
Commons Act 2006	
s 15	3.32, 5.1
s 15(2)	5.35
s 15(3)	5.35
s 15(4)	5.35
s 15(7)	4.6
s 15(7)(b)	5.35
Compulsory Purchase Act 1965	11.51
s 13	6.61
County Courts Act 1984	
s 15	13.20
s 21(1)	13.20
s 69	A3.1–A3.4
s 138	3.2, 12.29
Criminal Justice and Public Order Act 1994	
s 61	13.17
s 68	13.17
Criminal Law Act 1977	
s 6	13.16
s 6(1)(a)	13.16
s 6(2)	13.16
s 12(1)(a)	13.16
s 12(2)	13.16
s 12A	13.16
s 12A(2)(c)	13.16
s 12A(4)(c)	13.16
s 12A(6)(c)	13.16
Defective Premises Act 1972	10.48, 11.2, 11.21–11.25
s 1	11.21
s 4(1)	11.22–11.25

Defective Premises Act 1972—*continued*		Highways Act 1980	5.33
s 4(2)	11.24	s 31	3.33, 5.1, 5.31, 5.34
s 4(3)	11.24	s 31(3)	5.31
s 4(3)(b)	11.24	s 31(5)	5.31
s 4(4)	11.25	s 31(6)	5.31
s 4(6)	11.23	Housing Act 1980	
s 6(3)	11.22	s 69	13.16
Disability Discrimination Act 1995		s 89	13.22
s 19	12.39	Housing Act 1985	6.1, 6.39, 6.42, 6.43, 8.54
s 22	12.39	Pt IV	6.39
s 23	12.39	s 24	6.44
Distress for Rent Act 1737		s 32	3.1
s 18	3.2	s 79(1)	6.39
		s 79(2)	6.39
Electricity Act 1989		s 79(3)	6.38, 6.40, 6.41, 8.54, 9.20
s 10	3.35	s 79(4)	6.42
Environmental Protection Act		s 80	6.39, 6.40
1990	11.58–11.60	s 81	6.39
s 79	11.58	s 82	6.43
s 79(7)	11.59	s 82A	6.43
s 80(2)(a)	11.59	s 83	6.43
s 80(2)(b)	11.60	s 83(1)(b)	6.43
s 80(2)(c)	11.59, 11.60	s 84	6.43
s 80(4)	11.58	s 84(3)	6.43
s 81(2)	11.59	s 85(1)–(3)	6.43
Equality Act 2006		s 86	6.43
s 46	12.39	s 86(2)(a)	6.43
		s 87	6.43
		ss 87–90	8.54
Family Law Act 1996	6.65, 9.54	ss 91–92	6.43, 8.54
s 30(2)	6.66	s 93	8.54
s 30(3)	6.66	s 96	8.54
s 30(4)	6.66, 9.47	ss 97–101	8.54
s 30(7)	6.66	ss 102–103	8.54
s 30(8)	6.67	s 108	8.54
s 30(9)	6.66	s 112(1)	6.39
s 31(2)	6.69	Sch 1	6.39
s 31(3)	6.69	Sch 1, para 2	6.42
s 31(8)	6.67	Sch 1, para 2(1)–(3)	6.27
s 31(10)(a)	9.4	Sch 1, para 3	6.42
s 31(10)(b)	9.4	Sch 1, para 4	6.42
s 33	6.65, 6.70	Sch 1, para 5	6.42
s 33(1)(a)	6.68	Sch 1, para 12	6.42
s 33(1)(b)	6.66	Sch 2	6.43
s 33(3)	6.68	Housing Act 1988	3.2, 3.19, 6.38, 6.49,
s 33(5)	6.67		6.53–6.55, 8.57
s 33(6)	6.68	s 5(3)	8.57
s 33(7)	6.68	s 6	8.57
s 33(8)	6.67	s 7(4)	6.55
s 33(10)	6.68	s 8	6.55
s 34(2)	6.69, 9.37	s 9(1)	6.55
ss 35–38	6.65	s 9(2)	6.55
Finance Act 2003		s 9(3)	6.55
s 42(1)	11.48	s 9(4)	6.55
s 44(2)	11.50	s 18	8.57
s 44(4)	11.50	s 18(3)	8.57
s 44(5)(a)	11.50	s 24(2)	6.54
s 44(6)	11.50	s 24(3)	6.55, 8.57
s 44(8)	11.50	s 24(4)	8.57
s 48(1)	11.49	ss 27–28	12.40
s 48(2)	11.48	s 34(4)	6.49
s 48(2)(b)	11.49	s 36(1)	6.47
s 77	11.49	Sch 2	6.55
		Sch 3	6.54

Housing Act 1988—*continued*	
Sch 3, para 3	6.55
Housing Act 1996	
Pt V	6.45
Pt VII	6.42
s 124(2)	6.45
s 124(3)	6.45
s 125(2)	6.45
s 125(5)	6.45
s 125A	6.45
s 126	6.45, 6.46
s 127(2)	6.46
s 128	6.46
s 129	6.46
ss 131–133	6.46
s 134	6.46
ss 143B–143F	6.43
Housing and Regeneration Act 2008	
s 316	6.56
Sch 16	6.56
Immigration and Asylum Act 1999	
Pt VI	6.42
s 4	6.42
Increase of Rent and Mortgage Interest (War Restrictions) Act 1915	1.3
Insolvency Act 1986	
Pt I	12.39
s 178(2)	12.35
s 178(3)	12.37
s 178(3)(a)	12.35
s 178(4)	12.36
s 252	12.39
s 285	12.39
s 315(1)	12.35
s 315(2)(b)	12.37
s 315(3)	12.36
s 315(3)(b)	12.36
s 336(4)	6.70
s 336(5)	6.70
Sch B1	12.39
Interpretation Act 1978	
s 7	12.27
Sch 1	11.51
Land Charges Act 1972	
s 2(7)	9.6
s 4(8)	9.6
Land Compensation Act 1973	
s 29(2)	11.53
s 29(4)	11.53
s 33	11.53
s 37(1)	11.52
s 37(2)(a)	11.52
s 37(3)	11.52
s 37(5)	11.52
Land Registration Act 1925	9.32, 9.40
s 70(1)	9.5
s 70(1)(g)	9.5, 9.32, 9.40
s 75	5.1
Land Registration Act 2002	9.41
s 28	9.32

Land Registration Act 2002—*continued*	
s 29(1)	9.32
s 29(2)(a)(i)	9.32
s 32	9.4, 9.5
s 96(1)	5.1
s 116	9.32, 10.31
s 131(1)	9.42
s 131(2)(c)	9.42
Sch 3	9.40
Sch 3, para 2	9.32, 9.40, 9.41
Sch 3, para 2(b)	9.40
Sch 3, para 2(c)	9.40
Sch 4, para 3(2)	9.42
Sch 4, para 6(2)	9.42
Sch 6	5.1
Landlord and Tenant Act 1730	
s 1	3.2
Landlord and Tenant Act 1925	
s 146	3.2
Landlord and Tenant Act 1927	
s 19	3.2, 10.8
Landlord and Tenant Act 1954	6.3
Pt II	3.2, 6.2
s 23(1)	6.2, 9.47
s 24	3.2
ss 24–28	6.14
s 38(4)	6.4
s 38A(1)	6.4
s 43(1)(b)	6.14
s 69(1)	6.2
Landlord and Tenant Act 1985	
s 8	3.2, 8.37, 10.48
s 9	8.37, 8.56
s 11	3.2, 8.37, 8.56
Landlord and Tenant Act 1988	
s 1	3.2
Landlord and Tenant (Covenants) Act 1995	3.2
Law of Property Act 1925	
146	12.29
s 1(2)	3.24, 7.4
s 53(1)(c)	10.16
s 54	3.24
s 54(1)	4.30
s 54(2)	4.30
s 62	2.4, 5.2, 7.3, 9.34–9.36, 10.1
s 82	6.18
s 136	10.15
s 139	9.46
s 146	12.27
s 149(6)	3.4
s 196	12.27
Law of Property (Miscellaneous Provisions) Act 1989	
s 2	3.25, 4.30, 4.33
Law Reform (Frustrated Contracts) Act 1943	
s 1(2)–(3)	12.34
Leasehold Property (Repairs) Act 1938	3.2
Limitation Act 1939	4.21
Limitation Act 1980	3.19, 5.16
s 15	5.15
Sch 1, para 4	5.23

Limitation Act 1980—*continued*	
Sch 1, para 5	3.2, 3.19, 5.16
Sch 1, para 8(1)	5.15
Sch 1, para 8(4)	4.21, 4.22
Local Government Act 1992	
s 69(1)	11.39
Local Government (Miscellaneous Provisions) Act 1976	
s 19(2)	5.2
Local Government Finance Act 1988	
s 43(1)	11.38
Local Government Finance Act 1992	
s 3	11.39
s 4	11.39
s 6	11.39
s 6(2)(d)	11.40
s 6(2)(e)	11.40
s 6(3)	11.40
s 6(5)	11.39
s 7	11.39
Mobile Homes Act 1983	6.1, 6.38, 6.56–6.60, 8.59, 10.10
s 1(1)	6.56
s 1(2)	6.57
s 1(3)	6.57
s 1(4)	6.57
s 1(5)	6.57
s 1(6)	6.57, 6.59, 8.59
s 2	6.57, 8.59
s 2(1)	6.58, 8.59
s 2(2)	6.59, 8.59
s 2(3)	6.59
s 3(1)	6.56, 6.57, 9.20
s 3(2)	6.56
s 3(3)	6.56
s 3(4)	6.56
s 5(1)	6.56
Sch 1	6.56, 6.58, 6.59, 8.59
Pt I	6.56, 6.58, 8.59
para 1	8.59
para 2	8.59
para 2(1)	6.58
para 2(2)	6.58
para 2(3)	6.58
para 3	6.58
para 4(3)	6.58
para 6	6.58
para 6(2)	6.58
para 6(3)	6.58
para 6(4)	6.58
para 7	6.58
para 8	8.59
para 8(1)	10.8
para 8(1B)	10.8
para 8(2)	8.59
para 9	8.59
para 10(1)–(3)	8.59
paras 11–15	8.59
para 16	8.59
para 21	8.59
Pt II	6.59, 8.59

Occupiers' Liability Act 1957	4.13, 5.9, 6.1, 6.25, 6.28, 7.2, 7.11, 8.2, 8.38, 11.2–11.20, 11.23, 11.26, 12.3, 13.2
s 1(1)(a)	11.17
s 1(2)	11.9
s 1(3)	6.25
s 1(3)(b)	11.4
s 2(1)	8.37, 11.9, 11.14, 11.15, 11.17
s 2(2)	11.3, 11.7
s 2(3)	11.5, 11.13
s 2(4)	11.5
s 2(4)(a)	11.5
s 2(4)(b)	11.5
s 2(5)	11.5
s 3(1)	11.15, 11.16
s 3(4)	11.15
s 5	8.37, 8.38, 11.15, 11.16
s 5(1)	8.38
s 5(2)	8.38
Occupiers' Liability Act 1984	6.1, 7.2, 11.2, 11.7, 11.15, 11.16, 11.18–11.20, 11.26
s 1(3)	11.18
s 1(4)	11.18
s 1(5)	11.18
s 1(6)	11.18
s 1(8)	11.18
Open Spaces Act 1906	
s 10	4.19, 5.2
Petroleum Act 1998	2.1
Police and Criminal Evidence Act 1984	2.1
Prescription Act 1832	5.1
s 2	5.27, 5.28
Protection from Eviction Act 1977	6.1, 6.37, 6.62, 13.16
s 1(1)	13.16
s 1(2)	13.16
s 1(3)	13.16
s 1(3A)	13.16
s 1(3B)	13.16
s 1(3C)	13.16
s 2	13.16
s 3	13.16
s 3(1)	13.16
s 3(2)	13.16
s 3(2A)	13.16
s 3(2B)	13.16
s 3A	12.18, 13.16
s 3A(7)(a)	6.23
s 3A(7)(b)	12.5
s 3A(7A)–(7C)	13.16
s 4(2A)	13.22
s 4(3)–(5)	13.22
s 4(7)–(10)	13.22
s 5	6.23, 12.5, 12.13, 12.18, 12.25
s 8(2)	13.16
Protection from Harassment Act 1997	13.16
Public Health Act 1875	
s 164	5.2
Public Health Act 1964	
s 164	4.19

Race Relations Act 1976		Supreme Court Act 1981	
s 29	12.39	s 38	12.29
Rent Act 1977	6.38, 6.47, 6.49, 6.50, 6.52		
s 19	6.22, 6.47, 8.55	Telecommunications Act 1984	
s 19(3)–(7)	6.47	Sch 2	3.35
s 19(5)(c)	6.47	Torts (Interference with Goods) Act 1977	
s 19(6)	6.47		
s 103	6.48	s 12	13.9
s 104	6.48	s 13	13.9
s 106	6.48	Sch 1	13.9
s 106A	6.48	Town and Country Planning Act 1990	
s 122	8.55	s 171C(1)	11.54
Sch 15	6.51	s 171C(2)	11.54
Rent (Agriculture) Act 1976	6.38, 6.49–6.54, 8.56	s 171D	11.54
		s 171E(4)	11.54
s 1(1A)	6.50	s 171G	11.54
s 2(1)	6.50	s 172(2)	11.55
s 2(2)–(4)	6.50	s 173(4)	11.55
s 3(2)–(3)	6.52	s 173(5)	11.55
s 5	6.51	s 179(1)	11.55
s 6(1)	6.51	s 179(4)	11.55
s 7(2A)	6.51	s 183	11.56
s 7(3)	6.51	s 187A(1)	11.57
s 7(4)	6.51	s 187A(2)	11.57
s 7(5)	6.51	s 336(1)	11.54, 11.55
s 9	6.52	Tribunals, Courts and Enforcement Act 2007	3.19
ss 13–16	6.52		
s 23	6.50	Pt 3	3.2
s 34	6.50	Sch 12	8.45
Sch 2, para 1	6.50	Trusts of Land and Appointment of Trustees Act 1996	3.28
Sch 2, para 3	6.50		
Sch 3, para 1	6.50	s 12	3.28–3.30
Sch 3, para 2	6.50	s 12(1)	3.30
Sch 3, para 3	6.50	s 12(2)	3.28
Sch 3, para 4	6.50	s 13	3.29, 3.30
Sch 4	6.51	s 13(7)	3.29
Sch 5	6.51, 8.56	s 14	3.29
Sch 5, para 5	8.56		
Sch 5, para 6	8.56	Unfair Contract Terms Act 1977	3.2, 8.50–8.52, 11.17
Sch 5, para 6(1)	8.37		
Sch 5, para 7(1)	8.56	ss 2–4	8.51
Sch 5, para 7(2)	8.56	Sch 1, para 1(b)	8.51
Sch 5, para 10	8.56		
Sch 5, para 12(4)	8.56	Value Added Tax Act 1994	
		s 4(1)	11.42
Settled Land Act 1925	3.27	s 5(2)	11.42
Sex Discrimination Act 1975		Sch 9	11.43
s 20	12.39		
Supply of Goods and Services Act 1982	3.2, 8.53, 8.55	Water Resources Act 1991	
		s 160	3.35
s 13	8.53		
s 15(1)	8.45		

TABLE OF STATUTORY INSTRUMENTS

References are to paragraph numbers.

Civil Procedure Rules 1998, SI 1998/3132	
r 6.3	13.21
Pt 16	13.21
r 16.3(2)	13.21, A3.1
PD 16, para 7.3(1)	13.21
Pt 24	13.21
Pt 55	13.21
r 55.1(b)	13.21, 13.22
r 55.2(1)(a)(iii)	13.21
r 55.2(1)(b)	13.21
r 55.3(1)	13.20
r 55.3(2)	13.20
r 55.4	13.21
r 55.5(2)	13.21
r 55.7(1)	13.21
r 55.7(2)	13.21
r 55.8	13.21
r 55.21(2)	13.19
PD 55, para 2.1	13.20, 13.21
PD 55, para 2.6	13.21
Sch 1	
RSC Ord 45	
r 3(2)	13.22
RSC Ord 54	
r 3(1)(a)	13.22
RSC Ord 113	
r 7	13.22
Sch 2	
CCR Ord 26	
r 17(1)	13.22
Council Tax (Exempt Dwellings) Order 1992, SI 1992/558	11.39
Furniture and Furnishings (Fire) (Safety) Regulations 1988, SI 1998/1324	A1.2
Mobile Homes (Written Statement) (England) Regulations 2006, SI 2006/2275	6.57
Mobile Homes (Written Statement) Regulations 1983, SI 1983/749	6.57
Notices to Quit (Prescribed Information) Regulations 1988, SI 1988/2201	12.18
Regulatory Reform (Business Tenancies) (England and Wales) Order 2003, SI 2003/3096	6.4
Unfair Terms in Consumer Contracts Regulations 1994, SI 1994/3159	3.2
Unfair Terms in Consumer Contracts Regulations 1999, SI 1999/2083	3.2, 8.50–8.53, 10.8, 11.17
reg 6(2)	8.18, 8.52

Chapter 1

INTRODUCTION

1.1 Until now licences regarding the use and occupation of land have received relatively cursory treatment in academic and practitioner texts.[1]

1.2 In part the reasons are historical. Traditional analysis distinguished personal (eg contractual) rights – which, with certain exceptions, bind only the immediate parties and their privies – and proprietary rights/interests – which bind the whole world, including the grantor's successors, except someone with a superior title. Licences were thought to fall exclusively into the former category. Only comparatively recently has the ability of a licence, whilst essentially personal in nature, to emulate, in certain circumstances and in certain respects, a proprietary right – eg the ability to bind third parties – been recognised (see Chapter 9). Licences straddle – not always comfortably – the personal and the proprietary.

1.3 Also, licences came rather late on the scene.[2] It is only in the last hundred years or so – coinciding with the start of statutory intervention in the landlord and tenant relationship[3] – that their potential as a mechanism for regulating the occupation of land became recognised. That intervention gave particular impetus to the development of the licence, which became used as a means/attempted means of avoiding statutory control. In part also the licence received little attention because of its (perceived) lack of commercial importance; the classic licence was gratuitous and/or short term and, as a result, was rarely the subject of litigation before the last century. Licences are the residual category of rights in relation to property.

1.4 Principally, however, it is thought the licence received scant treatment as a discrete subject because it was (and is) the least homogenous of all rights over property. There is no single set of rules as to the creation, termination and attributes of licences as there is in relation to (say) easements or leases. Also, the sheer versatility of the licence – the most 'chameleonic'[4] of all rights regulating the use/occupation of land – hinders easy classification. Licences range from the ephemeral (eg informal house visits) to the permanent.

---

[1] A notable exception is Dawson and Pearce *Licences Relating to the Occupation or Use of Land* (Butterworths, 1979).
[2] A licensee is 'a legal creature who probably rarely engaged the attention of the courts before 1852 or for some time thereafter': *Manchester Airport plc v Dutton* [2000] QB 133, at 149.
[3] Starting with the Agricultural Holdings (England) Acts 1875 and 1883 and (in the residential sphere) the Increase of Rent and Mortgage Interest (War Restrictions) Act 1915.
[4] Gray and Gray *Elements of Land Law* (Oxford University Press, 5th edn, 2009), at para 10.3.2.

Uniquely they may be granted to defined person(s), or to a group whose composition changes over time (eg the inhabitants of a particular area) or to the public generally. They may confer rights of occupation (even, exceptionally, possession – see Chapter 2) or merely limited rights of entry for a specific purpose. They may be gratuitous, contractual or ancillary to a traditional proprietary right or interest. They may do no more than give the licensee a defence to an action in trespass by the owner or impose substantial obligations on one or both parties towards the other and strangers.

1.5 In the residential sphere, the licence is the mechanism that governs the relationship between (eg) owners and informal visitors/lodgers, hotel guests and service occupiers. In agriculture, they take often the form of share farming agreements and grasskeeps. In the commercial context, they are typically found in franchise agreements, partnerships, building contracts and agreements relating to market stalls, advertising hoardings, front-of-house rights and so on. Indeed it is difficult to think of any type of right to use land that can take the form of a proprietary interest/right (eg leases, easements, profits, customary rights, town/village greens, public rights of way) that cannot instead take the form of a licence.

1.6 This variety of function is the best testimony to the licence's usefulness. However, it is perhaps little wonder, given its malleability, that there have been few comprehensive treatments of such a disparate subject. This book tries to go some way to filling that gap.

1.7 The time is ripe to do so because of the increasing prevalence and sophistication of licences in modern times. Of course they retain their traditional function in the domestic sphere. However, their role in long-term agreements and sophisticated multi-party commercial transactions (eg joint ventures, partnerships, land development contracts etc) is increasingly appreciated.

1.8 It is also considered an opportune time for such a book because over the last few decades the subject of licences has been one of the most dynamic areas in land law. For instance, from the 1950s (starting with *Errington v Errington and Woods*[5]) attempts were made to assimilate contractual licences and proprietary interests, despite blithe assertions at the time that: 'The question of the position of a contractual licensee vis a vis a third party is not likely to become a matter of so great importance.'[6] These developments seemed sufficiently established by the 1980s that learned authors asserted confidently: 'All the indications now are that contractual licences are capable of binding successors in title as equitable interests ... the courts appear to be well on their way to creating a new and highly versatile interest in land ...'[7] Yet only 5 years

---

[5] [1952] 1 KB 290; *Re Sharpe* [1980] 1 WLR 219.
[6] Maudsley 'Licences to Remain on Land' (1956) 20 Conv 280.
[7] *Megarry & Wade: The Law of Real Property* (Sweet & Maxwell, 5th edn, 1984), at p 808.

later *Ashburn Anstalt Ltd v Arnold*[8] put the quietus to the *Errington* 'heresy'.[9] Also, in the last few decades courts have struggled to regulate informal family arrangements concerning land, initially by means of the (inferred or even imputed) contractual licence[10] but latterly by the use of estoppel, itself a controversial development insofar as such 'licences' have been held to bind third parties.[11] Furthermore from about the 1950s – but reaching its zenith with the decision in *Street v Mountford*[12] – courts have sought to formulate the appropriate test to distinguish leases and licences, initially by reference to whether the parties intended their arrangement to be purely personal or to create an interest in land[13] but latterly by reference to the substance of the agreement and specifically whether it granted exclusive possession. Yet at the same time, it was acknowledged that a licence may, in exceptional cases, confer possession. A further controversial[14] development of the licence – and a further blurring of the distinction between personal and proprietary rights – occurred more recently in *Manchester Airport plc v Dutton*,[15] as a result of which licensees with a right to occupy land that confers control (but not, necessarily, possession as traditionally defined) may now claim possession against strangers, a remedy hitherto thought to be confined to persons with factual possession or the right to possession. Licences retain their capacity to surprise.

1.9 What is more the licence has been and will continue to be at the forefront of the debate as to the nature of possession and the defining characteristics and attributes of proprietary rights/interests, particularly in light of the so-called 'non-proprietary' lease in *Bruton v London & Quadrant Housing Trust*.[16]

1.10 This book does not try to resolve those issues but intends rather to provide a practical guide as to the identification and classification of licences, their attributes and the effect such designation has on the respective rights and obligations of the licensor and licensee towards each other and third parties.

1.11 This, however, is far from the last word on the subject: the law of licences will not remain static. In the coming years, further clarification can be expected (eg) as to what acts/circumstances are sufficient to give rise to an implied licence, preventing the running of time for limitation/prescription etc purposes; the circumstances in which a licence binds the licensor's successors on the basis of constructive trust and/or tortious interference with contractual relations; the

---

[8] [1989] Ch 1, overruled (on a different point) *Prudential Assurance Co Ltd v London Residuary Body* [1992] 2 AC 386.
[9] *IDC Group Ltd v Clark* [1992] 1 EGLR 187, at 189M, aff'd [1992] 2 EGLR 184.
[10] See eg *Tanner v Tanner* [1975] 1 WLR 1346; *Chandler v Kerley* [1978] 1 WLR 693; *Hardwick v Johnson* [1978] 1 WLR 683; contrast *Horrocks v Forray* [1976] 1 WLR 230.
[11] See eg *Megarry & Wade: The Law of Real Property* (Sweet & Maxwell, 7th edn, 2008), at para 16-006.
[12] [1985] AC 809.
[13] See eg *Cobb v Lane* [1952] 1 All ER 1199.
[14] See Gray and Gray *Elements of Land Law* (Oxford University Press, 4th edn, 2005), at para 3.51: 'an unprincipled erosion of the historic concept of possession.'
[15] [2000] QB 133.
[16] [2000] 1 AC 406.

degree of control necessary to give the licensee standing to sue strangers in trespass; the parties' implied obligations (if any) as to the suitability/fitness for purpose or the condition, maintenance and repair of the land; when a dated notice is impliedly required to terminate a licence and so forth.

1.12 Of course licences are not immune from developments in other areas, eg as to the scope for proprietary estoppel in the commercial sphere after *Cobbe v Yeoman's Row Management Ltd*;[17] the statutory control of contract terms; and the impact of human rights legislation on a public owner's ability to seek possession against its licensees. The possible future implementation of the recommendations in the Law Commission's Consultation Paper *Easements, Covenants and Profits à Prendre*[18] and in its *Renting Homes: The Final Report*[19] – which recommends the creation of a generic 'occupation contract' to replace residential tenancies and licences – will also have implications for its future development.

1.13 For the present, however, although hitherto largely unheralded, the licence is now established as a flexible and pragmatic tool, highly adaptable to the circumstances and the parties' needs. Licences form a discrete, albeit disparate, category of rights regulating the use/occupation of land. Their importance is becoming increasingly recognised.

1.14 The law of licences is important to all concerned with the use and management of land: landowners, public authorities, developers, professionals and their legal advisers. Its importance is only likely to increase in the future.

---

[17] [2008] 1 WLR 1752. Compare the extrajudicial observations of Sir Terence Etherton's extrajudicial observations to the Chancery Bar Association 2009 'Constructive Trust and Proprietary Estoppel: The Search for Clarity and Principle' and Lord Neuberger's 2009 lecture 'The Stuffing of Minerva's Owl? Taxonomy and Taxidermy in Equity'.
[18] Law Com No 186 (TSO, 2008).
[19] Law Com No 297 (TSO, 2006).

Chapter 2

THE NATURE AND TYPES OF LICENCES

The nature of the licence	2.1
The concept of the licence	2.2
Distinguishing licences from other private rights/interests	2.5
Distinguishing licences and public rights	2.7
Types of licences	2.8
Bare licences	2.11
Contractual licences	2.13
Licences coupled with an interest	2.21
Estoppel licences	2.24
Licences and possession	2.29
The relevance of possession	2.29
Factual possession	2.32
The right to possession	2.36

THE NATURE OF THE LICENCE

2.1 An intrusion by one person onto another's land is a trespass unless justifiable by law. Justification may be provided by virtue of a common-law[1] or statutory[2] right of entry, a public right (eg of way), a proprietary right/interest or a licence.

The concept of the licence

2.2 'Licence' may be used to denote both the operative act of the licensor that creates the right to use the land ('... grant licence ...') and the nature of the rights – and the resulting relationship of the parties – thereby created. The former is considered in Chapter 4; the latter is considered here.

2.3 A licence is, fundamentally, a permission granted by one person to another to enter, use or occupy land and which does not amount to the creation of some greater (proprietary) right/interest. The classic definition is, in

---

[1] Eg an owner's right of entry onto neighbouring land to abate a nuisance; the public's right of entry into a common inn or tavern; the right of entry to recapture one's goods wrongfully placed by someone on his land. A common-law defence of necessity may be available in exceptional circumstances: *Southwark LBC v Williams* [1971] Ch 734, at 743.

[2] Eg police powers of entry under the Police and Criminal Evidence Act 1984; oil extraction licences under the Petroleum Act 1998; access orders under the Access to Neighbouring Land Act 1992.

Vaughan CJ's words, a right that 'properly passeth no interest, nor alters or transfers property in any thing, but only makes an action lawful, which without it had been unlawful'.[3] It therefore confers immunity to a claim in trespass and, correspondingly, prevents or stops time running for limitation/prescription etc purposes (see Chapter 5). A licence is no more than a bundle of rights, which permit the use of land; it creates no distinct right/interest, unlike (say) a lease[4] or easement.

2.4 However, a licence may have effects beyond the immediate parties by (in rare cases) burdening the licensor's successors in title and giving rise to or altering the parties' rights (Chapter 9) and obligations (Chapter 11) towards strangers. Although, therefore, a licence is not a proprietary right (Chapter 9), certain types of licences in particular circumstances display some of the attributes of one. Furthermore licences are in some cases statutorily converted into proprietary rights/interests, eg some residential licences with security of tenure are converted into or deemed to be tenancies (see Chapter 6) and user licences can, in certain circumstances, mature into easements under the Law of Property Act 1925, s 62 (Chapter 9). But the greater objection to the use of Vaughan CJ's dictum as a definition of a licence is that it merely describes its incidents (ie effects); it gives little or no assistance in categorising a particular right as a licence or something else.

Distinguishing licences from other private rights/interests

2.5 There is no single, unifying set of characteristics of a licence that distinguishes it from proprietary (or public) rights/interests in land. Neither the duration of the rights, the persons able to exercise them nor the nature of the permitted activities provides a clear basis of distinction: some licences are permanent, as are some (not all[5]) proprietary rights/interests; (bare) licences and public rights may be exercisable by a particular group whose composition changes from time to time or by the public generally; both licences and proprietary interests may confer a right of possession (eg leases) or a mere limited right to use the land (eg easements); both licences and profits may entitle the grantee to remove things from the land. All types of rights capable of existing as proprietary (or public) rights/interests may, it is thought, take effect instead by way of licence; indeed the sort of rights capable of existing as licences are, if anything, rather wider (Chapter 3). The licence may grant a right of personal entry, (non-)exclusive occupation or, exceptionally, possession, permit the placing of things on/in the land, the removal of things from the land, the undertaking of works to it so as to alter its condition or the passage of materials (eg water, gas) through the land. As, however, a licence necessarily involves some entry onto another's land, a right to receive (rather than to pass) a flow of water etc is not a licence nor, it is thought, is a right to use electricity/telephone cables. Nor can a simple distinction be drawn based on

---

[3] *Thomas v Sorrell* (1673) Vaugh 330, at 351.
[4] *Old Groverbury Manor Farm Ltd v W Seymour Plant Sales & Hire Ltd (No 2)* [1979] 1 WLR 1397.
[5] Eg profits/easements in fee simple but not leases.

their incidents; as Chapter 9 considers, in certain cases licences may bind the licensor's successor and permit the licensee to sue third parties in trespass/nuisance, which traditionally were considered to be the attributes of a property right/interest.

2.6 For that reason no self-contained definition of a licence as a means of identification is possible except at such a level of abstraction as to be worthless in practice. A licence is best identified by a process of exclusion; it is a consensual right to enter/occupy land that is not some other (ie greater) type of right or interest. Licences in essence form a residual category of land rights: if a particular arrangement satisfies all the requirements for some other right/interest and contains no contrary indication, it is not a licence. Otherwise, it is. These requirements are considered in Chapter 3.

Distinguishing licences and public rights

2.7 A licence is a right derived from some consensual act by the licensor. Some public rights over land (eg public rights of way etc) may be – actually or presumptively – consensual in origin, eg by dedication, although the majority arise from the bare fact of user.[6] The difference (more fully explained in Chapter 5) is thought to turn on the nature of the consent. A licence consists of a permission to *use* land; consent giving rise to a public right is, to the *creation* of such right, irrevocable and is, in its nature, a public act.

TYPES OF LICENCES

2.8 The traditional classifications of licences are: bare (or gratuitous) licences; contractual licences; and licences coupled with an interest,[7] to which should now be added a fourth, namely estoppel licences. They are not, however, entirely mutually exclusive; a licence coupled with an interest is typically contractual in origin.

2.9 These categories are useful in identifying the rules applicable to the creation (Chapter 4), termination (Chapter 12) and certain incidents of the licence, eg whether its benefits and burdens pass to the parties' respective successors in title (Chapters 9 and 10) and the remedies available to the parties to enforce their rights. Different rules apply to each: '[i]t is not possible, having categorised something simply as a licence, to attribute to it fixed characteristics. The relationship is not identical in all cases. The incidents of a licence may vary according to the circumstances.'[8]

---

[6] Albeit such user may justify drawing inferences as to the owner's intention to create such right, eg by dedication.
[7] *Hounslow LBC v Twickenham Garden Developments Ltd* [1971] Ch 233, at 243.
[8] Dawson and Pearce *Licences Relating to the Occupation or Use of Land* (Butterworths, 1979), at p 3.

2.10 However, neither the categorisation of the right as a licence nor its classification as a particular type of licence is an end of the inquiry into its effects:[9]

> 'Whilst ... it is possible to identify certain features common to [say] all contractual licences it is not the case ... that all licences falling within [that category] although created in identical manner (ie by virtue of a contract) will have identical incidents.'

Account must be taken of its terms, the nature of the rights granted and the context in which it was created. Other principles may also affect the prima facie incidents of a particular licence, eg the concept of the executed licence (Chapter 13).

Bare licences

2.11 A bare or gratuitous licence best fits Vaughan CJ's classic description of a licence (see **2.3**); it is no more than a permission, which confers immunity to a claim in trespass, but something more than mere acquiescence (Chapters 4 and 5). For example, social visitors/dinner guests, customers entering a shop etc. It is an entitlement to enter/occupy land for which the licensee gives no consideration and/or is given without contractual intent. Bare licences form the residual category of licences.

Bare licence granted on terms

2.12 A licence granted on terms (eg 'you may use my field, but please keep the grass down') may be no more than bare licence coupled with a mere precatory request or the offer of a contractual licence ('you may use my land if you keep the grass down') the consideration for the right to use the land being the obligation to mow. In other cases (eg 'you may use my land if you do not disturb the neighbours') the proviso may be a condition of a (bare) licence and thus defines its scope. In such case the failure to abide by it may render the licensee a trespasser because he acts outside the scope of his permission or, in more serious cases, because such failure amounts to a disclaimer/renunciation of the licence (Chapter 4).

Contractual licences

2.13 A contractual licence is merely a particular type of contract, by which one party permits another to use/occupy land. It must be supported by consideration, entered into with contractual intent and sufficiently certain as to its terms (see Chapter 4). Such a licence is not distinct from the contract that creates it but is merely one of its terms.[10]

---

[9] Ibid, at p 25.
[10] *Millennium Productions Ltd v Winter Theatre (London) Ltd* [1946] 1 All ER 678, at 680 (rev'd on different grounds [1947] 2 All ER 331); *Hounslow LBC v Twickenham Garden Developments Ltd* [1971] Ch 233, at 245–246.

2.14 An arrangement, however, may not amount to a contractual licence if the right to use/occupy the land is attributable to some other relationship between the parties, e g trustee–beneficiary[11] or almshouse–object of charity[12] at least (in the latter case) where any payment for the occupation is minimal or tokenistic.[13]

Family arrangements and contractual intent

2.15 The distinction between bare, contractual and estoppel licences can be difficult to draw in relation to arrangements between family members/friends, where the inference of contractual intent may be inappropriate[14] or which involve acts of generosity/charity, e g *Booker v Palmer*[15] (accommodation offered to bombed-out family), *Cobb v Lane*[16] (sibling permitted to reside rent-free), *Heslop v Burns*[17] (owner permitted poor couple to reside and made notional entries for rent), *Marcroft Wagons Ltd v Smith*[18] (owner with no immediate need for house allowed deceased tenant's daughter to remain). However, the mere fact of a family/friendly relationship does not preclude contractual intent if the indicia of a contract are otherwise present.[19] If payment is made for the use of the land, even if it is below the open market rate, contractual intent may be inferred.[20] Payment at or near to that rate makes such inference easier to draw.

The imputation of contractual intent

2.16 Hitherto, however, courts generally inclined against finding contractual intent in relation to arrangements between family members/friends unless the indicia of a contract were clearly present.[21] This may be contrasted with the inclination in favour of non-contractual promises between such persons being intended to be relied on and thus capable of giving rise to a proprietary estoppel following *Thorner v Major*[22] (see Chapter 4).

2.17 However, during the period when contractual licences were thought automatically capable of binding the licensor's successors in title[23] and before the potential application of the estoppel licence was fully realised, courts in

---

[11] See **3.27–3.30**.
[12] See e g *Gray v Taylor* [1998] 1 WLR 1093, at 1097–1098.
[13] See the criticisms of *Gray v Taylor*, above: Loveland (2010) 74 Conv 234, at p 238 et seq.
[14] *Balfour v Balfour* [1919] 2 KB 521.
[15] [1942] 2 All ER 674.
[16] [1952] 1 All ER 1199.
[17] [1974] 1 WLR 1241.
[18] [1951] 2 KB 496. See also *Wheeler v Mercer* [1956] 1 QB 274.
[19] *Collier v Hollinshead* [1984] 2 EGLR 14; *Ward v Warnke* (1990) 22 HLR 496; *Parker v Clarke* [1960] 1 WLR 286.
[20] See e g *Collier v Hollinshead* [1984] 2 EGLR 14.
[21] *Balfour v Balfour* [1919] 2 KB 521.
[22] [2009] 3 All ER 945.
[23] See e g *Errington v Errington* [1952] 1 KB 290; see now *Ashburn Anstalt Ltd v Arnold* [1989] Ch 1 (overruled on a different point by *Prudential Assurance Co Ltd v London Residuary Body* [1992] 2 AC 386).

cases such as *Tanner v Tanner*,[24] *Hardwick v Johnson*[25] and *Chandler v Kerley*[26] strained – unnecessarily and inappropriately[27] – to fit family arrangements, to which the principles of proprietary estoppel were more suited,[28] into the straightjacket of contract in order to prevent the licensor (typically, the man) evicting the licensee (typically, his former mistress) from the quasi-matrimonial home or selling it free of her rights. In such cases the identification of consideration and contractual intent took on an air of unreality, the courts inferring and even imputing[29] them in circumstances where neither party intended their arrangements to have the attributes of a contract.

2.18 Estoppels, classically, apply to non-contractual arrangements intended to have legal consequences[30] – as in *Chandler v Kerley*[31] and *Hardwick v Johnson*[32] – and such cases should now be classified and dealt with accordingly. In that way the court has flexibility to fashion an appropriate remedy. If an equity is made out, the relief may take the form of a contractual licence but that is a remedial construct – a very different process from inferring a contractual licence as a matter of fact.

Consideration

2.19 A contractual licence requires consideration from the licensee in return for the right to use the land. This seemingly unexceptional point can, however, sometimes cause difficulty: the precise purpose of the licensee's payment must be ascertained. First, it may be a mere ex gratia payment if the parties lack contractual intent, as in *Marcroft Wagons Ltd v Smith*.[33] Second, a payment intended *solely* as a contribution to certain shared costs (eg in cases of sharing arrangements, household bills, utilities etc) is not in return for the right to use the land and is consistent with a bare licence.[34] If, however, it is expressly for both (or even not expressly for the former) then it may be regarded as being in part in return for such right; the consideration need not relate *solely* to it.[35]

---

[24] [1975] 1 WLR 1343.
[25] [1978] 1 WLR 683.
[26] [1978] 1 WLR 693. Although it was said there 'no question of estoppel arises ...' (at 697b), it is unclear why.
[27] *Horrocks v Forray* [1976] 1 WLR 230.
[28] See now *Thorner v Major* [2009] 3 All ER 945.
[29] See eg *Hardwick v Johnson* [1978] 1 WLR 683, at 690H.
[30] See Lord Neuberger's 2009 lecture 'The Stuffing of Minerva's Owl? Taxonomy and Taxidermy in Equity', at paras 23–25, and *Thorner v Major* [2009] 3 All ER 945.
[31] [1978] 1 WLR 693, at 697.
[32] [1978] 1 WLR 683, at 688.
[33] [1951] 2 KB 496. See also *Wheeler v Mercer* [1956] 1 QB 274.
[34] Compare *Bostock v Bryant* (1990) 61 P & CR 23, at 25; *West Wiltshire DC v Snelgrove* (1998) 30 HLR 57, at 60–62; *Vesely v Levy* [2007] EWCA Civ 367. In that case, it was said (at [49]) that the proper inference from the absence of payment specifically for the use of the land was that the parties did not intend to become landlord and tenant. That is unexceptional if it means merely that there was no consideration for the use of the land or no intention to create legal relations but is otherwise contrary to authority: *Street v Mountford* [1985] AC 809.
[35] See eg *Parker v Clarke* [1960] 1 WLR 286 (licensee provided consideration by selling land at undervalue to licensor and agreeing to share expenses).

Third, if the payment is merely tendered/accepted – and thus objectively intended – as compensation for the unauthorised use of the land, no contractual licence arises because contractual intent is absent.[36]

2.20 The fact the licensee may have some implied responsibility for the condition of the land (see **8.48**) as a result of the licence's creation, eg not to commit waste, is not thought to be consideration; such duties arise at common law and are usually not undertaken *in return for* the right to occupy the land but arise rather *as a result of* such occupation. Of course an express obligation to maintain, repair etc may be consideration.[37]

Licences coupled with an interest

2.21 A licence coupled with an interest arises where one party (A) acquires an interest in land belonging to another (B) that does not confer a right of possession or in chattels located on B's land. It therefore comprises two components: the 'interest' and an ancillary licence permitting entry onto the land for the purpose of enjoyment of the interest.[38]

2.22 It is now established that the interest must be proprietary. Previously, at a time when contractual licences (but not licences coupled with an interest) were thought to be incapable of specific enforcement,[39] courts attempted to extend this category to cases where the licensee had no discernible proprietary 'interest', eg a right to attend a creditors' meeting[40] or to watch a film.[41] In truth the 'interest' in such cases was no more than the purpose for which the right of entry was granted. Such attempts were rendered unnecessary by the recognition in *Hurst v Picture Theatres Ltd*[42] that equitable remedies (injunction, specific performance) are available to contractual licensees and are now universally regarded as inappropriate.[43]

2.23 Any proprietary interest is sufficient; so limited, interests in land (eg a profit to cut and carry away crops/minerals) or chattels[44] (eg ownership of cut timber or worked minerals) qualify. It is immaterial therefore whether the interest arises before or after the thing is severed from the land. The interest

---

[36] See by analogy *Westminster CC v Basson* (1992) 62 P & CR 57 (no lease).
[37] See eg *Polarpark Enterprises Inc v Allason* [2007] 2 EGLR 85, at [31]–[34].
[38] *Thomas v Sorrell* (1673) Vaugh 330, at 351: 'a licence to hunt in a man's park and carrying away the deer killed ... [or] to cut down a tree in a man's ground and to carry it away ... are licences as to the acts of hunting and cutting down, but to the carrying away the deer killed and the tree cut down, they are grants.'
[39] See eg *Wood v Leadbitter* (1845) 13 M&W 838.
[40] *Vaughan v Hampson* (1875) 33 LT 15.
[41] *Hurst v Picture Theatres Ltd* [1915] 1 KB 1.
[42] [1915] 1 KB 1.
[43] See the CA decision in *Millennium Productions Ltd v Winter Theatre (London) Ltd* [1946] 1 All ER 678, at 685; *Hounslow LBC v Twickenham Garden Developments Ltd* [1971] Ch 233; *Cowell v Rosehill Racecourse Co Ltd* (1937) 56 CLR 605, at 616 ('Fifty thousand people who pay to see a football match do not obtain fifty thousand interests in the football ground').
[44] *James Jones & Sons Ltd v Earl of Tankerville* [1909] 2 Ch 440, at 442; *Frank Warr & Co v London CC* [1904] 1 KB 713, at 722.

may be legal or equitable[45]. As the licence is ancillary to a proprietary interest, it arises automatically on the creation of that interest; and an interest in land must, of course, satisfy the relevant formal requirements for its creation.

Estoppel licences

2.24 There is a distinction between: (i) an orthodox (eg bare, contractual) licence whose revocation is prevented/limited by estoppel; (ii) an equity arising by (proprietary) estoppel entitling the representee to use/occupy another's land, prior to court order (the inchoate equity); and (iii) the relief granted by the court to give effect to such equity, which may be a proprietary right/interest in the land, a mere right of user/occupation or compensation.

2.25 As regards category (i) estoppels, it was from early days established that a licence may not be terminated in accordance with its terms if the licensee had detrimentally relied on the licensor's promise, eg that he might use the land permanently[46] or for as long as he wished.[47] The doctrine of estoppel was thus extended to protect the rights of certain licensees.[48] Their rights, moreover, appeared to be capable of protection against the licensor's successors in title who took with notice, whether they acquired title before or after the court order giving effect to the licensee's equity.[49] In such way these rights, variously categorised as a 'licence coupled with an equity', 'equitable licences' and 'licences by estoppel', appeared to have the attributes of proprietary rights, although it is doubtful whether that is appropriate,[50] particularly given that, as has since been held, contractual licences generally do not bind the licensor's successors.[51] The implications of the application of estoppel to orthodox licences are, however, beyond the scope of this book.

2.26 Category (ii) estoppels are equitable proprietary rights (Chapter 9). They arise, classically, where a landowner has led another to believe that he has some right/interest in the land or the right to occupy or use it, on which the other has relied to his detriment. Such cases are labelled here as 'estoppel licences' although that is, strictly, a misnomer; the estoppel does not give rise to a licence but to an inchoate equity, which may entitle the representee to use/occupy the land and for which he may seek the court's vindication.

---

[45] *Lowe v Adams* [1901] 2 Ch 598 (grant not by deed).
[46] *Plimmer v Wellington Corp* (1883–84) 9 App Cas 699.
[47] *Re Sharpe* [1980] 1 WLR 219, at 223.
[48] See eg *Inwards v Baker* [1965] 2 QB 29, at 37A–37B ('licence coupled with an equity'); *Jones v Jones* [1977] 1 WLR 438; *Williams v Staite* [1979] 1 WLR 291, at 296E.
[49] *Inwards v Baker* [1965] 2 QB 29; *Williams v Staite* [1979] 1 WLR 291; *Re Sharpe* [1980] 1 WLR 219.
[50] See eg *Megarry & Wade: The Law of Real Property* (Sweet & Maxwell, 7th edn, 2008), at paras 16-006, 16-033. Compare *Maharaj v Chand* [1986] AC 898 (licence between common-law husband and wife arising independently of the estoppel but protected by it assumed incapable of binding successors in title). A promissory estoppel requires for its application some extant legal relationship between the parties – *Morris v Tarrant* [1971] 2 QB 143, at 160.
[51] *Ashburn Anstalt Ltd v Arnold* [1989] Ch 1.

The Nature and Types of Licences

2.27 In practice, however, it is sometimes difficult to distinguish between category (i) and category (ii) estoppels – eg a promise to an existing licensee that he may use the land for as long as he likes may be construed as a promise not to enforce the terms of the current licence (category (i)) or the promise of a separate right, giving rise to an independent (category (ii)) inchoate equity – principally because the parties themselves rarely have this distinction in mind.

2.28 In further contrast, category (iii) rights, as declared/granted by the court to give effect to an inchoate equity, derive no special status from their source. Therefore if the representee is granted a right to use/occupy the land, its incidents are defined by its categorisation as either a proprietary right/interest or a personal right (eg contractual licence) and are thus determined by the order.

LICENCES AND POSSESSION

The relevance of possession

2.29 Formerly the right to possession or exclusive possession[52] was thought to mark the boundary between proprietary interests (eg leases) and non-proprietary rights, including licences.[53] The former was good against the whole world, except someone with a superior right; the latter bound only the parties and their privies. Possession was/is generally regarded as the hallmark of a proprietary estate/interest.[54]

2.30 That neat symmetry – which appears to involve some circularity of reasoning[55] – has now partially broken down:

(1) Whereas it was originally thought that a right to exclusive possession was inconsistent with a licence and necessarily took effect as a leasehold (or freehold) interest,[56] the House of Lords in *Street v Mountford*[57] recognised that a licence may in certain cases confer exclusive possession (below). Other jurisdictions, exhibiting greater doctrinal purity, maintain the view that 'a licence that gives exclusive possession is a contradiction in terms'.[58]

---

[52] The adjective 'exclusive' is thought merely to add emphasis: *Woodfall's Landlord & Tenant* (Sweet & Maxwell, looseleaf), at para 1.023. All possession is necessarily 'exclusive' – *JA Pye (Oxford) Ltd v Graham* [2003] 1 AC 419, at [41] – although there may be a joint right to possession.

[53] See eg *Street v Mountford* [1985] AC 809, at 816, 818; *Wettern Electric Ltd v Welsh Development Agency* [1983] 2 All ER 629, at 635.

[54] *JA Pye (Oxford) Ltd v Graham* [2003] 1 AC 419, at [40]; *Manchester Airport plc v Dutton* [2000] QB 133, at 146F.

[55] Namely a right to possession was proprietary because it bound third parties and it bound third parties because it was proprietary.

[56] *Lynes v Snaith* [1899] 1 QB 486, at 488, disapproved in *Cobb v Lane* [1952] 1 All ER 1199; *Heslop v Burns* [1974] 1 WLR 1241, at 1251–1252.

[57] [1985] AC 809.

[58] *Western Australia v Ward* (2002) 191 ALR 1, at [513]; *Radaitch v Smith* [1959] 101 CLR 209, at 223.

(2) Following *Bruton v London & Quadrant Housing Trust*[59] not all proprietary interests are capable of binding the whole world; the *Bruton* tenancy binds only the parties and their privies.

(3) Following *Manchester Airport plc v Dutton*[60] factual possession or the right to possession, at least as traditionally defined, is not always essential to maintain an action in trespass against intruders, as was hitherto thought. A licensee with a mere unexercised right of occupation conferring control – or, it follows, factual occupation conferring control – may be granted an order for possession if such remedy is necessary to vindicate his right. That does not extend to mere user licensees (eg with a right to enter to survey the land).[61] *Dutton* therefore clothes certain licensees who do not have (a right to) possession, as traditionally defined, with certain attributes of a proprietary interest.

(4) Nevertheless possession (as traditionally defined) is still necessary to maintain an action in nuisance against third parties following *Hunter v Canary Wharf Ltd*.[62] *Dutton* licensees may maintain an action in trespass against third parties, but not nuisance.

2.31 Accordingly the control required to confer standing on the licensee to bring a claim in nuisance/trespass may vary, depending on the claim and who it is brought against:

(1) Factual possession (see **2.32–2.35**), which even a bare licensee may have, has always been sufficient to maintain an action in trespass/nuisance against strangers with no title to land (eg intruders), but not the licensor, against whom the licensee must show a better *right* to possession (see **2.36**).

(2) Whereas possession (as traditionally defined) remains essential to bring a claim in trespass against the licensor, something less (ie a *Dutton* right of occupation conferring control) is sufficient as against third parties. The alternative view – that *Dutton* imports a lesser standard as to what constitutes 'possession' as against strangers – is inconsistent with dicta in *Pye v Graham*[63] that 'possession' is the same in trespass and adverse possession.

(3) A licensee who has a right to possession under the licence but whose licensor lacks title to the land cannot maintain an action against third parties in trespass (unless he has factual possession) but may do so against his licensor.

---

[59] [2000] 1 AC 406; *Kay v Lambeth LBC* [2006] 2 WLR 570.
[60] [2000] 1 QB 133.
[61] *Countryside Residential (North Thames) Ltd v Tugwell* (2000) 81 P & CR 2.
[62] [1997] AC 655.
[63] *JA Pye (Oxford) Ltd v Graham* [2003] 1 AC 419, at [42].

Factual possession

2.32 The bare fact of possession – even without title – confers on the possessor rights in relation to the use of the land that are good against the whole world, except someone with a superior title/right.[64] His possession is treated as prima facie evidence of seisin in fee simple; it is transmissible (eg by sale)[65] and has the attributes of a proprietary right/interest. Accordingly he can assert his right against an intruder who threatens to interfere with his possession and, if forcibly evicted, may sue to recover possession.

2.33 Thus a licensee in *actual* possession but who does not have a right to possession can maintain an action in trespass against third parties, except someone with a superior interest (but not his licensor, even one who lacks title). Hence one spouse in exclusive occupation of the matrimonial home, whilst not in possession as against the other spouse, nevertheless may have standing to sue a third party in trespass.[66]

2.34 'Possession' is necessarily indivisible and exclusive.[67] Accordingly the licensor and licensee cannot both be in possession of land at the same time but two or more licensees may be in joint possession. Factual possession means a sufficient degree of physical custody and (not necessarily direct[68]) control of the land.[69] Use of the land in the manner to be expected of a true owner, as opposed to someone with a limited interest, suffices.[70] The degree of control required depends on the circumstances and in particular the nature of the land:[71] there must be 'possession of the character of which the thing is capable'.[72] Control, in essence, signifies the ability to regulate access by others and carries with it some connotation of freedom from external control. The absence of such freedom is thought to explain why the grantees in *Shell-Mex and BP Ltd v Manchester Garages*[73] and *Esso Petroleum Co Ltd v Fumegrange Ltd*[74] lacked the right to exclusive possession and were thus licensees, not tenants.[75] A positive obligation on the occupier's part to undertake certain activities or a limitation on the period during which the rights are exercisable does not, however, signify an absence of such freedom[76] –

---

[64] *Asher v Whitlock* (1865) LR 1 QB 1, at 5. See eg *Thomas v DPP* (2009) *The Times*, November 25.
[65] *Asher v Whitlock* (1865) LR 1 QB 1, at 6, 7.
[66] *National Provincial Bank Ltd v Ainsworth* [1965] AC 1175, at 1232.
[67] *JA Pye (Oxford) Ltd v Graham* [2003] 1 AC 419, at [70].
[68] *Port of London Authority v Ashmore* [2009] EWHC 954 (Ch), rev'd in part (on a different point) [2010] EWCA Civ 30.
[69] *JA Pye (Oxford) Ltd v Graham* [2003] 1 AC 419, at [40]–[41].
[70] Ibid, at [76].
[71] See eg *Red House Farms (Thorndon) Ltd v Catchpole* [1977] 2 EGLR 125.
[72] *Lord Advocate v Young* (1887) 12 App Cas 544, at 556.
[73] [1971] 1 All ER 841.
[74] [1994] 2 EGLR 90.
[75] *NCP Ltd v Trinity Development Co (Banbury) Ltd* [2001] 2 EGLR 43, at 44J.
[76] *Dellneed Ltd v Chin* (1987) 53 P & CR 172.

such terms are found in many leases (eg shop units in malls). Where the grantor retains rights of entry, it is a question of fact/degree whether by doing so he retains possession (see Chapter 3).[77]

2.35 Possession is not synonymous with (even exclusive) occupation: a hotel guest/lodger may have exclusive occupation, but not possession, of his room. However, in relation to self-contained structures, sole occupation may imperceptibly shade into possession. Custody of the key to unoccupied premises may suffice.[78] Enclosure (or controlling the means of access) is usually, but not in all cases, necessary (nor, conversely, sufficient, eg if the owner reserves a general right of entry). For instance, user in such manner as to preclude any contemporaneous use by others (eg by ploughing)[79] may amount to possession.

The right to possession

2.36 Although *Street v Mountford*[80] establishes that a right of possession is not in all cases antithetical to a licence, nevertheless in most cases the grant of such right creates a lease rather than a licence unless:

(1) one of the other requirements for a tenancy is absent, ie a capable grantor[81] or a defined or ascertainable term;[82] or

(2) the grantee's 'possession' is, in reality, that of his grantor – eg a service occupier[83] in occupation of his employer's accommodation,

(see Chapter 3) in which case the occupier is a licensee. There may be other exceptions.[84] However, the suggestion that 'a licensee may have a right to exclusive possession without thereby becoming a tenant ... where the licence is

---

[77] See eg *Burns v Anthony* (1997) 74 P & CR D41; *Williams v Jones* [2002] 3 EGLR 69; *Alston & Sons Ltd v BOCM Pauls Ltd* [2008] All ER (D) 312 (Nov), at [74]–[77].

[78] NB: in relation to occupied land, the owner's retention of a key does not necessarily prevent an occupier having exclusive possession and thus being a tenant. The critical issue is the purpose(s) for which the key is retained – see Chapter 3.

[79] See eg *Seddon v Smith* (1877) 36 LT 168.

[80] [1985] AC 809.

[81] *MAFF v Matthews* [1950] 1 KB 148 (requisitioning authority unable to create leases). Contrast *Manchester Airport plc v Dutton* [2000] 1 QB 133, where the licensor was incapable of granting exclusive possession.

[82] *Prudential Assurance Co Ltd v London Residuary Body* [1992] 2 AC 386. Eg a building contract that grants the contractor possession of the site for the duration of the works: *Hounslow LBC v Twickenham Garden Developments Ltd* [1971] Ch 233.

[83] *Street v Mountford* [1985] AC 809, at 818F–818G.

[84] See eg *Leadenhall Residential 2 Ltd v Stirling* [2002] 1 WLR 499, at [22], where it was suggested that a prospective purchaser/tenant allowed to enter/remain on land pending negotiations may have a right to possession as licensee, rather than (as is usual) tenant at will. See also ibid, at [23], where it was suggested a lodger who shares accommodation with the licensor may be in possession of the part he occupies. See apparently to the same effect *Vesely v Levy* [2007] EWCA Civ 367, at [43]. Query, however, whether the licensees were merely in exclusive occupation rather than possession.

gratuitous'[85] appears wrong in principle; the bare licensee has no such *right* as against the licensor.[86] But a bare licensee may be in *factual* possession during the licence term,[87] eg if the arrangement is an act of generosity or friendship or under a family arrangement but lacks contractual intent, which prevents the creation of a lease.[88]

2.37 Finally it is worth noting that a licensee who is permitted to keep chattels on the licensor's land will nevertheless usually retain possession of them and thus may bring an action in relation to their conversion by a third party.[89]

---

[85] *Manchester Airport plc v Dutton* [2000] 1 QB 133, at 145F (per Chadwick LJ, dissenting). See also *Colchester BC v Smith* [1991] 2 All ER 29, at 53–54 (on appeal [1992] Ch 421).
[86] *Bolch v Smith* (1862) 7 Hurl & N 736, at 745–746; *Goldsack v Shore* [1950] 1 KB 708, at 714.
[87] *Booker v Palmer* [1942] 2 All ER 674; *Ramnarace v Lutchman* [2001] 1 WLR 1651, at [17].
[88] *Marcroft Wagons Ltd v Smith* [1951] 2 KB 496, as explained in *Street v Mountford* [1985] AC 809, at 820D.
[89] *Ashby v Tolhurst* [1937] 2 KB 242, at 250.

Chapter 3

LICENCES DISTINGUISHED FROM OTHER RIGHTS/INTERESTS

Licences and leases	3.2
The concept of exclusive possession	3.5
The nature of the right	3.6
Joint possession, licensees and sharing agreements	3.8
Terms negativing/indicating exclusive possession	3.13
Terms: shams	3.15
Terms: the parties' expressed intentions	3.16
Occupation pending negotiations	3.17
Licences and bailment	3.21
Licences and easements/profits	3.23
Licences and trusts	3.27
Customary rights	3.31
Town and village greens	3.32
Highways	3.33
Wayleaves	3.35
Matrimonial homes rights	3.37

3.1 Since licences constitute the residual category of rights to use property and are best identified by a process of exclusion (see **2.5–2.6**) it is necessary, when determining whether a particular right takes effect as a licence or something else, to consider whether it is capable of existing as a proprietary right/interest. Rights to occupy land may take the form of licences or leases; rights to use land may exist as licences, easements, profits or public rights. Some rights may only take effect as licences, eg:

(1) rights granted by a body that lacks legal capacity to create a proprietary right or interest (eg a lease);[1]

(2) rights that are in *substance* incapable of existing as a proprietary right/interest (eg a right merely to use land in common with others and which does not accommodate the grantee's other land[2] and is not a profit

---

[1] See eg *MAFF v Matthews* [1950] 1 KB 148; Housing Act 1985, s 32 (requisitioning authority). Lack of title, however, is not a question of capacity: *Bruton v London & Quadrant Housing Trust* [2000] 1 AC 406.

[2] See eg *Hill v Tupper* (1863) 2 Hurl & C 121.

in gross; a private right granted to a body whose composition changes from time to time, such as the members of an unincorporated association); and

(3) rights granted on *terms* that negate the creation of any greater interest (eg a right granted for a period that is insufficiently certain to take effect as a lease or easement/profit).[3]

It is therefore necessary to consider the grantor's capacity and the substance and terms of the right in order to categorise it properly as a licence or something else.

LICENCES AND LEASES

3.2 Despite recent changes to the statutory regimes granting security of tenure to certain residential, agricultural and business occupiers[4] the distinction between a lease and licence remains of great practical significance, eg:

(1) whether the grantor is entitled to possession as of right at the end of the term (security of tenure remains largely – not exclusively – confined to tenants);[5]

(2) the statutory rights/obligations implied into the parties' agreement;[6]

---

[3] See eg *Lace v Chantler* [1944] KB 368; *Berrisford v Mexfield Housing Co-Operative Ltd* [2010] EWCA Civ 811 (both leases). Although entry under a lease defective for lack of certainty of term followed by payment of rent may give rise to a periodic tenancy.

[4] Specifically, the phasing out of agricultural holdings under the Agricultural Holdings Act 1986 by agricultural tenancies under the Agricultural Tenancies Act 1995; the 1996 substitution of assured shorthold tenancies for assured tenancies as the default tenancy under the Housing Act 1988; and the 2004 amendments to the Landlord and Tenant Act 1954, Pt II allowing parties to commercial leases to contract out of s 24 protection without the need for court order.

[5] Certain residential licensees (eg mobile home occupiers, agricultural workers and occupiers of public authority housing) and pre-1996 agricultural licensees also enjoy security of tenure – see Chapter 6.

[6] For licences, Supply of Goods and Services Act 1982, Unfair Contract Terms Act 1977 and Unfair Terms in Consumer Contracts Regulations 1999, SI 1999/2083 (formerly the 1994 Regulations, SI 1994/3159). For leases, the 1999 Regulations, statutory rights of enfranchisement, statutorily implied obligation as to repair (Landlord and Tenant Act 1985, s 11) or fitness for purpose (Landlord and Tenant Act 1985, s 8). More generally, the application of statutory regulation concerning the parties' respective rights/duties on an application for permission to assign (Landlord and Tenant Act 1927, s 19; Landlord and Tenant Act 1988, s 1) and after assignment (Landlord and Tenant (Covenants) Act 1995); fetters on the grantor's right to terminate for breach (Leasehold Property (Repairs) Act 1938; Landlord and Tenant Act 1925, s 146); the grantee's right to remove fixtures attached to the land at the end of the term (see Chapter 13) and to seek relief from forfeiture (ibid; County Courts Act 1984, s 138); as well as his liability for double rent (Distress for Rent Act 1737, s 18) or double value (Landlord and Tenant Act 1730, s 1) for failing to give up possession at the end of the contract term.

(3) the grantor's right to distrain (or, in future, to implement the commercial rent arrears recovery scheme) for non-payment and, if so, its extent;[7]

(4) the parties' respective tortious/statutory duties towards third parties;[8] and

(5) whether/when time starts to run for limitation purposes in favour of a grantee.[9]

3.3 According to the classic definition in *Street v Mountford*,[10] the hallmarks of a lease are an agreement intended to create legal relations, by which one party with capacity to grant a lease[11] gives to another the right to exclusive possession of a particular area of land for a defined or ascertainable term, at a rent (or some other consideration[12]) and which is not attributable to some other relationship between the parties,[13] such as (eg) employer–employee,[14] vendor–purchaser,[15] almshouse–object of charity[16] or trustee–beneficiary (below). These exceptions are not exhaustive.[17] The agreement terms are ascertained by reference to the parties' objective intentions but the nature of the rights granted (ie whether a lease or licence) is, rather, a question of law.[18]

3.4 It follows that:

(1) An agreement that does not confer exclusive possession cannot be a lease but may be a licence or an easement/profit. However, whilst all lessees have exclusive possession, not all persons with exclusive possession are lessees (see **2.36**).

(2) An agreement that is uncertain as to the precise area to which it applies[19] or merely grants a non-exclusive right to use an area or a right to use an undefined part of a larger area cannot be a lease but may be a licence (or, in the latter two examples, easement).

---

[7] A licensor has no right to distrain absent express agreement and cannot in any event distrain against a third party's goods: *Euston Centre Properties v H&J Wilson* [1982] 1 EGLR 57, at 58. A landlord has an automatic right to distrain against both the tenant's and a third party's goods. After Pt 3 of the Tribunals, Courts and Enforcement Act 2007 is brought into force, the landlord's, but not the licensor's (if any), right will be subject to the statutory recovery scheme.
[8] See Chapter 11.
[9] Eg whereas time only starts to run in the former licensee's favour on the determination of the licence: see the special rule relating to oral periodic tenants in Limitation Act 1980, Sch 1, para 5.
[10] [1985] AC 809.
[11] Ibid, at 821B.
[12] *Prudential Assurance Co Ltd v London Residuary Body* [1992] AC 386.
[13] *Street v Mountford* [1985] AC 809, at 818E–818F, 827A–827B; *Cameron Ltd v Rolls-Royce plc* [2007] EWHC 546 (Ch), at [22].
[14] Ibid; *Norris v Checksfield* [1991] 1 WLR 1241. See Chapter 6 for more detail.
[15] See eg *Essex Plan Ltd v Broadminster* (1998) 56 P & CR 353.
[16] *Gray v Taylor* [1998] 1 WLR 1093.
[17] *Leadenhall Residential 2 Ltd v Stirling* [2002] 1 WLR 499, at 508.
[18] *Barnes v Barratt* [1970] 2 QB 657, at 671; *Bruton v London & Quadrant Housing Trust* [2000] 1 AC 406, at 413.
[19] *Clear Channel UK Ltd v Manchester City Council* [2006] 1 EGLR 27, at [12].

(3) An agreement that is not for a defined or ascertainable term (e g for 'life'[20] or 'the duration of the war',[21] or 'until the land is required for road widening'[22] or which restricts the exercise of a right to terminate until the occurrence of an uncertain event[23]) cannot be a tenancy for lack of certainty of term but may be a valid licence. A lease may, however, be created for a certain term but subject to early determination on the occurrence of an uncertain event.

(4) An agreement that, properly construed, purports to create a tenancy but is ineffective for want of a sufficiently certain term cannot be 'saved' by being treated as a licence:[24]

> 'The court is not ... justified in treating the contract as something different from what the parties intended and regarding it merely as a contract for the granting of a licence. That would be setting up a new bargain which neither of the parties ever intended to enter into.'

But the absence of a sufficiently certain term may justify the conclusion that the agreement, properly construed, creates a licence rather than a (defective) lease.

(5) A permanent right cannot be a lease[25] but may be an (irrevocable) licence, a fee simple subject to a rentcharge (if a fee is reserved)[26] or an easement/profit.

(6) An agreement that lacks contractual intent or consideration cannot be a lease but is, by definition, a (bare) licence,[27] e g an arrangement by which a local authority allowed an allotment holder to continue to use the land rent-free at his own risk on the understanding he would vacate on short notice when the authority required it.[28]

---

[20] Prior to 1925 such an interest was a freehold estate and since then converted into a term certain subject to early termination on death: Law of Property Act 1925, s 149(6).
[21] *Lace v Chantler* [1944] KB 368, at 372.
[22] *Prudential Assurance Co Ltd v London Residuary Body* [1992] AC 386.
[23] *Lace v Chantler* [1944] KB 368. The majority in *Berrisford v Mexfield Housing Co-Operative Ltd* [2010] EWCA Civ 811 held that a term restricting one party's right to terminate only in certain events cannot be enforced in contract independently of the purported lease, e g by injuncting a party from terminating in other circumstances.
[24] *Lace v Chantler* [1944] KB 368, at 371–372; *Berrisford v Mexfield Housing Co-Operative Ltd* [2010] EWCA Civ 811 at [32], [72]–[73], [85].
[25] *Sevenoaks Ry Co v London, Chatham & Dover Ry Co* (1879) 11 ChD 625, at 635–636 (further example of licence conferring exclusive possession).
[26] *Doe d Robertson v Gardiner* (1852) 12 CB 319, at 333.
[27] See e g *Foster v Robinson* [1951] 1 KB 149 (retiring tenant allowed to live on rent-free during retirement); *Marcroft Wagons Ltd v Smith* [1951] 2 KB 496; *Booker v Palmer* [1942] 2 All ER 674. Cf *Vesely v Levy* [2007] EWCA Civ 367, at [49].
[28] *Colchester BC v Smith* [1991] 2 All ER 29, at 53–54.

The concept of exclusive possession

3.5 'Exclusive possession' is considered at **2.34** et seq and for present purposes is to be distinguished from exclusive occupation[29] (although in practice exclusive occupation of a discrete area of land may shade into possession) and the exclusive right to do a particular thing on the land (eg operate a concession stand).[30]

The nature of the right

3.6 Certain rights are generally thought not to confer exclusive possession (absent exceptional circumstances) and thus take effect as licences, such as rights to operate market stalls[31] or concession stands, advertising hoardings,[32] front-of-house rights[33] and the right to operate an established business.[34] So too an agreement permitting the erection and maintenance of a structure connecting to the grantor's land (eg shop premises cantilevered over a river and resting on its retaining walls) has been held not to confer a right to possession of the ground on which the structure rests.[35]

3.7 Other rights, however, may take effect either as a licence or a lease, depending on the substance of the grant, the agreement terms and the circumstances in which it was created.[36] For instance, a right to extract minerals, together with ancillary rights of entry and occupation, is a licence[37] (or profit) whereas a right to possession for the purpose of extracting minerals may be a lease.[38] A right to occupy a houseboat or static caravan attached to land may be a lease or licence of a chattel (the boat or caravan) or the land, depending on the degree of annexation.[39] A right to moor a boat will usually be a licence unless (exceptionally) it confers the right to exclusive possession of the mooring/riverbed.[40] A shop manager will usually occupy as licensee – the

---

[29] *Scottish Widows v Stewart* [2006] EWCA Civ 999, at [63] ('Occupation is not the same as possession').
[30] See eg *Cobb v Lane* [1952] 1 All ER 1199, at 1201; *Frank Warr & Co v London CC* [1904] 1 KB 713, at 719–20.
[31] See eg *Smith v Northside Developments* (1988) 55 P & CR 164. Although the structure of the stall is important – see eg *Graysim Holdings Ltd v P&O Property Holdings Ltd* [1996] AC 329 (tenancy of a fixed, self-contained market stall).
[32] See eg *Wilson v Tavener* [1901] 1 Ch 578, at 581; *King v David Allen & Sons Billposting* [1916] 2 AC 54; contrast *Taylor v Pendleton Overseers* (1887) 19 QBD 288.
[33] See eg *Clore v Theatrical Properties Ltd* [1936] 3 All ER 483; *Frank Warr & Co v London CC* [1904] 1 KB 713.
[34] *Rossvale Ltd v Green* [1979] 1 EGLR 64.
[35] *London Development Agency v Nidai* [2009] EWHC 1730 (Ch).
[36] See eg the factors listed in *Woodfall's Landlord & Tenant* (Sweet & Maxwell, looseleaf), at para 1.023.2.
[37] *Hunts Refuse Disposal Ltd v Norfolk Environmental Waste Services Ltd* [1997] 1 EGLR 16.
[38] *Street v Mountford* [1985] AC 809, at 816G.
[39] *Chelsea Yacht & Boat Co Ltd v Pope* [2000] 1 WLR 1941. See **13.14**.
[40] Eg *Port of London Authority v Ashmore* [2009] EWHC 954 (Ch), rev'd on a different point [2010] EWCA Civ 30. Query as to a free mooring that allows a vessel to rotate 360 degrees, compared with a vessel moored at either end to a jetty which always occupies a certain irreducible minimum of riverbed during tidal changes.

employer being treated as retaining possession through him[41] – unless the business is in fact the 'manager's', in which case a term purporting to reserve possession to the grantor may be a sham.[42] The right to operate a shoppers' car park has also been held to be a licence,[43] as has the right to operate a petrol station shop and car wash,[44] but a right to exclusive possession for the purpose of undertaking such a business may be a lease.

Joint possession, licensees and sharing agreements

3.8 Where land (eg a student house) is occupied by two or more persons, they may be joint tenants (or joint licensees[45]) of the whole; or each may have separate, non-exclusive licences to occupy the whole;[46] or they may be tenants/licensees with the exclusive right to occupy individual parts (eg a specified bedroom), with non-exclusive rights to use the common areas.

3.9 In order for occupiers to be joint tenants (or joint licensees) the four unities must be present: the area of land, the nature of the rights and their start and end dates must be identical. If they are, the fact each executes a separate agreement with the owner is not fatal if execution of each was expressly/impliedly conditional on execution of the others. In that way seemingly non-exclusive licences can be read together as giving the grantees (joint) exclusive possession.[47] If any of these unities is absent (eg if each occupier has the sole right to use a particular part or their rights start/end on different dates or may be brought to an end independently of the others[48]) the agreements cannot create a joint right but take effect as several licences/tenancies of those individual parts or non-exclusive licences of the whole.[49]

3.10 In deciding whether separate agreements collectively grant exclusive possession the court takes into account 'the surrounding circumstances [including] the nature and extent of the accommodation and the intended and

---

[41] See eg *Rossvale Ltd v Green* [1979] 1 EGLR 64; *Ross Auto Wash Ltd v Herbert* [1979] 1 EGLR 95.
[42] See eg *Teasdale v Walker* [1958] 1 WLR 1076.
[43] *NCP Ltd v Trinity Development Co (Banbury) Ltd* [2001] 2 EGLR 43.
[44] *Esso Petroleum Co Ltd v Fumegrange Ltd* [1994] 2 EGLR 90.
[45] Eg if the grantor reserves the right to use it or allow others to use it in common with the grantees. However, where the residential accommodation is such that the occupiers must be mutually acceptable to each other (eg a single bedsit), such a term (which usually must be expressly reserved) is likely to be regarded as a sham: *Antoniades v Villiers* [1990] 1 AC 417.
[46] See eg *Mikeover Ltd v Brady* [1989] 3 All ER 618.
[47] *Antoniades v Villiers* [1990] 1 AC 417.
[48] *Somma v Hazlehurst* [1978] 1 WLR 1014, as explained in *Street v Mountford* [1985] AC 809, at 825.
[49] It is, as yet, not wholly certain whether a joint right may exist where each occupier is only liable for his several share of the combined fee (*Demeuren v Seal Estates* (1978) 7 HLR 83; *Antoniades v Villiers* [1990] 1 AC 417, at 460B) or not (*Antoniades v Villiers*, at 466B, 469H, 474F; *Mikeover Ltd v Brady* [1989] 3 All ER 618). The fact each occupier is only liable for his 'share' is a fair indicator that the use of separate agreements is not a sham.

actual mode of occupation ...'.[50] Such a finding is easier if the agreements are executed contemporaneously (but this is not decisive if they replaced earlier agreements with the same occupiers executed at different times[51]) or the premises are only suitable for occupation by persons who are mutually acceptable and self-selecting.

3.11 Changes in the identity of occupiers who are joint tenants/licensees present particular problems. In such case, none of them may terminate without the other's consent during the fixed term.[52] An arrangement substituting an existing occupier for a new one may take effect as a surrender (lease) or agreement to rescind (licence) and re-grant, which requires all parties' consent.[53] If the new body of occupiers sign fresh agreements at the same time on identical terms, they may become joint tenants/licensees.[54] In reality that will rarely be the appropriate inference if the new occupier or the terms on which he occupies are not known to/agreed by the remaining occupiers. Even if the remaining occupiers select the new person, they may not be joint tenants/licensees if they do so merely for their/the owner's convenience.[55]

3.12 Changes in occupation can also present difficulties where the occupiers do not have a joint right at the outset. Where, say, two independent licensees are together entitled to occupy an area of land, the fact that one quits and the other then occupies the whole or pays both sets of licence fees will not necessarily result in him becoming tenant: his de facto occupation may (or may not) amount to possession; the extra payment may simply be in return for the owner not permitting anyone else to use the land.[56]

Terms negativing/indicating exclusive possession

3.13 Exclusive possession depends not only on the substance of the right but also the terms of the agreement. The fact that it uses language more appropriate to a lease or licence is irrelevant to its construction.[57] It is also inappropriate to consider whether the terms are more usually found in leases or licences.[58] What is critical is the degree of control conferred on the occupier or retained by the grantor (see **2.34**). Hence:

- A residential occupier with an exclusive right to occupy may be a tenant if the grantor provides neither attendance nor services.[59]

---

[50] *Stribling v Wickham* [1989] 2 EGLR 35, at 36.
[51] Ibid.
[52] In contrast, if the joint lease/licence is periodic, any one occupier may unilaterally terminate – see Chapter 12.
[53] *Stribling v Wickham* [1989] 2 EGLR 35, at 37.
[54] *Nicolaou v Pitt* (1989) 21 HLR 487.
[55] *Stribling v Wickham* [1989] 2 EGLR 35, at 37.
[56] *Smith v Northside Developments* (1988) 55 P & CR 164.
[57] *Bruton v London & Quadrant Housing Trust* [2000] 1 AC 406, at 413.
[58] *Crancour v De Silvaesa* (1986) 52 P & CR 204, at 230.
[59] *Street v Mountford* [1985] AC 809, at 818C.

- The reservation of a limited right of entry for specified purposes (eg to view the land or effect repairs) may indicate that the occupier has exclusive possession.[60] In contrast the absence of such reservation may indicate the owner retains possession, rendering one unnecessary.[61]

- The question, however, is one of degree.[62] If the owner provides services that require unrestricted access to the land, ie whether or not the occupier is present to allow him in,[63] the agreement takes effect as a licence – eg hotel proprietors who clean, service, inspect etc rooms.[64]

- If, however, the agreement otherwise grants exclusive possession and such services are provided under an entirely independent arrangement for which the occupier pays a separate fee (as is sometimes found in relation to residential 'hotels') the occupier may be a tenant.[65]

- A limitation on when the occupier may use the land may indicate exclusive possession was not granted. Of itself, however, it is rarely determinative[66] although taken with other factors may indicate the owner retains operational control and thus possession.[67] Such a restriction in the domestic sphere where the grantee is the sole occupier is likely to be regarded as a sham.[68]

- A right to relocate the occupier to other land during the term (if genuine) is also inconsistent with a lease.[69] In contrast a right to terminate the agreement conditional on the owner offering other land on the same terms may be either a lease or licence.[70]

- A term prohibiting the occupier from interfering with the owner's right to possession and control of the premises (if genuine) is also inconsistent

---

[60] Ibid, at 818D; *Addiscombe Garden Estates v Crabbe* [1958] 1 QB 513, at 524.
[61] *Venus Investments Ltd v Stocktop Ltd* [1996] EGCS 173.
[62] *Wells v Kingston upon Hull* (1874–75) LR 10 CP 402 (retention of management and control of graving docks).
[63] *Crancour v De Silvaesa* (1986) 52 P & CR 204, at 211.
[64] See eg *Luganda v Services Hotels* [1969] 2 Ch 209.
[65] See eg *Vandersteen v Agius* (1992) 65 P & CR 266.
[66] *Joel v International Circus and Christmas Fair* (1920) 124 LT 459; *Westminster City Council v Southern Railway Co* [1936] AC 511 (tenancy of railway station bookstall).
[67] *Shell-Mex and BP Ltd v Manchester Garages* [1971] 1 All ER 841, at 843, 846; *Esso Petroleum Co Ltd v Fumegrange Ltd* [1994] 2 EGLR 90; *NCP Ltd v Trinity Development Co (Banbury) Ltd* [2001] 2 EGLR 43. Compare *Westminster CC v Clarke* [1992] 2 AC 288.
[68] See eg *Aslan v Murphy (No 1)* [1990] 1 WLR 766 (excluding occupiers from bedsit for 90 minutes per day); but compare *Westminster CC v Clarke* [1992] 2 AC 288 (requirement that vulnerable occupiers comply with supervision given by the licensor, be in rooms by a certain time and prohibiting overnight guests indicative of licence).
[69] *Crancour v De Silvaesa* (1986) 52 P & CR 204, at 212; *Dresden Estates v Collinson* (1987) 55 P & CR 47; *Westminster CC v Clarke* [1992] 2 AC 288.
[70] *Dresden Estates v Collinson* (1987) 55 P & CR 47, at 53, 54.

with a lease.[71] However, a declaration in a written agreement that it does not grant exclusive possession is likely to be regarded as a mere label (as to which see below).[72]

- A term requiring the occupier to insure the owner against third party liability arising out of his operations has been held to be indicative of a tenancy.[73]

- A prohibition on subletting has also been held to be indicative of a lease,[74] as has one against parting with 'possession'.[75]

- Similar conclusions have been drawn in relation to covenants for quiet enjoyment[76] and a grantee's repairing covenant.[77]

- Terms prohibiting the creation of a nuisance or making alterations are consistent with both licences and leases.[78]

3.14 The form of the term may also be relevant: a covenant not to do something (eg share possession) may be a derogation from a right that otherwise exists (to possession) and thus implicit recognition of it;[79] a declaration that the grantee has no right to do such thing is not.

Terms: shams

3.15 A term or label purporting to create a licence rather than a lease may be rejected as a sham if it does not reflect the parties' true intentions. The parties may, of course, genuinely structure their arrangements so as to avoid granting security of tenure. It follows a term/agreement is not a sham *merely* because it is entered into for that very purpose.[80] A sham is one:[81]

> '... intended ... to give ... the appearance of creating between the parties legal rights and obligations different from the actual legal rights and obligations (if any) which the parties intended to create ... all the parties thereto must have had a common intention that the acts or documents are not to create legal rights and obligations which they give the appearance of creating.'

---

[71] *Manchester City Council v National Car Parks* [1982] 1 EGLR 94.
[72] *Family Housing Association v Jones* [1990] 1 WLR 779.
[73] *NCP Ltd v Trinity Development Co (Banbury) Ltd* [2001] 2 EGLR 43, at 45M.
[74] *Wigan BC v Green & Sons (Wigan) Ltd* [1985] 2 EGLR 242, at 246.
[75] *JA Pye (Oxford) Ltd v Graham* [2003] 1 AC 419, at [56].
[76] *Addiscombe Garden Estates Ltd v Crabbe* [1958] 1 QB 513, at 529.
[77] Ibid. Sed quaere, given an occupation licence may include a covenant for quiet enjoyment and possibly against derogation from grant (see Chapter 8) and a licensee may expressly be required to keep the land in repair. See eg *Wettern Electric Ltd v Welsh Development Agency* [1983] 2 All ER 629, at 632.
[78] *Scottish Widows v Stewart* [2006] EWCA Civ 999, at [62].
[79] See eg *JA Pye (Oxford) Ltd v Graham* [2003] 1 AC 419, at [56]; *Dellneed Ltd v Chin* (1987) 53 P&CR 172, 185.
[80] *Belvedere Court Mgmt Ltd v Frogmore Dvpts Ltd* [1997] QB 858, at 876.
[81] *Snook v West Riding Investments Ltd* [1967] 2 QB 766, at 802.

The question is whether the term was really intended to govern the parties' relationship,[82] as to which the fact it has not been enforced is relevant, but not determinative.[83] In broad terms the distinction is between (permissible) artificiality and (impermissible) artifice.[84] Artificiality, however, may be a factor indicating that the label/term in question is not genuine[85] and the court may take into account the reason(s) for incorporating the term when considering whether or not it was genuine. A finding of a sham implies dishonesty and should only be made with caution, taking into account the strong presumption that the terms reflect the parties' real intentions.[86]

Terms: the parties' expressed intentions

3.16 The classification of an agreement as a lease or licence does not depend on any additional intention beyond that expressed in the choice of terms.[87] Its true nature therefore is not merely decided by its label;[88] if it is in substance a lease, the fact it is called a licence is irrelevant.[89] On the other hand, the parties' expressed intentions are not wholly irrelevant: where their stated intention was not to grant exclusive possession and the purpose of the agreement, considered in light of the surrounding circumstances, was consistent with it, such intention was held to be conclusive against the creation of a tenancy.[90] Also, whilst the principles in *Street v Mountford*[91] have been said to apply to commercial/agricultural as well as residential land,[92] some difference of emphasis in the authorities is apparent and the tension between them remains to be fully resolved. Whereas in the residential sphere courts are astute to detect a sham, they are more inclined in other cases to take the parties' expressed intentions at face value. Thus if commercial bodies at arm's length acting on legal advice enter into an agreement that expresses their intentions as to its effect (usually, to create a licence), the court will require persuading that it is something else.[93]

---

[82] *National Westminster Bank v Jones* [2000] BPIR 1092, at 1108H.
[83] *AG Securities v Vaughan* [1990] 1 AC 417, at 463.
[84] *National Westminster Bank v Jones* [2000] BPIR 1092.
[85] Ibid, at 1102D.
[86] Ibid, at 1111F–1111H.
[87] *Bruton v London & Quadrant Housing Trust* [2000] 1 AC 406, at 413.
[88] *Facchini v Bryson* [1952] 1 TLR 1386, at 1390; *Street v Mountford* [1985] AC 809, 819E–819F ('If the agreement satisfied all the requirements of a tenancy, then the agreement produced a tenancy and the parties cannot alter the effect of the agreement by insisting that they only created a licence. The manufacture of a five-pronged implement for manual digging results in a fork even if the manufacturer, unfamiliar with the English language, insists that he intended to make and has made a spade').
[89] *Addiscombe Garden Estates v Crabbe* [1958] 1 QB 513, at 522.
[90] *Camden LBC v Shortlife Community Housing Ltd* (1992) 25 HLR 330.
[91] [1985] AC 809.
[92] *London & Associated Investment Trust v Calow* (1986) 53 P & CR 340, at 352; *Dellneed v Chin* (1987) 53 P & CR 172 (business); *Colchester BC v Smith* [1991] Ch 448, at 483–484 (aff'd [1982] Ch 421); *Ashdale Land Property Co v Mannus* [1992] 2 EGLR 5 (agricultural).
[93] *Clear Channel UK Ltd v Manchester City Council* [2006] 1 EGLR 27, at [29]; *Scottish Widows v Stewart* [2006] EWCA Civ 999, at [63].

Occupation pending negotiations

3.17 A prospective purchaser/tenant may be allowed to enter/remain in occupation before exchange/completion of some formal grant of a proprietary interest in land. In such cases, an issue may arise as to his status.

3.18 Before exchange, he will usually be a licensee or a tenant at will.[94] If exceptionally he occupies under a discrete agreement, independent of the intended transaction, that grants exclusive possession for a term, he may be a fixed-term/periodic tenant.[95] If, as in most cases, such arrangement is not severable from the negotiations, he will be a tenant at will (if it grants exclusive possession and is intended to create legal relations[96]) or (if not or if the parties expressly agree) a licensee.[97] A term entitling him to advance notice if the owner wishes to resume occupation in the interim is indicative of a licence rather than a tenancy at will.[98]

3.19 In reality the practical importance of the distinction between licences and tenancies at will is not so great following changes made by the Limitation Act 1980.[99] Neither is an 'interest in the land to which possession can be referred ...'.[100] Nevertheless differences remain. First, a tenant at will can maintain an action in trespass; a mere licensee – unless he is in factual possession or has a *Dutton* right of occupation (see Chapter 2) – may not. Similarly, a tenant at will may maintain an action in nuisance; a licensee – unless he has a right to possession or is in factual possession – may not. Third, a landlord under a tenancy at will that reserves a rent can distrain/implement the statutory recovery scheme in the Tribunals, Courts and Enforcement Act 2007 (when brought into force) whereas a licensor cannot, absent express agreement, and cannot in any event do so against a third party's goods.[101] Fourth, whereas a tenancy at will automatically terminates on the death of the sole owner/occupier,[102] a contractual licence may not. Fifth, a licensee may be entitled to some period of notice to terminate; a tenancy at will is terminable on demand.[103] Lastly, whereas a tenant at will of residential accommodation

---

[94] *Javad v Aquil* [1991] 1 WLR 100; *Cardiothoracic Institute v Shrewdcrest Ltd* [1986] 1 WLR 368; *Ramnarace v Lutchman* [2001] 1 WLR 1651, at [18].
[95] *Bretherton v Paton* [1986] 1 EGLR 172; *Cameron Ltd v Rolls-Royce plc* [2007] EWHC 546 (Ch).
[96] See eg *Essex Plan Ltd v Broadminster* (1998) 56 P & CR 353; *Ramnarace v Lutchman* [2001] 1 WLR 1651, at [16]–[17].
[97] Eg *Isaac v Hotel de Paris* [1960] 1 WLR 239 (no exclusive possession).
[98] *Parker v Parker* [2003] EWHC 1846 (Ch), at [296]; *Colchester BC v Smith* [1991] 2 All ER 29, at 51–52.
[99] Time now starts to run from the termination of the tenancy at will or licence. Contrast the position of an oral tenancy from year to year or other period: Limitation Act 1980, Sch 1, para 5.
[100] *Ramnarace v Lutchman* [2001] 1 WLR 1651, at [18].
[101] See n 7 above.
[102] *Woodfall's Landlord & Tenant* (Sweet & Maxwell, looseleaf), at para 6.071.
[103] Ibid, at paras 6.073–6.074A.

may have the protection of the Rent Acts (now Housing Act 1988)[104] a residential licensee does not have security of tenure except in the limited circumstances set out at **6.38** et seq.

3.20 Between exchange and completion the grantee may occupy either by virtue of his equitable interest arising from the agreement (if specifically enforceable), as tenant at will or licensee. Usually his status is the subject of express agreement[105] and such a term is, absent exceptional circumstances, decisive.[106]

LICENCES AND BAILMENT

3.21 An arrangement by which one person leaves his goods on another's land may take effect as a licence or a bailment. The principal importance of the distinction concerns the duties owed by the land owner in relation to the security of the chattels: a licensor generally owes no such duty;[107] a bailee undoubtedly does.

3.22 The distinction between a licence and bailment is more fully considered in Chapter 7. A licence gives the goods owner a right to leave them on the land; under a bailment, the custody of the goods passes to the landowner, usually in order that he may keep them or perform some service in relation to them. Accordingly the critical issue is the degree of control each party has over the goods whilst on the land; the landowner's possession of the land is not necessarily to be equated with possession of the goods.

LICENCES AND EASEMENTS/PROFITS

3.23 Whereas a right to exclusive possession may be a lease or licence, a mere (non-)exclusive right to use land may be a licence or easement. If the right is to a thing that is part of the land (e g minerals) or its natural product (e g crops) that is susceptible of separate ownership when severed or to the wild animals upon it, it may be a licence or profit.

3.24 A right may be a profit/easement if it satisfies the following requirements:[108]

---

[104] *Chamberlain v Farr* [1942] 2 All ER 567; *Parker v Parker* [2003] EWHC 1846 (Ch), at [265]. However, a tenant at will of business premises is not protected under the Landlord and Tenant Act 1954: *Wheeler v Mercer* [1957] AC 416.
[105] See e g Standard Conditions of Sale, 4th edn, cl 5.2.2 (licensee); *Street v Mountford* [1985] AC 809, at 827; *Essex Plan Ltd v Broadminster* (1998) 56 P & CR 353, at 355–356; *Cameron Ltd v Rolls-Royce plc* [2007] EWHC 546 (Ch).
[106] *Euston Centre Properties v H&J Wilson* [1982] 1 EGLR 57.
[107] *Ashby v Tolhurst* [1937] 2 KB 249; but the rule is not absolute – see *Appah v Parncliffe Investments Ltd* [1964] 1 WLR 1064. See **8.43–8.44**.
[108] *London & Blenheim Estates Ltd v Ladbroke Retail Parks Ltd* [1994] 1 WLR 31, at 36.

(1) There must be a dominant and servient tenement (although no dominant tenement is required for profits in gross[109]) and they must be in different ownership/occupation. Although the dominant tenement may be wholly or partially incorporeal, an easement cannot be appurtenant to a licence. If therefore the grantee owns no land – or none that the right benefits – it must be a licence[110] (if not a profit in gross).

(2) The right must confer a benefit on the dominant owner *as such*, not merely a personal benefit, ie it must accommodate the dominant tenement.[111] A mere private right of recreation wholly unconnected with any land owned by the grantee is therefore a licence.

(3) The right must be capable of forming the subject matter of a grant. A licence need not.[112] That is:

 (a) it must be of a type capable of existing as a profit/easement;[113]
 (b) it must be capable of reasonable definition.[114] A right that is too vague or dependent on the owner's will and subject to the exigencies of his/others' use of the land is a licence, not an easement;[115] and
 (c) it must not fall foul of the 'ouster principle'. Its precise formulation, however, is uncertain following *Batchelor v Marlow*[116] and *Moncrieff v Jamieson*,[117] considered in Chapter 7. A right that does (if not a freehold/leasehold grant) must be a licence.

(4) There must be a capable grantor and grantee; the grantor must have capacity to create the profit/easement.[118]

(5) The right must be held for an interest equivalent to a fee simple absolute in possession or a term of years absolute.[119] If therefore the right is too uncertain in duration to be capable of existing in grant (eg a right to extract minerals for as long as the owner permits) it must, in order to be effective, take effect as a licence.

---

[109] *Bettison v Langton* [2002] 1 AC 27.
[110] *Hill v Tupper* (1863) 2 Hurl & C 121.
[111] Again, with the exception of profits in gross. See for the most recent analysis of this requirement *Polo Woods Foundation v Shelton-Agar* [2009] EWHC 1361 (Ch).
[112] *Green v Ashco Horticulturalists Ltd* [1966] 1 WR 889, at 897.
[113] See for a list *Gale on the Law of Easements* (Sweet & Maxwell, 18th edn, 2008), at paras 1-74–1-75. The class is not closed: *Re Ellenborough Park* [1956] Ch 131, at 153.
[114] See eg *Pwllbach Colliery Co Ltd v Woodman* [1915] AC 634, at 649 (right to spread coal dust over land incapable of taking effect as an easement but capable of being licence).
[115] *Green v Ashco Horticulturalists Ltd* [1966] 1 WR 889.
[116] [2003] 1 WLR 764.
[117] [2007] 1 WLR 2620.
[118] See for an example of an incapable grantor *Mulliner v Midland Railway* (1879) 11 Ch D 611. Where the owner is a public/statutory body, the statutory powers by which it holds the land must be considered.
[119] Law of Property Act 1925, s 1(2).

(6) (Unless arising by prescription) it must be granted by deed.[120]

3.25 If any of (1)–(5) are not met,[121] the right may, on its proper construction, take effect as a licence. If, however, it is intended to take effect as an easement or profit, but is defective in some respect, it cannot be upheld as a licence but may be wholly ineffective.[122] If (6) is not met but the agreement is in writing satisfying Law of Property (Miscellaneous Provisions) Act 1989, s 2, it may take effect as a contract to create an easement or profit and may, pending completion, give rise to an equitable easement/profit.

3.26 If all the above requirements are met, the right may (not must) take effect as a profit/easement. It may be a licence instead if the parties so intend. The label used is relevant, but not determinative.[123] The wording of the grant may indicate its true form – eg an agreement which 'grant[ed] licence and consent' to a right capable of existing as an easement nevertheless was held to create a licence in *IDC Group Ltd v Clark*.[124] Its terms are also relevant; hence an expressed intention that the grantor's successors in title be bound by the right is indicative of a profit/easement rather than a licence.[125]

LICENCES AND TRUSTS

3.27 A person may be entitled to use/occupy land by virtue of his status as a beneficiary of the trust on which it is held. For example, a beneficiary absolutely entitled under a bare trust has such right, as do Settled Land Act tenants for life; a beneficiary who is not entitled to an interest in possession does not.

3.28 The Trusts of Land and Appointment of Trustees Act 1996 now determines the rights of beneficiaries in relation to the use/occupation of trust land. Section 12 provides that a beneficiary entitled to an interest in possession (including someone with an interest in an undivided share in land under a sub-trust) is entitled to occupy land if the purpose of the trust involves making the land available for his occupation (or a class of which he is a member) or it is held by the trustees so as to be so available. This does not apply if the land is 'unavailable' or unsuitable for his occupation (s 12(2)).

3.29 These rights are subject to the trustees' powers of regulation under the Trusts of Land and Appointment of Trustees Act 1996, s 13, which in turn are subject to the court's supervisory jurisdiction under s 14. Trustees are entitled (subject to the limitations in s 13(7) and to the requirement of reasonableness)

---

[120] Law of Property Act 1925, s 54. It must also be completed by registration to vest legal title to the easement.
[121] Except for (1)–(2) in relation to profits in gross.
[122] See by analogy *Lace v Chantler* [1944] KB 368.
[123] *IDC Group Ltd v Clark* [1992] 2 EGLR 184; compare the position (above) regarding leases.
[124] [1992] 1 EGLR 187, at 189M, aff'd [1992] 2 EGLR 184.
[125] Ibid.

to exclude/restrict the entitlement of one or more (not all) beneficiaries who have occupation rights under s 12. They may also impose reasonable conditions on a beneficiary in relation to his occupation (eg payment of outgoings/ expenses, obligations to maintain, payment of compensation to other beneficiaries or foregoing payments/benefits to which he would otherwise be entitled).

3.30 User, therefore, that is referable to a beneficiary's rights is not by way of licence, even where the trustees imposed conditions under the Trusts of Land and Appointment of Trustees Act 1996, s 13. A beneficiary who does not have s 12 rights in relation to the land (eg because he does not have an interest in possession or the purpose of the trust does not include making it available for his occupation) but is allowed to use it may be a licensee or tenant, according to the criteria set out above. That may also be true of a beneficiary who has s 12 rights but uses the land for something other than 'occupation' within s 12(1).

CUSTOMARY RIGHTS

3.31 Although the law of custom is not exclusively (or even predominantly) concerned with the use of private land, a right to enter land for certain purposes may arise by custom by virtue of immemorial usage.[126] To do so the right must be certain (as respects the nature of the user, the land to which it applies and the persons entitled to enjoy it), reasonable and have been enjoyed 'as of right' (ie without force, secrecy or permission) without interruption throughout legal memory,[127] although an evidential presumption may arise from proof of long usage.[128] Proof of public user by licence or an alleged right that is dependent on the owner's permission is therefore inconsistent with a customary right. Whereas a licence is a consensually-created right, a custom is, in essence, a form of local law, exercisable in perpetuity independently of the owner's will and arising by virtue of user without his or his predecessor's consent (see Chapter 5).

TOWN AND VILLAGE GREENS

3.32 A town or village green is land on which local inhabitants have acquired a customary right to enjoy lawful sports and pastimes. Such rights can be acquired by usage by a significant number of the inhabitants of a locality (or of a neighbourhood within a locality) 'as of right' for a continuous period

---

[126] See eg *Mercer v Denne* [1905] 2 Ch 538 (right to dry fishing nets on land); *Hall v Nottingham* (1875) 1 Ex D 1 (sports and pastimes).
[127] 12(1) *Halsbury's Laws* (4th edn reissue), at paras 606, 623.
[128] Ibid, at paras 607–608.

exceeding 20 years.[129] Greens have the same attributes as customary rights, namely public rights whose exercise neither derives from, nor is dependent on, the owner's will (see Chapter 5).

HIGHWAYS

3.33 Public rights of way, eg over footpaths, bridleways and highways, arise by statute, by (express or implied) dedication by the owner and acceptance by the public or by user 'as of right' for a continuous period of 20 years without interruption (absent sufficient evidence that the owner did not intend to dedicate) under the Highways Act 1980, s 31.

3.34 Such rights, although sometimes consensual in origin (eg by actual dedication), are not, unlike licences, derived from some revocable act by the owner. Indeed use with the owner's permission[130] (ie licence) is antithetical to their creation. The distinction therefore is between an irrevocable act (of dedication) and a permission that is expressly or impliedly revocable or finite (a licence). Further, rights arising by licence, unlike public rights, are derived from a grant of permission to the use in question, whereas the act of consent (dedication) is to the creation of (public) rights and is essentially a public act. The relationship between licences and public rights of way is more fully addressed in Chapter 5.

WAYLEAVES

3.35 Certain public utilities may, by statute, acquire rights – analogous to a licence/easement[131] – to lay and maintain on a person's land and use apparatus necessary for the discharge of their statutory functions. For example, electricity cables under the Electricity Act 1989, s 10, pipes under the Water Resources Act 1991, s 160 and telecommunications equipment under the Telecommunications Code (Telecommunications Act 1984, Sch 2). The various statutory schemes are self-contained codes and prescribe the nature of the rights acquired, the procedure for acquiring them and the conditions on which they are exercisable and provide for payment of compensation.

3.36 Such rights are distinguishable from licences in that they may be acquired compulsorily, under the relevant statutory scheme, and their exercise is not dependent on – or, in reality, derived from – the owner's will. Their terms are determined by statute/statutory procedure, although such procedure normally makes provision for certain matters (eg compensation) to be resolved,

---

[129] Commons Act 2006, s 15.
[130] Or possibly (for common-law dedication) toleration: *R v Broke* (1859) 1 F&F 514. Cf private rights arising by prescription or limitation – see Chapter 5.
[131] Albeit the utility has no dominant tenement which the right benefits, and is therefore incapable of existing as an easement in private law.

if possible, by agreement; such agreement, however, is merely of the particular matters and does not create the relationship of licensor–licensee. Of course the undertaker and the owner may in fact agree to enter into a licence, independent of the statutory scheme.

MATRIMONIAL HOMES RIGHTS

3.37 Where one party to a marriage or civil partnership (A) owns, lets or has a statutory right to occupy the matrimonial/quasi-matrimonial home, the non-owning spouse/partner (B) has (now statutory) rights of occupation. These are more fully considered in Chapter 6. At common law, a spouse's rights shared certain attributes with licences: both the licensee and the spouse may have standing to bring an action in trespass/nuisance against third parties; neither right binds third parties who have a superior interest in the land (eg mortgagees); and in both cases one spouse's occupation and that of certain licensees may be relied on by the other/the licensor to assert that his interest overrides that of third party purchasers of the land (see Chapter 9).

3.38 Nevertheless such rights are not licences[132] but are sui generis[133] (now statutory). They derive from the relationship of the marriage/civil partnership and are not dependent on A's consent. At common law a spouse's rights (unlike a licensee's) did not attach to any particular property but were to occupy such property as was the matrimonial home for the time being.[134] Furthermore such spouse (at common law) had no right to possession, or to maintain an action in trespass, as against A,[135] whereas certain licensees may, exceptionally, do so against their licensor. Also whereas one spouse's occupation could entitle the other to claim statutory security of tenure[136] a licensor cannot rely on his licensee's presence for those purposes, unless it amounts to constructive occupation by himself. Furthermore B's rights – unlike in most cases, the licensee's – are capable of binding A's successors in title, subject to registration (see Chapter 9). Finally, a spouse's rights at common law ended automatically on the termination of the relationship, death or judicial separation, whereas few licences (except bare licences and service occupancies) do – see Chapter 12.

---

[132] *National Provincial Bank Ltd v Ainsworth* [1965] AC 1175, at 1223, 1232, 1250–1251.
[133] Ibid, at 1232.
[134] Ibid, at 1245.
[135] Ibid, at 1224.
[136] See eg *Brown v Draper* [1944] KB 309.

Chapter 4

CREATION OF LICENCES

The licensor's status	4.2
Co-owners	4.3
Bare licences	4.4
Express licences	4.5
Unilateral licences	4.6
Implied licences	4.15
Contractual licences	4.24
Implied contractual licences	4.27
Contractual licences arising by conduct	4.28
Licences coupled with an interest	4.29
Estoppel licences	4.31
The expectation	4.33
The nature of the reliance	4.37
The nature of the detriment	4.38
Unconscionability	4.39
Relief granted	4.40

4.1 All licences, unlike proprietary rights, are *necessarily* derived from *actual* consent, objectively ascertained, and thus cannot be acquired by prescription.

THE LICENSOR'S STATUS

4.2 A licence granted by someone with no rights to the land is effective as between the parties (only); for the licensee to be able to assert his rights against third parties, in the limited circumstances where that is possible (see Chapter 9), the licensor must generally have – or act with the authority of someone who has – an immediate right to possession of the land. The nature/duration/terms of the licensor's right/interest will determine, as against persons with an equal or superior right, what sort of licences he is able to grant.

Co-owners

4.3 Where land is jointly owned (by A and B), a licence may be granted by one of them (A) to another person. In such case the licence is effective in estoppel between A and his licensee (see **8.25** et seq). B will be bound (only) if A had his actual or ostensible authority to grant it. The extent of that authority will vary according to the circumstances and in particular the nature of the licence (eg casual guests, lodgers[1]). If the licence was granted with B's authority, he must obviously terminate it before he can treat the licensee as a trespasser. If it was not, he can do so forthwith[2] even if the licence continues as between A and the licensee.[3] In those circumstances, if the licence is contractual the licensee may have an action against A, eg for breach of warranty of title/authority.

BARE LICENCES

4.4 A bare licence may arise expressly, by implication or by conduct. It can be granted to one or more persons or to the public generally or to a specified group, the composition of which changes from time to time (eg the inhabitants for the time being of X or the members from time to time of an unincorporated association).

Express licences

4.5 An express, bare licence is created by the licensor communicating his permission to the licensee by some means. Nothing more is generally required, eg by way of acceptance,[4] for the licensee to be able to act on it, unless it is framed as an offer or conditional on the licensee first signifying his acceptance (eg an invitation marked RSVP).

Unilateral licences

4.6 Most licences, however, are unilateral, ie granted without prior request, or subsequent express acceptance, by the licensee. A unilateral licence is, in effect, an unsolicited permission. It may be created expressly (by communication) or impliedly (eg by opening a gate). It is often used – or asserted to have existed – as a (usually temporary) expedient to stop time running against the licensor for limitation or prescription purposes.[5] In such cases the issue frequently encountered is whether the owner has adequately manifested his consent to the use and whether the other person's subsequent use of the land is attributable to it or, conversely, is 'as of right', ie without permission, stealth or force.

---

[1] Compare *Sanders v McDonald & Pringle* [1981] CLY 1534 (co-owner allowing lover to live in former quasi-matrimonial home); *Jolliffe v Willmett & Co* [1971] 1 All ER 478, at 483g–485.
[2] *Ferguson v Welsh* [1987] 1 WLR 1553, at 1563.
[3] See by analogy *Robson Paul v Farrugia* (1969) 20 P & CR 820, at 825; *Annen v Rattee* [1985] 1 EGLR 136 (both tenancies).
[4] *Lambeth LBC v Rumbelow* [2001] All ER (D) 176.
[5] Although the same is true in relation to public rights (eg of way) this expedient is ineffective to prevent the creation of town and village greens after 20 years' use 'as of right': Commons Act 2006, s 15(7).

Sufficient manifestation of consent

4.7 The owner must sufficiently manifest his permission by words, action or circumstances so that the reasonable observer would have appreciated that the user was by consent. A permission which is not manifested at all (or not sufficiently to bring it to the mind of the objective observer) is ineffective, even if the owner in fact subjectively consents. If, however, such consent comes to the user's attention or he is aware that the owner is acting in the belief that the use was consensual (eg by desisting from barring entry) he may be estopped from denying that fact if he fails to evince his intention not to rely on it.[6]

4.8 Consent can be manifest expressly or impliedly. Implied permission is dealt with at **4.15** et seq. Express consent can take a variety of forms, oral or written. If by way of notice, it must be sufficiently obvious in its location, prominence and terms to bring to the mind of the objective observer that the owner consented to the use. If communicated in writing (eg by e-mail or letter), it need not come to the user's actual attention so long as he in fact receives it. In broad terms, a letter that is lost in the post is not effective; a letter that is delivered (but for whatever reason not read) is; the owner takes the risk of non-delivery but thereafter the risk of non-communication is on the user. Permission that is to be communicated by the licensor's agent, who for whatever reason fails to pass it on to the user, is of course ineffective. If, however, it is given to the licensee's agent, it is effective even if he does not forward it to his principal.

The user's position

4.9 The user need not accept the licence: a man cannot be made a licensee against his will. However, once the licence is communicated or is objectively ascertainable (eg by conduct or from circumstances – below) the user must expressly or impliedly renounce/disclaim it. If he does so, his use thereafter may be 'as of right'.[7] If he does not his use, if consistent with the licence, will be consensual even if he did not subjectively intend to rely on it (or indeed intended not to rely on it).[8] Failure to renounce/disclaim may also estop the user from disputing that his use was by consent, but that is strictly unnecessary since so long as his use was consistent with a (sufficiently manifest) consent, it *was* in fact consensual; the owner need not prove that he subjectively believed that it was, as he would in order to raise an estoppel. In sum, once consent is

---

[6] See eg *Ellis v Lambeth LBC* (1999) 32 HLR 596, where, however, the alleged estoppel (by representation) failed on the facts.
[7] *BP Properties Ltd v Buckler* [1987] 2 EGLR 168. *Buckler* has been extra-judicially doubted. See eg Wallace 'Limitation Prescription and Unsolicited Permission' (1994) Conv 196; *Land Registration for the Twenty-First Century: A Conveyancing Revolution*, Law Com No 271 (TSO, 2001), at para 14.56, n 187. It was, however, accepted as correct in *Markfield Investments Ltd v Evans* [2001] 1 WLR 1321, at [12], and assumed to be correct in *Odey v Barber* [2008] Ch 175 .*Markfield Investments Ltd v Evans* [2001] 1 WLR 1321, at [12].
[8] *BP Properties Ltd v Buckler* [1987] 2 EGLR 168, at 171L–172B.

manifested (expressly or impliedly) and not rejected (expressly or impliedly) by the user, his use thereafter is consensual if the objective observer would regard it as such.

4.10 The user must, of course, be attributable to the licence, although that is usually easy to infer if it started only after the consent was given and is consistent with it.[9] Even, however, if the user pre-dated the licence, it may be inferred that its subsequent continuation was attributable to it so as to defeat a claim of adverse possession[10] or prescription.[11]

4.11 In the case of claimed public rights, the user need not be shown to have been subjectively aware of the licence or (in relation to implied licences) of the facts/circumstances from which it is to be inferred, so long as an objective observer would.[12] A licence may therefore be implied from acts/circumstances of which the user is in fact unaware. Although recently doubted (obiter),[13] that is thought to be true also in the case of private rights.[14]

Express disclaimer

4.12 The user may expressly renounce/disclaim the licence,[15] in which case any subsequent use may be 'as of right'. He may do so at any time, although a delay may result in his use in the interim period being treated as consensual, restarting the limitation period. A renunciation that occurs as soon as reasonably possible after the licence is created (not, it is thought, after he becomes subjectively aware of it, if later) may, however, not break the required continuity of user 'as of right'. If the licensee disclaims in writing, the above rules as to the allocation of risk apply (see **4.8**); the user takes the risk of non-delivery, but thereafter the risk is on the owner.

Implied disclaimer

4.13 Disclaimer may also be inferred from overt acts or circumstances that are sufficient to bring to the mind of the objective observer that the user does not rely on the licence. For instance, whilst a minor or temporary deviation from the licence terms may not do so, a user that is wholly inconsistent with that allowed or a sufficiently flagrant or repeated failure to observe its terms may;[16]

---

[9] *Odey v Barber* [2007] 3 All ER 543, at 561–562 (prescriptive easement).
[10] *BP Properties Ltd v Buckler* [1987] 2 EGLR 168, at 171–172 (adverse possession). Contrast *Doe d Dayman v Moore* (1846) 9 QB 555 (not cited in *Buckler*).
[11] *Rafique v Walton Estate* (1992) 65 P & CR 356, at 357 (prescriptive easement).
[12] *R (Beresford) v Sunderland CC* [2004] 1 AC 889.
[13] *J Alston & Sons Ltd v BOCM Pauls Ltd* [2009] 1 EGLR 93, at [125].
[14] See *BP Properties Ltd v Buckler* [1987] 2 EGLR 168, at 172A ('the rule that possession is not adverse if it can be referred to a lawful title applies even if the person in possession did not know of the lawful title ...').
[15] *Lambeth LBC v Rumbelow* [2001] All ER (D) 176; *Greenhalgh v Brindley* [1901] 2 Ch 324; *Smith v Colbourne* [1914] 2 Ch 573.
[16] See by analogy *Pavledes v Ryesbridge Properties Ltd* (1989) 58 P & CR 459, at 476 (no acceptance by conduct of proffered contractual licence on terms different than those de facto

the question is one of inferred intention. A disclaimer that is objectively manifest is effective even if the owner fails to appreciate its effect or is unaware of the facts/circumstances from which it is to be implied or believes that the user is consensual. However, the user may be estopped from asserting that his continued use was 'as of right' if he is aware of the owner's mistake and fails to draw it to his attention.

Unauthorised/part-unauthorised user

4.14 Use of a type wholly different to that permitted is, of course, not attributable to it (whether or not it amounts to an implied disclaimer) and thus may be 'as of right'. Where the use is in part unauthorised/excessive it is a question of degree/inference whether that amounts to implied renunciation/disclaimer or is merely an unauthorised mode of exercising the rights granted. The question is whether the user is nevertheless still referable to the permission.[17] However, it appears there must be a change in the nature of occupation for an initially consensual user to become 'as of right'.[18]

Implied licences

4.15 A bare licence may be created informally, eg by 'a nod or a wave or by leaving open a gate or even a front door'.[19] An implied licence is, in essence, the conveying of permission by non-verbal means. In such cases, the licence *arises out of* the facts that justify the implication; they are not merely *evidence* from which an express licence may be inferred.[20] The permission must be *actual* permission, objectively determined and arising by necessary inference.[21] Permission may be granted even though the owner did not subjectively intend to consent, if the reasonable observer would regard him as having done so and such objective intention was sufficiently manifest. In practice, however, the converse situation is more usual: the owner faced with a claim in prescription/limitation asserts that he consented to the use; the user disputes that any such consent was sufficiently apparent.

4.16 For consent to be implied, the owner's permission must be unequivocal and objectively manifest. In summary:

(1) There must be either (a) some overt act by the owner or (b) some circumstances from which permission may be inferred. It is not enough

---

enjoyed). Compare *Harvey v Plymouth CC* [2010] EWCA Civ 860, at [22], where it is tentatively suggested that a licensee who is acting outside the scope of the licence may nevertheless remain a 'visitor' for purposes of the Occupiers' Liability Act 1957, albeit not one to whom the licensor owes the common duty of care.

[17] *Trustees of the Grantham Christian Fellowship v Scouts Association Trust Corpn* [2005] EWHC 209 (Ch), at [33] (whether licence terminated automatically for breach).

[18] *Allen v Matthews* [2007] EWCA Civ 216, at [86]–[87] (whether part-unauthorised user sufficient to amount to adverse possession).

[19] *R (Beresford) v Sunderland CC* [2004] 1 AC 889, at [75].

[20] *Lambeth LBC v Rumbelow* [2001] All ER (D) 176.

[21] *J Alston & Sons Ltd v BOCM Pauls Ltd* [2009] 1 EGLR 93, at [51], [56].

that the facts are consistent with permission – they must be probative of it.[22] The consent must be a *necessary* inference and the facts must be sufficient to justify it.[23] The owner's subjective (but unexpressed) consent is not enough.

(2) The user must have appreciated (or a reasonable observer would have understood) that the owner consented to his use. It is not essential therefore that the user is personally aware of the permission or the facts from which it is inferred so long as the objective observer would have appreciated that his use was consensual. Although recently doubted,[24] that is thought to be true in relation to claimed private as well as public rights.[25] This was adopted as the appropriate working test in *Lambeth LBC v Rumbelow*,[26] which relied on the first instance decision in *R (Beresford) v Sunderland City Council*.[27] Although that decision was reversed on appeal,[28] the *Beresford* formulation has been repeated in subsequent cases.[29] It is, however, a moot point whether this second requirement adds anything since the first-stage test will only be met if consent was known to the user or an objectively justifiable inference.

These requirements are rarely met in practice. In most cases the acts/circumstances relied on as giving rise to the licence are equivocal – particularly in cases of inaction – because they are equally consistent with an implicit acknowledgment that the user has an existing *right* to undertake those activities or (in the case of public land) with an intention of encouraging/ facilitating an activity which the public has a right to undertake.[30] Where therefore there is some other credible justification for the use, such as some other (actual or claimed) right, a licence is unlikely to be implied.

Overt conduct justifying the inference of consent

4.17 Consent may be manifested by overt conduct. For example:

- By taking a fee in return for the use of the land (unless payment was made pursuant to some *existing* right of entry), although such cases are probably rather instances of contractual licences arising by conduct.[31]

---

[22] *Hicks Developments Ltd v Chaplin* [2007] 1 EGLR 1, at [33].
[23] *J Alston & Sons Ltd v BOCM Pauls Ltd* [2009] 1 EGLR 93, at [138].
[24] Ibid, at [125], [133].
[25] *BP Properties Ltd v Buckler* [1987] 2 EGLR 168, at 172A.
[26] See also *BANES v Nicholson* [2002] All ER (D) 327 (Feb).
[27] [2001] 1 WLR 1327, at [43].
[28] [2004] 1 AC 889.
[29] *Batsford Estates (1983) Ltd v Taylor* [2005] 2 EGLR 12, at [26]; *Colin Dawson Windows Ltd v King's Lynn BC* [2005] EWCA Civ 9; *Hicks Developments Ltd v Chaplin* [2007] 1 EGLR 1.
[30] *R (Beresford) v Sunderland CC* [2004] 1 AC 889.
[31] *Gardner v Hodgson's Kingston Brewery Co Ltd* [1903] AC 229.

- By preventing access to the land from time to time, from which the inference may be drawn that access at other times was by consent.[32] It is uncertain whether that is also true if the owner uses the land intermittently to the factual exclusion of others but without prohibiting entry; the answer may be one of fact and degree.[33]

- The inference of consent is readily made if the user enters/remains in occupation pending negotiations for the grant of some proprietary right or interest in the land, particularly if the owner undertakes works to facilitate his use.[34] Such licence may terminate when negotiations end, although when that occurs may sometimes be uncertain.[35] More often the decision to terminate negotiations and the licence requires some communication.[36] However, termination of the latter does not always automatically follow the termination of the former[37] – hence in *Canadian Pacific Railway v The King*[38] a use remained consensual after negotiations ended by virtue of the fact the owner indicated during them that if they did not progress satisfactorily it would give a date for the occupier to quit.

- Where the owner, having threatened to eject the occupier, desists, e g by discontinuing possession proceedings in response to the user's assertion that he has permission to be there.[39] Although a similar inference was drawn in *Batsford Estates (1983) Ltd v Taylor*[40] where the owner refrained from taking steps to evict the occupier who claimed an *existing* right to use the land (in that case, a tenancy), that is considered doubtful since neither party appears to have objectively intended to enter into a fresh relationship of licensor–licensee. If the user claims to be a contractual licensee he may be estopped from denying that subsequently.[41] Nevertheless a licence will not be implied if to do so would be inconsistent with the owner's intentions, objectively ascertained. The mere fact the user is a breach of some prohibition ('no ball games'), which the owner tolerates, is not of itself enough; it must be possible, as in the cases cited above, to infer the owner has changed his mind, which in most cases will require some overt act on his part.[42]

---

[32] *R (Beresford) v Sunderland CC* [2004] 1 AC 889, at [5], [83]; *Mills v Silver* [1991] Ch 284, at 282c; *R (Lewis) v Redcar and Cleveland BC* [2010] 2 All ER 613, at [83].
[33] *R (Lewis) v Redcar and Cleveland BC* [2010] 2 All ER 613, at [23]–[28].
[34] *BANES v Nicholson* [2002] All ER (D) 327 (Feb); see also *Colin Dawson Windows Ltd v King's Lynn BC* [2005] EWCA Civ 9, at [39]. A tenancy at will may arise instead if the requirements of exclusivity and contractual intent are met – see Chapter 3.
[35] See e g *BANES v Nicholson* [2002] All ER (D) 327 (Feb) (occupier held still to be licensee 5 years after desultory discussions began for grant of lease as active negotiations, which had petered out, were still under consideration).
[36] See e g *Sandhu v Farooqui* [2004] 1 P & CR 19, at [20].
[37] See e g ibid.
[38] [1931] AC 414.
[39] See e g *Lambeth LBC v Rumbelow* [2001] All ER (D) 176; *Westminster CC v Basson* (1990) 62 P & CR 57; *Batsford Estates (1983) Ltd v Taylor* [2005] 2 EGLR 12, at [25].
[40] [2005] 2 EGLR 12.
[41] See e g *Ofulue v Bossert* [2009] AC 990, at [100].
[42] For an example see *Lambeth LBC v Rumbelow* [2001] All ER (D) 176.

- Where the parties have dealt with the land on the assumption that the user was a licensee, eg if the owner undertakes repairs at his request[43] or accedes to his invitation to apportion rates between the land occupied by the licensee and licensor respectively[44] or where the occupier acts in accordance with the owner's wishes, such as by modifying his conduct when asked.[45] However, not all dealings that acknowledge the owner's *title* justify the inference of consent. For example, an offer by the squatter to pay for his use of the land or to let/purchase it will not of itself make him the owner's licensee;[46] a fortiori if the offer is not accepted.[47] The dealings must implicitly acknowledge the existence of a *relationship* of licensor–licensee between the parties.

4.18 In contrast, consent was not/may not be inferred:

- by virtue of the user entering/remaining in occupation, where one party refused outright an offer to grant/take an interest in the land;[48]

- from an agreement between the owner and squatter to erect a barrier between the occupied land and the rest of the owner's land;[49]

- from visits by the owner's contractors who were not authorised to manage the land by virtue of their failure to object to the user;[50]

- from negotiations to grant the user a right/interest in the land where the owner was in fact unaware of his presence – one cannot infer permission to an occupation of which the owner is ignorant;[51]

- from *mere* inaction by the owner in the face of the user.[52] This of itself amounts to toleration or acquiescence rather than permission. Whilst it has been suggested that mere acquiescence may, over time, amount to 'tacit permission'[53] preventing adverse rights being acquired[54] it is thought

---

[43] As in *Lambeth LBC v Rumbelow* [2001] All ER (D) 176.
[44] *East Sussex CC v Miller* (1991) June *Legal Action* 13. Although the result there could have been justified on the basis the occupier had not shown the necessary animus for limitation purposes. *Pavledes v Ryesbridge Properties Ltd* (1989) 58 P&CR 459, at 480–481 (asking owner to undertake repairs to boundaries to keep out squatters).
[45] See eg *Pulleyn v Hall Aggregates (Thames Valley) Ltd* (1992) 65 P & CR 276 (squatter allowed sailing clubs to use car park at owner's request). Although the case was decided on the basis the squatter lacked the required animus possidendi, an alternative explanation is that he had impliedly accepted the owner as his licensor.
[46] *JA Pye (Oxford) Ltd v Graham* [2003] 1 AC 419, at [46].
[47] See for an example *Wallis's Cayton Bay Holiday Camp Ltd v Shell-Mex and BP Ltd* [1975] QB 94.
[48] See eg *JA Pye (Oxford) Ltd v Graham* [2003] 1 AC 419.
[49] *Hicks Developments Ltd v Chaplin* [2007] 1 EGLR 1.
[50] *Clowes Developments (UK) Ltd v Walters* [2005] EWHC 669 (Ch).
[51] *Tower Hamlets LBC v Barrett* (2006) 1 P & CR 132, at [66]–[68].
[52] See eg *Edwards v Railway Executive* [1952] AC 737, 746 ('repeated trespass of itself confers no licence'). See also the analysis in *Mills v Silver* [1991] Ch 284, at 288–290, 291.
[53] See eg *Lowery v Walker* [1911] AC 10, at 12, 13–14; *Canadian Pacific Railway Co v The King*

that is no longer good law following *Beresford*,[55] although when coupled with other acts or circumstances inaction may amount to implied consent in fact. Nevertheless inaction in the face of a trespass may give rise to an estoppel (proprietary/by acquiescence) although if the trespass is deliberate the trespasser will usually not believe he has the right to use the land, which is highly relevant to the question of unconscionability and whether he detrimentally relied on the owner's failure to act.[56]

- to an actual use of which the owner is unaware, although the owner may of course have given general consent to such use by the public or to a class of persons to which the user belongs; or

- where the user is attributable to some other existing or claimed right to use the land (eg as tenant with security of tenure, as the owner of a prescriptive right or as adverse possessor).

In reality, however, the differences between some of the examples in this and the preceding paragraph can be small (eg between acceding to a request to apportion rates and to physically apportion the land). It is unnecessary, however, to attempt to reconcile them since each case is a question of fact and inference, taking into account the totality of the parties' acts and the background circumstances.

Encouragement etc as overt conduct

4.19 Conduct that facilitates, encourages or regulates the use in question (eg marking out sports fields for recreational use) may be ambiguous as to whether it amounts to (a) implied consent, (b) implicit acknowledgement that the user has an existing right to undertake such activities,[57] eg in relation to publicly owned land,[58] or (c) an intention to create permanent rights, eg by dedication. Accordingly such acts, at least in relation to land to which the public may have/claim existing rights,[59] are often ambiguous and therefore insufficient to amount to permission. The appropriate inference, however, as to the owner's intention depends on the identity of the owner and user(s), the nature of the land, the use in question and the owner's acts. For example, since private owners are not expected to facilitate beneficial public activities, the inference to be drawn in cases of private and public land is likely to be different;

[1931] AC 414, at 424, 428; *Morris v Tarrant* [1971] 2 QB 143, at 159–160 ('No doubt a situation may arise in which failure to take steps to evict a trespasser whose presence is known may amount to tacit permission to remain').

[54] *Alfred F Beckett Ltd v Lyons* [1967] Ch 449.
[55] *R (Beresford) v Sunderland CC* [2004] 1 AC 889.
[56] *Lester v Woodgate* [2010] EWCA Civ 199, at [39].
[57] *R (Beresford) v Sunderland CC* [2004] 1 AC 889, at [48]–[49], [60], [85]; *Herrington v BRB* [1972] AC 877.
[58] Ibid, at [49]: public ownership a 'highly material' factor.
[59] Eg the statutory trusts for pubic recreation under Public Health Act 1964, s 164 and Open Spaces Act 1906, s 10.

encouragement/facilitation in the former case is more likely to be evidence of implied permission in the absence of any colourable basis for some existing right to use the land.

Circumstances justifying the inference of consent

4.20 A licence may arise from circumstances from which consent can be inferred.[60] However, if the user was originally as of right, supervening circumstances alone will rarely (if ever) justify the inference that it was subsequently consensual.[61]

4.21 For many years a squatter was deemed to have occupied with the owner's implied consent if his use was not inconsistent with the owner's present/future intended use of the land.[62] That is no longer the case as a result of amendments made originally to the Limitation Act 1939 but now contained in the Limitation Act 1980, Sch 1, para 8(4): a licence may not be implied as a matter of *law* merely because the squatter's use is not inconsistent with the owner's plans for the land.

4.22 However, the Limitation Act 1980 expressly permits a 'finding to the effect that a person's occupation of any land is by implied permission ... in any case where such a finding is justified on the actual facts of the case'.[63] Whilst that leaves open the possibility of consent being inferred as a matter of *fact* where (as in *Leigh v Jack*[64]) the squatter's use was not inconsistent with the owner's intended use of the land, it is now clear that such intentions are generally irrelevant to whether the squatter is in adverse possession.[65] The highest it can be put is that if the squatter is aware of a special purpose to which the owner uses/intends to use the land and his use does not conflict with that, 'it remains a possible, if improbable inference'[66] that he lacked the required animus to be in adverse possession.

4.23 In reality, circumstances alone rarely justify the inference of consent. Nevertheless there are some examples. For instance:

- Persons who have/reasonably believe they have legitimate business with the occupier have permission to approach the front door of a dwelling[67] in the absence of a locked gate/warning sign.[68] This does not extend to entry

---

[60] *R (Beresford) v Sunderland CC* [2004] 1 AC 889, at [59]. Contrast Lord Walker at [83].
[61] *R (Lewis) v Redcar and Cleveland BC* [2009] EWCA Civ 3, at [58]–[59]: 'it is not possible to infer precario simply from the context. Once the owner is on notice of a public use "as of right" he must act positively if he wishes to avoid that acquiescence which is at the root of the concept'; rev'd (on a different point) [2010] 2 All ER 613.
[62] See e g *Wallis's Cayton Bay Holiday Camp Ltd v Shell-Mex and BP Ltd* [1975] QB 94.
[63] Limitation Act 1980, Sch 1, para 8(4).
[64] (1879) 5 Ex D 264.
[65] *Buckinghamshire CC v Moran* [1990] Ch 623; *JA Pye (Oxford) Ltd v Graham* [2003] 1 AC 419.
[66] *JA Pye (Oxford) Ltd v Graham* [2003] 1 AC 419, at [45].
[67] *Robson v Hallett* [1967] 2 QB 939, at 951, 953–954.
[68] *Lambert v Roberts* [1981] 2 All ER 15, at 19.

into the building itself[69] or presumably the common parts of a block of flats, at least where entry is through a communal door. The permission can be limited ('no canvassers/unauthorised personnel') or excluded ('no entry'), eg by notice.

- There is similarly prima facie implied permission to enter business premises normally open to the public (eg shops) during trading hours for purposes connected with the business conducted there.[70] In both this and the preceding example a person who enters for legitimate business does so as the owner's visitor rather than as member of the public.[71]

- By allowing someone whose current right to use the land (eg as tenant or licensee) has expired to remain, if circumstances are such that the owner's decision to desist from taking action is attributable to an act of generosity or friendship.[72] Mere inaction, however, is insufficient of itself in these circumstances.[73]

- Courts have also been prepared to infer licences by virtue of the fact the owner and the user were family members/friends,[74] but whilst that doubtless makes the inference easier to draw the better justification for such cases is that the user lacks the necessary qualities to be capable of giving rise to adverse rights. The question is ultimately one of inference: in cases of ouster/dispossession, the fact the user and owner are family/friends is most unlikely to be justify an implication of consent.

- Use of the foreshore for minor purposes (eg picking sea coal) otherwise than by virtue of a customary public right may also be justified on this basis.[75]

- So too a local practice between local hill farmers of giving access to each other's land.[76]

CONTRACTUAL LICENCES

4.24 The rules as to the creation of contractual licences are those for contracts generally and are therefore briefly mentioned. A contractual licence may arise expressly, by implication[77] or by conduct. As with contracts generally, the licence may be bilateral (where the offer of a licence is expressly accepted) or

---

[69] *Great Central Ry Co v Bates* [1921] 3 KB 581, at 582.
[70] *Davis v Lisle* [1936] 2 KB 434, at 440.
[71] *R v Roberts* (1978) 67 Cr App R 228, at 231.
[72] See eg *Foster v Robinson* [1951] 1 KB 149.
[73] *J Alston & Sons Ltd v BOCM Pauls Ltd* [2009] 1 EGLR 93.
[74] See eg *Morris v Pinches* [1969] 212 EG 1141.
[75] *Alfred E Beckett Ltd v Lyons* [1967] 1 Ch 449, as explained in *Mills v Silver* [1991] Ch 284, at 283–284.
[76] *Mills v Silver* [1991] Ch 284, at 293D–293E.
[77] *Horrocks v Forray* [1976] 1 All ER 737, at 742.

unilateral (where acceptance is inferred from the offeree entering and using the land in the manner authorised). The parties must be identified or identifiable; accordingly a contractual licence, unlike a bare licence, cannot be granted to a fluctuating body of persons, eg the members for the time being of an unincorporated association.[78]

4.25 A licence 'in gross' need not be in any particular form[79] as it is not an interest in land (see Chapter 9); it may thus be created orally or in writing or by implication or conduct. Where, however, it is merely part of a larger transaction (eg a term of a lease or coupled with an interest in land), the formalities rules applicable to that type of transaction must be observed, unless it is severable and entirely independent of the remainder.

4.26 There must, of course, be a meeting of minds with the contract terms reasonably clearly made out and an intention to create legal relations. A contractual licence, however, needs only the barest terms to be effective: identification of land, permitted use (although a general right of entry may be inferred in the absence of some express or implied limitation as to the purposes for which the licensee is entitled to enter) and consideration. Nevertheless no binding agreement will arise if it lacks certainty, either because its terms are too vague or it is manifestly incomplete in some material respect, eg because important terms have been left unresolved or further agreement on outstanding matters is expressly contemplated, unless the parties intend to be bound in the interim/in any event or such terms would be implied.

Implied contractual licences

4.27 A contractual licence may arise by implication but 'there has to be shown a meeting of the minds of the parties with a definition of the contractual terms reasonably clearly made out with an intention to affect the legal relationship'.[80] A licence may also be an implied term of a larger transaction if such right would spell out in express words what the contract, read against the relevant background, would reasonably be understood to mean,[81] eg because the right 'goes without saying' or is necessary to give business efficacy to the contract (eg where the licensee is required to perform services to the licensor that require his presence on the land).

Contractual licences arising by conduct

4.28 A contractual licence may occasionally arise by conduct, eg by the tender/acceptance of a fee in return for the right to use the land. An offer of a licence may be accepted by conduct, eg by the offeree subsequently entering and using the land in the manner intended, even if the offer contemplated

---

[78] See by analogy *Camden LBC v Shortlife Community Housing Ltd* (1992) 25 HLR 330, at 342 (lease).
[79] See eg *Wells v Kingston upon Hull* (1874–75) LR 10 CP 402.
[80] *Horrocks v Forray* [1976] 1 WLR 230, at 236D.
[81] *A-G of Belize v Belize Telecom Ltd* [2009] 2 All ER 1127, at [21].

acceptance by some other means (eg by signing and returning the proffered written licence agreement).[82] Even if the intended form of acceptance was meant to be a condition of the offer the licensor may waive it expressly or impliedly, eg by permitting the licensee to take up occupation. An offer to renew an expired licence may be impliedly accepted (in the absence of any colourable right to continue to use the land) by the licensee continuing to use the land. If, however, the user is already using/occupying the land 'as of right', acceptance will not be inferred merely by virtue of his continued use of the land after the offer is made,[83] unless he modifies his conduct consistent with the proffered terms. Nor, of course, will a licence arise by conduct by virtue of the offeree's continued presence on the land if the offer is expressly rejected[84] or he has some independent, existing or claimed right to be there (eg under an unexpired lease/licence).

LICENCES COUPLED WITH AN INTEREST

4.29 A licence may be coupled with some proprietary interest in land (typically, a profit, eg growing crops) or chattels (eg cut timber or severed minerals). In such cases the grantor must be able (or must act with the authority of someone who is able[85]) to create/convey the interest. In the case of chattel interests, he must also have the right to permit the grantee to enter the land.

4.30 The nature of the interest determines the manner in which it must be created or transferred. That is:

- Title to chattels may be transferred by gift or contract. The contract may be oral or written.[86] A gift must be perfected by deed or by vesting possession of the chattel in the donee.

- A contract to grant an interest in land must, with certain exceptions,[87] comply with the Law of Property (Miscellaneous Provisions) Act 1989, s 2, ie must be contained in writing, signed by the parties setting out all terms expressly agreed.

- Legal interests in land must be created by grant (which must be by deed and, where necessary, completed by registration)[88] or prescription. Whilst

---

[82] *Wettern Electric Ltd v Welsh Development Agency* [1983] 2 All ER 629.
[83] *Pavledes v Ryesbridge Properties Ltd* (1989) 58 P&CR 459, at 476. Contrast the position (above) in relation to bare licences under *BP Properties Ltd v Buckler* [1987] 2 EGLR 168.
[84] Compare *Glossop v Ashley* [1921] 2 KB 451.
[85] See eg *Wood v Manley* (1839) 11 Ad & El 34 (purchase of chattels from a landlord exercising his right to distrain; sale terms entitling purchaser to enter land to remove chattels agreed by tenant; tenant's action in trespass against purchaser entering land to remove chattels failed).
[86] *James Jones & Sons Ltd v Earl of Tankerville* [1909] 2 Ch 440, at 442.
[87] Eg leases for less than 3 years taking effect in possession at the best rent reasonably obtainable without taking a fine.
[88] Law of Property Act 1925, s 54(1), (2).

a licence cannot be acquired by prescription, an easement or profit can and an interest so acquired can confer on the user, as a necessary incident, an ancillary licence.

There are no formalities for the licence itself but if the purported grant/transfer of the interest is ineffective by virtue of the failure to comply with the formalities required for *its* creation, so too is the licence.

ESTOPPEL LICENCES

4.31 Proprietary estoppel is not exclusively (or even predominantly) concerned with licences but with expectations of rights/interests in/over property generally. It is therefore dealt with in outline only. 'Orthodox' licences whose revocation is prevented by estoppel are outside the scope of this book.

4.32 Although no single formulation is free from objection, a proprietary estoppel may arise where one person (A) has changed position by taking/desisting from taking action in the reasonable but mistaken belief that he has/will have[89] some – not necessarily proprietary – right or interest in another's (B's) land, which B caused or encouraged by statement or conduct or by standing by (in circumstances where he could be expected to speak) if he knew or ought to have known that A would rely on that belief and as a result it would be unconscionable for him to enforce his strict legal rights against A to the land. The requirements of expectation, reliance and detriment are, to a certain extent, interdependent.[90]

The expectation

4.33 The expectation must relate to specific property (or type of property, e g 'my fields') but need not be of any specific type of right or interest.[91] A belief by A that he has a right to use land that in law amounts to a licence appears to be sufficient.[92] A mere promise to provide for A or that A would always have a home (without reference to any specific property) is not.[93] Where the promise is of a future right/interest in land, changes in its composition before the expectation crystallises (typically, on death) may affect the form of relief but do not prevent the equity arising so long as there remains identifiable property to which the promise may be said to apply, unless it now comprises

---

[89] See, however, *Thorner v Major* [2009] 3 All ER 945, at [20] for the suggestion that representations of a future benefit are more properly analysed in terms of constructive trust rather than proprietary estoppel.
[90] *Gillett v Holt* [2001] Ch 210, at 225.
[91] *Plimmer v Wellington Corp* (1883–84) 9 App Cas 699, at 713–714. See *Thorner v Major* [2009] 3 All ER 945, at [9], [61], [102].
[92] See, however, the criticism in *Megarry & Wade: The Law of Real Property* (Sweet & Maxwell, 7th edn, 2008), at paras 16-006, 16-033. In such case presumably no question of the application of the Law of Property (Miscellaneous Provisions) Act 1989, s 2 applies – see *Cobbe v Yeoman's Row Management Ltd* [2008] 1 WLR 1752.
[93] *Coombes v Smith* [1986] 1 WLR 808, at 818D.

something entirely different or later events justify giving the promise a different effect. Such changes may, however, affect the form of relief granted.[94]

4.34 There must be a sufficient (express or implied) representation on which the recipient might reasonably have been expected to rely. In cases of standing by, the owner's silence in circumstances when he could be expected to speak may amount to an implicit representation/encouragement.[95]

4.35 In the commercial sphere it is thought highly improbable (if not practically impossible) following *Cobbe v Yeoman's Row Management Ltd*[96] that a sufficient representation will be made when parties (a) are in negotiations for a formal contract or (b) have concluded an agreement that (i) is incomplete in some material respect or (ii) is (expressly or implicitly) subject to contract or otherwise not intended to be immediately binding.[97] Since both parties will appreciate there is no contract between them they understand (or will be taken to understand) that the other's statements are not intended to be relied on and thus they take the risk by doing so. The representee must at least believe that he *has* a legally enforceable right (although even then the representor may not be bound if he did not cause it and was unaware of it) – a mere expectation of one if negotiations conclude successfully is insufficient. Nor does mere unconscionable behaviour give rise to an equity.

4.36 In contrast, parties in the domestic sphere are more likely to intend or foresee that their promises will be relied on without them being reduced to a contract.[98] What the representor's (B's) words/acts would reasonably have conveyed to the representee (A)[99] and whether they were intended to be relied upon is to be judged objectively. B need not subjectively intend A to rely on his promise and B's subjective understanding or intentions as to what his words/acts convey is irrelevant. It is enough that B's words would reasonably have been understood by A as intended to be taken seriously as an assurance that could be relied on,[100] or were sufficiently clear and unequivocal[101] or were 'clear enough'[102] when judged in context, including A's knowledge of B's character.[103] Where the words used are capable of more than one meaning, A

---

[94] *Thorner v Major* [2009] 3 All ER 945.
[95] Ibid, at [55].
[96] [2008] 1 WLR 1752.
[97] See *Herbert v Doyle* [2010] EWCA Civ 1095, at [56]–[59], [64]–[66], [89]–[91].
[98] *Cobbe v Yeoman's Row Management Ltd* [2008] 1 WLR 1752, at [66]–[68]. Contrast the judicial inclination against finding that such parties contracted with each other – see Chapter 2.
[99] Eg whether a statement as to his future acts was a promissory assurance or no more than a statement of current intention – *Cobbe v Yeoman's Row Management Ltd* [2008] 1 WLR 1752, at [2], [74].
[100] *Thorner v Major* [2009] 3 All ER 945, at [5], per Lord Hoffman.
[101] Ibid, at [15], [18], per Lord Scott, [84], per Lord Neuberger.
[102] Ibid, at [26], per Lord Rodger, [56], per Lord Walker.
[103] Ibid, at [3] ('The fact [B] spoke in oblique and allusive terms does not matter if it was reasonable for [A] given his knowledge of [B] and the background circumstances, to have understood him to mean not merely that his present intention was to leave [A] the farm but that he definitely would do so').

will not be deprived of all relief if he reasonably relied on one interpretation, but in such case relief may be granted on the basis that is least beneficial to him.[104]

The nature of the reliance

4.37 A must have relied on the statement/promise, although it need not have been the sole inducement. Accordingly it is no answer that he would have acted in the same way had no promise been made. But no reliance is shown if A would have acted in the same way had B expressly withdrawn his promise before A acted on it.[105] Nor if A has an existing right/interest in the land (such as a licence[106]) and B makes no promise of a further or different right. Although A has the legal burden of proving he relied on the promise, that will be inferred if promise and detriment are proven; the evidential burden then shifts to B to prove A did not.[107]

The nature of the detriment

4.38 The detriment must consist of more than merely the loss of the promised right/interest. It must be sufficiently substantial to justify the intervention of equity[108] but need not be financially quantifiable.[109] A must have acted (eg by spending money on B's land or giving up rights over other land) or desisted from acting (eg by failing to make alternative provision) on the strength of the promise. The degree of detriment suffered and whether B knew or ought to have been aware that A was relying on his statement/promise are factors relevant in the assessment of unconscionability.

Unconscionability

4.39 A must give credit for countervailing benefits received as a result of their dealings (eg the free use of B's land in the interim).[110] If, of course, the expectation was only of a right to use B's land for a period of time that has since passed or until certain events or circumstances that have in fact come about ('until I return from abroad') or for so long as certain conditions are satisfied which no longer apply (eg 'as long as you are my employee'[111]), the equity is discharged as A had no expectation of being able to use B's land beyond then.

---

[104] Ibid, at [86].
[105] *Wayling v Jones* (1995) 69 P & CR 170.
[106] *E&L Berg Homes Ltd v Grey* [1980] 1 EGLR 103.
[107] *Coombes v Smith* [1986] 1 WLR 808, at 821.
[108] *Thorner v Major* [2009] 3 All ER 945, at [15].
[109] *Gillett v Holt* [2001] Ch 210, at 232.
[110] See eg *Sledmore v Dalby* (1996) 72 P & CR 196.
[111] See by analogy *Uglow v Uglow* [2004] EWCA Civ 987 (promise to leave property on death dependent on parties remaining in partnership).

Relief granted

4.40 The 'estoppel licence', as used here, is the inchoate equity that crystallises before judgment once the elements of expectation, reliance and detriment exist, as distinct from the manner in which the court decides to give effect to the equity. The maximum permissible relief is to have made good A's expectation. If therefore it is subjectively understood to be of a specific type of right (eg licence as distinct from, say, a lease or easement) the court cannot grant any greater interest. In practice that is rarely the case. The court must do justice to both A and B.[112] It is not bound to give effect to A's expectation, although the presumption is in favour of it doing so if the parties' arrangements fell not far short of an enforceable contract, the expectation and the detriment being in effect bargained for. In such case the parties may be regarded as having agreed the two were broadly proportionate unless that is clearly not so (eg an extravagant promise in return for a modest detriment).[113] In most cases, however, the discretion is at large. If (eg) B's promise was not specific or the promised benefit was disproportionately greater than A's detriment, the court may give A a quantum meruit sum representing the value of his loss/B's benefit or (only) a proportion of what B promised,[114] taking into account the degree to which B's conduct can be properly said to be unconscionable, the extent of A's expectation and detriment and the need for some proportionality between the two.[115]

---

[112] *Jennings v Rice* [2003] 1 P & CR 100, at [48].
[113] Ibid, at [45].
[114] Ibid, at [47].
[115] *Sutcliffe v Lloyd* [2008] EWHC 1329 (Ch), at [4].

Chapter 5

LICENCES AND ADVERSE RIGHTS

General	5.1
The nature of consent	5.3
The quality of consent necessary to prevent the acquisition of adverse rights	5.4
User in excess of the licence	5.5
Licences and limitation	5.15
General	5.15
Limitation by licensee against licensor	5.16
Limitation against true owner	5.19
Limitation in favour of third parties	5.23
Licences and prescription	5.25
Licensees and prescription	5.25
Licensors and prescription	5.29
Prescription by third parties	5.30
Licences and public rights of way	5.31
Licences and town or village greens	5.35
Custom	5.38

GENERAL

5.1 Public rights and proprietary rights/interests – but not mere licences – may be acquired over another's land by virtue of long user 'as of right'. For example:

(1) a squatter may acquire possessory title to land after 12 years' exclusive possession;[1]

(2) prescriptive easements and profits may be acquired as a result of 20 or 40 years' user at common law, under the Prescription Act 1832 or by virtue of the doctrine of lost modern grant;

(3) public rights of way may be acquired by dedication/deemed dedication and acceptance;[2]

---

[1] See now, however, in relation to registered land, Land Registration Act 1925, s 75 (where possession first acquired more than 12 years before October 2003) and Land Registration Act 2002, s 96(1) and Sch 6 (subsequent taking of possession).

[2] At common law or under Highways Act 1980, s 31.

(4) customary rights over land (eg to hold fairs[3] or to dry fishing nets[4]) may be acquired by the inhabitants of a particular locality from user from time immemorial, which in practice may be presumed on proof of use throughout living memory or even 20 years,[5] so long as it is not shown to have originated after 1189; and

(5) town/village greens may be created under the Commons Act 2006, s 15 by use for lawful sports and pastimes by a significant number of the inhabitants of a locality (or a neighbourhood within it) for a period of at least 20 years.

5.2 These doctrines arose independently of each other. English law never developed a consistent theory of prescription.[6] As a result, the principles applicable to their creation are not necessarily identical and care is needed when importing concepts derived from one to another.[7] However, at a certain level of abstraction some common principles apply:

(1) The user, to give rise to an adverse right/interest, must have been 'as of right', which so far as relevant means without the owner's permission, as distinct from acquiescence or toleration.[8] Use pursuant to licence (except possibly an estoppel licence[9]) cannot mature into such right or interest, however long it continues.[10]

(2) Such permission may be express (oral,[11] in writing or by notice) or implied by overt acts or circumstances (see Chapter 4).

(3) The use must not be attributable to some existing common-law or statutory right or interest. For example, where a local authority holds land on statutory trust for public recreation (eg under Public Health Act 1875, s 164; Open Spaces Act 1906, s 10) it is considered – although the point was left open in *R (Beresford) v Sunderland CC*[12] and *R (Lewis) v Redcar and Cleveland BC*[13] – that such use is both referable to and explicable by such trusts and thus not as of right, there being an alternative legal basis to a claimed customary etc right for such activity. In contrast where the land has not been appropriated for recreation purposes, thereby engaging the statutory trusts, but has been allowed to be used as such, the public's use may over time mature into a public right unless it was by licence.[14] The

---

[3] *Wyld v Silver* [1963] Ch 243.
[4] *Mercer v Denne* [1905] 2 Ch 538, at 580.
[5] *R v Oxfordshire CC ex parte Sunningwell PC* [2000] 1 AC 335, at 350.
[6] Ibid, at 349G.
[7] *R (Beresford) v Sunderland CC* [2004] 1 AC 889, at [34].
[8] *R v Oxfordshire CC ex parte Sunningwell PC* [2000] 1 AC 335, at 358G.
[9] See **5.4(8)–(9)**.
[10] But see the exception in Law of Property Act 1925, s 62 – Chapter 9.
[11] With one exception, where a prescriptive profit/easement is based on 40 years' user – see **5.28**.
[12] [2004] 1 AC 889, at [9], [30].
[13] [2010] 2 WLR 653, [2010] 2 All ER 613.
[14] *Attorney-General v Teddington UDC* [1989] 1 Ch 66, at 69–70.

position is less clear where land is held under the Local Government (Miscellaneous Provisions) Act 1976, s 19(2) (which authorises an authority to 'make ... facilities provided ... available for such persons as [it] thinks fit either without charge or on payment of such charge as [it] thinks fit').

(4) Correspondingly where the use is attributable to a statutory right – whether or not the user is aware of that fact – a licence may not be implied since there is some other legal basis for it (see Chapter 4).

(5) Nor is one likely to be implied if the user is asserted to be attributable to some other right or interest, whether or not it exists in fact.[15] In such case the question is whether it is appropriate to infer that the parties intended to enter into some new relationship. If not – as is usual – such use may be 'as of right', although a user who has claimed some finite interest in the land, eg as lessee, may well be estopped from asserting that his use thereafter gave rise to a prescriptive right/adverse possession.

(6) A permission given at any time during the prescription period is generally sufficient – for as long as it continues – to prevent the subsequent user being 'as of right'.[16] If, however, a user originally started 'as of right' then at least in the context of public rights subsequent circumstances alone will rarely, if ever, justify the conclusion that its use thereafter was permissive.[17]

(7) The user need not have any subjective belief that he has an existing right.[18]

(8) The use must have the necessary attributes:

 (a) In adverse possession, the squatter must have factual possession and an intention to possess (see Chapter 2).
 (b) For other adverse rights the user must have been continuous in the *Hollins v Verney*[19] sense of being in the manner to be expected of someone with an existing right, although this precise requirement has been left uncertain as a result of *R (Lewis) v Redcar and Cleveland*.[20] The mere fact the users of claimed public rights deferred

---

[15] See eg *Marcroft Wagons Ltd v Smith* [1951] 2 KB 496; *Burrows v Brent LBC* [1996] 1 WLR 1448, at 1454F–1454G.
[16] See eg *R (Beresford) v Sunderland CC* [2004] 1 AC 889, at [46].
[17] *R (Lewis) v Redcar and Cleveland BC* [2009] EWCA Civ 3 (overruled on a different point, [2010] 2 WLR 653, [2010] 2 All ER 613), at [58]–[59]: 'it is not possible to infer precario simply from the context. Once the owner is on notice of a public use "as of right" he must act positively if he wishes to avoid that acquiescence which is at the root of the concept.'
[18] *R v Oxfordshire CC ex parte Sunningwell PC* [2000] 1 AC 335, at 355–356 (town and village greens but considering authorities on highways); *Bridle v Ruby* [1989] 1 QB 169 (prescription); *R (Lewis) v Redcar and Cleveland BC* [2010] 2 WLR 653, [2010] 2 All ER 613.
[19] (1884) 13 QBD 304, at 315; *R v Oxfordshire CC ex parte Sunningwell PC* [2000] 1 AC 335, at 352–353.
[20] [2010] 2 WLR 653, [2010] 2 All ER 613, at [31], [33], [65], [67]–[69], [75], [114], [116].

to others rightfully using the land is not of itself fatal to such claim,[21] but taken with other factors may indicate that the user lacked this quality.

(c) The user need not, however, be adverse to the owner's interests.[22] Public rights may arise from the use of land held by a public authority (but not appropriated to such uses) which it promoted as beneficial to the common good,[23] eg recreation. So too, an individual may acquire adverse rights over another's land by using it as the owner intended it to be used (eg for parking), although if – rarely – that intention extended to its use by the public, such use may be by implied consent or the user may lack the required characteristics ((a) and (b) above) to give rise to a right/interest arising by prescription or limitation.[24]

THE NATURE OF CONSENT

5.3 The qualities sufficient to defeat a claim to an adverse right may not be the same in all cases.[25] Nevertheless where permission is alleged, it is generally necessary to ask whether:

(1) it was sufficiently manifested (see Chapter 4);

(2) it had the necessary quality of precariousness (see **5.4**);

(3) it permitted the acts on which the claimed right is based (see **5.7–5.12**); and

(4) if so, whether/when it came to an end.

The quality of consent necessary to prevent the acquisition of adverse rights

5.4 As regards the quality of the consent required to prevent the user being 'as of right', some general comments may be made:

(1) Permission cannot be inferred from *mere* inaction by the owner in the face of the user. Something more is necessary (see Chapter 4). Nor can it be inferred from a (mistaken) express/implied acknowledgement by the owner that such a right existed,[26] although in practice the distinction

---

[21] *R (Lewis) v Redcar and Cleveland BC* [2010] 2 WLR 653, [2010] 2 All ER 613.
[22] *R (Beresford) v Sunderland CC* [2004] 1 AC 889, at [90].
[23] See eg *R (Beresford) v Sunderland CC* [2004] 1 AC 889.
[24] See eg *Pulleyn v Hall Aggregates (Thames Valley) Ltd* (1993) 65 P & CR 276.
[25] *R (Beresford) v Sunderland CC* [2004] 1 AC 889, at [51] ('The conclusion ... depend[s] on the nature of the permission, objectively assessed or construed').
[26] *R (Beresford) v Sunderland CC* [2004] 1 AC 889.

(2) Permission may be express or implied. An implied bare licence is a form of unilateral licence. An express unilateral licence[27] is normally granted for the purpose of preventing subsequent use of the land maturing into a legal right. Implied unilateral licences are usually first raised in retrospect by the owner who asserts that the past use on which the claimed right is based was at least in part impliedly consensual and therefore not 'as of right'.

(3) Permission which prevents a user being 'as of right' is not synonymous with consent. For example, 'consent' (if not sufficiently manifested) may be consistent with mere toleration/acquiescence or implicit recognition of an existing right (eg a 'Public entry' notice). It may merely signify the user was not contentious.

(4) Where there have been dealings between the owner and the user concerning the land or their use of it during the prescription period, it is a question of fact and inference whether the former impliedly recognised the latter's rights or (conversely) the latter implicitly acknowledged the owner's right to control its use and, thus, that his use was precarious. For example, if access to the land was always locked, but the key was asked for/given *as a matter of right*, the user may be 'as of right'.[28] Conversely if by retaining the key the owner was implicitly exercising the right to control access, the use is permissive.[29] The proper inference is not always easy to draw in practice. A practice of deference by one party to the other's use is equivocal; it may be explicable on the basis of courtesy/neighbourliness rather than some implicit acknowledgement of the existence (or otherwise) of the user's right[30] or, conversely, of a licence.

(5) In public rights of way, a consent may, if intended to be permanent, constitute an act of dedication.[31]

(6) In other cases, although there are statements that precario is, classically, 'revocable at will'[32] or grants consent 'for a limited period'[33] as opposed to 'a permanent irrevocable permission attributable to a lost grant',[34] a perpetual (contractual) licence may be granted – see Chapter 6. In such

---

[27] See eg *BP Properties Ltd v Buckler* (1988) 55 P & CR 337.
[28] *Roberts v Fellowes* (1906) 94 LT 279.
[29] See eg *Wood v Waud* (1849) 3 Exch 748 (evidence that water only intended to flow as long as owners had no use for it inconsistent with claimed prescriptive right to receive such flow).
[30] *R (Lewis) v Redcar and Cleveland BC* [2010] 2 WLR 653, [2010] 2 All ER 613, at [36], [77], [96], [106], [116].
[31] *R (Beresford) v Sunderland CC* [2004] 1 AC 889, at [38], [47]; *R (Godmanchester TC) v Secretary of State for the Environment* [2008] 1 AC 221, at [63], referring to 'the inference that the landowner *had* given permission, not merely temporarily but on a permanent basis, for the user' (emphasis in original).
[32] *R (Beresford) v Sunderland CC* [2004] 1 AC 889, at [57]; see also at [58].

case the question is not then one of prescription, but whether the user was within (or was treated as being within) the scope of the licence.[35] A gratuitous, general permission unlimited in time will usually be regarded as impliedly terminable and thus use pursuant to it is at the licensor's will.

(7) According to Lord Scott in *R (Beresford) v Sunderland City Council*,[36] 'consent' may be consistent with the creation of prescriptive rights in two other circumstances. First, a use that is pursuant to uncompleted contract to grant a proprietary right/interest (or, possibly, also a purported but invalid grant of such a right/interest) is not precario. Arguably, however, if the uncompleted contract is specifically enforceable, the equitable right/interest which it confers on the grantee[37] provides an alternative justification for the user, obviating the need to attribute it to some prescriptive right or (conversely) some revocable permission by the grantor.

(8) Second, user consequential upon a promise by the owner of some existing/future right/interest in land which gives rise to an inchoate equity was said not to be permissive (although it is in a sense consensual), at least where the promisee was led to believe he would be able to enjoy the rights in perpetuity.[38] If that is right, then an estoppel licensee may acquire a prescriptive right/interest at the end of the relevant period.

(9) However, in such circumstances the court may instead infer some other (non-estoppel) licence entitling the representee to use the land. If so, time will not run in his favour, at least until the owner purports to terminate.[39] Hence in *Sandhu v Farooqui*[40] a person allowed into occupation who paid a deposit and mortgage instalments in the belief that completion had taken place was held to have occupied under a licence that was terminable (on notice) once the parties ceased to proceed towards completion.

(10) The requirement of permanence in (8) is thought to be critical and, it is considered, should apply in the circumstances considered in (7). Otherwise a promise of – or an uncompleted contract to grant – a finite interest/right (eg for 25 years) could, during the period of the intended user, give rise to

---

[33] *R v Oxfordshire CC ex parte Sunningwell PC* [2000] 1 AC 335, at 351. See also *Bright v Walker* (1834) 1 Cr M & R 211, at 219 ('... a grant, or of a licence, written or parol, for a limited period').
[34] *Gardner v Hodgson's Kingston Brewery Co Ltd* [1903] AC 229, at 239.
[35] *Mills v Silver* [1991] Ch 271, at 282E.
[36] [2004] 1 AC 889, at [38]. The other members of the House did not express a view. See also *Cullen v Cullen* [1962] IR 268.
[37] *Walsh v Lonsdale* (1882) LR 21 ChD 9.
[38] *R (Beresford) v Sunderland CC* [2004] 1 AC 889, at [37]. Where an implicit representation is relied on, it may often be more difficult to regard it as a promise of a permanent right.
[39] Whether a user can be said to be adverse if revocation of an (orthodox) licence is prevented by promissory estoppel is beyond the scope of this book.
[40] [2004] 1 P & CR 19.

greater (ie permanent) rights by prescription than was contracted for/promised or would be granted by the court in giving effect to the equity (see **4.40**).

(11) The implication of (7) and (8) is that a user can sometimes prescribe even though he has a contractual or equitable entitlement to use the land. The difference with a licence is that the consents considered here are not consents to do the thing itself but agreements/representations to convey an interest, albeit ineffective in law; pending completion/satisfaction of the equity the grantee/promisee unlike the licensee has no (at least, legal) *entitlement* to use the land, which prescription provides.

User in excess of the licence

5.5 Even though the owner has granted permission to use his land, the user may be adverse if it was unauthorised (eg) because the licence has come to an end or its scope was exceeded or it was not granted to the particular person(s) on whose use the claimed right is based. The question in each case is: what does the licence authorise?

Limited duration

5.6 Permission may be granted for a single event or series of events or for a certain period of time. It may be granted for an indefinite period but terminable on notice or may terminate automatically after a reasonable period of time. An indefinite right may be expressly revoked or may come to an end as a result of a change of circumstances from which its termination may fairly be implied.[41] If the user was originally by permission it is a question of fact and inference whether it has continued as such.[42] The termination of the licence is considered in detail in Chapter 12.

5.7 Where the licence arises impliedly from circumstances it may continue for as long as they exist, but that does not always follow; it may merely justify a single entry or user for only a certain period of time. If the former, whether a change of circumstances automatically determines the licence or whether the parties must be aware of such change before any continued user becomes adverse is as yet unresolved.[43]

5.8 Conversely a user which was originally consensual may become adverse despite the continuation of the licence if the owner transfers the land to a successor who takes free of it (Chapter 9) or because the user was not the original licensee or a valid assignee (Chapter 10). A contractual licence, unlike a bare licence, generally does not automatically end on the assignment of the land by the licensor or the purported (but invalid) assignment of the right to

---

[41] *Healey v Hawkins* [1968] 1 WLR 1967.
[42] Ibid.
[43] Compare **4.16(2)** as to the need for the licensee to be aware of the existence of a unilateral licence or the facts from which it is inferred.

use it by the licensee. It may, however, be possible to infer the grant of some new licence by/to the original parties' successors in such cases. And of course the user may be estopped from asserting that his use was adverse if, when challenged, he claims to be able to rely on the licence.

Limited scope

5.9 A licensee may exceed the physical or purposive restrictions of his licence. If he occupies other land of his licensor during the licence term, the parties may impliedly agree to vary the original licence terms so as to include it. If that inference is not possible, his use may be so inconsistent with the licence terms as to amount to its implied disclaimer – see Chapter 4 – eg if the licensed land is merely used as an adjunct of (or ancillary/incidental to) the extra land. That is a question of degree and inference. If, however, his use is severable, the use of the extra land (only) may be adverse.[44] A licensee who exceeds the scope of his licence may be at least pro tanto a trespasser or the impermissible activities may be so indivisible from the remainder that his presence is, as a whole, unauthorised. However, in *Harvey v Plymouth CC*[45] it was tentatively suggested that a person who pursues such activities may remain a 'visitor' for the purposes of the Occupiers' Liability Act 1957, albeit not one to whom the occupying licensor owes the common duty of care.

5.10 A licensee who enters or uses the land for some unauthorised purposes or engages in some unauthorised activity may over time acquire a prescriptive right to continue it.[46] However, a minor deviation from the licence terms is unlikely to have that effect or amount to a disclaimer. The question, again, is one of degree and inference, eg as to the relative importance of the (un)authorised uses, whether one is ancillary to the other, to what extent they are severable etc. A licensee who is given a right to enter for general or unspecified purposes and who enters for several purposes, only some of which were contemplated by the parties at the time of the grant,[47] does not start to prescribe against the licensor at least until he actively pursues those unauthorised purposes.[48]

5.11 In contrast a mere breach by the licensee of the terms of a contractual licence may not render his subsequent user adverse unless/until the licensor

---

[44] Cf *Smirk v Lyndale Developments Ltd* [1975] Ch 317 (adverse possession by lessee of landlord's land outside demise presumed to be accretion to lease). The rationale of the presumption has variously been said to be based on the tenant's obligation to protect his landlord's rights, estoppel or because the opportunity to encroach derives from the lease – see *Jourdan's Adverse Possession* (LexisNexis UK, 2003), at paras 25-04–25-09. Whether the presumption applies to licences is as yet unresolved.
[45] [2010] EWCA Civ 860, at [22].
[46] See eg *Rose v Krieser* [2002] 212 DLR (4) 123, at [47] (uncompleted grant of easement followed by enjoyment of a materially different right).
[47] *Byrne v Kinematograph Renters Society Ltd* [1958] 1 WLR 762, at 776.
[48] *JA Pye (Oxford) Ltd v Graham* [2003] 1 AC 419, at [59].

elects to terminate.[49] However, the distinction in such cases between a wholly unauthorised use and a mere breach of the licence terms may sometimes be difficult to draw.

Permission to limited persons

5.12 In cases of alleged public prescriptive rights, the question sometimes arises whether the owner's grant of permission to some users prevents the public's use, taken as a whole, from being 'as of right'. Such acts may, of course, rebut any inference of an intention to dedicate in cases of public rights of way or may, if known to others, evince the owner's implied opposition to their use and thus render it contentious (ie vi) and not 'as of right'. In other cases, however, the grant of permission to only some users does not (it is considered) prevent a prescriptive public right arising from the others' use of the land because those invited onto the land do not enter *as* members of the public but *as* the owner's invitees; accordingly the *public's* use remains adverse.

5.13 In contrast, in cases of claimed prescriptive easements, the grant of permission to one or more (but not all) of the co-owners of the alleged dominant land is nevertheless thought to prevent a prescriptive right arising since the dominant owners' use was not, taken in its entirety, as of right.

5.14 Where adverse possession is claimed, the fact the owner continues to use/allow others to use the land during the relevant period will often prevent the squatter displaying the necessary animus possidendi (unless he does so with the squatter's permission) or acquiring factual possession of the land. If, however, he does, time will not stop running in his favour unless/until the owner effectively resumes possession.[50] Whether he does so is a question of fact and degree.[51]

LICENCES AND LIMITATION

General

5.15 A person in exclusive possession of land but without lawful right/title/authority bars the owner's title and his right to recover possession at the end of the statutory period[52] and (where land is unregistered) acquires a title based on his own possession.[53]

---

[49] *Lakshmijjt v Sherani* [1974] AC 605.
[50] *Markfield Investments Ltd v Evans* [2001] 1 WLR 1321.
[51] See the authorities referred to in *J Alston & Sons Ltd v BOCM Pauls Ltd* [2009] 1 EGLR 93, at [74]; see also *Roberts v Swangrove* [2007] EWHC 513 (Ch), at [45].
[52] 12 years from accrual of the cause of action in relation to unregistered land: Limitation Act 1980, s 15. For registered land, however, see n 1 above.
[53] Limitation Act 1980, Sch 1, para 8(1).

Limitation by licensee against licensor

Possession during the subsistence of the licence

5.16 Unless his use is in some respects unauthorised a licensee of course cannot be in adverse possession during the subsistence of his licence;[54] his use is consensual and therefore not 'as of right'.[55]

Continued use after licence expires

5.17 However, after the licence expires his continued use of the land may be adverse unless some new right[56] or interest arises in his favour. Specifically:

(1) Occasionally the former licensee's use may change after the licence expires. If – as in *Pye v Graham*[57] – he assumes effective control of the land or the licensor ceases to exercise such control leaving the licensee in factual possession he may acquire possessory title even though his former licence merely conferred a right of user/non-exclusive occupation.

(2) If, however, there is no change in the nature of his user, the type of licence will determine whether he can acquire possessory title or prescriptive rights (if either).

(3) As a variation on (2), if in substance the rights granted were capable of amounting to exclusive possession but for some term in the licence agreement (eg entitling the licensor to relocate the licensee) then the licensee may be in exclusive possession once it comes to an end even though he continues to use the land in the same manner as before.

(4) The effect of the former licensor's contemporaneous use of the land (personally or through others) with the former licensee is referred to in **5.14**.

(5) There is conflicting dicta as to the circumstances in which a licensee who is subjectively unaware that his licence has expired and therefore erroneously believes his use is with consent and does not subjectively intend to possess to the exclusion of the licensor can have the necessary

---

[54] *Moses v Lovegrove* [1952] 2 QB 533, at 544; *Hughes v Griffin* [1969] 1 WLR 23, at 30 ('Time cannot run ... in favour of a licensee and therefore he has no adverse possession'); *JA Pye (Oxford) Ltd v Graham* [2003] 1 AC 419, at [37] ('It is clearly established that the taking or continuation of possession by a squatter with the actual consent of the paper title owner does not constitute dispossession or possession by the squatter for the purpose of the [Limitation] Act [1980]').

[55] *Buckinghamshire CC v Moran* [1989] 3 WLR 152, at 162G, per Slade LJ. Contrast the rule in relation to oral periodic tenants, in whose favour time starts to run from the end of the first year or other period of the tenancy or from the last receipt of rent, whichever is the later: Limitation Act 1980, Sch 1, para 5.

[56] See **13.3**.

[57] *JA Pye (Oxford) Ltd v Graham* [2003] 1 AC 419, at [58].

intention to possess. In *Wretham v Ross*[58] and *J Alston & Sons v BOCM Pauls Ltd*[59] it was held that he may, unless as a result of that mistake he intends only to occupy the land temporarily until required by the licensor which makes his occupation something less than possession in law (although unlikely)[60] or he desists from exercising full control over the land. In contrast, in *Clowes Developments (UK) Ltd v Walters*[61] a former licensee was held to lack the necessary animus because his erroneous belief in the licence's continuation meant that he intended to occupy only for so long as the owner allowed him to. The first approach is considered correct – the required intention is merely to possess and requires no subjective appreciation by the squatter that his use is unlawful nor inquiry into his knowledge of the owner's intentions (except where he knows of the owner's future plans for the land[62]). In contrast an intention to possess indefinitely, if possible, but coupled with an acceptance that if the licensor demands possession because he needs the land it will have to be given up is sufficient animus possidendi.

(6) It follows that a licensee whose licence confers a right of possession may be in adverse possession after it ends even if he subjectively believed that it was continuing since he nevertheless intends to possess to the exclusion of the licensor. Hence in *Ofulue v Bossert*[63] the squatter's mistaken belief he was the tenant did not prevent him having the necessary animus.

Effect of grant/renewal of licence after limitation period expires

5.18 Once the former licensor's title is barred, it cannot be revived by the grant of a fresh licence to the former licensee, although if such licence continues for the full statutory period, the licensor will in turn acquire possessory title as against him. Nevertheless it may be that such a licence can, even before then, give rise to an estoppel preventing the licensee from claiming possessory title if he enjoys its benefits.[64]

Limitation against true owner

5.19 A licensor who has no title to the land may be in adverse possession as against the true owner by virtue of his licensees' use of the land, his own use and/or his control of access to it or a combination of these factors. A series of licences, none of which individually confers exclusive possession on the

---

[58] [2005] EWHC 1259 (Ch), at [44].
[59] [2009] 1 EGLR 93, at [98]–[104].
[60] Compare the requisite intention – as defined in *JA Pye (Oxford) Ltd v Graham* [2003] 1 AC 419, at [43], [77] – ie to possess the land for the time being so far as is reasonably practicable and the process of law will allow.
[61] [2005] EWHC 669 (Ch), at [38]–[40].
[62] *Buckinghamshire CC v Moran* [199] Ch 623 (whether squatter displays animus possidendi if his use is consistent with owner's intended future use of land).
[63] [2008] EWCA Civ 7, at [63]; on appeal [2009] UKHL 16, at [67].
[64] *Colchester BC v Smith* [1991] 2 All ER 29, at 61–63. See generally *Jourdan's Adverse Possession* (LexisNexis UK, 2003), at ch 19 as to whether time may run against a party who is estopped.

licensees, may together amount to the assumption of possession by the licensor. As between the licensor and licensees, the former is in possession as against the true owner, at least during the subsistence of the licence(s). The licensees' presence is treated as constructive possession by the licensor[65] even if they use/occupy the land for their own purposes rather than on his behalf, eg as agent.[66]

5.20 It is thought that is so (although the contrary was tentatively suggested in *Roberts v Swangrove*[67]) also in the case of a licensor who grants bare licence(s); although not in receipt of the rents/profits he may be in constructive possession through his licensee(s) since the grant of such licences may amount to the exercise of exclusive dominion and control by him over the land.

5.21 As between the licensor and licensee, the latter is estopped from disputing the former's title, whether or not he in fact owns the land (see **8.25** et seq). Once the licence ends, a former licensee who remains in possession begins to prescribe against the former licensor, who may nevertheless recover possession until either he abandons possession (if he has not in the meantime acquired possessory title)[68] or the former licensee in turn acquires possessory title against him. Whether or not he has abandoned possession is a question of fact and inference.

5.22 If the licensor does so before the true owner's title is barred, a licensee who remains in possession may 'tack on' the licensor's period of adverse possession (ie during the continuation of his licence and any previous licence granted by the licensor) to his own if there is continuity of possession. In that way the licensee may claim possessory title as against the true owner at the end of the relevant period, measured from when time first started to run against him.

Limitation in favour of third parties

5.23 Where, in contrast, a third party is in adverse possession of the licensor's land during the subsistence of the licence, he prescribes against both the licensor and licensee, at least if (as is usual) the licensee does not have a right to exclusive possession. The statutory rules as to the running of time against reversionary estates or interests[69] have no application since the licensee has no intervening title against which the squatter may prescribe – see Chapter 9.

---

[65] See eg *Roberts v Swangrove* [2007] EWHC 513 (Ch), at [33].
[66] See eg *Sze To Chun Keung v Kung Kwok Wai* [1997] 1 WLR 1232, at 1235. Contrast the position where the licensor seeks to rely on the licensee's occupation in order to claim an overriding interest – see Chapter 9.
[67] [2007] EWCA Civ 513 (Ch), at [34].
[68] *Mount Carmel Investments Ltd v Peter Thurlow Ltd* [1988] 1 WLR 1078. See the discussion in Jourdan's *Adverse Possession* (LexisNexis UK, 2003), at paras 20-55–20-60 as to the effect of abandonment by the squatter after the limitation period has expired.
[69] Limitation Act 1980, Sch 1, para 4; see eg *Fairweather v St Marylebone Property Co Ltd* [1963] AC 510.

5.24 For the situation where the licensor uses the land (either personally or through his licensee(s)) at the same time as the squatter, see **5.14**.[70]

LICENCES AND PRESCRIPTION

Licensees and prescription

5.25 Whereas limitation has extinctive effect, prescription is a means by which profits and easements may be acquired over another's land. Prescription (at common law and under the doctrine of lost modern grant) is based on the presumption/fiction of grant by the owner of the right in question.[71] Prescription is, in essence, a 'gap-filling' rule; it provides a justification for a user where none otherwise exists. That, however, is unnecessary where such user is referable to some other right, such as a licence – see **5.2(1)–(3)** and **5.37**. In that case the user is 'of right' not 'as of right' (ie as *if* of right)[72].

Meaning of consent

5.26 Accordingly user by permission, ie licence, but not mere acquiescence or toleration,[73] however long persisted in, cannot mature into a prescriptive right. The evidence must be probative of the fact the user was as of right.[74] In particular courts are more ready to ascribe an owner's failure to act to implied permission rather than toleration or acquiescence based on good neighbourliness, friendliness or generosity, in relation to minor or infrequent intrusions[75] (at least where private – rather than public – rights are claimed) or to find that such user does not manifest the qualities required (see **5.2(8)(b)**).[76] However, in a proper case (eg where the use was frequent and/or substantial), the mere existence of neighbourly relations between the owner and user may not prevent the latter acquiring prescriptive rights.

5.27 Obviously a use is not 'as of right' if permission is granted from time to time: each renewal rebuts the presumption that may otherwise arise that it was as of right. Even a once-and-for-all consent for a finite/indefinite period or

---

[70] See the authorities referred to in *J Alston & Sons Ltd v BOCM Pauls Ltd* [2009] 1 EGLR 93, at [74].
[71] *Gardner v Hodgson's Kingston Brewery Co Ltd* [1903] AC 229, at 239; *R v Oxfordshire CC ex parte Sunningwell PC* [2000] 1 AC 335, at 349–350.
[72] *Cumbernauld & Kilsyth DC v Dollar Land (Cumbernauld) Ltd* (1992) SC 357, [1992] SLT 1035, at 1042.
[73] *Mills v Silver* [1991] Ch 271, at 279H–280A.
[74] *Odey v Barber* [2008] Ch 175, at [36]. Note, however, that the absence of consent is not synonymous with user 'as of right'; if the owner overtly attempts to prevent its continuance or makes clear his opposition to it, the user may be contentious and thus not as of right: *Newnham v Willison* (1987) 56 P & CR 8; *Smith v Brudenell-Bruce* [2002] 2 P & CR 51. See the analysis in *Gale on the Law of Easements* (Sweet & Maxwell, 18th edn, 2008), at paras 4-86–4-87.
[75] See eg *Costagliola v English* (1969) 210 EG 1425.
[76] Alternatively the court may regard the minor/infrequent user consider as not having the requisite quality discussed in **5.2(7)(b)**. See eg *Mills v Silver* [1991] Ch 271, at 284E.

even, it is thought, for a single occasion may be sufficient to prevent the required continuity of user as of right.[77] If entry follows a request for permission, consent can be inferred merely by the owner desisting from preventing it. So too if he regularly bars access to the land for a certain period of time it may be easy to infer that its use at other times was with his permission.[78] The same may be true where he uses it occasionally to the factual exclusion of others, although the question then may be one of degree.[79]

Form of consent

5.28 Not every consent, even if objectively manifest, defeats a claim in prescription:

(1) Where 20 years' user is relied on, any consent (whether written or oral) given either at the start of the period or during it (either from-time-to-time or once-and-for-all) may do so.

(2) User for the longer period of 40 years is absolute and indefeasible unless enjoyed by *written* consent.[80]

(3) Nevertheless a user that has continued for 40 years does not give rise to prescriptive rights if permission is given or if it continues during that period on a common understanding that it is (and continues to be) permissive. Parol permission given *prior* to the period, however, does not have that effect.[81]

Licensors and prescription

5.29 A licensor who has no title to the land may acquire prescriptive rights over it by virtue of his licensee's use, as well as his own if he has other land which such rights accommodate. The rule that prescriptive rights may only be claimed as appurtenant to a fee simple (with the exception of profits in gross) means the licensee – who has no proprietary interest (see Chapter 9) – cannot acquire rights over a third party's land on his own account but only on behalf of his licensor's land.[82]

Prescription by third parties

5.30 A third party who prescribes during the subsistence of the licence necessarily does so against the licensor as well as the licensee, at least if the

---

[77] Permission granted by an occupying tenant suffices under Prescription Act 1832, s 2 or lost modern grant: *Ward v Kirkland* [1967] Ch 194.
[78] *Goldsmith v Burrow Construction Ltd* (1987) *The Times*, July 31.
[79] *R (Beresford) v Sunderland CC* [2004] 1 AC 889, at [5]; *R (Lewis) v Redcar and Cleveland BC* [2010] 2 All ER 613, at [23]–[28].
[80] Prescription Act 1832, s 2 (rights of way).
[81] *Gardner v Hodgson's Kingston Brewery Co Ltd* [1903] AC 229, at 239.
[82] *Gale on the Law of Easements* (Sweet & Maxwell, 18th edn, 2008), at para 4-76.

licence does not confer exclusive possession. By comparison where land is let the issue is whether the landlord acquiesced in the relevant user, which in turn depends on whether he was (or ought to have been) aware of – and could have taken steps to prevent – it.[83]

LICENCES AND PUBLIC RIGHTS OF WAY

5.31 Public rights of way may arise by statute, dedication/acceptance at common law or statutorily 'deemed' dedication. At common law, proof of long user by the public as of right was evidence from which an intention to dedicate may (but need not) be inferred.[84] Now, however, under the Highways Act 1980, s 31 a presumption of dedication arises from 20 years' continuous user 'as of right' unless the owner sufficiently manifests an intention not to dedicate during that period.[85]

5.32 As stated above (**5.4**) 'consent' per se to the use is neither antithetical to nor conclusive in favour of the existence of public rights. It may exemplify the landowner's intention to dedicate if it is permanent or irrevocable.[86] It does not if it is temporary or revocable,[87] which may be manifest (eg) by preventing public access from time to time[88] or by indicating that the continued use is subject to the (non-)occurrence of some future event (eg payment of a fee), the continuation of certain conditions or is subject to his control.[89]

5.33 Since at common law an actual intention to dedicate was necessary, proof that the user was attributable to toleration or acquiescence prevented any inference of such an intention.[90] That, however, does not imply that a tolerated user is not as of right, or that toleration was synonymous with permission, merely that there had been no dedication despite the user being as of right.[91] The nature of the consent, objectively ascertained,[92] is critical. The question is: what inference is to be drawn from the owner's acts (or failure to act) as to his intention (or not) to dedicate? In most cases a failure to act will be more

---

[83] *Williams v Sandy Lane (Chester) Ltd* [2007] 2 P & CR 27. Query as to the application by analogy of this rule to cases where the licensee has a right to exclusive possession.
[84] *Folkestone Corp v Brockman* [1914] AC 338.
[85] See the (non-exhaustive) means by which he may do so in s 31(3), (5) and (6) of the 1980 Act.
[86] See n 31 above. However, an intention to dedicate may be inferred from 'consent' which consists of mere acquiescence; a sufficient manifestation of such consent by overt acts by the owner is unnecessary.
[87] *Mann v Brodie* (1885) 10 App Cas 378, at 392; *Attorney-General v Antrobus* [1905] 2 Ch 188, at 205–206; *R (Beresford) v Sunderland CC* [2004] 1 AC 889, at [39], [45].
[88] *R (Beresford) v Sunderland CC* [2004] 1 AC 889, at [83]; *R (Godmanchester TC) v Secretary of State for the Environment* [2008] 1 AC 221, at [13], [89].
[89] See eg *Barraclough v Johnson* (1838) 8 Ad & El 99.
[90] *Folkestone Corp v Brockman* [914] AC 338. The 1980 Act, in contrast, makes it unnecessary to infer actual dedication and in the absence of specific rebutting evidence to treat user as of right as sufficient to establish a public right.
[91] *R v Oxfordshire CC ex parte Sunningwell PC* [2000] 1 AC 335, at 358G.
[92] See by analogy *R (Beresford) v Sunderland CC* [2004] 1 AC 889, at [51].

consistent with acquiescence/toleration or implicit acknowledgement that a public right exists rather than the implied grant of some limited/revocable permission.[93]

5.34 Conversely the absence of permission is not synonymous with user 'as of right', eg if the owner manifests his objection to the use, eg by treating the public as trespassers or barring access, the user is contentious and/or he manifests an intention not to dedicate, thereby rebutting the presumption that would otherwise arise under the Highways Act 1980, s 31, whether or not the means used to do so are those specified in the Act.

LICENCES AND TOWN OR VILLAGE GREENS

5.35 New town and village greens can be created by user 'as of right' by a significant number of inhabitants in a locality for lawful sports and pastimes for a continuous period of 20 years.[94] In the case of an application under Commons Act 2006, s 15(2) the period of 20 years is that immediately before the application. However, where there has been enjoyment 'as of right' for 20 years, the owner cannot prevent it continuing as such by subsequently granting unilateral permission.[95]

5.36 With that exception, the requirement that the user be as of right prevents the creation of new greens on the basis of user under a licence. The same distinction is to be drawn between a (sufficiently manifest) permission, on the one hand, and mere acquiescence/toleration[96] or implicit acknowledgement that such rights exist, on the other.

5.37 Where the land is publicly owned the analysis at **5.2(3)** is engaged. The doctrine of prescription operates in the absence of an alternative explanation as to a lawful entitlement to do the acts complained of.[97] The rights of recreation enjoyed by the public under the statutory trusts are subject to the local authority owner's power either to regulate such usage or to appropriate the land to other use, in which case they cease. Their exercise is, in that sense, precarious but is nevertheless for the time being 'of right' rather than '*as* of right'. As the basis of prescription is acquiescence by the owner in the assertion of the (alleged) right[98] if the right to do that thing already exists and the user in

---

[93] *Mann v Brodie* (1885) 10 App Cas 378, at 386; *R (Godmanchester TC) v Secretary of State for the Environment* [2008] 1 AC 221, at [62].
[94] Commons Act 2006, s 15(2).
[95] Commons Act 2006, s 15(7)(b). In such case his recourse is to try to bar access for the requisite period (as to which see s 15(3) and (4)).
[96] *R v Oxfordshire CC ex parte Sunningwell PC* [2000] 1 AC 335, at 359 (decided under predecessor Act).
[97] *Gardner v Hodgson's Kingston Brewery Co Ltd* [1903] AC 229, at 239–240; *Brocklebank v Thompson* [1903] 2 Ch 344, at 350 ('it has been held that a regular usage of 20 years *unexplained and uncontradicted* may be sufficient to justify the finding of the existence of an immemorial custom') (emphasis added).
[98] *R v Oxfordshire CC ex parte Sunningwell PC* [2000] 1 AC 335, at 353.

question is attributable to it, it is considered the owner does not (in any relevant sense) acquiesce in what he cannot *prevent*, unless and until the land is appropriated to other uses.

CUSTOM

5.38 The requirement that, in order to establish a customary right, the user must be as of right requires the same distinction in **5.36** to be drawn. For instance, a claimed right to a *licence* to enter land admits of the need for the owner's consent and is thus incapable of existing as a custom.[99] Also, proof that the public has hitherto paid for the right to use land will usually indicate that such use was by permission.[100] If, however, such payment was merely a *condition* of a purported *right* the user may have been as of right.[101] The critical issue is thus whether it is proper to infer that the public was *entitled* to use the land on tendering the fee or (more likely) whether the owner could even then refuse entry.

---

[99] *Mills v Colchester Corpn* (1867) LR 2 CP 476, at 486.
[100] Ibid (failed claim to right to be *permitted* to fish on payment of a fee).
[101] See eg *Tyrone v Smith* (1838) 9 Ad & El 406; *Elwood v Bullock* (1844) 6 QB 383.

Chapter 6

OCCUPATION LICENCES

Introduction	6.1
Business licences	6.2
General	6.2
Typical business licences	6.8
Agricultural licences	6.16
Licences subject to conversion	6.18
Exceptions	6.19
The effect of the application of the Agricultural Holdings Act 1986	6.20
Residential licences	6.21
Lodgers	6.21
Holiday accommodation	6.23
Mobile structures	6.24
Occupation referable to some other relationship	6.26
Residential licensees with security of tenure	6.38
Matrimonial home rights	6.65

INTRODUCTION

6.1 The traditional classification of licences (bare, contractual, coupled with an interest[1] and now estoppel licences) principally assists in determining how they may be created and terminated, the remedies available to the parties to enforce their rights and whether their benefit and burden are capable of passing to successors in title. An alternative method of classification distinguishes occupation licences (here) and user licences (Chapter 7). Although the difference may be one of degree – and occupation means things in different contexts[2] – this distinction helps determine:

---

[1] *Hounslow LBC v Twickenham Garden Developments Ltd* [1971] Ch 233, at 241.
[2] 'The word "occupy" is a word of uncertain meaning. Sometimes it denotes legal possession in the technical sense ... At other times "occupation" denotes nothing more than physical presence in a place for a substantial period of time': *Madrassa Anjuman Islamia of Kholwad v Johannesburg Municipal Council* [1922] 1 AC 500, at 504. '"[O]ccupation" is a concept which may have different connotations according to the nature and purpose of the property which is claimed to be occupied': *Abbey National Building Society v Cann* [1991] 1 AC 56, at 73, per Lord Oliver. But '[i]n the ordinary meaning of the word a person is in "occupation" of premises if he in fact uses them and is able to control the day to day use of them by other persons': *Valuation Commissioner (Northern Ireland) v Fermanagh Protestant Board of Education* [1969] 1 WLR 1708, at 1729G.

(1) Whether the licensee may have standing to sue third parties in trespass.[3]

(2) On whom the duties of care under the Occupiers' Liability Acts 1957 and 1984 fall.[4]

(3) Who is liable as between the licensor/licensee of business premises for non-domestic rates (see **11.38**).

(4) Whether the licence fee may be subject to VAT (see **11.42** et seq.)

(5) Whether the licence attracts security of 'tenure'. Statutory intervention protects occupation (not mere user), principally where that is by way of lease but occasionally protection is extended to licensees whose occupation has, like lessees, the necessary attribute of permanence to justify intervention.[5] With one (now repealed) exception, the statutory protection of licensees is restricted to *residential* occupation (see below). How licences are protected varies: the Mobile Homes Act 1983 limits the circumstances in which the licensor may, with the court's sanction, terminate the licence; under the Housing Act 1985 residential licences of public authority accommodation are treated as secure tenancies; and under the Agricultural Holdings Act 1986 qualifying licences were, by statutory process, converted into tenancies from year to year. In addition, certain residential licensees have a residual degree of statutory protection under the Caravan Sites Act 1968 or the Protection from Eviction Act 1977. These are considered at **6.60** et seq and **13.16** respectively. The assimilation of residential tenancies and licences, however, is partial: not all residential licences have security of tenure and the distinction between tenancies and licences remains critical in many other respects.[6]

Rights of user/occupation which fall foul of the 'ouster principle' and are thus incapable of existing as easements but which may amount to licences are dealt with in **7.6** et seq.

BUSINESS LICENCES

General

6.2 The Landlord and Tenant Act 1954, Pt II provides for the continuation of non-contracted out business tenancies notwithstanding the expiration of the contract term. Licences, however, are exempt from protection under the Act.[7] Thus a licence granted for business purposes automatically expires at the end of the contract term.

---

[3] See Chapters 2 and 9.
[4] See Chapter 12.
[5] Contrast e g licensees of holiday accommodation or short-term local authority hostels.
[6] See e g **3.2**.
[7] Landlord and Tenant Act 1954, s 23(1); see definition of 'tenancy' ibid, s 69(1); *Shell-Mex and BP Ltd v Manchester Garages* [1971] 1 WLR 612, at 615, per Lord Denning MR.

Distinguishing leases and licences

6.3 Although the *Street v Mountford* test applies in the commercial sphere as in the residential,[8] some differences of emphasis remain. First, residential premises are more often wholly self-contained units and thus sole occupation is more often capable of shading into possession.[9] Second, multiple-occupancy residential premises are more likely to be susceptible of use only by persons who are mutually acceptable/self-selecting. If such persons occupy on identical terms they may collectively have joint right to possession (see **3.8** et seq) rather than individual, non-exclusive licences.[10] A series of individual licences of business premises more often reflects the reality of the situation. Third, courts are less astute to detect a sham in the commercial sphere and should not be influenced by the fact the Landlord and Tenant Act 1954 only protects tenancies.[11] The nature of the business occupier's rights is to be ascertained without reference to the statutory implications.[12] Finally, courts are more likely to take at face value an expressed intention not to grant exclusive possession in a contract entered into between commercial parties at arm's length with the benefit of legal advice.[13] Where, therefore, businessmen have genuinely structured their dealings so as to fall within the exceptions to *Street v Mountford*, courts will give effect to their intention to create a licence rather than lease.[14]

---

[8] *London & Associated Investment Trust v Calow* (1986) 53 P & CR 340, at 352; *Dellneed Ltd v Chin* (1987) 53 P & CR 172; contrast *Dresden Estates v Collinson* (1988) 55 P & CR 47.
[9] See e g *Venus Investments Ltd v Stocktop Ltd* [1996] EGCS 173; *First Real Estates (UK) Ltd v Birmingham CC* [2009] EWHC 817 (Admin).
[10] *Hunts Refuse Disposal Ltd v Norfolk Environmental Waste Services Ltd* [1997] 1 EGLR 16, at [18]: '[The construction of the agreement] is not to be undertaken in a vacuum, but rather with a proper regard to the context in which the issue arises ... while one would ordinarily expect that someone in occupation of a small house for a fixed term at a rent had exclusive possession, one would I suggest have no such preconceptions about a person given the right to tip rubbish in the excavated parts of a large plot of land, on other parts of which, it would seem, quarrying was continuing.'
[11] *Shell-Mex and BP Ltd v Manchester Garages* [1971] 1 WLR 612.
[12] Ibid, at 619: 'It may be that this is a device which has been adopted by the plaintiff company to avoid possible consequences of the Landlord and Tenant Act 1954, which would have affected a transaction being one of landlord and tenant; but, in my judgment, one cannot take that into account in the process of construing such a document to find out what the true nature of the transaction is. One has first to find out what is the true nature of the transaction and then see how the Act operates upon that state of affairs, if it bites at all. One should not approach the problem with a tendency to attempt to find a tenancy because unless there is a tenancy the case will escape the effects of the statute.'
[13] *Clear Channel UK Ltd v Manchester City Council* [2006] 1 EGLR 27; *Scottish Widows v Stewart* [2006] EWCA Civ 999.
[14] See e g *Essex Plan Ltd v Broadminster* (1998) 56 P & CR 353: owner granted option for lease and allowed grantee to use the land pending its exercise; occupation held to be ancillary to the option and hence analogous to occupation pending completion of sale. Sed quaere.

76   *Land Licences*

6.4 Nevertheless where there is a serious prospect of challenge to the form of agreement[15] the better practice, rather than purportedly granting a licence, is to grant an excluded tenancy under s 38(4)[16] or, where appropriate,[17] a tenancy at will.[18]

Nature of the right

6.5 Certain types of commercial rights are generally held not to confer possession and thus take effect as licences, e g front-of-house rights, the right to operate a business, such as pleasure boats on a lake,[19] rights to occupy an undefined part of a larger area (e g concession stands), rights to erect/use advertising hoardings and similar structures,[20] parking/mooring rights and so forth (see **3.6**).

6.6 In other cases the *substance of the grant,* rather than the nature of the right, is determinative. So (e g) in *Hunts Refuse Disposal Ltd v Norfolk Environmental Waste Services Ltd*[21] an exclusive right to tip waste on a site was held not to confer exclusive possession. And in *Manchester City Council v National Car Parks*[22] and *National Car Parks Ltd v Trinity Developments (Banbury) Co Ltd*[23] rights to operate car parks were held not to confer possession. In such cases a different form of grant could have taken effect as a tenancy, limited to the particular user. However, the distinction between a mere right to undertake an activity and a right of exclusive possession subject to a restriction on user can sometimes be difficult to draw in practice, particularly in relation to oral agreements.[24]

6.7 In other, probably most, cases where neither the type of rights granted nor the nature of the grant is determinative the agreement terms, insofar as they indicate who has possession, are likely to be critical – see **3.13**.

---

[15] Unless of course the operation of the 1954 Act would be excluded on other grounds, e g agreements for 6 months or less, tenancies of agricultural holdings, farm business tenancies and mining leases.

[16] For the relevant rules, see s 38A(1) and SI 2003/3096.

[17] Its use other than in the classic situations where a party allowed to enter/remain on land pending negotiations for the grant/renewal of some right/interest in land or between contract and completion may well be unduly risky.

[18] *Manfield & Sons Ltd v Botchin* [1970] 2 QB 612.

[19] Eg *Hill v Tupper* (1863) 2 Hurl & C 121.

[20] See for a recent example *London Development Agency v Nidai* [2009] EWHC 1730 (Ch).

[21] [1997] 1 EGLR 16.

[22] [1982] 1 EGLR 94.

[23] [2002] 2 P & CR 18.

[24] Compare *Daly v Edwardes* (1900) 83 LT 548: 'free and exclusive licence or right to the use of all the refreshment rooms [etc] in the [theatre] together with the free right of access thereto' held to create an exclusive licence; *Clore v Theatrical Properties Ltd* [1936] 3 All ER 483: the words 'demise and grant unto the lessee the free and exclusive use of all the refreshment rooms ... for the purposes of the supply to and accommodation of visitors to the theatre' also held to create a licence; see also *Frank Warr & Co v London CC* [1904] 1 KB 713.

Typical business licences
Partnership

6.8 Premises used by a partnership, but which is not partnership property, may be owned by some (but not all) of the partners. As the traditional partnership lacks legal personality, it cannot acquire land or rights. Such arrangements may take the form of a lease[25] or trust between the owning and non-owning partners or their nominee (eg a company owned by the partners). Usually, however, the non-owning partners each have non-exclusive contractual licences for the purpose of carrying on the partnership business[26] as an express or, more often, implied term of the partnership agreement.

6.9 Such licences automatically terminate upon an individual partner's death or resignation.[27] These licences may be collectively terminable at any time on reasonable notice unless, on the true construction of the partnership/licence agreement(s), the owning-partners are required to make the land available to the partnership throughout its continuation. They may be terminated by a general dissolution (subject to the non-owning partners having sufficient time, if necessary, to use the land in order to wind up the partnership business) or on the completion of the winding-up. Even so, a licensee-partner who is excluded during the winding-up period may be refused injunctive relief to reinstate him, if circumstances warrant.[28]

Shared or serviced office accommodation

6.10 The use of shared/serviced offices takes a variety of forms, from a mere right to use office equipment to a right that grants possession of a self-contained area. Agreements by which the owner provides services that require unrestricted access to the land or reserves rights to use/allow others to use the land, however, do not grant possession and take effect as licences.

Shops, market stalls and concession stands

6.11 An exclusive right to occupy a self-contained commercial unit or a defined area within a shop[29] may take effect as either a licence or a lease (if it confers possession),[30] as may agreements for the use of kiosks (eg railway station newspaper stands, flower stalls and bookstalls) and immovable, self-contained market-stalls. However, possession will not be conferred by a right to occupy an area that is not self-contained (eg a concession area within a

---

[25] See eg *Pocock v Carter* [1912] 1 Ch 663.
[26] *Harrison-Broadley v Smith* [1964] 1 WLR 456.
[27] Although in the latter case depending on the terms of the partnership agreement and the period of notice of resignation required, he may have a reasonable period of time afterwards to vacate.
[28] See eg *Latchman v Pickard* [2005] EWHC 1011 (Ch).
[29] *Piper v Muggleton* [1956] 2 QB 659; but compare *Smith v Northside Developments* (1988) 55 P & CR 164.
[30] See *Graysim Holdings Ltd v P&O Property Holdings Ltd* [1996] AC 329.

shop) or to station/use a mobile unit (eg a food van at a sports event or a traditional barrow-stall in a market) or vending machine within a larger area (eg a station concourse).

Advertising hoardings

6.12 Occasionally the right to use an area to site hoardings or display advertising may take the form of a lease.[31] Usually, however, rights to erect/maintain a hoarding on a site[32] (particularly if the precise location of the structure is not determined by the agreement) or to display advertising on a structure or wall[33] do not confer exclusive possession of the land where they are situated and thus take effect as licences.[34]

Front-of-house rights

6.13 Front-of-house rights, likewise, usually do not to confer exclusive possession either because, properly construed, they merely grant the exclusive right to conduct the particular activity in question[35] or because the owner retains control over the land that is sufficient to amount to possession. The question in each case, however, is one of construction.

Mineral rights

6.14 The right to extract minerals may take effect as a lease[36] or licence coupled with an interest, depending on whether it confers possession of the land (or the relevant stratum) or a mere right of entry to work and carry away the minerals.[37] In the later case the right to remove minerals is a profit, to which the right of entry onto the land to work them is ancillary.

Building licences

6.15 Agreements to provide building services almost invariably include express/implied terms entitling the contractor to enter the land and/or requiring the owner to make it available for the duration of the works. Usually these take effect as licences, although a demise may sometimes be created, eg if the works

---

[31] See eg *Taylor v Pendleton Overseers* (1887) 19 QBD 288. See also the reference in *Clear Channel UK Ltd v Manchester City Council* [2006] 1 EGLR 27, at [4].
[32] See eg *Wilson v Tavener* [1901] 1 Ch 578, at 581; *King v David Allen & Sons Billposting* [1916] 2 AC 54; *Kewal Investments Ltd v Arthur Maiden* [1990] 1 EGLR 193, at 194 where a contention that a right to use an advertising hoarding was a tenancy was described as 'misconceived'; *London Development Agency v Nidai* [2009] EWHC 1730 (Ch).
[33] See eg *Wallshire v Advertising Sites* [1988] 2 ELGR 167 where the nature of the right was not argued.
[34] Or, in relation to rights to maintain structures on another's land, easements.
[35] See eg *Isaac v Hotel de Paris* [1960] 1 WLR 239 (hotel night bar). Compare the authorities at n 29 above.
[36] Although mining leases are excluded from Landlord and Tenant Act 1954, ss 24–28 – s 43(1)(b).
[37] Eg *Hunts Refuse Disposal Ltd v Norfolk Environmental Waste Services Ltd* [1997] 1 EGLR 16.

necessitate that the contractor has exclusive possession/control of the site, provided the term is certain. A right of possession for a fixed period of time for the purpose of undertaking works may be a lease. A right of possession for the duration of the works, which is uncertain at the outset, however, cannot and must be a licence.[38] Rights/obligations typically found in such licences are considered in Chapter 8.

AGRICULTURAL LICENCES

6.16 Agreements to occupy agricultural land entered into before 1 September 1995 or to which the transitional provisions of the Agricultural Tenancies Act 1995[39] apply may be protected by the Agricultural Holdings Act 1986. Agreements entered into after then are subject to the 1995 Act, if applicable. That Act applies only to tenancies,[40] but since it grants only limited security of tenure in any event, the imperative for owners now to use licences as a means of avoiding statutory protection has significantly reduced.

6.17 In contrast under the 1986 Act, which granted substantial security of tenure, licences were often used as an alternative to *Gladstone v Bower*[41] tenancies for that very purpose. However, only certain categories of licence were exempt; others were, by statutory alchemy, converted into tenancies from year to year. It is therefore necessary, in this context, to determine whether a particular agreement creates a lease or licence (as to which the principles in *Street v Mountford*[42] apply[43]) and, if the latter, whether it qualifies for conversion.

Licences subject to conversion

6.18 A licence that satisfies the following conditions takes effect, with necessary modifications, as a tenancy from year to year,[44] unless it falls into one of the exceptions in **6.19**. Those conditions are:

---

[38] *Prudential Assurance Co Ltd v London Residuary Body* [1992] 2 AC 386; contrast *Canadian Imperial Bank of Commerce v Bello* (1991) 64 P & CR 48.
[39] Agricultural Tenancies Act 1995, s 4(1), as amended.
[40] See the definition in Agricultural Tenancies Act 1995, s 38.
[41] [1960] 2 QB 384.
[42] [1985] AC 809.
[43] *Colchester BC v Smith* [1991] Ch 448, at 483–484 (aff'd [1982] Ch 421); *Ashdale Land Property Co v Mannus* [1992] 2 EGLR 5.
[44] Agricultural Holdings Act 1986, s 2.

(1) The licence must be sufficiently certain as to its terms, entered into with contractual intent[45] and supported by consideration[46] (which may take the form of services[47]). No minimum period is required.[48]

(2) It must confer a right of occupation, as distinct from mere user.[49]

(3) It must concern an identifiable area of land, of which the licensee has exclusive occupation;[50] a mere exclusive right to *use* the land for agricultural purposes (not amounting to occupation) during the subsistence of the licence is not enough.[51] Accordingly the typical farming partnerships and share farming agreements do not qualify as the grantee's rights are not exclusive.[52] Whether the owner's reserved rights prevent the licensee having exclusive occupation is a question of fact and degree: a right to plough or graze animals will; a mere right of way will not.[53] This need for exclusivity substantially restricts (if not eliminates) the number of licences that can convert following *Street v Mountford*.[54] Exclusive occupation may often shade into exclusive possession, which is the hallmark of a tenancy and since none of the established exceptions – where exclusive possession does not create a tenancy – are likely to apply, the number of licences that satisfy this requirement but do not amount to leases is likely to be small. Possibly the intended effect of the requirement is to catch grazing/mowing licences which are not, by being limited to some specified period of the year, excluded by s 2(3) (below).[55]

(4) The land must be agricultural in nature.[56]

(5) It must be used for agricultural purposes, subject to such exceptions as do not affect its character.

---

[45] *Collier v Hollinshead* [1984] 2 EGLR 14 (family relationship; payment of annual sum for occupation which was more than nominal but far below market rent sufficient to create intention to enter into legal relations).

[46] *Goldsack v Shore* [1950] 1 KB 708.

[47] *Verrall v Farnes* [1966] 1 WLR 1254.

[48] See e g *Crawford v Elliott* [1991] 1 EGLR 13 (licence to occupy during X's life).

[49] Agricultural Holdings Act 1986, s 2(1); hence in *Milton (Peterborough) Estates Co Ltd v Harris* [1989] 2 EGLR 299 a licence to cut and remove a crop did not qualify.

[50] *Bahamas International Trust Co Ltd v Threadgold* [1974] 1 WLR 1514, at 1527H.

[51] *McCarthy v Bence* [1990] 1 EGLR 1.

[52] *Harrison-Broadley v Smith* [1964] 1 WLR 456. In that case it was said the owning partner could not grant a joint licence to himself and the non-owning partner that confers exclusive possession on them jointly. Sed quaere. Contrast the position in relation to leases, where A may grant a lease to A and B jointly – Law of Property Act 1925, s 82.

[53] *Secretary of State for Social Services v Beavington* [1982] 1 EGLR 13.

[54] [1985] AC 809.

[55] *McCarthy v Bence* [1990] 1 EGLR 1, at 3M.

[56] For the definition see Agricultural Holdings Act 1986, s 1(4), which in turn refers to s 96(1)'s non-exhaustive definition of 'agriculture'.

(6) It must be used for the purpose of a trade or business.[57]

(7) The licence must be capable 'with the necessary modifications' of taking effect as an agreement for a tenancy from year to year; that is, the agreement, if converted, must not become something radically different.[58] This excludes licences granted to purchasers pending completion[59] or in return for one-off,[60] as distinct from periodic,[61] consideration. Payment in kind (eg periodic rendering of services) may qualify.

Exceptions

6.19 A licence will not convert if:

(1) the licensor has an interest less than a tenancy from year to year;[62]

(2) it is granted for use during the licensee's continuance in any office, appointment or employment held under the licensor;[63] or

(3) it is a grazing or mowing agreement within the Agricultural Holdings Act 1986, s 2(3)(a), ie one made expressly or impliedly in contemplation of the use of the land:

   (a) for grazing/mowing only (or both) and incidental purposes (eg erecting shelters, sowing etc); and

   (b) for some specified period of the year. Any period of less than a year will do; the dates need not have agricultural significance or be specified precisely, eg a 'summer' grasskeep is good. A series of separate licences for successive periods, each less than a year but which aggregate to more than a year, do not convert even if there is no 'gap' between them or the licensee does not vacate the land between the end of one and the start of the next. But each period should be specified by separate agreement; an agreement that contemplates multiple periods totalling more than a year or gives the licensee the right to renew and thus to use the land for more than one

---

[57] In the alternative to (4)–(6) the land may be designated as agricultural land under Agriculture Act 1947, s 109.
[58] *Harrison-Broadley v Smith* [1964] 1 WLR 456, at 467; it 'must remain recognisably the same agreement after the necessary modifications have been made' (ibid, per Pearson LJ); and 'must be capable of being modified ... consistently with its own terms': *Goldsack v Shore* [1950] 1 KB 708, at 713, per Lord Evershed MR.
[59] See *Bahamas International Trust Co Ltd v Threadgold* in the Court of Appeal [1974] 3 All ER 428, at 434, per Megaw LJ.
[60] *Davies v Davies* [2002] EWCA Civ 1791.
[61] *Mitton v Farrow* [1980] 2 EGLR 1.
[62] Agricultural Holdings Act 1986, s 2(3). But a licensor whose licence has itself converted under s 2 may qualify.
[63] Ibid, s 1(1).

year in total does not qualify. However, a mere expectation of renewal for such a period without any contractual right to do so may.[64]

The effect of the application of the Agricultural Holdings Act 1986

6.20 Only the most cursory mention of the effect of the Act's application to converted licences can be given. Reference should be made to specialist texts for a proper treatment. In short summary, the principal effects are as follows:

(1) *Security of tenure*. Licences converted into tenancies from year to year can only be brought to an end in the manner provided by the Act. Specifically:

 (a) Either party may serve notice to quit, which, with certain exceptions,[65] must expire at least 12 months from the end of the current year of the tenancy.[66]

 (b) An owner's notice can take one of two forms. First, it may specify one or more of the eight Cases in Sch 3 to the Act. In such case, provided the recipient within one month gives notice to arbitrate or counter-notice the notice will only take effect if the owner can make out one/more of them.

 (c) Second, the owner may serve an 'unqualified' notice. If the recipient gives counter-notice within one month the notice will be ineffective unless the Agricultural Lands Tribunal consents to its operation, which it may do (only) if the owner makes out one or more of the grounds in s 27(3) and it is reasonable for him to seek possession.[67]

(2) *Rent control*. There is no limit on the parties' freedom of contract as to rent at the outset. However, not more than once every 3 years thereafter the rent may be adjusted by arbitration to the open market rent.[68] This will only take effect on the date from which the converted tenancy could have been terminated by notice to quit served on the date arbitration was demanded, provided the arbitrator was appointed by then. Separately, an owner may seek an increase in rent to take account of the value of improvements undertaken by him.[69]

(3) *Compensation*. Four statutory rights to compensation, which cannot be excluded by agreement, are provided by the Act. First, a tenant who is not in default and vacates following notice to quit by the owner may be

---

[64] *Scene Estates Ltd v Amos* [1957] 2 QB 205.
[65] Agricultural Holdings Act 1986, s 25(2), (3).
[66] Although the parties may agree to treat a short notice as valid or one party may be estopped from disputing its validity. See e g *In re Swanson's Agreement* [1946] 2 All ER 628; *Elsden v Pick* [1980] 1 WLR 898.
[67] Agricultural Holdings Act 1986, s 27(2).
[68] Ibid, s 12 and Sch 2.
[69] Ibid, s 13.

entitled to compensation for disturbance.[70] Second, tenants are entitled to compensation upon vacating the holding for certain improvements undertaken by them provided the relevant conditions are met.[71] Third, tenants are entitled to compensation for loss of milk quota[72] or for increasing the value of the holding by adopting more beneficial systems of farming than required by the agreement or (if none) than carried out on comparable holdings.[73] Finally, owners may claim compensation for dilapidations or deterioration in the value of the holding or damage caused by the tenant's failure to observe the rules of good husbandry.[74]

RESIDENTIAL LICENCES

Lodgers

6.21 Lodgers comprise an apparently disparate category of occupiers, including the casual short- or long-term house visitor, hotel and guest-house occupants, students in college/bedsit accommodation, occupiers of hostels/almshouses/old people's homes/some sheltered accommodation, flat/house sharers and a paying lodger with sole use of his room.[75] These cases have in common the fact that the occupiers may have a right of (even sole) occupation but do not have a right to possession because the owners:

(1) reserve the right to provide services (eg cleaning, maintenance etc) which require unrestricted access to the land[76] in the sense of being able to enter whether or not the occupier is present;[77]

(2) retain general control of the land, eg by reserving the right to use – or allow others to use – it in common with the occupier;

(3) do not grant the exclusive use of a defined area, eg shared houses without allocated rooms;

(4) retain supervisory control over the occupier in respect of his occupation or more generally provide services that include some significant care-component, eg to persons who are vulnerable by reason of age, illness, dependency etc,

or a combination of some/all of these factors.

---

[70] Ibid, ss 60–63.
[71] Ibid, ss 64–69 and Schs 7–9.
[72] Ibid, s 13 and Sch 1.
[73] Ibid, s 70.
[74] Ibid, ss 71–73.
[75] See eg *Woodfall's Landlord & Tenant* (Sweet & Maxwell, looseleaf), at para 1.028 for more examples of lodgers.
[76] *Huwyler v Reddy* (1996) 65 P & CR D3.
[77] *Crancour v De Silvaesa* (1986) 52 P & CR 204, at 211.

6.22 Whether an occupier has a right of possession or merely occupation is often a question of fact and degree. Typically the hotel/guest-house owner provides services and reserves rights of access which are sufficiently extensive and/or unqualified so as to retain possession.[78] However, if services are provided under a separate agreement for a separate consideration, as is sometimes found in residential hotels and certain types of sheltered accommodation,[79] the occupier may be in possession, at least if it is not a condition of his occupation that he enters into such agreement. Certain lodgers hitherto had a degree of statutory protection from eviction under the Rent Act 1977, s 19 (restricted contracts) – see **6.46–6.47**.

Holiday accommodation

6.23 Similar principles apply to rights to occupy self-contained holiday accommodation, which may, despite their short term, be leases (albeit without security of tenure[80]) or licences, depending on the nature and extent of the owner's reserved rights.

Mobile structures

6.24 The right to occupy a caravan, houseboat or similar structure may be licence (if not a lease) of the land or, sometimes, merely of the structure itself. It is a question of fact whether a particular structure is a chattel or fixture.[81] That in turn depends on the degree and purpose of its annexation to the land, as to which see **13.14**.

6.25 A licence to reside in a caravan etc (whether a chattel, fixture or part of the land) includes the right to use the land where it is situated. The extent of that right/the land depends on the circumstances. Subject to the terms of the agreement, however, a mere right to occupy a structure which remains a chattel will usually not of itself confer a right to possession of the land. If the structure is a chattel, the licensee may only be in occupation of it[82] and not the land for the purposes of the Occupiers' Liability Act 1957, depending on the licence terms and in particular the degree of control he has over the area occupied by the structure. See generally Chapter 11.

Occupation referable to some other relationship

6.26 An agreement that grants (or appears to grant) possession may nevertheless be a licence if the occupation is referable to some other relationship between the parties, such as that of employer–employee or prospective vendor–purchaser. The list is not exhaustive, e g offices holders may

---

[78] See e g *Marchant v Charters* [1977] 1 WLR 1181.
[79] *Vandersteen v Agius* (1992) 65 P & CR 26.
[80] See below. Note notice to terminate under Protection From Eviction Act 1977, s 5 is unnecessary: s 3A(7)(a).
[81] *Reynolds v Ashby & Son* [1904] AC 466.
[82] Occupiers' Liability Act 1957, s 1(3); see *Pratt v Richards* [1951] 2 KB 208 (scaffolding).

also be licensees,[83] as well as live-in care providers[84] and persons whose right to occupy arises from their membership of the organisation that owns the land.[85]

Service occupiers

6.27 The most frequently encountered example is the service occupier. An employee who occupies his employer's premises may be a service tenant, a service occupier or a licensee. A service tenant is simply a tenant (who may therefore have statutory security of tenure) who provides services to the owner that do not require him to occupy the land. A service occupier is a type of licensee whose employment does require occupation (below). He has no security of tenure unless he is an agricultural worker or works for certain types of public bodies (below).[86] An employee who is neither a service occupier nor a service tenant is a licensee (eg a seasonal agricultural worker whose non-exclusive occupation of his employer's accommodation is not required in order to perform his duties but is merely a benefit in kind).

6.28 The service occupier was treated in *Street v Mountford*[87] as not having a right to exclusive possession by virtue of the fact that the owner-employer retains constructive possession through him. Nevertheless the service occupier may be personally in occupation so as to be able to maintain in his own name an action in trespass against third parties and/or for the purposes of the Occupiers' Liability Act 1957.[88]

Test for service occupier

6.29 Service occupation requires a sufficient nexus between the occupier's employment duties and his residence. An employee who lives in his employer's accommodation is a service occupier if either: (a) it is essential to the performance of his duties that he occupies that accommodation[89] or accommodation within that area; or (b) it is an express term of his employment contract that he does so and his occupation enables him better to perform his duties to a material degree.[90] This is to be contrasted with accommodation provided to an employee as an inducement or remuneration in kind[91] but which he is not obliged to occupy.

6.30 An express term requiring occupation must be genuine. The test is objective; it is not enough that the term is expressed to be for the purpose of promoting the better performance of those duties or was included for that

---

[83] *Street v Mountford* [1985] AC 809, at 818, 827.
[84] See eg *Vesely v Levy* [2007] EWCA Civ 367.
[85] *Koeller v Coleg Elidyr* [2005] EWCA Civ 856.
[86] Ie those not specified in Housing Act 1985, Sch 1, para 2(1)–(3).
[87] [1985] AC 809, at 818E.
[88] See eg *Wheat v E Lacon & Co Ltd* [1966] AC 552. See more generally Chapter 2.
[89] *South Glamorgan CC v Griffiths* [1992] 2 EGLR 232.
[90] *Valuation Commissioner (Northern Ireland) v Fermanagh Protestant Board of Education* [1969] 1 WLR 1708, at 1722.
[91] *Norris v Checksfield* [1991] 4 All ER 327, at 330d.

reason.[92] Nor, conversely, is it necessary that his occupation has *in fact* had that effect[93] (although that may shed light on whether the term was genuine[94]). The test, rather, is whether the term was, objectively viewed, intended to promote – and was reasonably capable of promoting – the better performance of those duties.[95]

6.31 In reality both tests in **6.29** are different ways of expressing the same concept, namely whether the employee is contractually required – expressly or impliedly – to live in his employer's accommodation. (Only) if it is essential to the performance of his duties that he does so is such a term likely to be implied; (only) an express term that meets the test in **6.30** will be regarded as genuine (ie non-sham). Whilst it has been suggested that an employee is not a service occupier if he would chose to live in the accommodation anyway,[96] it is considered that merely makes it more difficult (where the employment contract is silent) to imply a term, since in such case it may be neither essential to the performance of the contract nor so obvious as to go without saying that he does.

6.32 It is irrelevant that his right to occupy is separate from his employment contract (so long as the one is expressly/impliedly conditional on the other) as is the fact that he pays (or a deduction from wages is made) for the use of the accommodation.[97]

6.33 Typically the requirements in **6.29** are found to have been met where eg: (a) the employee's residence provides some element of security (eg caretakers, pub managers); (b) his presence enables him to respond quickly, if required, out of hours to emergencies or contingencies (eg caretakers); (c) such accommodation is needed to store equipment, tools or materials which his job requires that he has to hand; or (d) his presence provides a public interface for the employer. These are not mutually exclusive.[98] In each case the particular benefit that his occupation confers must be relevant to his duties as employee.

Date for applying test

6.34 A service occupier may become a service tenant (or vice versa) if the nature of his employment duties – insofar as they impact on his need to occupy the accommodation – changes from time to time. An express term requiring occupation which was genuine at the outset may cease to be so by virtue of changes in his employment duties; conversely a term which did not qualify at the outset may do so subsequently as a result of such changes. The question is

---

[92] *Wragg v Surrey CC* [2008] EWCA Civ 19, at [41]–[42].
[93] Eg a caretaker may never *in fact* have had to attend at short notice after hours.
[94] Or in the absence of an express term whether there is a factual basis to imply one.
[95] *Wragg v Surrey CC* [2008] EWCA Civ 19, at [46].
[96] *Hughes v Greenwich LBC* (1992) 65 P & CR 12; aff'd [1994] 1 AC 704.
[97] *Thompson (Funeral Furnishers) v Phillips* [1945] 2 All ER 49; *Norris v Checksfield* [1991] 4 All ER 327, at 332h.
[98] See for a list of examples considering the requirements *Woodfall's Landlord & Tenant*, n 75 above, at paras 1.029.4–1.029.5.

whether, at the time the nature of his occupation is challenged, the occupation was still referable to his employment and the term requiring him to live there and whether there was/is any change/intended change in the purpose/nature of that occupation.[99]

Occupation in anticipation of performing duties

6.35 It is not essential that the employee is *immediately* assisted in the performance of his duties, eg an employee may be a service occupier if allowed into occupation in anticipation of securing qualifications which would allow him to undertake duties that would require him to occupy the premises. However, in such case he may cease to be a service occupier if it later becomes apparent he will not do so or that prospect becomes too uncertain or remote.[100]

Post-employment occupation

6.36 A term requiring the employee to occupy his employer's accommodation may have a 'limited after-life' so as to survive, for some time, the ending of the employment relationship.[101] Even a lengthy period of occupation after the employment ends may not give rise to a tenancy or some other contractual licence if attributable to the employer's generosity/charity or if the parties did not intend subsequently to create legal relations.[102]

Effect of service occupation

6.37 A service occupier's right of occupation determines automatically when his employment ends; notice under the Protection from Eviction Act 1977 is not required.[103] That is so even if the termination is unlawful.[104] The rule in *Hurst v Picture Theatres Ltd*[105] and *Winter Garden Theatres (London) Ltd v Millennium Productions Ltd*[106] that a court may not assist the licensor who unlawfully terminates the licence to recover possession does not apply to a service occupier who has been unlawfully dismissed; his right of occupation is conditional on the continuation of the employment contract[107] (however terminated) and in any event that contract is not one the court will specifically enforce.

---

[99] *Greenfield v Berkshire CC* (1996) 28 HLR 691.
[100] *Norris v Checksfield* [1991] 4 All ER 327, at 330–331.
[101] *Elvidge v Coventry CC* [1993] 3 WLR 976, at 981E–981F, explaining *South Glamorgan CC v Griffiths* [1992] 2 EGLR 232.
[102] *Thompson (Funeral Furnishers) v Phillips* [1945] 2 All ER 49.
[103] *Norris v Checksfield* [1991] 4 All ER 327.
[104] *Ivory v Palmer* [1975] ICR 340.
[105] [1915] 1 KB 1.
[106] [1948] AC 173; see generally Chapter 12.
[107] *Rokewood Nurseries v Burrell* [1955] EGD 304.

Residential licensees with security of tenure

6.38 Residential licensees, with certain exceptions, do not have security of 'tenure' and thus the licensor has an unfettered right to recover the land at the end of the licence term.[108] Nevertheless certain types of licensees are protected by statute, specifically:

- some licensees of public authority accommodation, under the Housing Act 1985;[109]

- licensees of private accommodation who had restricted contracts, under the Rent Act 1977;

- agricultural workers who occupy their employer's accommodation, under the Rent (Agriculture) Act 1976 or Housing Act 1988;

- licensees with the right to station a mobile home on a pitch, under the Mobile Homes Act 1983; and

- licensees of caravans or caravan sites not protected by the 1983 Act may have a residual degree of protection under the Caravan Sites Act 1968, Pt I.

Public authority accommodation

Licences treated as secure tenancies

The application of the Housing Act 1985

6.39 A tenancy is protected under the Housing Act 1985, Pt IV if/so long as the 'landlord condition' and 'tenant condition' are met and it is one by which a dwelling-house[110] (or part of one) is let as a separate dwelling.[111] Schedule 1 provides exemptions from protection. The 'tenant condition' requires that the occupier is an individual who occupies the dwelling as his only or principal home.[112] The 'landlord' condition is satisfied if the grantor is one of a number of stipulated public bodies.[113]

---

[108] Subject to the miscellaneous fetters referred to at **12.38–12.39** and limitations as to the manner of its exercise in **13.15** et seq.
[109] Housing Act 1985, s 79(3).
[110] Housing Act 1985, s 112(1). Obviously other types of licence (eg to store goods) do not qualify: *Fletcher v Brent LBC* [2006] EWCA Civ 960, at [42].
[111] Housing Act 1985, s 79(1). See, however, the exceptions in s 79(2) of and Sch 1 to the Act. For the application of this requirement in the case of licences, see *Woodfall's Landlord & Tenant*, n 75 above, at paras 25.017, 25.019.
[112] Housing Act 1985, s 81. In the case of joint tenants, at least one of them must satisfy the residence condition.
[113] Eg local authorities, new town corporations, housing action trusts, urban development corporations, charitable housing trusts and certain housing associations and co-operatives: Housing Act 1985, s 80, as amended.

Application to licences

6.40 The Housing Act 1985 also applies to licences to occupy a dwelling-house or part of a dwelling house (whether or not supported by consideration) as they apply in relation to tenancies.[114] Accordingly the licensor must be one of the specified authorities or bodies[115] and the licensee(s) must be an individual or individuals. The arrangement must be consensual; thus where an owner charges a squatter for use and occupation pending possession proceedings, no licence capable of conversion into a secure tenancy was created.[116]

6.41 In addition the licence must confer exclusive possession[117] but as the vast majority of agreements that do so are leases, following *Street v Mountford*, it follows that few licences will qualify for protection under s 79(3). The requirement of exclusive possession means that a non-exclusive licence will not qualify for protection, eg a licence to occupy a room in a hostel.[118] Nor will a licence to occupy a room in a house with the shared use of communal facilities, since the room alone is not a dwelling but only part of one and the licensee does not have exclusive use of the whole.[119] Similarly, a licence granted to a secure tenant to occupy other accommodation whilst his flat was being renovated was held not to be for use a separate dwelling but only in conjunction with his flat.[120] In contrast where a secure tenant was granted a licence of another flat as a temporary expedient for his own safety and pending the outcome of possession proceedings, that flat was held to be a separate dwelling and thus the licence qualified for protection under s 79(3).[121]

6.42 The Housing Act 1985 specifies a number of licences which are excluded from statutory protection. These include:

- service occupation agreements granted by certain types of bodies[122] (although such service occupiers may not have 'possession' in any event – see **2.36(2)**);

- land acquired for development that is used in the interim as temporary housing accommodation;[123]

- an arrangement in pursuance of any function under Pt VII of the Housing Act 1996 (homelessness) or under s 4 or Pt VI of the

---

[114] Housing Act 1985, s 79(3).
[115] Ibid, s 80.
[116] *Westminster CC v Basson* (1990) 23 HLR 225.
[117] *Westminster CC v Clarke* [1992] 2 AC 288.
[118] Ibid.
[119] *Parkins v Westminster CC* [1998] 1 EGLR 22.
[120] *Tyler v Royal Borough of Kensington & Chelsea* (1990) 23 HLR 380, at 385–386.
[121] *Langridge v Mansfield DC* [2008] HLR 541.
[122] Housing Act 1985, Sch 1, para 2.
[123] Ibid, Sch 1, para 3.

Immigration and Asylum Act 1999, unless the owner notifies the occupier that it is to be regarded as a secure tenancy;[124]

- a licence to occupy an almshouse granted by/on behalf of a charity which is authorised to maintain the dwelling-house as an almshouse but has no power to grant tenancies;[125] and

- licences granted as a temporary expedient to someone who entered the dwelling-house or other land as a trespasser, whether or not he previously had a licence to occupy that or another dwelling-house.[126]

The implications of the Housing Act 1985's application

6.43 The Act modifies certain of the parties' contractual rights in relation to licences that are converted into secure tenancies:

- First, a secure tenant may not, with certain exceptions, assign or sublet his interest.[127]

- Second, a qualifying person may succeed to the tenancy on the death of a secure tenant.[128]

- Third, and most importantly, the Act modifies the owner's right to recover possession at the end of the contract term (eg by effluxion of time, termination for breach or notice to quit). On termination, a periodic secure tenancy of the same dwelling-house on the same terms (so far as compatible with a periodic tenancy, but excluding any right to forfeit) and between the same parties arises automatically.[129] To recover possession the owner must first serve notice[130] and obtain a possession order, which can only be granted on proof of one/more of the grounds in the Housing Act 1985, s 84 and Sch 2.[131] An order can only be made under Grounds 1–8 if it is reasonable to do so,[132] under Grounds 9–11 if suitable alternative accommodation is available when it takes effect and under Grounds 12–16 if both these conditions are met. The court has extensive powers to adjourn[133] or, at any time before the order is executed, postpone the date of possession and/or stay/suspend the order or its execution on

---

[124] Ibid, Sch 1 paras 4, 5.
[125] Ibid, Sch 1, para 12.
[126] Ibid, s 79(4).
[127] Ibid, ss 91–92.
[128] Ibid, s 87.
[129] Ibid, s 86. The period of the tenancy is the same as that for which rent was payable under the contract – s 86(2)(a).
[130] Ibid, s 83. The court may allow the notice to be amended or dispense with service if just and equitable to do so – ss 84(3), 83(1)(b).
[131] Ibid, s 82.
[132] Note further restrictions apply where Grounds 2 or 2A are relied on.
[133] Except in relation to Grounds 9–11: Housing Act 1985, s 85(1).

terms and subsequently to rescind or discharge it, if appropriate.[134] The court may also make a demotion order for a period of up to one year, during which the landlord may, by following the statutory procedure, obtain possession as of right.[135]

- Fourth, certain secure tenants have the right to buy the freehold or an extended lease of their accommodation.

6.44 The Act does not, however, provide a scheme for rent control although the public authority's exercise of its statutory power to set charges for the accommodation[136] may in a particular case be subject to judicial review. For a detailed consideration, reference should be made to the relevant specialist texts.

Licences treated as introductory tenancies

6.45 Periodic tenancies granted by public bodies operating an introductory tenancy regime under the Housing Act 1996, Ch 1, Pt V that would otherwise be secure tenancies are, with certain exceptions, treated as introductory tenancies during their first year[137] or until one of the events stipulated in s 125(5) occurs. Section 126 extends the scheme to licences to occupy dwelling-houses (whether or not granted for consideration) that meet the above criteria, except ones granted as a temporary expedient to someone who entered the dwelling-house or any other land as a trespasser, whether or not beforehand he had a licence to occupy that or another dwelling-house.

6.46 During the introductory period, the owner has a right to possession[138] subject to compliance with the Act's formalities.[139] The occupier's recourse is to require the owner to review its decision to seek possession.[140] If, however, the trial period is successfully completed without being extended or a possession order made, the occupier becomes a secure tenant. There are also provisions restricting assignment of the introductory tenancy[141] and providing for succession on death.[142]

Restricted contracts

6.47 These are of historical interest only; few (if any) survive today and none have been created since 15 January 1989.[143] Restricted contracts included licences[144] by which an individual was permitted, in consideration of a fee

---

[134] Housing Act 1985, s 85(1)–(3).
[135] Ibid, s 82A; Housing Act 1996, ss 143B–143F.
[136] Ibid, s 24.
[137] Housing Act 1996, s 124(2), (3). The period may be extended – ss 125(2), 125A.
[138] Ibid, s 127(2).
[139] Ibid, s 126.
[140] Ibid, s 128. The review decision may itself be judicially reviewed – s 129.
[141] Ibid, s 134.
[142] Ibid, ss 131–133.
[143] Unless entered into pursuant to a contract made before then – Housing Act 1988, s 36(1).
[144] *Marchant v Charters* [1977] 1 WLR 1181; *Luganda v Service Hotels Ltd* [1969] 2 Ch 209.

which included payment for the use of furniture or services,[145] to occupy exclusively[146] as a residence a dwelling (or part of a dwelling)[147] falling within the rateable value limits of the Rent Act 1977.[148] The requirement that the premises be occupied as a 'residence' had the effect of excluding from protection certain lodgers, eg hotel guests but not occupiers of residential hotels, who may have been protected.[149]

6.48 Security of tenure varied according to the date the licence was created:

(1) for pre-27 November 1980 contracts, it took the form of postponing the operation of an owner's notice to terminate, once the restricted contract had been referred to the rent tribunal and, at the tribunal's discretion, in other cases where a specific application was made for an extension of the period of time when the notice took effect;[150] and

(2) for contracts entered into subsequently the court had the power, when making an order for possession or at any time prior to execution, to stay/suspend its execution or postpone the date for possession for such period(s), not exceeding 3 months in total, as it thought fit.[151]

Agricultural workers

6.49 The Rent (Agriculture) Act 1976 applies to qualifying licences granted before 15 January 1989 or pursuant to a contract entered into before then or to persons who at the time were protected occupiers or statutory tenants of the same licensor under the Act.[152] The Housing Act 1988 applies to qualifying licences granted thereafter. Service occupiers who are agricultural workers may thus be protected under these Acts. In broad terms, the Rent (Agriculture) Act 1976 gives such licences much of the protection afforded to regulated tenancies under the Rent Act 1977 and the Housing Act 1988 gives assured agricultural occupiers very similar security to assured tenants.

---

[145] Rent Act 1977, s 19.
[146] Ie to the exclusion of all others. Accordingly if a number of residents are granted collectively the exclusive right to occupy a dwelling (as distinct from a number of individual, non-exclusive licences) they may have a restricted contract.
[147] Whether or not it also granted the right to share other parts of the house in common with others – Rent Act 1977, s 19(6).
[148] See, however, the exceptions in Rent Act 1977, s 19(3)–(7).
[149] The provision of board by the hotel owner, if it formed a substantial proportion of the fee, would usually also exclude the lodger from protection – Rent Act 1977, s 19(5)(c). *Luganda v Services Hotels* [1969] 2 Ch 209.
[150] Rent Act 1977, ss 103, 104. The tribunal could abridge the period of deferment in the event of the licensee's misconduct – s 106.
[151] Ibid, s 106A.
[152] Housing Act 1988, s 34(4).

Occupation under the Rent (Agriculture) Act 1976

6.50 In order to qualify as a protected occupier:

- The licensee must be a 'qualifying worker' (broadly, someone who worked in agriculture[153] full-time[154] or as a permit worker for at least 91 out of the last 104 weeks[155]) or who was a qualifying worker at any time during the licence's subsistence.

- He must have a 'licence',[156] ie a contract under which he is granted the right to occupy a dwelling-house (or part of a dwelling-house) as a residence. It is immaterial that the licence contains other (eg employment) terms nor need it be in return for a separate consideration.[157] Service occupiers may thus be protected.

- The licence must be a 'relevant' licence, ie one under which the licensee has the exclusive occupation of a dwelling-house (or part of one) as a separate dwelling[158] and which, had it been a tenancy, would be a protected tenancy under the Rent Act 1977[159] but for certain exceptions, eg low rent.[160]

- The dwelling-house must be in 'qualifying ownership';[161] the occupier's employer must either own it or have an arrangement with the owner for its use as housing accommodation for persons employed by him in agriculture.[162]

6.51 An occupier who meets the above criteria becomes a statutory tenant after his protected occupancy has determined (eg as a result of the termination of his employment).[163] The terms of the statutory tenancy are set out in Sch 5 to the 1976 Act. No order for possession can be made against a protected occupier or statutory tenant except on certain specified grounds[164] which follow (with some exceptions) the mandatory and discretionary grounds for regulated tenancies in the Rent Act 1977, Sch 15. The court's powers are also similar: where a claim is brought on discretionary grounds it can adjourn

---

[153] For the non-exclusive definition of 'agriculture', see Rent (Agriculture) Act 1976, s 1(1)(a).
[154] As defined Rent (Agriculture) Act 1976, Sch 3, para 4.
[155] Ibid, Sch 3, para 1. Protection is extended to agricultural workers incapable of whole-time work in agriculture as the result of a qualifying injury/disease and persons who give up a secure occupancy in return for a new licence: ibid, s 2(2)–(4) and Sch 3, para 2.
[156] Ibid, s 2(1).
[157] Ibid, s 34. The entry into the employment contract itself provides consideration for the licence. However, bare licences may not qualify as they do not confer the *right* to exclusive occupation: *Goldsack v Shore* [1950] 1 KB 708, at 711.
[158] As defined in Rent (Agriculture) Act 1976, s 23.
[159] Ibid, Sch 2, para 1.
[160] Ibid, Sch 2, para 3.
[161] Ibid, s 2(1).
[162] Ibid, Sch 3, para 3.
[163] Unless the owner falls within one of the categories in ibid, s 5.
[164] Ibid, s 6(1) and Sch 4.

proceedings[165] and on granting an order for possession or at any time before execution may stay/suspend its execution or postpone the date for possession on terms,[166] in either case for such period(s) as it thinks fit. If the terms imposed are complied with the court may, if it thinks fit, subsequently discharge or rescind the order.[167]

6.52 The Rent (Agriculture) Act 1976 also modifies the parties' common-law and contractual rights by incorporating, with some modifications, the system for registered rents in the Rent Act 1977,[168] providing for rights of succession on the death of the protected occupier[169] and the effect of the determination of a licensor's leasehold interest.[170]

Assured agricultural occupancies under the Housing Act 1988

6.53 The Housing Act 1988, in contrast to the parallel, but separate, scheme of protection provided by the Rent (Agriculture) Act 1976, confers on assured agricultural occupancies almost identical protection to that of assured tenants.

6.54 The 1988 Act uses many of the concepts in the 1976 Act. A licence qualifies as an assured agricultural occupancy if:

- it confers the right to occupy exclusively a separate dwelling as a residence and is one which, had it been a tenancy, would have been an assured tenancy but for certain exceptions;[171]

- the licensee is an agricultural worker, ie a 'qualifying worker' as defined in the 1976 Act;[172] and

- the dwelling is in 'qualifying ownership' as defined in the 1976 Act.[173]

6.55 An assured agricultural occupancy enjoys similar protection to that afforded to assured tenancies.[174] Provision is made for succession by spouses, civil partners and certain members of the occupier's family.[175] The owner may not recover possession after the employment or the licence term ends except by first serving notice of intention to bring proceedings[176] and obtaining a court

---

[165] Ibid, s 7(2A).
[166] Ibid, s 7(3), (4).
[167] Ibid, s 7(5).
[168] Rent (Agriculture) Act 1976, ss 13–16.
[169] Ibid, s 3(2)–(3).
[170] Ibid, s 9.
[171] Housing Act 1988, s 24(2).
[172] Ibid, Sch 3.
[173] Ibid.
[174] Housing Act 1988, s 24(3). However, a licensee's notice terminating his employment is not treated as a notice to quit the dwelling.
[175] Subject to conditions of prior residence: ibid, Sch 3, para 3.
[176] Ibid, s 8.

order, which can only be granted if one of the statutory grounds is made out[177] and, if discretionary, it is reasonable to order possession.[178] The court may adjourn proceedings[179] and, on granting an order or at any time before execution, may stay or suspend the order (or its execution) or postpone the date for possession on conditions,[180] in either case for such period(s) as it thinks fit. If the conditions are complied with it may discharge or rescind the possession order, if appropriate.[181]

Mobile Homes Act licensees

6.56 The Mobile Homes Act 1983 contains a comprehensive code for the protection of certain licensees of mobile homes parks. It applies to an agreement which entitles an individual to station a mobile home on land forming part of a protected site[182] and to occupy it as his only or main residence.[183] It does not therefore apply to a licence to occupy the owner's mobile home or (it is thought) a bare licence.[184] The licence may be enforced against the original owner's successors in title[185] and its benefit may pass by lawful assignment[186] or succession.[187]

6.57 Where the Act applies, the licensor must give the licensee within the period specified in s 1(3), (4) of the Act a written statement in prescribed form[188] setting out (inter alia) the parties' names and addresses, particulars of the land on which the home is to be stationed, the express terms to be contained in the agreement, the terms implied by s 2 and such other terms as may be prescribed.[189] An express term which is not set out in the written statement is unenforceable by the owner or any person within s 3(1) unless the court orders otherwise under s 2(3).[190]

---

[177] Ibid, Sch 2. Ground 16 is omitted. Under Ground 9 (suitable alternative accommodation) it is enough if the occupier will have the same protection as an assured agricultural occupier.
[178] Ibid, s 7(4).
[179] Ibid, s 9(1).
[180] Ibid, s 9(2), (3).
[181] Ibid, s 9(4).
[182] The provision excluding land owned by a local authority and used as a travellers' site was repealed by Housing and Regeneration Act 2008, s 316 and Sch 16. The definition otherwise has the same meaning as in the Caravan Sites Act 1968 – Mobile Homes Act 1983, s 5(1). 'Protected site' does not include a site which requires, but lacks, planning permission: *Balthasar v Mullane* (1985) 51 P & CR 107. However, a site without a site licence is nevertheless protected: *National By-Products Ltd v Brice* (1983) 46 P & CR 281.
[183] Mobile Homes Act 1983, s 1(1) and Sch 1, Pt I.
[184] *Balthasar v Mullane* (1985) 51 P & CR 107.
[185] Mobile Homes Act 1983, s 3(1), (2).
[186] Ibid, s 3(2).
[187] Ibid, s 3(3)–(4).
[188] Or one substantially to like effect. See the Mobile Homes (Written Statement) (England) Regulations 2006, SI 2006/2275 and (for Wales) Mobile Homes (Written Statement) Regulations 1983, SI 1983/749.
[189] Mobile Homes Act 1983, s 1(2). In default, the occupier may apply for an order that he does so – s 1(6).
[190] Ibid, s 1(5).

6.58 There are implied into an agreement to which the Act applies the terms set out in Sch 1, Pt I notwithstanding any express provision to the contrary.[191] Those terms (inter alia) provide as follows:

(1) the right to station the mobile home on a protected site subsists until determined in accordance with the following;[192]

(2) if the site owner's estate/interest is insufficient to enable him to grant the right for an indefinite period, the period for which it subsists shall not continue beyond the date when his estate/interest determines;[193]

(3) if planning permission for the use of the protected site as a site for mobile homes is granted for a finite period of time, the period for which the right subsists shall not extend beyond its expiration;[194]

(4) if, however, before the end of the period in (2) and (3), there is a change in circumstances which allows a longer period 'account shall be taken of that change';[195]

(5) the occupier is entitled to terminate the agreement by giving at least 4 weeks' written notice;[196]

(6) the owner is entitled to terminate the agreement forthwith if the court is satisfied that:

   (a) the occupier has breached a term of the agreement and failed to comply with the owner's notice to remedy within a reasonable period of time and that it is reasonable for the agreement to be terminated;[197]
   (b) the occupier is not occupying the mobile home as his only or main residence and (in England) that it is reasonable for the agreement to be terminated;[198]

(7) the owner is also entitled to terminate the agreement:[199]

---

[191] Ibid, s 2(1).
[192] Ibid, Sch 1, Pt I, para 1.
[193] Ibid, Sch 1, Pt I, para 2(1).
[194] Ibid, Sch 1, Pt I, para 2(2).
[195] Ibid, Sch 1, Pt I, para 2(3).
[196] Ibid, Sch 1, Pt I, para 3.
[197] Ibid, Sch 1, Pt I, para 4(3).
[198] Ibid, Sch 1, Pt I, para 6.
[199] Ibid. See, however, para 6(3), (4) regarding the court's power to adjourn if it considers that it would be reasonably practicable for particular repairs to be carried out to the mobile home that would result in this ground no longer being made out which the occupier indicates an intention to effect.

(a) (in England) forthwith if the court is satisfied that having regard to its condition the mobile home is having a detrimental effect on the amenity of the site and that it is reasonable for the agreement to be terminated;

(b) (in Wales) at the end of the 'relevant period'[200] if the court is satisfied that having regard to its condition the mobile home is having a detrimental effect on the amenity of the site or is likely to do so before the end of the next relevant period;

(8) where the agreement is terminated under (5)–(7) the occupier may recover any advance payment that relates to the post-termination period.[201]

Implied terms other than as to termination are mentioned in Chapter 8.

6.59 The court may also, on the application of either party within the relevant period,[202] order that there be implied into the agreement terms concerning the matters referred to in Sch 1, Pt II of the Act[203] or make an order varying or deleting any express term or (in the case of a term to which s 1(6) applies) provide for it to have effect (if appropriate, subject to any variation specified in the order).[204]

Caravan Sites Act 1968

6.60 Part I of the Caravan Sites Act 1968 provides a residual degree of protection for occupiers of caravans on caravan sites. It applies to individuals entitled under any licence or contract ('a residential contract') (a) to station a caravan on a protected site[205] and occupy it as a residence or (b) to occupy as a residence a caravan stationed on any such site.[206] Category (a) includes licences protected by the Mobile Homes Act 1983; category (b) is wider. Holiday users – who do not occupy units as their residence – are not protected. The Act's application to bare licensees is doubtful.[207]

6.61 The Act provides that where a residential contract is terminable by notice by either party, such a notice is of no effect unless it is given not less than 4

---

[200] Ibid, Sch 1, Pt I, para 6(2): the period of 5 years from the date of the agreement and each succeeding period of 5 years thereafter.
[201] Ibid, Sch 1, Pt I, para 7.
[202] As defined in ibid, s 2(3A).
[203] Ibid, s 2(2).
[204] Ibid, s 2(3).
[205] Caravan Sites Act 1968, s 1(2), as amended, ie any land for which a site licence is required under Caravan Sites and Control of Development Act 1960, Pt I or would be required but for certain exemptions but not sites for which the planning permission or site licence permits holiday use or use for only part of the year. It is implicit that there must be planning permission to use the land for caravans: *Balthasar v Mullane* (1985) 51 P & CR 107. The land, however, may be protected where the absence of a site licence is the fault of the owner in failing to secure planning permission: *Hooper v Eaglestone* (1977) 34 P & CR 311.
[206] Caravan Sites Act 1968, s 1(1).
[207] 'Entitled' in s 1(1) whilst capable of including rights arising by bare permission more naturally connotes a right exercisable against the owner's will.

weeks before it is expressed to expire.[208] The restriction does not apply to fixed-term licences, which expire automatically by effluxion of time or to the exercise of a right to terminate for breach.

6.62 The Protection from Eviction Act 1977 does not apply to any premises that consist of a caravan stationed on a protected site.[209] Nevertheless the 1968 Act provides similar protection. It provides that a person is guilty of an offence if:

(1) during the subsistence of a residential contract he unlawfully deprives the occupier (and certain related parties[210]) of his/their occupation of a caravan on a protected site which he/they has/have the right to occupy;

(2) after the expiration or determination of the contract, he enforces (otherwise than by proceedings) any right to exclude the occupier from the protected site or caravan or removes or excludes the caravan from the site;[211] or

(3) whether during the subsistence of the contract or after its expiration or determination he does acts likely to interfere with the peace or comfort of the occupier or persons residing with him or persistently withdraws/withholds services/facilities reasonably required for occupation of the caravan on the site as a residence with the intent of causing the occupier to abandon occupation, or remove it from site or refrain from exercising any right or pursuing any remedy in respect thereof,

unless (in relation to (1) and (2)) he believed and had reasonable cause to believe that the occupier had ceased to reside on the site.[212]

6.63 The owner of a protected site or his agent also commits an offence if, during the subsistence of a residential contract or after its expiration or determination, he:

(1) does acts likely to interfere with the peace or comfort of the occupier or persons living with him; or

(2) persistently withdraws/withholds services/facilities reasonably required for the occupation of the caravan as a residence on the site,

and (in either case) he knows or has reasonable cause to believe that the conduct is likely to cause the occupier to do any of the things mentioned in

---

[208] Caravan Sites Act 1968, s 2. See the exception in relation to acquiring authorities acting under the Compulsory Purchase Act 1965, s 13: Caravan Sites Act 1968, s 5(3).
[209] Caravan Sites Act 1968, s 5(5).
[210] Ibid, s 3(2).
[211] Ibid, s 3(1)(a), (b).
[212] Ibid, s 3(4).

6.62(3).[213] It is a defence to show that the defendant had reasonable grounds for doing the acts or withdrawing/withholding the relevant services/facilities.[214] These restrictions do not apply to the enforcement of rights arising otherwise than on the expiration/determination of the licence or to anything done pursuant to a court order.[215]

6.64 If in proceedings brought by the owner of a protected site after the expiration or determination of a residential contract the court makes an order enforcing his right to exclude the occupier from the site or from any caravan or to remove or exclude any caravan from the site, it may (without prejudice to any other power to postpone the operation of the order or suspend its execution) suspend enforcement of the order for such period not exceeding 12 months from the date of the order as it considers reasonable.[216] In exercising that power the court may impose such terms and conditions (eg as to periodic payments) as it considers reasonable.[217] The court may from time to time terminate, reduce or extend this period (for up to 12 months at any one time) or vary the terms imposed.[218] In doing so it must have regard to all the circumstances, in particular those in s 4(4). Absent special reasons, the court should make no order as to costs when making any order under s 4(1).[219]

Matrimonial home rights

6.65 A spouse's (originally common-law) rights to occupy a matrimonial home owned by the other – sometimes loosely (but inaccurately) described as a licence[220] – are now set out in the Family Law Act 1996. The Act confers 'home rights' on non-owning spouses and civil partners. It also entitles the court to make occupation orders in the circumstances specified in ss 33 and 35–38 of the Act.

6.66 These rights apply to a dwelling-house that is, or is (or at one time was) intended to be, the matrimonial/civil partnership home[221] which one spouse/civil partner (A) owns,[222] leases or has a statutory right to occupy and in which the other (B) has no such right or interest or a mere beneficial interest.[223] In such case, B's rights are:

---

[213] Ibid, s 3(1)(c), (1A).
[214] Ibid, s 3(4A).
[215] Ibid, s 3(5).
[216] Ibid, s 4(1). Such power is not to be exercised if there is no site licence in force for the site and the exemptions for gypsies and other local authority sites do not apply – ibid, s 4(6).
[217] Ibid, s 4(2).
[218] Ibid, s 4(3).
[219] Ibid, s 4(5).
[220] *National Provincial Bank Ltd v Ainsworth* [1965] AC 1175, at 1223–1224, 1239, 1250.
[221] Family Law Act 1996, ss 30(7), 33(1)(b).
[222] Unless he is merely a trustee and has no beneficial interest in it.
[223] Family Law Act 1996, s 30(9).

- (if in occupation) not to be excluded from the home without court sanction and (if not) to return to occupy the home, with the court's consent;[224]

- to have his/her occupation treated as occupation by A (eg to preserve A's statutory security of tenure);[225] and

- to have his/her rent/mortgage payments treated as payments by A.[226]

6.67 Those rights end upon the earlier of:

- A's death;

- the termination of the marriage/civil partnership; or

- the termination of A's right to occupy the land,[227]

although in the first two cases the court has discretion to extend B's rights beyond the relevant event.[228]

6.68 Either party may apply to court for enforcement of his or her rights or to restrict or terminate the other's rights of occupation.[229] Such an order can be made for a fixed or indefinite period or until a specified event occurs.[230]

6.69 B's home rights are capable of binding A's successor in title if A has a proprietary right/interest in the land.[231] B's rights are a charge on A's interest and have the same effect as an equitable interest.[232] They bind volunteers but as against purchasers must be protected by notice (registered land) or Class F land charge (unregistered land), which is rarely done in practice. The court, in deciding to make an order under the Family Law Act 1996, s 33(5) extending B's home rights, should have regard to the interests of A's successors in title. They in turn may apply to court to restrict or terminate B's rights.[233]

6.70 In the event of A's bankruptcy, B's rights bind A's trustee but he can apply under s 33 to restrict or terminate them. In the first year after the

---

[224] Ibid, s 30(2).
[225] Ibid, s 30(3).
[226] Ibid, s 30(4).
[227] Ibid, ss 30(8), 31(8).
[228] Ibid, s 33(5), (8).
[229] Ibid, s 33(1)(a), (3). The court must have regard to the factors in s 33(6). See, however, the restriction in s 33(7) as to the exercise of this discretion in certain circumstances.
[230] Ibid, s 33(10).
[231] Ie not if A's rights are merely contractual or statutory.
[232] Family Law Act 1996, s 31(2), (3).
[233] Ibid, s 34(2).

bankruptcy the court has a general discretion[234] but thereafter the interests of A's creditors ought to prevail absent exceptional circumstances.[235]

---

[234] Insolvency Act 1986, s 336(4).
[235] Ibid, s 336(5).

Chapter 7

USER LICENCES

Introduction	7.1
User licences and easements/profits	7.3
General	7.3
Licences and the ouster principle	7.6
Types of user rights	7.11
Access	7.11
Limited activities	7.12
Rights to place/erect something on the land	7.13
Licences to remove things from land	7.16

INTRODUCTION

7.1 'User licences', as a type, typically (a) grant a mere right of entry, (b) permit some limited activity on the land, (c) authorise the placing, erection or retention of some chattel or structure on the land or (d) allow the removal of something from it. The first three can take the form of bare, contractual or estoppel licences; the fourth is, classically, a licence coupled with an interest.

7.2 Such rights do not generally amount to occupation (eg for the purposes of the Occupiers' Liability Acts 1957 and 1984), a fortiori possession, either because they are too ephemeral or limited in scope and/or because the licensor retains general control of the land. However, the distinction between mere use and occupation is one of degree and even user licences may involve some element of exclusivity, eg:

(1) to undertake a particular activity on the land (eg an exclusive concession);

(2) to use a particular area that is not physically divided from the remainder of the licensor's land and therefore not capable of separate occupation/control (eg theatre seats, pipes, cables etc); or

(3) for the duration of the period the right is in fact exercised (eg a shared bathroom).

USER LICENCES AND EASEMENTS/PROFITS

General

7.3 Whereas occupation rights may be either leases or licences, the critical distinction in relation to arrangements involving the mere use of land is between licences and easements/profits (although licences can ripen into easements/profits under the Law of Property Act 1925, s 62 if the licensee subsequently acquires an interest in the land to which the right is ancillary and both the benefited and burdened land have a common owner[1]). This distinction is of principal importance in determining whether the rights are capable of binding the grantor's successors in title: easements/profits are (subject, if necessary, to registration); licences generally are not (see Chapter 9).

7.4 User rights that are, in substance, incapable of existing as an easement/profit (see **3.24**) may take effect as licences. For example, rights:

- not held for an interest equivalent to a fee simple absolute or term of years[2] (eg 'until I require the land back');

- that do not accommodate the licensee's land, if any[3] – an easement cannot exist in gross;[4]

- that are not capable of being the subject matter of a grant, eg whose exercise is subject to the exigencies of the owner's business and others' use of the land;[5]

- (possibly) of mere recreation and amusement unconnected with any land owned by the grantee;[6]

- which impose some corresponding positive obligation on the landowner (eg a right to use a swimming pool);[7] or

- that fall foul of the ouster principle (below).

However, a right that is in substance capable of existing as an easement/profit but which is not granted for an interest in fee simple or term of years absolute will not be held to create a valid licence if it was intended to take effect as an easement or profit.[8] Nevertheless the lack of a sufficiently certain term may be

---

[1] See eg *Hair v Gillman* [2000] 3 EGLR 74 and below at **9.34**.
[2] Law of Property Act 1925, s 1(2).
[3] Unless the right is capable of existing as a profit in gross.
[4] *London & Blenheim Estates Ltd v Ladbroke Retail Parks Ltd* [1994] 1 WLR 31, at 36H.
[5] *Green v Ashco Horticulturalists Ltd* [1966] 1 WLR 889, at 897–898.
[6] Cf *Re Ellenborough Park* [1956] Ch 131; *Jackson v Mulvaney* [2003] 1 WLR 360 (maintenance of garden).
[7] *Moncrieff v Jamieson* [2007] 1 WLR 2620, at [47].
[8] See by analogy *Lace v Chantler* [1944] KB 368; *Berrisford v Mexfield Housing Co-Operative Ltd* [2010] EWCA Civ 811 (leases).

a factor in favour of construing the agreement as a licence. However, an easement is not invalid merely because the instrument fails to specify properly the dominant[9] or servient tenement[10] if they are ascertainable by extrinsic evidence (although such omissions may also favour construing the agreement as a licence).

7.5 If both the substantive and formal requirements for an easement/profit are met, the right may still be a licence, on its proper construction, eg if the benefit/burden is expressed to be personal to the original parties or the form of grant ('grant licence') so indicates.[11]

Licences and the ouster principle

7.6 Rights that are too extensive to amount to easements by virtue of the 'ouster principle' may take effect as licences, if not freehold or leasehold interests. An easement cannot – but a licence can – give exclusive, unrestricted use of a piece of land.[12] In most cases rights that fall foul of the principle, because the owner is ousted from his enjoyment of the affected land, usually confer a right of exclusive occupation if not possession, ie not mere user. However, the difference is sometimes one of degree and since, moreover, the principle is encountered in relation to easements, to which user licences are the nearest equivalent, they are dealt with here rather than in the previous chapter. Examples of rights held to violate the principle include:

- the right to make an embankment on another's land to support a railway or tramway;[13]

- the right to maintain a layer of silt over land in order to undertake ship-breaking operations;[14]

- the right to use a flat roof as ancillary to a dwelling, the owner reserving merely rights of entry to repair;[15]

- an unlimited right to deposit and repair vehicles within a defined area.[16] However, differing results have been reached in relation to storage rights;[17] and

---

[9] *Gale on the Law of Easements* (Sweet & Maxwell, 18th edn, 2008), at paras 1-10–1-12.
[10] Ibid, at paras 1-21–1-22.
[11] *IDC Group Ltd v Clark* [1992] 2 EGLR 194.
[12] *Hanina v Morland* (unreported) 22 November 2000, CA, at [17]–[18]; *Reilly v Booth* (1890) 44 Ch D 12. See **2.36**.
[13] *Taff Vale Railway v Cardiff Railway* [1917] Ch 299.
[14] *Thomas W Ward Ltd v Alexander Bruce (Grays) Ltd* [1959] 2 Lloyds Rep 472.
[15] *Hanina v Morland* (unreported) 22 November 2000, CA, at [34].
[16] *Copeland v Greenhalf* [1952] Ch 488.
[17] Contrast *A-G of Southern Nigeria v John Holt & Co (Liverpool) Ltd* [1915] AC 599, at 617; *Wright v Macadam* [1949] 2 KB 744; and *Grigsby v Melville* [1972] 1 WLR 1355, at 1363F–1365A (obiter) (exclusive right of storage in cellar likely to fall foul of ouster principle).

- the exclusive right to park an unlimited number of vehicles during working hours on land.[18]

But whether, in any case, the right falls foul of the principle is a question of fact and sometimes degree[19] and authorities in relation to parking/storage rights may need to be reconsidered in light of recent dicta in the House of Lords (see **7.8**).

7.7 Of course the right to undertake *any* activity on another's land may, to some degree, prevent *an* ordinary use by the owner, particularly if the servient tenement is defined as the specific area of land over which the rights are actually enjoyed (eg the route of the way or the line of the pipes).[20] Something more is needed for the principle to apply. Earlier cases considered whether the right amounted to joint occupation[21] or the whole beneficial user of the land.[22] This approach concentrated principally on the extent of the grantee's rights rather than what the grantor retained, although even then account was taken of who had possession.[23] Other cases adopted a different test, namely whether the grantee's rights were so extensive as to deprive the grantor of any reasonable use of the land.[24] This formulation was adopted by the Court of Appeal in *Batchelor v Marlow*[25] and requires the identification of some specific, reasonable use that the grantor could make of the land contemporaneously with the grantee.[26]

7.8 That test, however, was recently disapproved (obiter) by Lord Scott in *Moncrieff v Jamieson*, who preferred a more restrictive formulation of the principle, namely whether the grantor was excluded from possession or control (not mere occupation) of the land in question.[27] However, whilst Lords Scott and Neuberger's judgments in *Moncrieff*[28] cast doubt on the reasoning in *Batchelor v Marlow*, for the present it remains binding,[29] at least below Supreme Court level.

---

[18] *Batchelor v Marlow* [2003] 1 WLR 764; *Central Midland Estates Ltd v Leicester Dyers Ltd* [2003] 2 P & CR DG1, at [31]–[32]. Contrast *Newman v Jones* (unreported, cited *Handel v St Stephens Close Ltd* [1994] 1 EGLR 70, at 72).

[19] *Hanina v Morland* (unreported) 22 November 2000, CA, at [17]; *Hair v Gillman* [2000] 3 EGLR 74, at 75G ('The authorities fall on one side or the other of an ill-defined line between rights in the nature of an easement and rights in the nature of an exclusive right to possess or use').

[20] *Moncrieff v Jamieson* [2007] 1 WLR 2620, at [54], [57], [59].

[21] *In re Ellenborough Park* [1955] 3 WLR 892, at 901.

[22] *Copeland v Greenhalf* [1952] Ch 488, at 498.

[23] Ibid.

[24] *London & Blenheim Estates Ltd v Ladbroke Retail Parks Ltd* [1992] 1 WLR 1278, at 1288. See for a more recent example *P&S Platt v Crouch* [2004] 1 P & CR 18 (right to moor boats, erect signs and fish a section of riverbank held not to deprive the owner of any reasonable user of the land).

[25] [2003] 1 WLR 764.

[26] *Polo Woods Foundation v Shelton-Agar* [2009] EWHC 1361 (Ch), at [124].

[27] [2007] 1 WLR 2620, at [59]–[60]. See also ibid, at [140], [143]–[144], [147], per Lord Neuberger.

[28] *Moncrieff v Jamieson* [2007] 1 WLR 2620, at [59], [139]. See also Hill-Smith 'Rights of Parking and the Ouster Principle after Batchelor v Marlow' [2007] Conv 223.

[29] *Polo Woods Foundation v Shelton-Agar* [2009] EWHC 1361 (Ch), at [121].

7.9 Even so, the argued residual user in *Batchelor* was weak[30] compared with that suggested in *Moncrieff*.[31] Possibly, therefore, on marginally different facts, such rights may satisfy even the *Batchelor* test and thus be capable of taking effect as easements rather than leases/freeholds or licences. The issue is most often encountered in relation to parking/storage rights but even in that context rights (a) to park a fewer number of cars or store a smaller number of chattels than the land has capacity for;[32] (b) whose exercise is limited to a shorter period of time than in *Batchelor*; or (c) (possibly) that is not exclusive (eg on a first-come basis) will not fall foul of the *Batchelor* formulation of the ouster principle.

7.10 The particular relevance in this context is as follows: the *Batchelor* test creates a potentially wide category of rights that are too extensive to be easements yet insufficiently extensive to amount to a leasehold/freehold grant (because the grantor retains possession/control, even though he has no reasonable use of the land) and which therefore take effect as licences. In contrast rights that fall foul of the *Moncrieff* formulation because they confer possession on the grantee will generally not take effect as licences (unless granted for an indefinite term, since no other relevant exception to the rule in *Street v Mountford*[33] is likely to apply) but rather as freehold or leasehold grants. The scope for agreements to take effect as licences by virtue of the *Moncrieff* formulation of the ouster principle is significantly narrower.

TYPES OF USER RIGHTS

Access

7.11 The simplest form of licence entitles the licensee to enter or cross the licensor's land (eg a dinner invitation, permission to retrieve a ball or to drive though a field). Such rights are highly circumscribed: the licensee prima facie cannot place anything on or remove anything from the land or alter it so as to make it more convenient for his use[34] unless expressly agreed or necessarily implied. Nevertheless he will be owed the common duty of care under the Occupiers' Liability Act 1957 (see Chapter 11) and a contractual licensee may also be owed duties in relation to the condition and suitability of the land for those purposes (see Chapter 8). Such rights prima facie are not exclusive but

---

[30] [2003] 1 WLR 764, at [16]–[17].
[31] [2007] 1 WLR 2620, at [59].
[32] See eg *Newman v Jones* (unreported, cited *Handel v St Stephens Close Ltd* [1994] 1 EGLR 70, at 72); *London & Blenheim Estates Ltd v Ladbroke Retail Parks Ltd* [1992] 1 WLR 1278, at 1288C. An exclusive right to park in a single parking bay would appear to fall foul of the ouster principle applying *Batchelor v Marlow*, but the position is open to doubt: *Moncrieff v Jamieson* [2007] 1 WLR 2620, at [145].
[33] [1985] AC 809.
[34] Contrast the rights of the dominant owner: *Gale on the Law of Easements*, n 9 above, at para 1-91.

the licensor may be contractually obliged to regulate the behaviour of other licensees insofar as they may prevent or hinder the licensee in exercising his rights (see Chapter 8).

Limited activities

7.12 It is difficult to imagine any right to do some positive act on someone else's land that cannot, by the use of appropriate language, take the form of a licence. By way of example:

- Recreational activities, such as the right to watch plays, sporting and other events (eg a season ticket or ticket for a single event) are (usually contractual) licences.[35] For example, in *Krell v Henry*[36] the right to use rooms for a day to watch the Coronation was held to be a contractual licence, capable of frustration by the event's postponement.

- Rights to survey, measure and undertake tests to the land.[37]

- Rights to operate pleasure boats on a river.[38]

- Rights to pass or discharge materials through/on the licensor's land.

- Rights of members of an unincorporated association to use land held for the association's purposes. The rights of the members inter se are contractual. The right to use the association's facilities is by way of licence, subject (usually) to regulation by the association's rules or by committee authorised by the constitution. Such licence terminates automatically on cessation of membership.

Such rights are prima facie not exclusive unless that is expressly agreed or necessarily implied, eg from the nature of the activities or the physical characteristics of the land.

Rights to place/erect something on the land

Parking/storage rights

7.13 Arrangements between two parties whereby A's chattels are to be kept on B's land may take the form of a licence, lease,[39] easement[40] or, occasionally, bailment:

---

[35] *Winter Garden Theatre (London) Ltd v Millennium Productions Ltd* [1948] AC 173, at 189. Although the sole right to use a theatre box is sometimes a term of a debenture and could theoretically take the form of a demise.
[36] [1903] 2 KB 740, at 750.
[37] *Countryside Residential Ltd v Persons Unknown* (2000) 81 P & CR 2.
[38] *Hill v Tupper* (1863) 2 H&C 121.
[39] See eg *Hilton v John Smith & Sons (Norwood) Ltd* [1979] 2 EGLR 44.
[40] *Moncrieff v Jamieson* [2007] 1 WLR 2620, at [47], [75], [137].

(1) To take effect as a lease the grantee must have exclusive possession of a defined area[41] for a term. However, the grant of an exclusive, unlimited right of storage does not *necessarily* confer possession according to *Moncrieff v Jamieson*.[42] Something more may be needed, such as the right to control access (eg a lock-up garage or storage unit).

(2) Parking/storage rights typically throw up two issues in the context of easements: the ouster principle (above) and the absence of a dominant tenement which the right accommodates. The grantee must own land in the vicinity that is capable of being benefited by the right if it is to take effect as an easement.[43] Even so, rights to park in a public car park or to store goods in a commercial storage facility are not acquired by the grantee in his capacity as owner of dominant land[44] and thus (quite apart from the typical form and terms of such agreements) do not take effect as easements but as contractual licences.[45]

(3) A licence to store goods entitles the owner to leave them on another's land; a bailment, in contrast, passes custody of the goods to the recipient and may only incidentally involve the use of land. The practical importance of the distinction lies in the different duties owed in relation to the safety and security of the goods[46] and whether the recipient may enforce against them for unpaid fees.

A licensor who retains possession of the land does not necessarily have possession or custody of goods on it. The distinction – which is most frequently encountered in relation to parking/storage rights – therefore depends on the parties' respective control of the goods whilst present on the land. All the circumstances of the case are to be considered, eg whether the car owner/land owner has keys for the vehicle; who may decide where the goods are stored on the land; their respective rights (if any) to move the goods from place to place on the land; whether the goods owner has (un)restricted access to them and/or the right to remove them without notice; whether the landowner provides security for (or has operational control over) the site; and even the physical layout of the storage facility and the level of fees charged. Thus (eg) in *Southampton Cargo Handling Ltd v Lotus Cars Ltd*[47] a landowner was held to be a bailee, having operated secure, guarded commercial storage facilities, access to which by the vehicle owners was restricted to certain hours of operation.

Nevertheless normal arrangements to park a vehicle in commercial car parks have been fairly consistently held to be licences, not bailments

---

[41] See *Simpson v Fergus* (2000) 79 P & CR 398 where this requirement was not met.
[42] [2007] 1 WLR 2620, at [55]. See also *Harley Queen v Forsyte Kerman* [1983] CLY 2077. An owner who, under the *Batchelor v Marlow* formulation of the objective principle, is deprived of any reasonable use of the land may nevertheless remain in possession.
[43] *LeStrange v Pettefar* (1939) 161 LT 300.
[44] Ibid.
[45] See eg *Ashby v Tolhurst* [1937] 2 KB 242, at 249.
[46] See as to the licensor's duties **8.43–8.44**.
[47] [2008] 2 Lloyd's Rep 532.

(although a bailment may occur when the landowner has keys for the vehicle, eg valet parking).[48] Similarly a right to station a caravan on a holiday park will usually be a licence rather than a bailment, unless access to it is restricted to certain periods of time, in which case the land owner may be a bailee of the caravans during the other periods.[49] So too, the right to use a self-contained area in commercial self-storage facilities, access to which is controlled by the goods owner, may be a licence (or lease) but is unlikely to amount to a bailment.

Licences to place structures on land

7.14 Rights to place, erect or use structures on/in another's land (eg scaffolding, mobile phone masts, conducting media etc) may take the form of easements (eg of support, for the passage of water etc if the grantee has land in the vicinity which the rights accommodate), licences[50] or leases if, exceptionally, the grantee has possession of the land where they are sited.[51] Certain undertakers have statutory powers to acquire similar rights in furtherance of their statutory duties – see **3.35–3.36**.

7.15 Ownership of the structure may remain vested in the licensee or pass to the landowner under the principle *quicquid plantatur solo solo cedit* – see **13.11**. In the former case the licensee is entitled and obliged to remove them at the end of the licence term; in the latter case he is not unless, in either case, the licence terms provide otherwise (see Chapter 13). Ancillary rights of access for maintenance, repair and renewal during the licence term will be implied, if not expressly granted.

Licences to remove things from land

7.16 A right to extract/sever and remove something in, on or which is part of another's land may take effect as a licence coupled with an interest (ie profit) or an easement – depending on the application of the criteria in **3.24** and **7.4–7.5** above – or a mere licence.

7.17 The right may be a profit if it is to remove (a) something from the land (eg unsevered minerals, growing crops etc) or (b) wild animals on it (eg fish, game), which (in either case) are capable of ownership separately from the land itself by being worked/reduced into possession, as distinct from something immediately capable of independent ownership, eg cut crops/timber, severed

---

[48] See eg *Ashby v Tolhurst* [1937] 2 KB 242; *Tinsley v Dudley* [1951] 2 KB 18, at 26; *The Rigoletto* [2000] 2 Lloyd's Rep 532. But contrast *Mendelsohn v Normand* [1970] 1 QB 177 (bailment).
[49] Eg *Halbauer v Brighton Corpn* [1954] 1 WLR 1161, at 1165–1166 (undercover winter storage; vehicle owner prohibited from visiting without prior permission).
[50] *Wilson v Tavener* [1901] 1 Ch 578; *King v David Allen & Sons Billposting* [1916] 2 AC 54; *Wallshire v Advertising Sites* [1988] 2 EGLR 167. See also *London Development Agency v Nidai* [2009] EWHC 1730 (Ch), at [49]–[51]. A right to pass materials through media may be a licence; a right merely to receive a flow is not.
[51] See eg *Taylor v Pendleton Overseers* (1887) 19 QBD 288 and the reference in *Clear Channel UK Ltd v Manchester City Council* [2006] 1 EGLR 27, at [4].

minerals or wild animals already reduced to ownership by possession (all of which may be chattel interests). Both types of interest are capable of comprising the 'interest' element of a licence coupled with an interest – see **2.23**. The right may be an easement if it cannot be a profit because the thing the grantee is entitled to extract is incapable of separate ownership in that form (eg a right to take water from a flowing river), not having been already appropriated by the land owner (eg by containment in a pond or tank).

7.18 A right to remove something from the land is a licence if it fails to meet the substantive requirements for the creation of an easement or profit[52] or is expressed to be personal to the parties or is otherwise intended to take effect as such.

---

[52] See **3.24(1)–(5)** and the text accompanying n 8 above. Note that certain profits may exist in gross, ie without the need for a dominant tenement.

Chapter 8

THE LICENCE TERMS

Bare licences	8.1
Contractual licences	8.4
Ascertaining the terms	8.5
Particular terms	8.13
The licensor's obligations	8.25
The licensee's obligations	8.45
Statutory control of terms	8.50
Estoppel licences	8.60
The basic equitable right	8.61
The relief	8.63
Licences coupled with an interest	8.64

BARE LICENCES

8.1 A bare licence confers immunity to a claim in trespass but does not except in that limited sense confer on the licensee 'rights' in relation to the land.[1] Nevertheless its creation may give rise to statutory or common-law rights and duties between the parties (see Chapter 11) and if the licensee is forcibly evicted before being given a reasonable time to vacate the licensor commits a trespass to his person and/or goods.

8.2 A licence granted on terms that the licensee is to act/refrain from acting in a particular manner may be a contractual licence, the licensee providing consideration by observing (or promising to observe) those terms. In contrast, a bare licence may be granted on terms which are not promissory obligations but are merely conditions of the licence and/or define its scope.[2] In such case a

---

[1] *Goldsack v Shore* [1950] 1 KB 708, at 714 ('if the nature of the privilege given is a mere licence unsupported by consideration, it cannot strictly be stated that any "right" to occupy land has been conferred at all'); *Bolch v Smith* (1862) 7 Hurl & N 736, at 745–746 ('Permission involves leave and licence but it gives no right. If I avail myself of permission to cross a man's land I do so by virtue of a licence, not as of right. It is an abuse of language to call it a right; it is an excuse or licence, so that the party cannot be treated as a trespasser').

[2] *Wilkie v LPTB* [1947] 1 All ER 258, at 260: 'It is the mere grant of a revocable licence subject to a condition that while the licence is being enjoyed, certain consequences should follow. That is not contractual but a term or condition of the licence and if anyone makes use of the licence he can only do so by being bound by that condition.' See **2.12**.

licensee's failure to observe them renders him a trespasser and potentially liable to a claim in restitution or damages for use and occupation.[3]

8.3 The terms of the bare licence depend on the parties' intentions. The manner in which such intentions are ascertained is akin to the process of contractual interpretation (below). It is thought terms may be implied, at least those which represent the parties' obvious, but unexpressed, intentions. Certain terms, however, are common to all bare licences:

(1) First, a bare licence is, by definition, terminable by either party at any time, even if purportedly granted for a longer period, and may automatically determine on the occurrence of certain events (eg death or the sale of the land) subject to the licensee having a grace period in which to quit/cease using the land – see **12.52** et seq.

(2) Second, as a bare licence is in its nature a personal permission to the licensee, it cannot be assigned nor may the licensee allow others to enjoy its benefit – a permission to A, logically, cannot justify B's presence on the land.

(3) However, the licence may, properly construed, extend to others or authorise the licensee to allow others onto the land on the licensor's behalf. Neither is a true exception to the above rule; in both cases the licensor is the true invitor.

CONTRACTUAL LICENCES

8.4 A licence supported by consideration entered into by parties who are ad idem and intend to enter into legal relations confers a contractual right on the licensee to use the land, unless affected by some vitiating factor (eg fraud, duress, misrepresentation, mistake, unconscionable bargain, undue influence etc). No formalities are required for its creation as it is not an interest in land (see Chapter 9).

Ascertaining the terms

8.5 The rules governing the interpretation of contractual licences are those for contracts generally and for that reason are taken shortly.

Incorporation of terms

8.6 The question occasionally arises whether a term not expressly agreed nor arising by implication, custom or prior course of dealings between the parties

---

[3] See, however, *Harvey v Plymouth CC* [2010] EWCA Civ 860, at [22] for the tentative suggestion that not every act beyond the scope of the licence automatically renders the licensee a non-'visitor' for the purposes of the Occupiers' Liability Act 1957.

has been incorporated into the licence (e g standard conditions referred to on a parking ticket or set out on a notice at the entrance to the land). If it is, the term binds even though it has not in fact come to the licensee's attention. To do so, however, the ticket, notice etc must be of a type the licensee subjectively knows contains/refers to contract terms or the objective reasonable observer would expect it to do so.[4] If the licensee was aware that it contains writing and the licensor has done what was reasonably sufficient to give him notice of the conditions, they will be incorporated.[5] Whether the licensor has done so is a question of fact: the more unusual/onerous the term, the greater the onus on him to take reasonable steps to bring them to the licensee's attention.[6] Incorporation is to be judged in light of the acts/circumstances existing at the time the licence was created,[7] although exceptionally if the licensee subsequently becomes aware of the unincorporated 'terms' and that the licensor intended them to bind yet fails to object he may be estopped from denying their incorporation or they may be incorporated by implied variation.

Construction of terms

8.7 The meaning and effect of the licence terms are determined by the process of contractual construction.[8] The purpose of construction is to ascertain the parties' (objective) common intentions. That process may involve determining the meaning of particular terms or the broader task of ascertaining, in light of those terms and the context in which the licence was created, their common intentions.[9]

8.8 The question in both cases is: what would a reasonable person, with the background knowledge reasonably available to the parties at the time of the contract, have understood them to be using the language in the licence to mean?[10] The parties' subjective belief or understanding as to their meaning is irrelevant, at least in relation to written licences[11] (although if one party's belief is known to/shared by the other it may form the basis of an estoppel, e g by convention). Whilst the meaning of a written licence is to be ascertained from the document itself, the court may also look, at least in cases of uncertainty, at the background and context (the factual matrix) surrounding its creation.[12] That includes anything that would have affected the way in which the language

---

[4] Compare *Parker v South Eastern Ry* (1877) 2 CPD 416 (bailment: railway luggage office ticket); *Thornton v Shoe Lane Parking Ltd* [1971] 2 QB 163 (personal injury: exemption clause in parking ticket).
[5] *Chitty on Contracts* (Sweet & Maxwell, 30th edn, 2008), at para 12-013.
[6] *J Spurling Ltd v Bradshaw* [1956] 1 WLR 461.
[7] See *Olley v Marlborough Court Ltd* [1949] 1 KB 532 (personal injury to hotel guest: notice terms in hotel room not incorporated; contract entered into when register signed).
[8] For a comprehensive treatment, see *Chitty on Contracts*, n 5 above, at paras 12-041–12-094.
[9] *Staffordshire AHA v South Staffordshire Waterworks Co* [1978] 1 WLR 1387, at 1399H, citing with approval from the judgment of Buckley J in *Re Spenborough UDC's Agreement* [1968] Ch 139.
[10] *Investors Compensation Scheme Ltd v West Bromwich BS* [1998] 1 WLR 896, at 912H–913F.
[11] See, however, *Carmichael v National Power* [1999] 1 WLR 2042, at 2050H–2051A and *Thorner v Major* [2009] 3 All ER 945, at [82] in relation to oral contracts.
[12] See e g *Cartwright v Merthyr Tydfil BC* (unreported), CA, 22 May 2000, at [12]–[14] (physical

used in the licence would have been understood by a reasonable man.[13] Although evidence of pre-contract negotiations, including what was said or done during them, may not be used as a construction aid[14] it may be used to establish that a fact, which may be relevant as background, was known to the parties.[15] Background material may also help to conclude that the syntax/words used were wrong; in such case, where it is clear both that the licence contains a mistake and what a reasonable person would have understood the parties to have meant, the court may correct the mistake as a matter of construction.[16] Where that is not possible, equitable rectification[17] may apply, as it does to contracts generally.

Express terms

8.9 Except where controlled by statute (below) the parties are free to agree such terms as they think fit. The traditional classification of contract terms (conditions, warranties and intermediate terms)[18] and the remedies available to enforce them apply to contractual licences. So too contractual principles of waiver, election and estoppel: e g one party to the licence may elect to treat the other's breach of condition as a breach of warranty by affirming the licence, in which case both remain liable to observe its terms, subject to the innocent party's right to claim damages.[19]

Implied terms

8.10 Traditionally, terms have been implied where necessary on grounds of business efficacy[20] or because they reflect the parties' obvious, but unexpressed, intentions.[21] Where (e g) a mechanism necessary to make the licence workable is unintentionally omitted, such term may be implied.[22]

8.11 More recently, however, the Privy Council has made clear that the purpose of implication is to spell out the meaning of an agreement so that the fundamental question (which the traditional bases are but ways of expressing) is whether the implied term would make clear expressly what the agreement

---

extent of a street trading licence ascertained by reference to surrounding facts); *Lymington Marina Ltd v Macnamara* [2007] EWHC 704 (Ch), at [62] (on appeal [2007] EWCA Civ 151).
[13] *Investors Compensation Scheme Ltd v West Bromwich BS* [1998] 1 WLR 896.
[14] *Chartbrook Ltd Persimmon Homes Ltd* [2009] 4 All ER 677, at [42].
[15] Ibid.
[16] Ibid, at [21]–[24].
[17] For the relevant principles, see *Swainland Builders Ltd v Freehold Properties Ltd* [2002] 2 EGLR 71, at [33]; *Chartbrook Ltd Persimmon Homes Ltd* [2009] 4 All ER 677, at [48].
[18] *Chitty on Contracts*, n 5 above, at paras 12-019–12-040.
[19] *Dudley Port Warehousing Co Ltd v Gardner Transport & Distribution Ltd* [1995] EGCS 5 (licensor's failure to undertake works in breach; licensee who elected to affirm by continuing to occupy the premises remained liable for licence fee).
[20] See e g *Liverpool City Council v Irwin* [1977] AC 239.
[21] *Lymington Marina Ltd v Macnamara* [2007] 2 All ER (Comm) 825, at [37]. See to the same effect *Rickman v Brudenell-Bruce* [2005] EWHC 3400 (Ch), at [20].
[22] See e g *Donington Park Leisure Ltd v Wheatcroft & Sons Ltd* [2006] All ER (D) 94 (Apr), at [38].

would reasonably be understood to mean, read against the relevant background.[23] Nevertheless a mere common assumption (eg that premises are sound) is not enough to warrant implying a warranty (usually by the licensor) to that effect:[24] that is only appropriate if it is proper to infer that he assumed responsibility for its condition. Given the fundamental differences between leases and licences, authorities as to the terms implied in the former are of uncertain application here.[25]

8.12 Where the *licence itself* is said to be an implied term of a wider contract both its existence and terms are determined by application of the above principles. Such an implication has recently been justified under the doctrine against derogation from grant,[26] although the decision is controversial.[27]

Particular terms

Scope of the licence

8.13 In the classic words of Vaughan CJ a licence 'makes an action lawful which without it had been unlawful'.[28] That in turn depends on the scope of the licence – eg the area of land concerned[29] and the nature of the permitted activities[30] – which are questions of construction. See **5.5** et seq. For example:

- a licence to use/occupy certain land may impliedly include the right to use the licensor's other land/facilities if necessary in order to enjoy the rights granted (eg for access);[31]

- a permission to carry out works on the licensee's own land[32] may impliedly include the right to use the licensor's land to erect scaffolding necessary to undertake those works;[33] and

---

[23] *A-G of Belize v Belize Telecom Ltd* [2009] 2 All ER 1127, at [15]–[27].
[24] *Morris Thomas v Petticoat Lane Rentals* (1986) 53 P & CR 238.
[25] See eg *Graham v Northern Ireland Housing Executive* (1986) 8 NIJB 93, which refused to extend to licensors the landlord's common-law immunity in relation to the state and condition of the premises established in *Cavalier v Pope* [1906] AC 428.
[26] *Donington Park Leisure Ltd v Wheatcroft & Sons Ltd* [2006] All ER (D) 94 (Apr).
[27] See Dixon (2006) 70 Conv 374.
[28] *Thomas v Sorrell* (1673) Vaugh 330, at 351.
[29] See eg *Cartwright v Merthyr Tydfil BC* (unreported), CA, 22 May 2000. The onus may be on the licensor to make the limitations of the licence clear; if he does not, and the licensee acts in a way reasonably believing he is entitled to do so, he may not be a trespasser. See eg *Pearson v Coleman Bros* [1948] 2 KB 359 (child injured at circus by unwittingly entering a restricted area).
[30] *Gould v McAuliffe* [1941] 2 All ER 527; *The Carlgarth* [1927] P 93, at 110 ('When you invite a person into your house to use the staircase, you do not invite him to slide down the banisters, you invite him to use the staircase in the ordinary way in which it is used').
[31] See for an example *Donington Park Leisure Ltd v Wheatcroft & Sons Ltd* [2006] All ER (D) 94 (Apr).
[32] Eg where the licensee's land is bound by a restrictive covenant or the parties also stand in the relationship of lessor–lessee.
[33] See eg *Europa 2000 Ltd v Keles* [2005] EWCA Civ 1748, at [31].

- it is thought, by analogy with easements, that a licence to use a driveway, track or road will not of itself include a right to park, although a right to stop temporarily to (un)load may be implied if the way does not permit the licensee to drive directly onto the land intended to be accessed.[34]

Rights taking effect as licences are not limited to those which permit personal entry by the licensee. For example, a right to project something over the licensor's land (eg overhanging eaves) or to pass something through it (eg water[35]) or to discharge something on it (eg foul water) may take effect as a licence (or an easement).

8.14 The issue sometimes arises as to the parties' respective rights in relation to things found by the licensee on/in the land (eg treasure, jewellery) of which the parties were unaware when the licence was granted and which are not the subject of the licence. In such cases, a licensor in possession has a superior right to things attached to the land, unless the licence grants the licensee the right to remove them. Such right will only exceptionally be implied.[36] Where an express right to dig is given, it is a question of construction whether that includes the right to carry away and, if so, to what things/materials it applies.[37] In contrast a licensee with a general right of entry may be entitled to things found on (not in) the land unless the licensor makes clear, expressly or impliedly, his intention to control the land and anything on it.[38]

Exclusivity

8.15 There is no presumption that a licence is exclusive; if anything, the presumption is that it is not.[39] Exclusivity may, of course, be expressly agreed[40] (although such a term must be scrutinised closely[41]) and may sometimes be implied (eg hire of a single room).

8.16 An exclusive licence entitles the licensee to prevent the licensor using or granting others the right to use the land for the same purposes.[42] It will not, however, give the licensee standing directly to prevent others using the land

---

[34] See by analogy *Bulstrode v Lambert* [1953] 1 WLR 1064; *Handel v St Stephens Close Ltd* [1994] 1 EGLR 70, at 71G (easements).
[35] Query whether the passage of an electrical charge over another's land involves any 'entry' so as to be capable of taking effect as a licence.
[36] See eg *Waverley BC v Fletcher* [1995] 4 All ER 756.
[37] See eg *Elwes v Brigg Gas Co* (1886) 33 ChD 562, at 568–569 (ancient vessel).
[38] *Waverley BC v Fletcher* [1995] 4 All ER 756, at 758–759.
[39] See by analogy *Duke of Sutherland v Heathcote* [1892] 1 Ch 475, at 485, per Lindley LJ ('An exclusive right ... can no doubt be granted but such a right cannot be inferred from language which is not clear and explicit') (profit à prendre).
[40] See eg *Altman v Royal Aquarium Society* (1876) 3 Ch D 228: licensor gave licensee 'the sole right of exhibiting [in an exhibition hall] and selling' a certain type of goods.
[41] *Reid-Newfoundland Co v Anglo-American Telegraph Co* [1910] AC 560: an 'exclusive right ... to build ... and operate as many lines of telegraph for the purposes of the business of the telegraph company as [it] may deem necessary' held not to prevent the licensor operating his own telegraph lines.
[42] It may of course be exclusive as to only one or the other only, not both.

unless he has a right of exclusive possession or sole occupation conferring control[43] or the circumstances in which the other licensees acquired their rights amount to a tort (eg conspiracy or tortious interference/inducement) by them against him.[44] If the licensee has exclusive user rights (but not sole occupation or possession), he may restrain the licensor from using or granting others the right to use the land in competition with him or in a way that unreasonably interferes with his rights. However, he cannot restrain other licensees using the land in that manner unless they personally committed a tort, eg by acquiring their rights knowingly in breach of his contract. If the licence is not exclusive the licensor may of course use the land or allow others to use it at the same time and/or for the same purposes as the licensee,[45] although some limitations may be implied on that right, eg to prevent unreasonable interference with the licensee's rights. Where the licensee cannot himself sue in trespass the licensor may be under a duty to take reasonable steps to restrain third parties whose acts unreasonably interfere with the licensee's rights.[46]

Assignment and sub-licences

8.17 These are considered in Chapter 10.

Termination

Right to terminate

8.18 A licence (unlike a lease, but like a profit/easement) may be granted in perpetuity.[47] The vast majority of licences, however, are either for a fixed, periodic or indefinite term but (in the latter case) impliedly determinable. Where the licence contains an express provision as to termination, the question is one of its construction.[48] The licence may be terminable generally or on the occurrence of a particular event[49] and, in the latter case, termination may occur automatically (eg service occupancies on the termination of employment[50]) or at one or both party's election (eg an informal licence granted during a relationship).[51] For instance, it is a question of construction whether a licence granted to a prospective purchaser to enter land in anticipation of exchanging contracts for the acquisition of an interest in it terminates automatically on the failure of negotiations or only once notice of election to terminate is given.[52]

---

[43] *Manchester Airport plc v Dutton* [2000] 1 QB 133.
[44] See (by analogy) *Crestfort Ltd v Tesco Stores Ltd* [2005] 3 EGLR 25; Chapter 9.
[45] *Carr v Benson* (1868) 3 Ch App 524, at 532; *Thorpe v Brumfitt* (1873) 8 Ch App 650.
[46] *Cartwright v Merthyr Tydfil BC* (unreported), CA, 22 May 2000.
[47] See eg *Llanelly Ry & Dock Co v London & North Western Ry Co* (1874–5) LR 7 HL 550.
[48] *Winter Garden Theatres (London) Ltd v Millennium Productions Ltd* [1948] AC 173, at 204.
[49] *Sandhu v Farooqui* [2004] 1 P & CR 19, at [20].
[50] *Norris v Checksfield* [1991] 4 All ER 327, at 333c.
[51] See eg *Hardwick v Johnson* [1978] 1 WLR 683, at 689F–689H, 692F.
[52] Compare *BANES v Nicholson* [2002] All ER (D) 327; *Sandhu v Farooqui* [2004] 1 P & CR 19, at [20].

The duration of the licence is a 'core term' for the purpose of the Unfair Terms in Consumer Contracts Regulations 1999,[53] reg 6(2).[54]

8.19 If the licence contains no express term as to whether/how it is terminable, the first question is whether or not it is irrevocable. Occasionally the view has been propounded that a contract that was not expressed to be terminable was rebuttably presumed to be permanent.[55] The modern rule, however, is that there is no general *presumption* for or against revocability.[56] Nevertheless where the licence is silent, the onus is on the party asserting it is terminable:[57] 'An agreement which is silent about determination will not be determinable unless the facts of the case, such as the subject matter of the agreement the nature of the contract or the circumstances in which the agreement was made, support a finding that the parties intended it to be determinable ...'[58] The burden, however, is not high.[59] Indeed only rarely will a contractual licence be held to be irrevocable. Ultimately the question is one of construction[60] or intention.[61] Hence in the *Winter Gardens* case a licence to use a theatre which gave the licensee the power to extend the period but contained no express power for the licensor to terminate was held to be impliedly terminable by him on reasonable notice.[62] So too indefinite licences to discharge waste at fixed rates were held to be impliedly terminable by the licensor in *Beverley Corpn v Richard Hodgson & Sons Ltd*[63] and *Re Spenborough UDC's Agreement*.[64]

8.20 By way of further example:

- A licence is very likely terminable if no term is specified but it reserves a periodic licence fee.[65]

---

[53] SI 1999/2083.
[54] *Baybut v Eccle Riggs Country Park Ltd* [2006] All ER (D) 161 (Nov), at [23].
[55] *Llanelly Ry & Dock Co v London & North Western Ry Co* (1874–5) LR 7 HL 550; contrast *Winter Garden Theatres (London) Ltd v Millennium Productions Ltd* [1948] AC 173, at 195; *Staffordshire Area Health Authority v South Staffordshire Waterworks Co* [1978] 1 WLR 1387, at 1395H–1396B.
[56] *Re Spenborough UDC's Agreement* [1968] Ch 139, at 147E–147F.
[57] Ibid, at 147C–147D.
[58] Ibid, at 147D, 147F.
[59] *Australian Blue Metal Ltd v Hughes* [1963] AC 74, at 98: 'It is true that it does not require very much to induce a court to read into an agreement of a commercial character, either by construction or by implication, a provision that the arrangements between the parties, whatever they may be shall be terminable only upon reasonable notice.' Note, however, this concerned specifically whether the licence was terminable forthwith or on reasonable notice.
[60] See e g *Colcheseter & East Essex Co-op Ltd v Kelvedon Labour Club & Institute Ltd* [2003] EWCA Civ 1671, at [9], per Buxton LJ.
[61] *Staffordshire AHA v South Staffordshire Waterworks Co* [1978] 1 WLR 1387, at 1399H, per Goff LJ.
[62] *Winter Garden Theatres (London) Ltd v Millennium Productions Ltd* [1948] AC 173.
[63] (1972) 225 EG 799.
[64] [1968] Ch 139.
[65] Note, however, that the period of notice may not be the same as the period for which the licence fee is paid/calculated – see Chapter 12.

- A licence may be permanent if granted in consideration of a capital sum or equivalent[66] (eg transfer of land in return for a right to park). That may be so even if it also reserves a periodically payable fee.

- However, a one-off consideration may in fact be capitalised, advance payment of the licence fee over the intended (but unexpressed) contract term. Such term may be ascertained by comparing the licence fee and market rates for such a right.[67]

- If a one-off consideration is substantially below the market rate for a permanent right, the licence may be terminable, possibly subject to a minimum period of enjoyment.

- A licence that is expressed to be periodic is unlikely to be subject to an implied term that it last for a minimum number of periods.[68]

- A licence may not be terminable during the subsistence of some other relationship between the parties. For example, mutual licences given in connection with the grant of reciprocal fixed-term leases may not be terminable independently of those leases.[69] However, that is a question of construction, eg whether a non-owning partner's licence to use land for partnership purposes is terminable during the subsistence of the partnership[70] – see Chapter 6.

- If a licence is granted for a fixed term or is expressly terminable on certain specified events, a general right of termination at any time on reasonable notice is unlikely to be implied.[71]

- Commercial licences, particularly ones that contain no provision to adjust the licence fee for inflation/changes of circumstances, are likely to be impliedly terminable on reasonable notice.[72]

8.21 The parties may agree to suspend or vary their contractual right to terminate; such an agreement provides its own consideration as the new term is

---

[66] *Llanelly Ry & Dock Co v London & North Western Ry Co* (1874–5) LR 7 HL 550; *Skipton BS v Clayton* (1993) 66 P & CR 223 (sale of land at undervalue in return for right to occupy rent-free for life, albeit as tenant).

[67] Eg one-off payment of £1,200 for right to park; market rate £100 pm; likely inference one-year, fixed-term licence.

[68] *Baybut v Eccle Riggs Country Park Ltd* [2006] All ER (D) 161 (Nov), at [49].

[69] See eg *Colchester & East Sussex Co-op Ltd v Kelvedon Labour Club & Institute Ltd* [2003] EWCA Civ 1671.

[70] *Harrison-Broadley v Smith* [1964] 1 WLR 456.

[71] *Winter Garden Theatre (London) Ltd v Millennium Productions Ltd* [1948] AC 173; *Colchester BC v Smith* [1991] 2 All ER 29, at 51–52; *Jani-King (GB) Ltd v Pula Enterprises Ltd* [2007] EWHC 2433, at [60] et seq; *ServicePower Asia Pacific Pty Ltd v ServicePower Business Solutions Ltd* [2009] EWHC 179 (Ch), at [25]–[27]. See eg *Colchester and East Sussex Co-Operative Society Ltd v Kelvedon Labour Club* [2003] EWCA Civ 1671.

[72] *Beverley Corpn v Richard Hodgson & Sons Ltd* (1972) 225 EG 799; *Re Spenborough UDC's Agreement* [1968] Ch 139.

capable of benefiting either party. For instance, in *Endstaff Ltd v Anglo Overseas Group Properties Ltd*[73] where the parties to a monthly periodic licence agreed for the licensee to pay the fee in advance in return for a discount, the appropriate inference was their rights to terminate were suspended during the period covered by the advance payment; accordingly the licensee who quit early was not entitled to be reimbursed any part of it.

8.22 Of course principles of estoppel may also affect the parties' rights: a revocable licence may become irrevocable (at all or for a period) by virtue of a supervening equity if one party (usually the licensee) relied on the other's promise not to terminate the licence and as a result it would be inequitable for the other now to do so.[74]

Termination for breach

8.23 Contractual principles govern the right of termination for breach of the licence terms; the suggested implication, by analogy with leases, of a right to *forfeit* was described as 'novel' in *Donington Park Leisure Ltd v Wheatcroft & Sons Ltd*.[75] Accordingly a breach may entitle the innocent party to terminate the licence if: (a) it contains an express right to terminate in those circumstances; (b) the term broken is a condition or is an intermediate term and the breach is sufficiently serious; or (c) the breach amounts to a repudiation of the licence, which the innocent party accepts. Of course, he may instead elect to affirm and seek damages/specific enforcement of its terms, in which case the licence continues.[76]

Manner of termination

8.24 Chapter 12 considers how terminable licences may be brought to an end.

The licensor's obligations

Title

8.25 A form of estoppel in pais applies between the parties so as to prevent them from denying that they stand in the relationship of licensor–licensee.[77] The estoppel has two principal effects: it prevents the licensor from denying the licensee's rights under the licence[78] and the licensee from disputing his licensor's title to grant them.[79] It applies notwithstanding the licensor has no title to the

---

[73] [2008] EWCA Civ 243.
[74] See eg *Plimmer v Wellington Corp* (1883-84) 9 App Cas 699, at 714; *Ramsden v Dyson and Thornton* (1886) LR 1 HL 129.
[75] [2006] All ER (D) 94 (Apr), at [51].
[76] *Dudley Port Warehousing Co Ltd v Gardner Transport & Distribution Ltd* [1995] EGCS 5.
[77] *Terunnanse v Terunnanse* [1983] 1 All ER 651, at 654; *Sze To Chun Keung v Kung Kwok Wai David* [1997] 1 WLR 1232.
[78] *Cartwright v Merthyr Tydfil BC* (unreported), CA, 22 May 2000, at [21], per Hale LJ.
[79] See eg *Clark v Adie (No 2)* (1877) 2 App Cas 423; *Sze To Chun Keung v Kung Kwok Wai David* [1997] 1 WLR 1232, at 1235E–1235F.

land, even if the licensee is aware of that fact. If the licensor subsequently acquires sufficient title to grant the licence, the estoppel is fed.

8.26 It follows the licensee may not rely on that lack of title as a defence to an action on the licence (eg for possession or licence fee arrears) and the licensor may not prevent or interfere with the licensee's use of the land during the term on the basis that his grant was ineffective as against third parties. The estoppel applies during the licence term and subsequently in relation to rights/duties arising in that period.

8.27 It ceases to apply, however, if claim is made against the licensee by someone with a superior title in relation to his use of the land during the licence term.[80] Nor does it prevent him, whether during or after the end of the contract term, asserting that the licensor's (eg leasehold) title has come to an end,[81] although the better view would appear to be that if he first used/occupied the land by virtue of the licence, he must be (actually or constructively) evicted by a superior owner or cease to use the land before disputing the licensor's title.[82] Nor does the estoppel apply where the question of title arises between the parties not in the relationship of licensor–licensee but (say) as vendor–purchaser, eg where one party is allowed into occupation between exchange and completion as licensee.[83]

8.28 The estoppel binds (only) the parties and persons claiming under them. Thus an assignee of the licence takes the benefit of (and is bound by) the estoppel.[84] A sub-licensee is similarly bound in relation to the licensor's right to terminate/claim possession but not in relation to other claims, eg for distress.[85] But as a licensor's successor does not claim under him and the licence is not an interest in land the successor is not generally bound (see Chapter 9). If the licensor is himself bound by estoppel in relation to a third party (eg because he is himself a licensee), his licensee's position is the same as that of the sub-licensee considered above: he is bound by a third party's termination/claim to possession of the land but not other claims.

Quiet enjoyment, not to interfere etc

8.29 Although there are dicta that the covenant for quiet enjoyment is inconsistent with a licence,[86] it is though such a term may be implied if the licensee has a right to possession or possibly sole occupation. Hence in *Smith v*

---

[80] *Industrial Properties (Barton Hill) Ltd v Associated Electrical Industries Ltd* [1977] QB 580.
[81] See by analogy *Nat West Bank v Hart* [1983] QB 773.
[82] *Doe d Johnson v Baytup* (1835) 3 Ad & El 188.
[83] *Nesbitt v Mablethorpe UDC* [1917] 2 KB 568, at 579.
[84] See by analogy *Mackley v Nutting* [1949] 2 KB 55 (tenant by assignment).
[85] Compare *Doe d Knight v Smythe* (1815) 4 M&S 347 and *Doe d Johnson v Baytup* (1835) 3 Ad & El 188 (both ejectment); *Tadman v Henman* (1893) 2 QB 168, at 171 (licensee not bound by right to distrain as against his licensor). See, however, the criticism of the latter decision in relation to tenancies by estoppel in *Megarry & Wade: The Law of Real Property* (Sweet & Maxwell, 7th edn, 2008), at para 17-097, n 531.
[86] And therefore an express term to that effect is indicative that the agreement is a lease:

Nottinghamshire CC[87] the implied term was held to prevent the licensor disturbing its licensees' occupation of student bedsit accommodation by making excessive noise during exams.

8.30 The scope of a licensor's implied obligation is thought, similarly to a lessor's, to extend to the licensor's own acts and to the acts of those claiming under him (eg other licensees) which unreasonably interfere with the licensee's rights, but not persons with a superior title. But whereas a lessor is only liable for the *lawful* acts of those claiming under him a licensor's covenant may not be so limited, at least if it extends to licences that do not confer standing on the licensee to sue in trespass. In such case the licensor's obligation may include taking reasonable steps to prevent those persons unreasonably interfering with the licensee's exercise of his rights at least in relation to activities that take place on land which the licensor controls.[88] The covenant – where it exists – is likely to require the licensor to:

- make the land available to the licensee and not actively to prevent or hinder the exercise of his rights.[89] Where he is entitled to transfer the licensee to another area, the alternative site must be reasonably suitable and reasonably comparable to the original;[90] and

- ensure/take reasonable steps to ensure the land remains available to the licensee for the intended purposes,[91]

although such terms could be justified instead simply by applying ordinary principles of contractual interpretation/implication (see **8.10–8.11**). The relevant rules in the context of licences await enunciation by the courts.

8.31 The covenant is thought to be inapposite in relation to non-exclusive occupation licences and mere user licences. Nevertheless such a licensor will be under a similar implied obligation not to prevent/hinder the licensee's exercise of his rights and to make the land available for the licensee's use (although the content of the obligation may differ as between these licences and those considered at **8.29–8.30**). He is likely to be under a similar obligation to take reasonable steps to prevent third parties unreasonably interfering with the

---

Addiscombe Garden Estates v Crabbe [1958] 1 QB 513, at 529; see also *Shell-Mex and BP Ltd v Manchester Garages* [1971] 1 WLR 612, at 618.

[87] (1981) *The Times*, November 13.

[88] *Cartwright v Merthyr Tydfil BC* (unreported), CA, 22 May 2000, at [20]. Contrast *Chartered Trust Plc v Davies* (1997) 76 P & CR 396, at 409 (derogation from grant in lease). A lessor is generally not liable in negligence for damage deliberately caused by third parties in the absence of some special relationship or unless the injury to the lessee is the inevitable and foreseeable result of his act/failure to act: *King v Liverpool CC* [1986] 1 WLR 890. Nor does he impliedly covenant with one lessee to enforce the covenants of other lessees: *O'Leary v Islington LBC* (1983) 9 HLR 86.

[89] *Cartwright v Merthyr Tydfil BC* (unreported), CA, 22 May 2000, at [18]; see also (by analogy) *Euston Centre Properties v H&J Wilson* [1982] 1 EGLR 57, at 58.

[90] See by analogy *Dresden Estates v Collinson* (1987) 55 P & CR 47, at 54 (lease).

[91] Eg *Cartwright v Merthyr Tydfil BC* (unreported), CA, 22 May 2000, at [20], [29].

licensee. Given the number of possible variables and the current paucity of authority, no general principles can be formulated; each case turns on its facts.

8.32 In relation to both categories of licences the licensor will be impliedly obliged:

- not to purport to revoke it otherwise than in accordance with its terms;[92] and

- not of his own motion to take steps that prevent the licensee exercising his rights over the land under the rule in *Stirling v Maitland*,[93] eg by assigning the land to a third party who takes free of the licence (see Chapter 9).

Non-derogation from grant

8.33 It has been doubted whether the doctrine can apply in this context or is limited to proprietary interests.[94] It was applied to what was described as a licence coupled with an interest in *Donington Park Leisure Ltd v Wheatcroft & Sons Ltd*,[95] although the decision has been criticised and that categorisation is itself doubtful, as the licence was merely a term of a lease.[96]

8.34 In reality often much of the substance of the obligation can be read in to licences applying standard principles of contractual implication/interpretation.[97] Account will be taken of the nature and extent of the licence, its terms[98] and the circumstances known to the parties when it was created.[99] For instance, the licensee may be entitled to use the licensor's other land for such purposes as are necessary to enjoy his rights, and the licensor may be prohibited from engaging in conduct inconsistent with the purposes for which the licence was granted or rendering the land in question materially less fit for those purposes. It will not, however, prohibit the licensor from granting similar rights or using the land himself for those purposes unless the licence is, properly construed, exclusive.[100]

8.35 In *Donington Park*, the doctrine was held to prevent the licensor restricting the number of available access routes to the licensed area (a car

---

[92] *Hurst v Picture Theatres Ltd* [1915] 1 KB 1.
[93] (1864) 5 B&S 841, at 852.
[94] *Megarry & Wade: The Law of Real Property*, n 85 above, at para 34-004; Dixon (2006) 70 Conv 374, at p 377.
[95] [2006] All ER (D) 94 (Apr).
[96] (2006) 70 Conv 374, at pp 377–378.
[97] See eg *Europa 2000 Ltd v Keles* [2005] EWCA Civ 1748, at [31].
[98] See by analogy *Platt v London Underground Ltd* [2001] 2 EGLR 121, at 122E–122F (lease of a kiosk). Express terms will often be decisive as to its scope although such terms must be construed so as to be consistent with the 'irreducible minimum' of rights implicit in the agreement: *Petra Investments Ltd v Rogers* [2003] 2 EGLR 120, at 126L–126M.
[99] See by analogy *Chartered Trust plc v Davies* [1997] 2 EGLR 83, at 87C.
[100] See by analogy *Romulus Trading Co Ltd v Comet Properties Ltd* [1996] 2 EGLR 70, as qualified in *Petra Investments Ltd v Rogers* [2003] 2 EGLR 120, at 227.

park) and justified the implication of a term entitling the licensee to assign (although such terms could simply have been implied on the basis that they represented the parties' obvious but unexpressed intentions). More controversially the principle was held to entitle the licensee to register a restriction against the licensor's registered title to give teeth to the licensor's obligation not to transfer the land. This, however, seems wrong in principle since the result is to give the licence a substantive, proprietary effect it otherwise lacks and to fetter the licensor's power (not right) to assign his interest free of the licence (Chapter 9), blurring the distinction between contractual and proprietary rights.[101]

Fitness for purpose

8.36 A licensor may of course expressly warrant the condition of the land or its suitability for the licensee's purposes.[102]

8.37 Common law disfavours the implication of such terms into leases[103] in part because the lessee is usually best able to determine the land's suitability for his purposes and/or may usually undertake works required to make it fit. That, however, is not true of most licensees and accordingly such terms are more likely to be implied, eg on grounds of business efficacy.[104] Conversely where Parliament *has* acted in this context, such intervention is largely confined to leases.[105] The licensor may of course owe the common duty of care in tort under the Occupiers' Liability Act 1957, s 2(1) in respect of the safety of the licensee and his goods (see Chapter 11) and any equivalent implied contractual duty of care is presumed to be the same,[106] unless the parties expressly agree otherwise.[107]

8.38 At common law licensors were held to have impliedly warranted that the land was safe for the intended purposes,[108] although the 1957 Act has largely (not entirely) obviated the need for such a term.[109] The precise formulation of

---

[101] See the criticism of this part of the decision at (2006) 70 Conv 374, at pp 380–381.
[102] See e g *Dudley Port Warehousing Co Ltd v Gardner Transport & Distribution Ltd* [1995] EGCS 5.
[103] *Southwark LBC v Mills* [2001] 1 AC 1. See the exception for residential lettings of furnished accommodation (*Smith v Marrable* (1843) 11 M&W 5: reasonably fit for habitation at start of term) and lettings of premises in the course of construction (*Perry v Sharon Developments* [1937] 4 All ER 390: fitness for habitation, quality of workmanship and suitability of materials used). See for a further possible exception in the case of public authority lessors: *Lee v Leeds CC* [2002] 1 WLR 1488.
[104] *Wettern Electric Ltd v Welsh Development Agency* [1983] 2 All ER 629, at 637–638.
[105] See e g Landlord and Tenant Act 1985, s 8 (fitness for habitation), s 11 (repairs). *Bomford v South Worcestershire Assessment Committee* [1947] All ER 299. See for exceptions Landlord and Tenant Act 1985, s 9 (s 8 applicable to agricultural workers' tied accommodation) and Rent (Agriculture) Act 1976, Sch 5, para 6(1) (applying s 11 of the 1985 Act). See also below the statutory terms implied into certain residential licences with security of tenure.
[106] Occupiers Liability Act 1957, s 5.
[107] *Maguire v Sefton MBC* [2006] 1 WLR 2250, at [24].
[108] See n 110 below.
[109] See e g *Wettern Electric Ltd v Welsh Development Agency* [1983] 2 All ER 629, at 636–637.

the licensor's duty varied in such cases[110] but (as stated) is now presumed to be the common duty of care.[111] It applies to the land and to fixed and moveable structures on it.[112]

8.39 The implied contractual duty may, in appropriate cases, extend beyond the safety of the licensee's person and goods, eg as to the suitability of the land for the licensee's intended purposes or that its use for such purposes is legal.[113] The existence and scope of the duty is in each case sensitive to the facts. For example:

- In *Wettern Electric Ltd v Welsh Development Agency*[114] a warranty of fitness for purpose was implied in a short-term licence of commercial premises used whilst works to the occupier's existing unit (which he rented from the licensor) were undertaken, where the licensor knew the use to which they would be put.

- In contrast in *Morris Thomas v Petticoat Lane Rentals*[115] no such term was implied into a licence intended to resolve a prior dispute as to the licensee's occupation where the licensee knew the nature and condition of the premises in advance.

- In lump sum building contracts, the licensor/owner does not warrant to the builder/licensee that the land is suitable for the works; the builder takes the risk of them being more costly etc than envisaged and must do all works necessary to bring about the contracted result.[116] Nor does the owner owe him a duty to warn as to the condition of the land.[117] That is an example of a wider principle that no warranty is likely where the licensee is better able to judge the suitability of the land for the intended purposes.

---

[110] See eg *Francis v Cockrell* (1870) LR 5 QB 501, at 513–514 (collapse of grandstand at racecourse; implied duty that the structure should be reasonably fit for purpose except for latent defects not discoverable by reasonable care); *Maclenan v Segar* [1917] 2 KB 235 (fire in hotel; implied duty that premises are as safe for the intended purposes as reasonable care and skill could make them); *Gillmore v LCC* [1938] 4 All ER 331, at 333 (injury due to overpolished floor; implied duty to take reasonable steps to see that the premises are in all respects safe for the intended purpose). Note, however, that club members do not owe each other contractual duties to ensure that club premises are safe: *Shore v Ministry of Works* [1950] 2 All ER 228.
[111] Occupiers' Liability Act 1957, s 5(1); *Maguire v Sefton MBC* [2006] 1 WLR 2250 (no absolute warranty by the licensor that machines provided for licensee's use would be safe or warranty that his independent contractors would take reasonable care; common duty of care under s 5 discharged by engaging apparently competent contractors).
[112] Occupiers' Liability Act 1957, s 5(2).
[113] Eg the intended use would amount to a breach of planning control, breach of covenant in the licensor's headlease or, due to the condition of the premises, a statutory nuisance. Absent express warranty, no such responsibility is owed by the lessor: *Edler v Auerbach* [1950] 1 KB 359 (illegality); *Hill v Harris* [1965] 2 QB 601 (breach). Contrast the liability of the vendor of goods: *Niblett v Confectioners Materials Co Ltd* [1921] 3 KB 387 (trade mark infringement).
[114] [1983] 2 All ER 629.
[115] (1987) 53 P & CR 238.
[116] *Tharsis Sulphur & Copper Co v M'Elroy & Sons* (1878) 3 App Cas 1040.
[117] *Thorn v London County Council* (1876) 1 App Cas 120.

- In storage licences, the licensor may be under a duty to take reasonable care to ensure the land is fit for the reception and storage of the goods, eg watertight.[118]

- However, the content of the duty in each case may vary depending on the circumstances. It may be sufficient for the licensor to guard against or warn of a particular hazard rather than remedy it.[119]

8.40 More generally, a licensor is unlikely to covenant impliedly that the premises are suitable for the licensee's purposes if the unsuitability is due to some special requirement/sensitivity of the licensee or (possibly) a latent defect in the premises of which the licensor is unaware or where the licensee had the opportunity to inspect the premises in advance to assess their fitness. The answer will be sensitive to the circumstances, eg who is in occupational control and whether the licensee is able to undertake the necessary works to make the land fit for his purposes.

Repair and maintenance

8.41 A licensor may impliedly undertake to repair and maintain the land. However, as leases usually contain no such implied duty[120] and statutory intervention here is largely confined to residential lettings, it is only likely to be implied into licences where warranted by the particular circumstances. The retention of occupational control by the licensor or the *right* to enter to maintain/repair the land is not of itself sufficient to imply an *obligation* to do so.[121] Conversely if the licence fee is calculated or a service charge is paid on the basis the licensor will undertake repairs/maintenance such a term may be implied[122] but not if he merely reserves the right to charge for such work.[123] More generally, a licensor is unlikely to owe such a duty to a licensee who has a right to possession and is able undertake works to the premises. But a residential licence that grants a right of (even sole) occupation (eg of a hotel room) may well contain such a term at least if the licensee cannot undertake such works. A general obligation to maintain/repair is more difficult to imply into mere user licences, although the licensor may be impliedly obligated to undertake works (if he is able) which are necessary in order for the licensee to be able to enjoy his rights. Each case, however, turns on its facts, both as to the existence and the scope of such term.

8.42 Where the licensor retains adjacent land he may be under an implied duty in relation to its repair and condition. For example:

---

[118] *AMF International v Magnet Bowling* [1968] 1 WLR 1028, at 1040.
[119] See by analogy *Benjamin's Sale of Goods* (Sweet & Maxwell, 7th edn, 2006), at para 11–057.
[120] *Duke of Westminster v Guild* [1985] QB 688.
[121] See by analogy *Woodfall's Landlord & Tenant* (Sweet & Maxwell, looseleaf), at para 13.007.1 (lessors).
[122] *Murphy v Hurley* [1992] 1 AC 369.
[123] *Duke of Westminster v Guild* [1985] QB 688.

- if that is necessary for the protection of the licensee or the land which he has the right to use (eg a common roof above serviced office accommodation) – in such case he may be bound to take reasonable care to ensure the other land does not injure the licensee or prevent him exercising his rights;[124]

- where the retained land is a necessary means of access to the land that is the subject of the licence (eg the common parts of a building used as bedsits), the licensor is likely to be obliged to use reasonable care to keep it reasonably safe;[125] and

- the licensor may be required to use reasonable care to keep in repair and proper working order common facilities (eg utilities, ventilation etc) which the licensee is entitled to use.[126]

Security

8.43 Licensors are not, without more, liable for the security of the land or the licensee's goods;[127] in this respect their duty is different to that of a bailee.[128] One obvious exception is the innkeeper, whose liability for his guest's goods is that of an insurer, subject to well-known statutory and common-law limitations.[129] Also the proprietors of lodgings/boarding houses may be under an implied duty to take reasonable care for the safety of their guests' goods, eg by keeping the common entrance door shut/locked and in repair so as to prevent entry by thieves.[130]

8.44 As well the licensor may owe a duty of reasonable care in respect of the security of the goods/site: (a) on ordinary negligence grounds; or (b) where the basis to imply such a term exists, eg where he receives/stores goods on land he controls for reward (eg commercial storage facilities).[131] Where, in contrast, the licensee has a sole right of occupation/possession of a self-contained area the licensor is unlikely to owe such a duty in relation to that area, although if it is part of a larger area within his control he may be responsible for the security of the site generally.

---

[124] See by analogy *Woodfall's Landlord & Tenant*, n 121 above, at para 13.004.
[125] *Morris Thomas v Petticoat Lane Rentals* (1987) 53 P & CR 238, at 256.
[126] *Liverpool City Council v Irwin* [1977] AC 239.
[127] *Ashby v Tolhurst* [1937] 2 KB 242; *Tinsley v Dudley* [1951] 2 KB 18.
[128] *Mendelsohn v Normand* [1970] 1 QB 177.
[129] 67 *Halsbury's Laws* (5th edn), at paras 197–204.
[130] See eg *Scarborough v Cosgrove* [1905] 2 KB 805, at 811; *Appah v Parncliffe Investments Ltd* [1964] 1 WLR 1064.
[131] *Southampton Cargo Handling Ltd v Lotus Cars Ltd* [2008] 2 Lloyd's Rep 532, at [91].

The licensee's obligations

Payment of licence fee

8.45 The licensee must pay the licence fee or provide other agreed consideration (eg services) in return for the right to use the licensor's land. If no fee was expressly agreed, the court may imply a term that he pay a reasonable sum.[132] A licensee has an equitable right of set-off if the licensor is himself in breach,[133] unless that right is expressly excluded by the licence terms. Furthermore the licensor may not distrain for arrears against the licensee's goods (unless expressly agreed)[134] and may not in any event do so against a third party's goods.[135]

Licensee estopped from denying licensor's title

8.46 See **8.25–8.28**.

Responsibility for the condition of the premises

8.47 Licensees are rarely under an implied general duty to maintain and repair the premises, particularly if they have merely a right of user or non-exclusive occupation.[136] Indeed as tenants are generally under no such duty[137] even a licensee with exclusive occupation or possession is unlikely to be bound.

8.48 Nevertheless a licensee may be responsible for particular conditions, eg:

- In tort, for damage/deterioration which he negligently caused.

- Where he is permitted to install/use conducting media through the licensor's land he may, if not contractually liable to keep it in repair, be practically obliged to do so to avoid committing a trespass or nuisance, eg from the escape of water from the pipes.[138]

---

[132] See eg Supply of Goods and Services Act 1982, s 15(1). See **8.53** as to the Act's application in this context.
[133] See by analogy *British Anzani (Felixstowe) Ltd v International Marine Management (UK) Ltd* [1980] QB 137; *Smith v Muscat* [2003] 1 WLR 2853 (leases).
[134] Nor implement the commercial rent arrears recovery procedure when Tribunals, Courts and Enforcement Act 2007, Sch 12 comes into force.
[135] *Euston Centre Properties v H&J Wilson* [1982] 1 EGLR 57, at 58. Such a person is not bound by the estoppel between the licensor and licensee. *Tadman v Henman* (1893) 2 QB 168.
[136] *Addiscombe Garden Estates v Crabbe* [1958] 1 QB 513, at 523 ('It seems inappropriate that a mere licensee should be saddled with an obligation to repair').
[137] *Hill & Redman's Law of Landlord and Tenant* (LexisNexis Butterworths, looseleaf), at para A[3327].
[138] See *Jones v Pritchard* [1908] 1 Ch 630, at 638 (easement). The position may be different if he merely uses the pipes in common with the licensor. Cf *RH Buckley & Sons v N Buckley & Sons* [1898] 2 QB 608 (easement).

- A residential licensee with a sole right of possession/occupation (but not, say, a short-term occupant, eg a hotel guest) may be under a duty akin to the tenant's obligation to use the land in a tenant-like manner. That is not a duty to repair per se but requires him to 'do the little jobs around the place which a reasonable tenant would do',[139] eg mending dripping taps, unblocking sinks etc.

- Certain exclusive licensees of agricultural land are subject to an implied duty of good husbandry.[140]

- A licensee may be liable for voluntary waste, ie deliberate or negligent acts that damage the land or substantially alter its character,[141] excluding fair wear and tear and damage arising from the reasonable and proper use of the land for the purposes intended.

8.49 A licensee who is allowed to erect a structure on the licensor's land may be impliedly liable to make good any damage caused by doing so. However, a licensee is not generally liable – or entitled – to remove the structure at the end of the term (see Chapter 13) but if it is expressly agreed that he do so, he is likely to be impliedly responsible to reinstate the land.

Statutory control of terms

Unfair Contract Terms Act 1977 and Unfair Terms in Consumer Contracts Regulations 1999

8.50 A contractual licence's terms are potentially subject to statutory regulation under the Unfair Contract Terms Act 1977 and the Unfair Terms in Consumer Contracts Regulations 1999.[142] Their impact is beyond the scope of this book; it is appropriate only to note their application.

8.51 The 1977 Act applies principally to contract clauses and non-contractual notices that (so far as relevant) purport to exclude or limit one party's liability for death/personal injury and to standard terms that entitle him to render a substantially different performance from that promised or no performance at all. Certain terms are rendered wholly ineffective; others are ineffective except to the extent they are reasonable. Sections 2–4 apply to all contracts bar (inter alia) those 'relat[ing] to the creation or transfer of an interest in land'.[143] Contractual licences do not create such interests and where they have proprietary effect, that is because of circumstances outside the licence (see Chapter 9). Accordingly mere contractual licences are caught by the Act whereas licences coupled with an interest in land (not chattels) are not.

---

[139] *Warren v Keen* [1954] 1 QB 15, at 20.
[140] *Colchester BC v Smith* [1991] 2 All ER 29, at 56.
[141] For a full consideration see Dowding and Reynolds *Dilapidations: The Modern Law and Practice* (Sweet & Maxwell, 4th edn, 2008), at ch 21.
[142] SI 1999/2083.
[143] Unfair Contract Terms Act 1977, Sch 1, para 1(b).

8.52 The 1999 Regulations apply to contracts between a 'seller' or 'supplier' and a 'customer' and to express terms that are not individually negotiated – typically one party's (usually the licensor's) standard terms. Contracts to grant interests in land have been held to amount to a 'service' within the Regulations[144] – a fortiori licences to use/occupy land.[145] The Regulations require that terms must be 'fair' unless they are 'core terms' within reg 6(2), ie which concern the adequacy of the price/remuneration or the definition of the main subject matter of the contract. The duration of a licence is a 'core term' for these purposes.[146] Written terms that are not in 'plain and intelligible language' are construed against the 'proferens', usually the licensor.

Supply of Goods and Services Act 1982

8.53 It is likely (although as yet undecided) that a licence is also a 'service' under the Supply of Goods and Services Act 1982. It has been held that a residential tenancy is not,[147] but that has been distinguished in relation to the meaning of 'service' in the Unfair Terms in Consumer Contracts Regulations 1999[148] and the ratio – namely that the tenant occupies by virtue of his interest, not any service provided by the owner – is in any event distinguishable here. Nevertheless the practical impact of the Act's application is likely to be small. The court may imply a term for payment of a reasonable fee for the service (here, the right to use the land). However, the duty to provide the service with care and skill (s 13) would appear to add little, if anything, to the particular duties referred to above.[149]

Licences with security of tenure

Housing Act 1985 licences

8.54 Licences treated as secure tenancies under the Housing Act 1985[150] contain statutorily implied terms as to: rights of succession;[151] limits on the right to assign;[152] the right to take in lodgers/sublet;[153] the right to require the

---

[144] *R (Khatun) v Newham BC* [2005] QB 37 (accommodation provided by local authority under its duty under the homelessness legislation), distinguishing *Dunn v Bradford MDC* [2002] EWCA Civ 1137.
[145] See *R (Khatun) v Newham BC* [2005] QB 37, at [78].
[146] See eg *Baybut v Eccle Riggs Country Park Ltd* [2006] All ER (D) 161 (Nov), at [23].
[147] *Dunn v Bradford MDC* [2002] EWCA Civ 1137, at [52]; contrast *Camden LBC v McBride* [1999] CL 3737 (tenancy 'service' for the purpose of Unfair Terms in Consumer Contracts Regulations 1994, SI 1994/3159).
[148] *R (Khatun) v Newham BC* [2005] QB 37.
[149] *Dunn v Bradford MDC* [2002] EWCA Civ 1137, at [48].
[150] By virtue of Housing Act 1985, s 79(3).
[151] Ibid, ss 87–90.
[152] Ibid, ss 91–92.
[153] Ibid, s 93.

Restricted contracts under the Rent Act 1977, s 19

8.55 Services provided by the licensor under a restricted contract were subject to the Supply of Goods and Services Act 1982. Any furniture for which the licensee was obliged to pay was required to be of satisfactory quality. The 1977 Act also contained controls on the amount the licensor could charge[158] and on premiums.[159]

Agricultural workers

Agricultural workers under the Rent (Agriculture) Act 1976

8.56 An agricultural worker who continues to occupy accommodation after the end of his employment does so on the same terms as he did previously, except insofar as they relate to his employment. Other terms in the Rent (Agriculture) Act 1976, Sch 5 apply subject to any contrary written agreement.[160] The most important require the owner to provide facilities/services previously provided which are reasonably necessary for occupation[161] and to keep the dwelling in repair.[162] The licensee is obliged to use the premises only as a private dwelling[163] and may not assign, sublet or part with possession of it[164] and must give at least 4 weeks' notice to quit.[165] There are also detailed provisions in respect of rent.

Assured agricultural occupancies under the Housing Act 1988

8.57 Assured agricultural occupancies treated as assured tenancies[166] are subject to the same provisions in relation to the fixing of rent as for assured tenants.[167] There are also statutorily implied terms prohibiting the licensee assigning, subletting or parting with possession without the licensor's

---

[154] Ibid, s 96.
[155] Ibid, ss 97–101.
[156] Ibid, s 108.
[157] Ibid, ss 102–103.
[158] For further reference see *Woodfall's Landlord & Tenant*, n 121 above, at para 23.196 et seq.
[159] Rent Act 1977, s 122.
[160] See, however, the restrictions in Rent (Agriculture) Act 1976, Sch 5, para 12(4).
[161] Rent (Agriculture) Act 1976, Sch 5, para 5.
[162] Ibid, Sch 5, para 6; Landlord and Tenant Act 1985, s 11. Note also the statutory duty of fitness for habitation: s 9 of the 1985 Act.
[163] Rent (Agriculture) Act 1976, Sch 5, para 7(1).
[164] Ibid, Sch 5, para 7(2).
[165] Ibid, Sch 5, para 10.
[166] Housing Act 1988, s 24(3).
[167] Ibid, s 24(4).

consent.[168] The terms in the Housing Act 1988, s 5(3) apply to the statutory periodic tenancy arising after the contract term ends, subject to variation.[169]

Agricultural holdings

8.58 Licences converted into tenancies from year to year under the Agricultural Holdings Act 1986, s 2 are subject to the extensive range of provisions in the Act. As such rights/obligations are terms – and/or arise by virtue – of the tenancy, they are beyond the scope of this book. For details, reference should be made to the Act and specialist practitioner works.

Mobile homes occupiers

8.59 Licences to station and occupy a mobile home on a protected site may be protected under the Mobile Homes Act 1983.[170] The Act implies into such licences the terms set out in Sch 1, Ch 1 to the Act, which take precedence over any inconsistent express terms.[171] In addition the court can imply certain terms into the agreement.[172] It can also make such order as it considers just and equitable in the circumstances,[173] varying or deleting any express terms and/or providing that an express term that would otherwise be unenforceable has effect, subject to any specified variation.[174]

---

[168] Ibid, s 18(3). The landlord may unreasonably withhold consent – s 18.
[169] Ibid, s 6.
[170] See Chapter 6.
[171] Mobile Homes Act 1983, s 2(1). In summary the terms: (i) give the licensee the right to station the home on the pitch during the subsistence of the licence (s 2(1), Sch 1, Pt I, para 1); (ii) define the duration of the agreement where the site owner has a limited interest (ibid, para 2); (iii) entitle the licensee to sell/gift the home to a family member or someone approved by the licensor and regulate the process for seeking permission (ibid, paras 8, 9); (iv) limit the commission chargeable on sale (ibid, para 8(2)); (v) entitle the licensor, with court approval, to relocate the licensee to another comparable pitch in certain specified circumstances (ibid, para 10(1)–(3)); (vi) imply a covenant for quiet enjoyment (ibid, paras 11–15); (vii) limit the frequency of pitch fee reviews and the amount of any increase and prescribe the factors to be taken into account on a review (ibid, para 16 et seq); (viii) require the licensee to pay the pitch fee and other sums due and impose obligations as to the maintenance of the home and pitch and maintain records (ibid, para 21); and (ix) require the owner to (inter alia) provide certain information as to the pitch, any new pitch fee and charges for utilities/other services, repair the base and utilities serving the pitch/home, keep the common parts clean and tidy, consult about improvements and consult a qualifying residents' association on matters as to the operation management and improvement of the site.
[172] Mobile Homes Act 1983, s 2(2), Sch 1, Pt II. Specifically: (i) for quiet enjoyment; (ii) how much the licensee must pay and when; (iii) the review of those sums; (iv) the provision or improvement of services and their use by the licensee; (v) the preservation of the amenity of the site; (vi) the maintenance/repair of the site by the owner and the mobile home by the licensee; and (vii) access by the owner to the pitch.
[173] On an application by either party made within 6 months of the agreement or the date the written statement is given (whether or not in compliance with an order under s 1(6)).
[174] Mobile Homes Act 1983, s 2.

ESTOPPEL LICENCES

8.60 In ascertaining the terms of an estoppel licence it is necessary to distinguish between the basic equitable right that entitles the representee to seek relief – the inchoate equity – and the manner in which the court satisfies it.

The basic equitable right

8.61 An estoppel arises where a person relies on a representation that he has/will have an interest in the representee's land. Such circumstances give the representee the right to apply to the court for an order that he has rights over (or an interest in) that land or other relief. It is for the court to decide what if any rights etc to confer, although it will not grant greater relief than that promised. But what is the position of the representee before the application or the order is made?

8.62 It is inaccurate to refer to the 'terms' on which the representee uses/occupies the land before the court order giving effect to the equity. Rather, the basis on which it was understood that the representee would have rights in/to the land is a factor in determining whether the equity has arisen (eg whether the conditions on which it was understood the right etc would be granted are satisfied/still exist[175]), whether it has been discharged in the interim (eg because, taking into account the countervailing benefits, the representee has had sufficient satisfaction for it[176]) and whether/how the court ought to exercise its discretion in his favour (eg based on the parties' conduct[177]). For example, a representee will usually have no continuing expectation of a right etc that was dependent: (a) on certain conditions existing which have not been (or are no longer) met; (b) on him doing or refraining from doing something, with which he failed to comply; or (c) on the existence of a (business or personal) relationship between them that has since come to an end.

The relief

8.63 The court may fashion an appropriate remedy – both as to the nature of the rights/interest and the term on which it is held – in order to give effect to the equity in such way as it thinks fit. Although the court searches for the minimum equity to do justice,[178] that does not require it to be 'constitutionally

---

[175] Eg if the promise was that the representee could use the land for a certain period of time or until a certain event occurred or for so long as a certain state of affairs continues, his right to do so under the equity will end on the expiry of that time, the occurrence of that event or the state of affairs ceasing to exist.
[176] See eg *Watts & Ready v Storey* (1983) 134 NLJ 631.
[177] Eg the court may regard the representee's misconduct as barring his right to relief on the basis he fails to come to equity with clean hands (see eg *Willis v Willis* [1986] 1 EGLR 62; *Gonthier v Orange Contract Scaffolding Ltd* [2003] EWCA Civ 873) or misbehaviour (*Brynowen Estates Ltd v Bourne* (1981) 131 NLJ 1212; but compare the effect of misconduct after the remedy has been granted: *Williams v Staite* [1979] 1 WLR 291).
[178] *Crabb v Arun DC* [1976] Ch 179, at 198.

parsimonious' but recognises that it must be fair also to the owner.[179] The court may give effect to the expectation (which forms the 'maximum extent' of the relief[180]), discharge the detriment or fashion some other remedy between these two. Where, however, the equity arises out of dealings akin to a bargain, ie both the reliance and the expectation are specified with reasonable clarity, the court is likely to give effect to the latter if the representee has done what was asked of him, unless the expectation was wholly disproportionate to the detriment.[181] Where the relief takes the form of a specific right, eg licence,[182] the permitted activities, its duration and other terms are to be determined by the court.[183]

LICENCES COUPLED WITH AN INTEREST

8.64 A licence coupled with an interest will continue for as long as the interest component continues.[184] It cannot be revoked so as to defeat the grant to which it is appurtenant. Such licences were always regarded as an exception to the (now largely, if not entirely, defunct) rule that the licensor had the power (even if not the right) to terminate the licensee's entitlement to use/occupy the land.[185] Since the licence is essentially parasitic on – and supportive of – the interest, its scope and terms (if not express) are to be determined in light of the nature and terms of the interest. The licence is such as is reasonably necessary for the grantee to be able to enjoy that interest.[186] Such a licence will be assignable if, as is usual, the interest is assignable but may not be assigned separately from it (see Chapter 10).

---

[179] *Jennings v Rice* [2003] 1 P & CR 8, at [48].
[180] *Snell's Equity* (Sweet & Maxwell, 31st edn, 2005), at para 10-21.
[181] *Jennings v Rice* [2003] 1 P & CR 8, at [50]–[51].
[182] See eg *Williams v Staite* [1979] 1 WLR 291.
[183] But see *Jones v Jones* [1977] 1 WLR 438, at 442 where the court gave additional relief in support of the previously declared right.
[184] *James Jones & Sons Ltd v Earl of Tankerville* [1909] 2 Ch 440, at 442.
[185] *Wood v Leadbitter* (1845) 13 M&W 838. See now **12.40** et seq.
[186] See eg *Europa 2000 Ltd v Keles* [2005] EWCA Civ 1748, at [31] (obiter).

Chapter 9

THE BURDEN OF THE LICENCE

The licensor's successors in title	9.2
General	9.2
Bare licences	9.7
Contractual licences	9.8
Licences coupled with an interest	9.24
Licences and the mutual benefit and burden principle	9.26
Estoppel licences	9.29
Licences converted by the Law of Property Act 1925, s 62	9.34
Matrimonial home rights	9.37
Licences together with other interests	9.38
Licensee's interest	9.39
Licensor's interest	9.41
Persons with a superior interest to the licensor	9.43
Persons deriving title through the licensor	9.48
Persons with no right to use the land	9.51
Trespass	9.52
Nuisance	9.54

9.1 This chapter considers the circumstances in which the licence can be enforced – or give one or other party rights – against others, specifically:

- The licensor's successor in title: in what circumstances is he bound to honour the licence?

- Someone who would otherwise take free of a proprietary interest owned by the licensee or licensor; in what circumstances does the licensee's use of the land entitle him/the licensor to claim priority for that interest?

- Persons with a superior title to the licensor; does the licence bind them?

- Persons deriving title through the licensor, eg mortgagees.

- Those who, without any legal right, enter the land or interfere with the licensee's use of it.

THE LICENSOR'S SUCCESSORS IN TITLE

General

9.2 Whether the burden of a right is capable of passing to a successor depends, broadly, on whether it is contractual or proprietary in nature. Proprietary rights/interests are capable of binding the whole world except someone with a superior title; mere contractual rights are not. The burden of mere contractual obligations (eg to permit the use of one's land) generally cannot be assigned[1] and therefore such obligations do not generally run with the land;[2] proprietary obligations (eg restrictive covenants) may. Common-law remedies, such as damages, are only available against persons with whom there is privity of contract;[3] equitable remedies too are generally unavailable against successors, except in support of proprietary rights/interests.[4]

9.3 The passing of the burden of the licence to the licensor's successors therefore depends principally on whether it is contractual or proprietary in nature.[5] As considered in more detail below, bare and contractual licences – even those conferring a right to possession – are not proprietary and thus generally do not bind a licensor's successor[6] even if he buys with notice.[7] Estoppel licences and the 'interest' component of licences coupled with an interest are and thus can, in principle, bind successors.

The need to register – registered land

9.4 As bare and contractual licences are not proprietary rights, they cannot be protected by registration or notice against the licensor's registered title. The court in *Donington Park Leisure Ltd v Wheatcroft & Sons Ltd*,[8] however, controversially held that the contractual licensor's obligation not to transfer the land could be protected by restriction against its registered title, although as previously stated this is thought to be wrong.[9] Estoppel licences (ie inchoate equities) and matrimonial home rights can be protected by notice.[10] The

---

[1] *Linden Gardens Trust Ltd v Lenesta Sludge Disposals Ltd* [1994] 1 AC 85.
[2] *Rhone v Stephens* [1994] 2 AC 310.
[3] Although damages can be given against successors in lieu of equitable relief, where such relief is available in principle.
[4] *National Provincial Bank Ltd v Ainsworth* [1965] AC 1175.
[5] In contrast, the lack of a proprietary right is not fatal where the licensee claims against strangers in trespass; as discussed below (at **9.53**) a right of sole occupation appears to be sufficient.
[6] *Ashburn Anstalt Ltd v Arnold* [1989] Ch 1, overruled (on a different point) *Prudential Assurance Co Ltd v London Residuary Body* [1992] 2 AC 386.
[7] *National Provincial Bank Ltd v Ainsworth* [1965] AC 1175, at 1237E ('Notice itself does not create the right. To create the right over the land of another the right must (apart from statute) create a burden on the land ie an equitable estate or interest in the land') and 1261.
[8] [2006] All ER (D) 94, at [45].
[9] See **8.35**.
[10] Land Registration Act 2002, s 32 (estoppels); Family Law Act 1996, s 31(10)(a) (matrimonial homes rights). Note, however, that a spouse's matrimonial home rights cannot be an overriding interest by virtue of his or her occupation – Family Law Act 1996, s 31(10)(b).

interest component of a licence coupled with an interest (if in land) may – and may need to – be substantively registered.

9.5 It also follows that bare and contractual licences cannot be overriding interests.[11] Estoppel licences can, eg if the representee is in actual occupation.[12] In relation to licences coupled with an interest, the interest (if in land) may also be protected as an overriding interest if – exceptionally – the grantee is in actual occupation but only (since the Land Registration Act 2002) if he occupies the particular area of land to which the interest relates. In most cases, however, the ancillary licence will not give a right of occupation but mere user.

The need to register – unregistered land

9.6 Bare and contractual licences in unregistered land cannot be registered as a local land charge or protected by way of pending land action.[13] Matrimonial homes rights are registrable as Class F land charges and if unregistered are void against a purchaser.[14] An estoppel licence, although not registrable as a land charge,[15] may be registrable as a pending land action[16] and is capable of binding successors, except bona fide purchasers of the legal estate for value without notice. The 'interest' component of a licence coupled with an interest may, depending on its nature, require registration.

Bare licences

9.7 A bare licence is not, in strict legal sense, a 'right'[17] – proprietary or otherwise – and thus its burden cannot pass to the licensor's successor[18] even one who purportedly takes subject to it[19] unless he acquires in circumstances giving rise to a constructive trust.[20] Rather, the licensor's assignment of his interest will terminate the licence,[21] subject to the licensee having a reasonable

---

[11] *Canadian Imperial Bank of Commerce v Bello* (1992) 64 P & CR 48, at 52. Only proprietary interests qualified for protection under Land Registration Act 1925, s 70(1): *National Provincial Bank Ltd v Ainsworth* [1965] AC 1175, at 1197C. But see *Saed v Plustrade* [2002] 2 EGLR 19, at 21 (person with a right to park – whether an easement or licence – held to have overriding interest under s 70(1)(g)); possibly the better explanation is that the right was a term of an interest (lease) or the tenant's occupation of the demised premises sufficed under s 70(1)(g). If the latter, the result would now be different under the Land Registration Act 2002 as actual occupation can only protect rights in relation to the land in fact occupied – see below.
[12] *Singh v Sandhu* (unreported), CA, 4 May 1995.
[13] *Albany Construction Ltd v Cunningham* [2004] EWHC 3392.
[14] Land Charges Act 1972, ss 2(7), 4(8).
[15] *ER Ives Investments Ltd v High* [1967] 2 QB 379, at 395, 400, 405.
[16] *Haselmere Estates Ltd v Baker* [1982] 1 WLR 1109, at 1119–1120.
[17] See **8.1**.
[18] *Wallis v Harrison* (1838) 4 M&W 538, at 543.
[19] *Clowes Developments (UK) Ltd v Walters* [2005] EWHC 669 (Ch), at [36].
[20] Ibid, at [43] et seq.
[21] *Terunnanse v Terunnanse* [1968] AC 1086, at 1095–1096.

time to quit/cease using the land.[22] If he is not on the land when the licence terminates, he may be barred entry peremptorily[23] subject to his right to remove any possessions from it (see **13.7**).

Contractual licences

The general rule

The licence as a proprietary interest

9.8 The common-law rule,[24] which applied to both executed and executory contracts, was that a contractual licence did not create a proprietary interest or estate. Nevertheless later authorities, starting with *Errington v Errington and Woods*,[25] treated the licence as capable in equity of binding the licensor's successors, including purchasers who took with notice. *Errington* was followed by *Binions v Evans*,[26] in which a contractual licence was held to give rise to a constructive trust binding a purchaser who had agreed to honour it, and *DHN Food Distributors Ltd v Tower Hamlets LBC*,[27] where a contractual licensee was held to have a compensatable interest, arising by constructive trust, for the purposes of compulsory purchase legislation.

The current position

9.9 More recently, however, *Ashburn Anstalt Ltd v Arnold*[28] has returned the law to its position pre-*Errington* (which it was said was decided per incuriam[29]) and put 'the quietus to the heresy that a mere licence creates an interest in land [and] ... that parties to a contractual licence necessarily become constructive trustees'.[30] Although *Ashburn* has since been reversed on a different point,[31] this obiter dictum has been repeatedly affirmed.[32] Accordingly it is now clear a mere contractual licence of itself does not bind the licensor's successors, even those with notice.[33] Nor does it give rise to an estoppel, the burden of which

---

[22] *Webb v Paternoster* (1619) 2 Rolle 143.
[23] *Wallis v Harrison* (1838) 4 M&W 538.
[24] See eg *Frank Warr & Co v London CC* [1904] 1 KB 713; *King v David Allen & Sons Billposting Ltd* [1916] 2 AC 54; *Clore v Theatrical Properties Ltd* [1936] 3 All ER 483, at 490.
[25] [1952] 1 KB 290; *Re Sharpe* [1980] 1 WLR 219.
[26] [1972] Ch 359, at 367.
[27] [1976] 1 WLR 852, at 859.
[28] [1989] Ch 1.
[29] Ibid, at 22.
[30] *IDC Group Ltd v Clark* [1992] 1 EGLR 187, at 189M, aff'd [1992] 2 EGLR 184.
[31] *Prudential Assurance Co Ltd v London Residuary Body* [1992] AC 386.
[32] *IDC Group Ltd v Clark* [1992] 1 EGLR 187; *Canadian Imperial Bank of Commerce v Bello* (1992) 64 P & CR 48; *Lloyd v Dugdale* [2002] 2 P & CR 13.
[33] *Lloyd v Dugdale* [2002] 2 P & CR 13, at 52(4); *Ashburn Anstalt Ltd v Arnold* [1989] Ch 1, at 24D; *Canadian Imperial Bank of Commerce v Bello* (1992) 64 P & CR 48, at 51; *IDC Group Ltd v Clark* [1992] 1 EGLR 187.

may pass to the licensor's successor (below).[34] The reasoning in *Errington* and *Binions v Evans* can no longer be supported, although the results can, albeit on different grounds.[35]

9.10 Thus the licensor has the power (even if not, as against the licensee, the right) to assign his right/interest free of the licence. Even where the licensor is himself a contractual licensee, any prohibition in the sub-licence on assigning his interest will not void any such assignment as between the licensor and his successor.[36] Nor, however, does the assignment of the licensor's interest free of the licence terminate it (unless the licence expressly so provides) and thus he may be liable to the licensee under the rule in *Stirling v Maitland*[37] if the successor prevents the licensee using the land, having by his own act brought to an end the licensee's ability to exercise his rights.

Exceptions to the general rule

9.11 Nevertheless the successor may be bound: (a) by constructive trust; (b) if a new licence is created expressly/by implication between him and licensee; (c) if the licensee has security of tenure; or (d) in tort. These are considered below. Additionally the successor may be bound if the transfer is a sham, intended purely to defeat the licence and to give the appearance of a change in ownership that is not matched by reality.[38] He may also be bound if he gives an undertaking to the licensor to honour the licence which the licensee is entitled to enforce under one of the exceptions to the privity rule, but as these have no particular application to contractual licences and are rarely encountered in practice they are not dealt with here.

Constructive trust

9.12 A successor may be bound by the licence in constructive trust only in 'very special circumstances showing that [he] undertook a new liability to give effect to provisions for the benefit of third parties'[39] such that it would be inequitable for him not to do so. 'The court will not impose a constructive trust unless it is satisfied that the conscience of the estate owner is affected.'[40]

---

[34] *Baybut v Eccle Riggs Country Park Ltd* [2006] All ER (D) 161 (Nov), at [61].
[35] In *Errington v Errington and Woods* [1952] 1 KB 290 on the basis the occupier had either (i) an estate contract, (ii) an equity arising in estoppel or (iii) a beneficial interest, having paid the mortgage, which in each case was an overriding interest by virtue of actual occupation. *Ashburn Anstalt Ltd v Arnold* [1989] Ch 1, at 17B. *Binions v Evans* [1972] Ch 359 can now be justified a classic example of an *Ashburn* constructive trust – see text below.
[36] Contrast the effect of a prohibition on assignment in the licence itself – see Chapter 10.
[37] (1864) 5 B&S 841.
[38] Eg *Ferris v Weaven* [1952] 2 All ER 233; see also *National Provincial Bank Ltd v Hastings Car Mart Ltd* [1965] AC 1175, at 1223, 1240, 1257–1258.
[39] *IDC Group Ltd v Clark* [1992] 1 EGLR 187, at 190C; *Ashburn Anstalt Ltd v Arnold* [1989] Ch 1, at 23D.
[40] *Ashburn Anstalt Ltd v Arnold* [1989] Ch 1, at 25H. See, however, the doubts expressed in *Megarry & Wade: The Law of Real Property* (Sweet & Maxwell, 7th edn, 2008), at para 11-022 as to the appropriateness of applying principles of constructive trust in such circumstances.

9.13 A successor may be bound if he undertakes, expressly or impliedly, a new obligation[41] to give effect to the licence.[42] Such an inference cannot be drawn from 'slender materials'.[43] It is not enough therefore that the successor buys with notice of the licence.[44] Nor that he acquires the land expressly 'subject to' it[45] since that term may have been intended merely to qualify the vendor–licensor's covenant for title or to give vacant possession,[46] rather than to impose any obligation on the successor to honour it.[47]

9.14 No such undertaking was given on the facts, and hence the purchasers took free, in *King v David Allen & Sons Billposting Ltd*[48] and *Clore v Theatrical Properties Ltd*.[49] In contrast the successor was bound, having made such a promise, in *Binions v Evans*.[50] By way of further example, in *Bannister v Bannister*[51] a purchaser who sought to renege on his promise to the vendor to allow him to remain in the premises rent-free was found to be a constructive trustee for him. In *Lyus v Prowsa Developments Ltd*[52] a purchaser's promise to honour an executory contract (to sell part of the land) that would not otherwise have bound him was construed as a de novo obligation, giving rise to a constructive trust. In contrast, in *Chandler v Kerley*[53] a purchaser who bought at a discount on the understanding he could not evict the licensee was held bound by a contractual licence terminable on reasonable notice rather than constructive trust, such licence having arisen by virtue of direct dealings between the successor and licensee.[54] In the absence of an express promise to honour the licence one may be implied if (eg) the purchaser buys at a discount in consequence of the licensee's rights[55] but not if that merely reflects the nuisance value of recovering possession from the licensee.

---

[41] *Ashburn Anstalt Ltd v Arnold* [1989] Ch 1, at 23D.

[42] *Lloyd v Dugdale* [2002] 2 P & CR 13, at [52], point (3). It is sufficient if this stipulation is set out in the contract; it need not also be set out in the transfer: *Lyus v Prowsa Developments Ltd* [1982] 1 WLR 1044, at 1048G.

[43] *Ashburn Anstalt Ltd v Arnold* [1989] Ch 1, at 26E.

[44] See eg *Melbury Road Properties 1995 Ltd v Kreidi* [1999] 3 EGLR 108, at 109M.

[45] *Lloyd v Dugdale* [2002] 2 P & CR 13.

[46] Which requires possession to be given free of any adverse rights (*James Maccara Ltd v Barclays* [1945] KB 148) and in fact (*Cleadon Trust Ltd v Davis* [1940] Ch 940).

[47] *Lyus v Prowsa Developments Ltd* [1982] 1 WLR 1044, at 1051H. A fortiori the successor is not bound if the transfer expressly states that he is not required to give effect to the licence or, presumably, if he agrees to indemnify the vendor against any liability to the licensee under the rule in *Stirling v Maitland* (1864) 5 B&S 841, at 852.

[48] [1916] 2 AC 54.

[49] [1936] 3 All ER 483.

[50] Although the majority held the occupier was tenant for life. It was also true of the first purchaser in *Williams v Staite* [1979] Ch 291, at 296C (uncrystallised equity), but not the second (post-judgment licence) (at 296G) who was bound by it merely on the basis he had notice. The rules for estoppel licences, however, are different from contractual licences – see below.

[51] [1948] 2 All ER 133.

[52] [1982] 1 WLR 1044, at 1051C.

[53] [1978] 1 WLR 693.

[54] Ibid, at 696.

[55] *Ashburn Anstalt Ltd v Arnold* [1989] Ch 1, at 23F–23G; *Lloyd v Dugdale* [2002] 2 P & CR 13. See also *Williams v Staite* [1979] Ch 291, at 296B.

9.15 It is uncertain, however, whether the *mere* breach of such a promise is sufficient to affect the successor's conscience. Where, as in *Lyus v Prowsa*, the successor paid full value, the unconscionability (beyond a mere unfulfilled promise, which the licensee, as a stranger to the contract, cannot enforce) is not immediately apparent. In contrast it is clear where, as in *Binions v Evans*, the vendor relied on the promise in agreeing to sell and would be personally prejudiced if the purchaser reneged. So too where, as suggested in *Ashburn Anstalt v Arnold* and *Lloyd v Dugdale*, the successor obtains a benefit, such as by acquiring the property at a discount, by virtue of his promise to honour the licence. Accordingly it is considered that a mere unfulfilled promise, shorn of any element of detrimental reliance (as in *Binions*) or unfair benefit (as suggested in *Ashburn Anstalt* and *Dugdale*), is insufficient.

9.16 It is possible, however, that the 'benefit' is merely the acquisition of the land, although whether that is so where neither the decision to sell nor the terms of sale were influenced by the promise to honour the licence remains doubtful. Often there is no direct evidence that the land was sold at a discount or that any such discount was in return for the promise to honour the licence or that such promise influenced the decision to sell. It may be that the court will presume or readily infer that such decision and/or the terms of sale (including the price) were influenced by the promise, putting the onus on the successor to prove otherwise. If so the decision in *Lyus v Prowsa*, despite the absence of positive proof that the terms of sale were affected by the promise, can be justified, the successor having failed to prove that they were not. So too where it can be shown a discount was given, it may be presumed that it was (at least in part) in return for the promise unless the contrary is shown. If, however, the successor establishes that his promise did not influence the decision to sell or the terms of sale, it is arguable that no constructive trust arises (since he neither secured a benefit nor did the vendor suffer a detriment by virtue of his promise). If he does not, it may.

9.17 The constructive trust is not a true exception to the rule that the burden of the licence does not run; the successor is bound because he undertakes a *new* obligation, not because the existing burden *passes* to him[56] or because the licence has become a proprietary right/interest. It follows that if the successor is bound:

(1) The terms between him and the licensee are those he undertakes to honour, if different from the existing licence terms.[57] The onus will usually be on him to make clear if they are. The licensee is not bound to accept the successor's terms (eg if they are less favourable), but if he does, they (rather than the original licence terms) govern their ongoing relationship.[58]

---

[56] *IDC Group Ltd v Clark* [1992] 1 EGLR 187, at 190.
[57] Eg if the assignment requires the successor to allow the licensee to use the land for a longer (or shorter) term than the original contractual term.
[58] *Lyus v Prowsa Developments Ltd* [1982] 1 WLR 1044, at 1053H–1054A.

(2) The original licensor will not be liable to the licensee in the event the successor fails to comply with those new terms *to the extent that* they are more beneficial than the original terms. If, however, the new terms are materially less favourable than the old the licensee may have a claim against him for damages under the principle in *Stirling v Maitland*.[59]

(3) Since the constructive trust arises because the successor's conscience is bound, prima facie it binds only him, his estate and donees. If the successor sells without expressly requiring his purchaser to abide by the licence, that purchaser will not be bound even if aware of it[60] unless the circumstances in which *he* acquires the land are such as to give rise to a fresh constructive trust.[61]

New licences

9.18 A successor may also become bound if he otherwise acknowledges the licensee as *his* licensee and the licensee accepts that status.[62] In such case also the burden of the original licence does not pass but a new licence arises by novation between the successor and licensee, not necessarily on the same terms as the old[63] – see **10.23**. Accordingly the licensee may still have a claim in damages against the original licensor under *Stirling v Maitland*[64] if the new licence terms are materially less beneficial or more onerous than the original.

9.19 Such an agreement may be inferred from conduct,[65] eg if the successor allows the licensee to use the land and seeks to enforce the original licence terms/accepts payment of the licence fee without qualification or complies with the licensor's obligations under the original licence.[66] It will not be inferred if the successor expressly purports to accept payment from the licensee as damages for trespass.[67]

---

[59] (1864) 5 B&S 841.
[60] Cf the 'fallacy that, because an obligation binds a man's conscience, it therefore becomes binding on the consciences of those who take from him with notice of the obligation' – per Lord Wilberforce in *National Provincial Bank Ltd v Hastings Car Mart Ltd* [1965] AC 1175, at 1253. See also *Chattey v Farndale Holdings Inc* (1996) 75 P & CR 298, at 317. The point was left open in *Re Sharpe* [1980] 1 WLR 219, at 226G, and *Ashburn Anstalt Ltd v Arnold* [1989] Ch 1, at 24.
[61] See eg *Lyus v Prowsa Developments Ltd* [1982] 1 WLR 1044; *Chattey v Farndale Holdings Inc* (1996) 75 P & CR 298, at 315.
[62] *Clowes Developments (UK) Ltd v Walters* [2005] EWHC 669 (Ch), at [36].
[63] If the licensee merely continues to use the land as before the terms are likely to be same – the successor need not be subjectively aware of the terms of the licence so long as he is aware of its existence. See eg *Baybut v Eccle Riggs Country Park Ltd* [2006] All ER (D) 161 (Nov), at [55].
[64] (1864) 5 B&S 841, at 852. See also *Southern Foundaries (1926) Ltd v Shirlaw* [1940] AC 701, at 717; *Lyus v Prowsa Developments Ltd* [1982] 1 WLR 1044, at 1051E.
[65] See for an example in relation to unprotected mobile homes licences *Baybut v Eccle Riggs Country Park Ltd* [2006] All ER (D) 161 (Nov), at [51]–[57].
[66] See by analogy *Cornish v Stubbs* (1870) LR 5 CP 334 (leases).
[67] See by analogy *Westminster CC v Basson* (1990) 62 P&CR 57; *Vaughan-Armatrading v Sarsah* (1995) 27 HLR 631.

Licences with statutory security of tenure

9.20 Certain licences with security of tenure are capable of binding the licensor's successors either because statute expressly so provides[68] or because the licence is converted by statute into a tenancy.[69] These are discussed in Chapters 6 and 8.

Tort

The successor

9.21 Since the transfer to the successor will in most cases amount to a breach of contract by the licensor the successor may, in theory, be liable in tort for procuring that breach. That his interest is otherwise free of the licence is not a defence.[70] Nor that his subjective intention was not to damage the licensee but merely to enjoy the land free of the licence.[71] The successor's liability in tort does not have the effect of converting the licence into a proprietary interest although the licensee may have personal (including equitable) remedies against him.[72]

9.22 The successor must know of the licence and that he is, by taking a transfer, inducing a breach of contract; it is not enough that he knows he is procuring an act which in law amounts to a breach. Nor that he ought reasonably to have done so.[73] Knowledge for these purposes means actual or 'shut-eye' knowledge; negligence (even gross negligence) is not enough.[74] He need not, however, know all the licence terms or the licensee's identity.[75] It follows a successor is not liable if he is unaware of the licence or genuinely (if erroneously or even unreasonably[76]) doubts its existence or believes that it has – or by the time of completion will have – been validly terminated. His knowledge is to be judged – and liability crystallises – at the time contracts are exchanged. Knowledge acquired between contract and completion is irrelevant. Furthermore if the licence is only created during that period it is thought the successor has the defence of justification, by virtue of the superior right he acquires on exchange.[77]

---

[68] See eg Mobile Homes Act 1983, s 3(1).
[69] See eg Agricultural Holdings Act 1986, s 2(1), (2)(b); Housing Act 1985, s 79(3).
[70] See by analogy *BMTA v Salvadori* [1949] Ch 556 (chattels); *Esso Petroleum Co Ltd v Kingswood Motor (Addlestone) Ltd* [1974] QB 142, at 155–156 (solus agreement). Contrast *Miles v Bull (No 2)* [1969] 3 All ER 1585, at 1590. Compare *Midland Bank Trust Co v Green (No 3)* [1982] 1 Ch 529 (participation in conspiracy to defeat unregistered option by purchasing land).
[71] Cf *OBG Ltd v Allan* [2007] 4 All ER 545, at [43], [192].
[72] See by analogy *Crestfort Ltd v Tesco Stores Ltd* [2005] 3 EGLR 25 (sublease).
[73] *OBG Ltd v Allan* [2007] 4 All ER 545, at [39].
[74] Ibid, at [41].
[75] Ibid, at [192].
[76] Ibid; *L Meretz Investments v ACP Ltd* [2007] EWCA Civ 1303, at [124], [127].
[77] *Edwin Hill & Partners v First National Finance Corp* [1988] 3 All ER 801.

The successor's purchasers

9.23 Even where the successor is liable in tort his own purchaser will not as there is, by definition, no contract between the successor and licensee to interfere with and the licensee's loss accrued when the successor acquired the land.[78] Nor is the purchaser liable merely because his purchase prejudices the licensee's ability to seek an injunction against the successor, eg preventing his removal.[79]

Licences coupled with an interest

9.24 A licence that is ancillary to a proprietary interest in land will bind the owners for the time being of the land if the interest itself binds. The nature and terms of the particular interest will determine the formalities for its creation, whether its burden is capable of passing to successors and if so whether and how it must to be registered to do so. The licence itself need not, indeed cannot, be independently registered.

9.25 Where the interest is in chattels which remain on the licensor's land at the time he sells to the successor, the successor is not bound in contract or, it seems, in tort (ie conversion) to allow the goods owner to enter to remove them, nor does his taking of the land *of itself* amount to a conversion of them. Nevertheless, whilst there is old dicta that he is also not liable for refusing the goods owner's request to make them available the better view now appears to be that such a refusal following demand (a fortiori any dealing with/use of the goods by him) amounts to a conversion.[80]

Licences and the mutual benefit and burden principle

9.26 Although as a general rule the burden of a contractual obligation (in this case, to enjoy the land) is not assignable, it is possible for acceptance of the burden to be made a condition of the enjoyment of some corresponding benefit. In such case, acceptance of the benefit has the effect of making the burden pass. For instance, if adjoining owners agree that each shall have reciprocal rights (in the nature of licences[81]) over the other's land the burden of that right may be capable of passing to successors if they enjoy the corresponding benefit over the neighbouring land.

9.27 The burden may pass if it is a *condition* of the benefit which the successor enjoys, under the conditional benefits rule – see **10.21–10.22**. It may

---

[78] *Law Debenture Trust Corp v Ural Caspian Oil Corp Ltd* [1993] 1 WLR 138 (first instance), rev'd on different grounds [1995] 1 Ch 152.
[79] Ibid.
[80] *Thorogood v Robinson* (1845) 6 QB 769, at 777; *Clerk & Lindsell on Torts* (Sweet & Maxwell, 19th edn, 2006), at para 17-22. See **13.17** as regards the position after termination of the licence and any grace period.
[81] [1955] 1 WLR 213 (reciprocal rights to enjoy common drainage system passing through adjoining plots).

also pass under the mutual benefit and burden principle even if it is not a condition of the benefit but a mere covenant. To do so, however, the burden must be relevant or reciprocal to the exercise of the corresponding right which the successor enjoys, eg under his contract with his vendor.[82] The mere fact the benefit and burden are contained in the same document is not enough if they are, properly construed, independent. This requirement was recently formulated by the Court of Appeal in *Davies v Jones* as follows:[83]

> '(1) The benefit and burden must be conferred in or by the same transaction. In the case of benefits and burdens in relation to land it is almost inevitable that the transaction in question will be effected by one or more deeds or other documents.
>
> (2) The receipt or enjoyment of the benefit must be relevant to the imposition of the burden in the sense that the former must be conditional on or reciprocal to the latter. Whether that requirement is satisfied is a question of construction of the deeds or other documents where the question arises in the case of land or the terms of the transaction, if not reduced to writing, in other cases. In each case it will depend on the express terms of the transaction and any implications to be derived from them.
>
> (3) The person on whom the burden is alleged to have been imposed must have or have had the opportunity of rejecting or disclaiming the benefit, not merely the right to receive the benefit.'

9.28 The principle was applied recently in *Baybut v Eccle Riggs Country Park Ltd*[84] in relation to mobile homes licences by virtue of the fact the successor chose, when acquiring the land, to take the benefit of the caravan site and the income stream that it represented and undertook to the vendor-licensor to honour them.[85] Thus under the sale agreement the successor took the benefit of the licences conditionally on accepting the burdens. The authority is an example of the general proposition that:[86]

> '... one who takes the benefit of a licence to occupy the land granted to another in the form of an income stream ... by receiving periodical payments, will be bound by the burden to permit the licence-holder to occupy his pitch.'

It is not enough, however, that the licensor and his successor merely understand that the successor will honour the licence for the principle to apply; he must contract to do so.[87] Whether a mere covenant to do so in the sale agreement – shorn of any reciprocal benefit other than the acquisition of the land itself – is sufficient for the principle to apply may not yet be entirely certain. If it is, then constructive trust has little role in this context since in the circumstances where

---

[82] *Rhone v Stephens* [1994] 2 AC 310.
[83] [2010] 1 P&CR 423, at [27].
[84] [2006] All ER (D) 161 (Nov), at [51]–[57], [59].
[85] Such facts can, as was found, also result in the successor being bound in constructive trust/novation. An argument based on the mutual benefit and burden rule was, however, rejected at first instance in *IDC Group Ltd v Clark* [1992] 1 EGLR 187, at 190E–190G.
[86] *Davies v Jones* [2010] 1 P & CR 423, at [26].
[87] Ibid, at [28].

it arises the successor will also be bound under the mutual benefit and burden principle without the need to prove that his conscience is affected by the failure to honour his promise.[88]

Estoppel licences

Inchoate equity – unregistered land

9.29 In unregistered land the weight of authority favours the view that the equity, which arises as soon as the owner's conscience is affected,[89] is capable of binding his successors[90] except purchasers of a legal estate in the land for value without notice.[91] Such notice may be actual or constructive and may arise from the representee's use/occupation of the land.[92] Thus the owner's estate, devisees,[93] gratuitous transferees[94] and purchasers with notice may be bound.[95]

9.30 As stated above (Chapter 2), the application of estoppel principles in this context has been doubted; in particular why, if the burden of a (say, contractual) right – the licence – does not run, the burden of a mere *expectation* of such right can. The answer is thought to be that the estoppel does not create a licence properly so-called (the label 'estoppel licence' is a misnomer, albeit a useful one) but an equity. Although in principle it is capable of binding a successor the critical issue is whether it would be unconscionable for *him* to enforce his legal rights against the representee. It may be, where the expectation is of a right/interest that is in principle capable of binding successors. But it would not, where the understanding is that the representor is undertaking a merely *personal* obligation. For example, where the representee's expectation is of a mere licence and he is aware that such licences generally do not bind successors,[96] although in practice expectations are rarely, if ever, that clear.

---

[88] One possible advantage is that a constructive trust binds the successor throughout his ownership whereas it is as yet unresolved whether under the mutual benefit and burden principle, a successor can avoid the burden by renouncing the benefits acquired under the arrangement – compare *Halsall v Brizell* [1957] 1 Ch 169, at 182; *IDC Group Ltd v Clark* [1992] 1 EGLR 187, at 190G–190H; *Davies v Jones* [2010] 1 P&CR 423, at [32]–[34]. In reality, if the benefit and burden are contained in the sale contract by which the successor acquires the land, the possibility of him subsequently doing so in this context does not arise.

[89] *Re Sharpe* [1980] 1 WLR 219, at 225H.

[90] *Hopgood v Brown* [1955] 1 WLR 213; *Ward v Kirkland* [1966] 1 WLR 601, at 631–632; *Birmingham Midshires Mortgage Services Ltd v Sabherwal* (1999) 80 P & CR 256; *Lloyd v Dugdale* [2002] 2 P & CR 13, at [39].

[91] Spencer Bower and Turner *Estoppel by Representation* (LexisNexis Butterworths, 4th edn, 2004), at para VI.3.16 et seq; *Megarry & Wade: The Law of Real Property*, n 40 above, at para 16-031(ii).

[92] *Lyus v Prowsa Developments Ltd* [1982] 1 WLR 1044, at 1051C.

[93] *Jones v Jones* [1977] 1 WLR 438, at 442J, 443G.

[94] *Sutcliffe v Lloyd* [2008] EWHC 1329 (Ch), at [4].

[95] Spencer Bower and Turner, n 91 above, at para VI.3.16. See e g *Inwards v Baker* [1965] 2 QB 29, at 37F; *ER Ives Investments Ltd v High* [1967] 2 QB 379, at 400; *Shiloh Spinners Ltd v Harding* [1973] AC 691, at 721.

[96] See for a possible example *Maharaj v Chand* [1986] 1 AC 898, at 905C–906B. In that case the licence arose independently of the (promissory) estoppel (which prevented the licensor from exercising his right to terminate), neither of which ran against his successor.

9.31 The editors of *Estoppel by Representation*[97] suggest that the form of relief granted determines retrospectively whether the equity binds the successor: a proprietary right does; a personal right (eg contractual licence) does not. This is doubtful: it is the equity whose burden passes, not the form of relief by which the court, in its discretion, subsequently gives effect to it although the identity of the person against whom relief is sought is a relevant factor in determining whether/how the equity should be given effect to.

Inchoate equity – registered land

9.32 In relation to registered land, the weight of authority under the Land Registration Act 1925 favoured the view that the equity was capable of binding successors, eg as an overriding interest if the representee was in actual occupation.[98] Now, s 116 of the Land Registration Act 2002 declares 'for the avoidance of doubt' that equities arising by estoppel and mere equities – whenever created – have effect from the time of creation as an interest capable of binding successors, subject to the general rules as to the effect of dispositions on priorities. It follows such equities will be overridden by a registrable disposition for valuable consideration[99] (unless protected by notice,[100] restriction or actual occupation[101]), but not by a gratuitous disposition.[102]

Effect after judgment

9.33 As previously stated, the equity has no residual effect once it is given effect to by the court.[103] The form of relief therefore determines whether it is capable of binding successors and how (if at all) it must be protected to do so. The appropriate remedy is in the court's discretion; it may, if it deems appropriate, grant a personal licence,[104] which would therefore not bind successors – a factor that may militate against that form of relief.

---

[97] Spencer Bower and Turner, n 91 above, at para VI.3.22 et seq; *Baybut v Eccle Riggs Country Park Ltd* [2006] All ER (D) 161 (Nov), at [61]. See also Battersby (1991) Conv 36, at p 39.
[98] See eg *Thatcher v Douglas* [1996] NPC 406.
[99] Land Registration Act 2002, s 29(1).
[100] Ibid, s 29(2)(a)(i).
[101] Ibid, Sch 3, para 2. *Lloyd v Dugdale* [2002] 2 P & CR 13, at [39] (Land Registration Act 1925, s 70(1)(g)). However, an estoppel giving rise to a beneficial interest in the domestic (rather than commercial) sphere may be overreached: *Birmingham Midshires Mortgage Services Ltd v Sabherwal* (1999) 80 P & CR 256, at 262–263.
[102] Land Registration Act 2002, s 28.
[103] *Megarry & Wade: The Law of Real Property*, n 40 above, at para 16-033; Spencer Bower and Turner, n 91 above, at para VI.3.19; see eg *Maharaj v Chand* [1986] AC 898; contrast *Williams v Staite* [1979] Ch 291, at 296G, 300H (personal licence granted by court to give effect to equity bound purchaser subsequent to the order). The fact licences generally do not bind successors may be a factor against granting that form of relief: *Pascoe v Turner* [1979] 1 WLR 431, at 438–439.
[104] *Re Sharpe* [1980] 1 WLR 219, at 224G (relying on pre-*Anstalt* constructive trust cases). See also *Williams v Staite* [1979] Ch 291 (post-judgment equitable licence for life).

Licences converted by the Law of Property Act 1925, s 62

9.34 Licences may be converted into easements or profits under the Law of Property Act 1925, s 62[105] and, as such, bind the licensor's successors and/or prevent him/them from terminating those rights.

9.35 That will occur where: (a) a licence is granted over one plot of land (Whiteacre) for the benefit of other land (Blackacre), ie not merely for the licensee's personal benefit but for the more convenient use/occupation of Blackacre; (b) the rights are capable of existing as an easement or profit (eg not occupation rights that fall foul of the ouster principle – see **7.6** et seq); (c) both plots have a common owner; (d) the licensee subsequently acquires a freehold or leasehold interest in Blackacre; (e) the licence is actually enjoyed with or appertains to or is reputed to appertain to Blackacre at that time (although that may be shown if there was actual enjoyment some reasonable time before); (f) there was at the time of acquisition diversity of occupation between Whiteacre and Blackacre[106] or the right was continuous and apparent; and (g) the conveyance contains no contrary intention excluding s 62. If therefore Blackacre and Whiteacre have a common owner who grants a licence over Whiteacre in favour of the tenant of Blackacre (eg for access) and subsequently re-lets or sells the freehold of Blackacre to him, the licence, unless terminated beforehand, converts into an easement appurtenant to Blackacre.

9.36 A licence which is precarious in the sense that it is gratuitous and thus terminable at any time by Whiteacre's owner may thus convert under s 62; one that is precarious in the sense that the licensee can have no expectation of it continuing (eg because of the nature of the property over which it is to be enjoyed, such as a temporary facility) will not.[107]

Matrimonial home rights

9.37 Where one spouse/civil partner has a proprietary interest in land, the burden of the other's matrimonial home rights may pass to his successor. These rights have the attributes of an equitable charge and require protection by registration as a Class F land charge (unregistered land) or notice (registered land) – see **9.4** and **9.6**. A successor who is bound may nevertheless apply for an order restricting or terminating those rights under the Family Law Act 1996, s 34(2).

---

[105] *International Tea Stores Co v Hobbs* [1903] 2 Ch 165; *Goldberg v Edwards* [1950] Ch 247.
[106] Occupation of Whiteacre as licensee (eg as a purchaser allowed into occupation pending completion) is sufficient: *Lyme Valley Squash Club Ltd v Newcastle under Lyme BC* [1985] 2 All ER 405.
[107] Compare *Birmingham Dudley & District Banking Co v Ross* (1888) 38 ChD 295 (no expectation of right (to light) over land that was to be developed); *Wright v Macadam* [1949] 2 KB 744 (right over coal shed); *Hair v Gillman* [2000] 3 EGLR 74, at 75–77 (bare licence sufficient).

LICENCES TOGETHER WITH OTHER INTERESTS

9.38 A licensor or licensee may have a proprietary right/interest in the land that prima facie does not bind someone who subsequently acquires an interest in it for lack of registration, such as a licensee allowed into occupation pending completion of his unregistered contract to purchase the land. In such cases the licence, or rather the occupation by virtue of it, may nevertheless allow the licensor/licensee to claim priority in respect of his interest.

Licensee's interest

9.39 A licensee may claim priority in respect of his interest by virtue of the licence (or rather his resulting occupation) even if it is not 'coupled with' that interest,[108] eg if it is entered into subsequent to, and independently of, the interest. For instance, if the licensee has an equitable interest in unregistered land, his use of it pursuant to the licence may be sufficient notice of that interest, so as to bind subsequent purchasers of a legal estate.

9.40 In relation to registered land, such use, if it amounts to actual occupation, may make his registrable but unregistered interest an overriding one.[109] His occupation need not be by virtue of the interest;[110] occupation as licensee suffices. In order to have that effect the following conditions must be met:

- The licensee must actually occupy at the time the third party claiming priority acquires his interest.[111] Mere user, however intensive, falling short of occupation is insufficient.[112] 'Occupation' connotes physical presence that has some degree of permanence and continuity[113] but need not be exclusive.[114]

- He occupies on his own behalf, either personally or through an agent.[115] Occupation on behalf of the licensor is not enough.[116] Hence a service occupier is not in actual occupation for these purposes, but his employer may be.

---

[108] See eg *Donington Park Leisure Ltd v Wheatcroft & Sons Ltd* [2006] All ER (D) 94 (Apr) and the comment Dixon (2006) 70 P & CR 374.

[109] Unless the owner fails to disclose his interest on inquiry when he could have reasonably been expected to do so: Land Registration Act 2002, Sch 3, para 2(b). Land Registration Act 1925, s 70(1)(g) protected both unregistrable interests and registrable but unregistered interests; Sch 3 of the 2002 Act now specifies the types of interests capable of protection by actual occupation.

[110] See eg *Webb v Pollmount* [1966] 1 Ch 584, at 598 (unregistered option protected by occupation qua tenant).

[111] Land Registration Act 2002, Sch 3, para 2. Under Land Registration Act 1925 receipt of the rents and profits also qualified.

[112] *Holaw (470) Ltd v Stockton Estates Ltd* (2001) 81 P & CR 29.

[113] It is doubtful whether a lodger's occupation qualifies: *Hodgson v Marks* [1971] Ch 892, at 932E.

[114] *Williams & Glyn's Bank Ltd v Boland* [1981] AC 487.

[115] *Abbey National Building Society v Cann* [1991] 1 AC 56, at 93.

[116] See eg *Lloyd v Dugdale* [2002] 2 P & CR 13, at [45].

- His occupation is obvious on a reasonably careful inspection of the land or the interest is actually known to the purchaser.[117]

- (After October 2003) the occupation and the interest concern the same land.[118] If therefore the unregistered interest is over Blackacre and the licence concerns Whiteacre, Blackacre's successor will not be bound.

Licensor's interest

9.41 A licensor's interest may similarly be protected as an overriding interest by virtue of the *licensee's* sole occupation or by the use of the land by several licensees which together amounts to constructive occupation by the licensor. However, if the licensee is in sole occupation, it is thought that he must occupy on behalf of the licensor rather than on his own behalf.[119] Of course, the licensor may be in actual, personal occupation at the same time as the licensee(s).[120] If, however, the licensor is not in actual occupation, either personally or through his licensees, since the Land Registration Act 2002 came into force his mere receipt of the licence fees will not qualify for these purposes.

9.42 A licensor whose interest is protected by registration may, if faced with an application to alter or rectify his title by a third party, be in possession of the land by virtue of the licensee's use of the land, thereby bringing into effect the limitations on the power to correct the register in the Land Registration Act 2002, Sch 4, paras 3(2) and 6(2).[121] However, for these purposes the licensor must either retain possession or the licensee must possess on his behalf.

PERSONS WITH A SUPERIOR INTEREST TO THE LICENSOR

9.43 Where the licensor has less than a freehold interest in the land, the question may arise whether the licensee's rights bind someone with a superior interest. Normally no issue arises during the subsistence of the licensor's interest. If the licensor is himself a tenant/licensee with the right to possession or to grant the licence or acts with the (actual or ostensible) authority of the superior owner, the licensee has a defence to any action by that person. Note

---

[117] Land Registration Act 2002, Sch 3, para 2(c).
[118] Ibid, Sch 3, para 2 ('so far as relating to land of which he is in actual occupation ...'), reversing the effect of *Ferrishurst Ltd v Wallcite Ltd* [1999] Ch 355, at 372 (occupation of part of the land protects an interest in the whole under Land Registration Act 1925).
[119] Compare *Lloyd v Dugdale* [2002] 2 P & CR 13, at [44].
[120] *Williams & Glyn's Bank Ltd v Boland* [1981] AC 417, at 505E. A spouse with an unregistered interest may rely on the other spouse's occupation for the purposes of Land Registration Act 2002, Sch 3, para 2.
[121] Land Registration Act 2002, s 131(1), (2)(c).

that if the licensor is himself a licensee and the 'sub-licence' is of the whole of his rights for the remainder of the licence term it may take effect instead as an assignment of the licence.[122]

9.44 If the licence is granted in breach of the terms on which the licensor holds the land (eg as tenant[123]), the superior owner may be able to terminate his interest and evict both the licensor and licensee; the licensee has no standing to seek relief from forfeiture of the licensor's interest. If the superior owner elects not to terminate he may restrain the licensee from using the land only if (a) as between the licensor and the superior owner, the latter has the right to possession, (b) the licensee tortiously induced the breach (see **9.21–9.22**) or (c) the licensee's acts cause damage to the superior owner's reversionary interest.

9.45 The position regarding 'estoppel licences' (ie inchoate equities) is different. Although a proprietary interest, the equity usually does not bind someone with a superior interest to the representor as it is generally not unconscionable for that person to assert *his* legal rights unless his own conscience is bound, eg by standing by and knowingly allowing the representee to incur the detriment on the faith of the promise or because such promise was made on his behalf.

9.46 The licensee's right to use the land automatically ceases on the termination of the licensor's interest, eg for breach or by surrender/abandonment.[124] There are three exceptions:

- First, if the licensee has an estoppel that binds the superior owner (above).

- Second, if a new licence arises thereafter by novation between the licensee and the superior owner, eg by continued tender/acceptance of the licence fee.

- Third, if the licence is granted with the (actual or ostensible) authority of the superior owner to bind his interest. That the licensor has power to grant licences is not enough since prima facie they only bind his own

---

[122] See by analogy *Milmo v Carreras* [1946] KB 306 (purported sublease as assignment of lease).
[123] In covenants against sharing or parting with possession, 'possession' is to be given its strict legal meaning: *Clarence House Ltd v Nat West Bank* [2009] EWCA Civ 1311, at [32]. The grant of even a series of user licences is not a parting with possession nor is the grant of an occupation licence unless it entitles the licensee to occupy to the exclusion of all others. 'Sharing' for these purposes also means conferring of joint possession, which may be broken by allowing a third party into occupation to carry on a business: *Akici v LR Butlin Ltd* [2006] 1 WLR 201. A licence to erect an advertisement on the wall of a building was held not to constitute parting with possession of the wall in *Stening v Abraham* [1931] 1 Ch 470.
[124] *Kay v Lambeth LBC* [2006] 2 AC 465. Contrast the rule regarding subleases on the surrender of the headlease: *Mellor v Watkins* (1873-4) LR 9 QB 400; Law of Property Act 1925, s 139. However, the superior owner may be liable to the licensee for tortious inducement of the licensor's breach in such circumstances.

interest.[125] Nor does a licensor have ostensible authority to bind his superior merely because he is entitled to manage the property.[126] The licensor must act (actually or ostensibly) on behalf of the superior owner in granting the licence.

9.47 A licensor who is a tenant may lose statutory protection by virtue of the licensee's occupation. In general, security of tenure is conferred on tenants in actual/constructive occupation/residence. Where the licensor has a business tenancy, personal occupation for the purposes of the Landlord and Tenant Act 1954, s 23(1) is not essential; vicarious occupation through a licensee (e g an agent or manager) suffices. But where the licensee occupies on his own behalf the licensor cannot rely on that use. Nevertheless the licensor may remain in personal occupation of the particular area occupied by such licensee, depending on the extent of his reserved rights,[127] or of the whole land of which it forms part. For example, a licensor whose business consists of granting licences of parts of the premises (e g a hotel) will usually be in occupation of the whole of the land,[128] although it is a question of fact in each case:[129]

> '... the question whether [he] is sufficiently excluded, and the other is sufficiently present, for the latter to be regarded as the occupier in place of the former is a question of degree ... The types of property, and the possible uses of property, vary so widely that there can be no hard and fast rules. The degree of presence and exclusion required to constitute occupation, and the acts needed to evince presence and exclusion, must always depend upon the nature of the premises, the use to which they are being put, and the rights enjoyed or exercised by the persons in question ...
>
> Where the permission takes the form of a licence there will often be more room for debate [than in relation to subtenancies]. The rights granted by a licence tend to be less extensive than those comprised in a tenancy. In the nature of things, therefore, a licensor may have an easier task in establishing that he still occupies.'

A licensor will usually remain in residential occupation so as to retain security of tenure if the licensee is merely a lodger (e g friend, family member, partner) who lives with him. In such circumstances if the licensor temporarily vacates, the licensee's continued presence is relevant in determining whether he nevertheless remains in factual possession and/or has manifests an intention to return so as to retain security of tenure. If, however, the licensor evinces an

---

[125] See by analogy *Kay v Lambeth LBC* [2006] 2 AC 465; *Bruton v London & Quadrant Housing Trust* [2000] 1 AC 406.

[126] See by analogy *Islington LBC v Green* [2005] EWCA Civ 56, at [12], [18]–[21] (licensee granting *Bruton* sub-lease).

[127] See e g *Smith v Titanate Ltd* [2005] 3 EGLR 63 (owner not in occupation assuming residents were licensees, as reserved rights not unrestricted and exercisable only on reasonable notice).

[128] See e g *Groveside Properties Ltd v Westminster Medical School* [1983] 2 EGLR 68; *Linden v DHSS* [1986] 1 WLR 164.

[129] *Graysim Holdings Ltd v P&O Property Holdings Ltd* [1996] 1 AC 329, at 336B–336C, 336F.

intention no longer to live at the property (eg by granting a contractual licence of the whole), security of tenure will usually be lost notwithstanding the licensee's continued presence.[130]

PERSONS DERIVING TITLE THROUGH THE LICENSOR

9.48 Where the licensor's estate is subject to a proprietary right or interest (eg a charge or easement) or obligation (eg restrictive covenant) a bare or contractual licensee will be similarly bound,[131] whether it is created before or after the licence. Thus a chargee may recover possession in the event of the licensor's default free of the licensee's interest.[132]

9.49 The relative priorities of the 'interest' component of a licence coupled with an interest (if in land) and other proprietary rights/interests will depend on whether the competing rights/interests are legal or equitable and whether they are required to be (and are) protected by registration, notice etc and the order in which they are created/registered. For the relevant rules, reference should be made to a specialist text.

9.50 The rules as to the relative priorities of estoppel licences and other proprietary interests subsequently created by the representor are those applicable generally to proprietary estoppels and referred to briefly at **9.29** and **9.32**.

PERSONS WITH NO RIGHT TO USE THE LAND

9.51 In what circumstances does the licensor and/or licensee have standing to restrain a trespass on the land by a person with no right to be there or acts that interfere with its use and occupation? Since the issue predominantly arises in relation to contractual licences, the following is confined to them.

Trespass

Claim by the licensor

9.52 A licensor with a right to possession may sue in trespass third parties during the subsistence of the licence, even if the licensee is in factual possession

---

[130] See eg *Brown v Brash* [1948] 2 KB 247; *Thompson v Ward* [1953] 1 All ER 1169; *Colin Smith Music v Ridge* [1975] 1 All ER 290. Contrast the position regarding spouses and civil partners – Family Law Act 1996, s 30(4).
[131] See eg *Mander v Falcke* [1891] 2 Ch 554 (restrictive covenant binding occupier). The owner of the right/interest may exceptionally be bound in the circumstances considered at **9.46**.
[132] *Maharaj v Chand* [1986] 1 AC 898, at 908E: a licence is 'a personal right not amounting to a property interest diminishing the rights of the [licensor's] lessor and mortgagee ...'.

or, it appears, has a right of sole occupation falling short of possession.[133] If, however, the licence vests the right to possession in the licensee the licensor may not do so[134] unless the trespass threatens a permanent injury to the land/his interest[135] or takes place on land he retains. A licensor who has no legal right/interest in the land may sue if he is in factual possession, either personally or through his licensee(s).

Claim by the licensee

9.53 As explained at **2.45** et seq and **8.16**:

(1) A licensee who, exceptionally, has a right to possession may bring an action in trespass against third parties and the licensor (unless the latter is exercising a right of entry reserved by the licence agreement).[136] A mere right to use land (even an exclusive one) is insufficient, eg the sole right to operate boats on a lake.[137] Where, therefore, the parties to the licence share occupation, only the licensor may sue.

(2) A licensee in factual possession or occupation conferring control (see (3) below) may bring an action against third parties,[138] but not his licensor. Where both parties to the licence originally occupied the land simultaneously, the licensee will not assume factual possession merely because the licensor subsequently ceases to use the land, although he may do so if circumstances justify the conclusion that the nature of his occupation has changed.

(3) *Manchester Airport plc v Dutton*[139] controversially extended the remedy of possession to licensees with a mere unexercised right to enter and occupy land – falling short of possession as traditionally defined but conferring effective control – if the remedy was necessary in order to vindicate that right. In such case a licensor with possession would appear to have a concurrent right to sue the trespasser. More recently a licensee who exclusively occupied bedsit accommodation provided by the local authority was held to be able to exercise self-help to restrain a trespass in *Thomas v DPP*,[140] although it is in each case a question as to the degree and extent of his control; a lodger in a private house was held unable to

---

[133] It appears, following *Manchester Airport plc v Dutton* [2000] 1 QB 133, that the licensor and licensee have concurrent claims in trespass in such circumstances.
[134] *Cooper v Crabtree* (1882) 20 ChD 589 (landlord).
[135] Eg if it may bind his interest if it continues indefinitely unless something is done to prevent that or it operates as a denial of some right of the licence. Ibid; *Jones v Llanwrst UDC* [1911] 1 Ch 393. See the discussion in *John Smith & Co (Edinburgh) Ltd v Hill* [2010] EWHC 1016 (Ch).
[136] See eg *Marcroft Wagons Ltd v Smith* [1951] 2 KB 496, at 501; *Mehta v Royal Bank of Scotland* [1999] 3 EGLR 153.
[137] *Hill v Tupper* (1863) 2 H&C 121.
[138] *Asher v Whitlock* (1865) LR 1 QB 1; *Perry v Clissold* [1907] AC 73.
[139] [2000] 1 QB 133.
[140] (2009) *The Times*, November 25.

sue in *Allan v Liverpool Overseers*.[141] In comparison in *Countryside Residential (North Thames) Ltd v Tugwell*[142] a licensee with a mere right of access in order to survey and undertake technical investigations was held to lack standing.

(4) In other cases, where the licensee has no right to restrain the third party's use of the land, the licensor may owe him an implied duty to take reasonable steps to protect him from interference by such persons.[143]

Nuisance

9.54 A private nuisance is actionable primarily at the suit of someone with a proprietary interest in the land.[144] Accordingly bare and contractual licensees (and licensors who are themselves licensees) prima facie cannot sue, unless, exceptionally, they have a right to possession[145] or are in factual possession.[146] Hence in *Stockport Waterworks Co v Potter*[147] the grantee of water rights was unable to sue for interference with the purity of the stream; in *Malone v Laskey*[148] the licensee was held unable to bring an action in nuisance for injuries sustained by vibrations (although an action in negligence might have succeeded[149]); and in *Hunter v Canary Wharf Ltd*[150] licensees were held unable to sue for interference with television signals. A licensor with a proprietary interest may sue (concurrently with the licensee if the latter is in legal or factual possession, although in the former case the licensor's ability to sue for temporary nuisances is circumscribed[151]).

9.55 A person with a licence coupled with an interest in land may sue in nuisance for interference with that interest; actions that prevent or hinder the exercise of the licence are likely to amount to such an interference.

---

[141] (1874) LR 9 QB 180
[142] (2000) 81 P & CR 2.
[143] *Cartwright v Merthyr Tydfil BC* (unreported), CA, 22 May 2000.
[144] *Hunter v Canary Wharf Ltd* [1997] AC 655.
[145] [1997] AC 655, at 688, 692, 695, 703, 724. This category includes non-owning spouses/civil partners entitled to possession by virtue of an order under Family Law Act 1996: ibid, at 693G, 708D.
[146] *Foster v Warblington UDC* [1906] 1 KB 648; *Hunter v Canary Wharf Ltd* [1997] AC 655. De facto exclusive occupation is not synonymous with possession.
[147] (1864) 3 H&C 300.
[148] [1907] 2 KB 141.
[149] *Hunter v Canary Wharf Ltd* [1997] AC 655, at 696C–696D.
[150] [1997] AC 655.
[151] See n 135 above.

Chapter 10

THE BENEFIT OF THE LICENCE

Assignment of the licence	10.2
Bare licences	10.2
Contractual licences	10.4
Licences and the mutual benefit and burden principle	10.25
Licences coupled with an interest	10.28
Estoppel licences	10.30
Sub-licences	10.35
Bare licences	10.36
Contractual licences	10.39
Licences and the mutual benefit and burden principle	10.45
Licences coupled with an interest	10.46
Estoppel licences	10.47
Bruton tenancies	10.48

10.1 Chapter 9 considered the running of the burden of the licence. This chapter addresses the converse issue: who, apart from the licensee, can take its benefit – specifically, can he assign the right to use the land or allow others to use it as his sub-licensees or *Bruton* tenants?[1] Since the licensor's successor will usually wish to – and will – take free of the licence (see Chapter 9) the issue seldom arises regarding assignment of the licensor's rights.[2]

ASSIGNMENT OF THE LICENCE

Bare licences

10.2 A bare licence is a gratuitous permission that confers immunity to a claim in trespass. Its benefit therefore cannot be assigned, because there is no 'right' which can pass[3] and/or because the permission is personal to the licensee. Nevertheless it may be enjoyed by others if intended to extend to them, either concurrently with the licensee or consecutively. For example, a

---

[1] Note also the benefit of a licence which is converted into an easement or profit under Law of Property Act 1925, s 62 and licences with security of tenure which are treated as (or converted into) leases may also pass to successors in title. See Chapters 6 and 9.

[2] Eg an assignment of the income stream, the right to which is normally assignable absent an express term to the contrary: *Linden Gardens Trust Ltd v Lenesta Sludge Disposals Ltd* [1994] 1 AC 85, at 104H–105G.

[3] See **8.1**.

bare licence arising from circumstances and intended to accommodate the licensee's other land may inure for the benefit of the owner/occupiers for the time being of that land. In such case the benefit of the original licence does not *pass*; either it extended to them from the outset or the continuation of the circumstances from which it is inferred gives rise to a new or standing invitation to enter.[4] Furthermore the licensee may have the licensor's authority to invite others onto the land or to communicate his (the licensor's) invitation. Neither is a true exception to the rule that the benefit of a bare licence is incapable of passing; in both cases the invitor is the licensor.

10.3 A purported but ineffective assignment of a bare licence is thought to evince an intention by the licensee no longer to enjoy its benefits and thus amounts to a disclaimer, at least once it is communicated to the licensor. If so, the licensee may continue to enjoy the licence by resiling from the purported assignment before the licensor becomes aware of it.

Contractual licences

Assignment

10.4 Contractual principles determine whether the licensee's rights are assignable.[5] It is:[6]

> '... trite law that it is ... impossible to assign "the contract" as a whole ie both burden and benefit. The burden of a contract can never be assigned without the consent of the other party to the contract in which event such consent will give rise to a novation ...'

Thus, absent a novation, the licensee can only assign the benefits of the licence; the obligations (eg to pay the licence fee) remain with him, although the assignee may be concurrently liable to the licensor under the conditional benefits principle (below, at **10.22**) and may be liable to indemnify a licensee who is made to pay. Nevertheless whilst the licensor cannot be made to accept performance from a third party *in place of* the licensee, the licensee may be able to 'vicariously' perform his burdens (eg by requiring the assignee to pay the licence fee direct to the licensor), unless they require personal performance (eg a domestic servant)[7] or the exercise of rights (eg the use of the land) which are expressly or impliedly personal to him.

---

[4] See eg *ER Ives Investments Ltd v High* [1967] 2 QB 379, at 404. *Mellor v Watkins* (1873–74) LR 9 QB 400 (cited by Dawson and Pearce *Licences Relating to the Occupation or Use of Land* (Butterworths, 1979), at p 131 as an example of the benefit of a bare licence passing by assignment) is explicable on this basis.

[5] See for assignments by operation of law Treitel *The Law of Contract* (Sweet & Maxwell, 12th edn, 2007), at paras 15.070–15.075.

[6] *Linden Gardens Trust Ltd v Lenesta Sludge Disposals Ltd* [1994] 1 AC 85, at 103B, per Lord Browne-Wilkinson.

[7] *British Waggon Co v Lea & Co* (1880) 5 QBD 149, at 153. See generally *Chitty on Contracts* (Sweet & Maxwell, 30th edn, 2008), at paras 19-081–19-084.

Are the benefits assignable?

10.5 Assignability is a question of construction of the particular right: 'the benefit of some obligations ... under one contract may be assignable whilst at the same time others under the same contract may not: assignability is not a matter of all obligations arising under the contract or none at all.'[8] Nevertheless 'prima facie contractual rights to ... the ... occupation or use of land ... do not involve personal considerations and are capable of assignment'.[9] The right to assign may be expressly or impliedly excluded or limited.

Express prohibitions/limitations on assignment

10.6 An express prohibition on assignment may be absolute or qualified. It may be framed as a condition/stipulation that the right(s) cannot be assigned or a covenant by the licensee not to do so. In the latter case, the obligation should framed to include purported assignments if the licensor wishes to have a remedy for breach against the licensee (eg termination) since an attempted assignment of contractual rights contrary to the licence terms is ineffective (below) and thus not a breach of a covenant against 'assignment' per se.[10]

10.7 Both the (purported) assignment and the prohibition must be construed to determine if one falls foul of the other. A prohibition against assigning 'the licence' will usually be construed as meaning its benefits[11] and prima facie includes both accrued and future rights (eg the right to the future use of the land), unless the clause indicates otherwise.[12] Such a prohibition may not prevent the licensee declaring himself trustee of its benefits[13] unless it expressly so provides, although such a trust would not entitle the 'assignee' to use the land in breach of contract.

Qualified prohibitions on assignment

10.8 Where the licensor's consent to the assignment is required it must be sought beforehand, even if it could not be legitimately withheld.[14] With the

---

[8] *Don King Productions Ltd v Warren* [2000] Ch 291, at 319A (first instance).
[9] *Chitty on Contracts*, n 7 above, at para 19-055; Dawson and Pearce, n 4 above, at p 134. See also *Tolhurst v Associated Portland Cement Manufacturers (1900) Ltd* [1903] AC 414, at 420; *J Miller Ltd v Laurence & Bardsley* [1966] 1 Lloyd's Rep 90, at 94; *Lymington Marina Ltd v Macnamara* [2006] EWHC 704 (Ch), at [65] (on appeal [2007] EWCA Civ 151). Contrast *Dorling v Honnor Marine Ltd* [1963] 2 All ER 495, at 502 (first instance); *Donington Park Leisure Ltd v Wheatcroft & Sons Ltd* [2006] All ER (D) 94, at [44]; *ER Ives Investments Ltd v High* [1967] 2 QB 379, at 404.
[10] *Hendry v Chartsearch Ltd* [1998] EWCA Civ 1276, at [34]. See also *Linden Gardens Trust Ltd v Lenesta Sludge Disposals Ltd* [1994] 1 AC 85, at 108F.
[11] *Linden Gardens Trust Ltd v Lenesta Sludge Disposals Ltd* [1994] 1 AC 85, at 103E.
[12] *Don King Productions Ltd v Warren* [2000] Ch 291, at 319C–319D. Compare *Flood v Shand Construction Ltd* [1996] EWCA Civ 1241; *Helstan Securities Ltd v Hertfordshire CC* [1978] 3 All ER 262.
[13] See by analogy *Gentle v Faulkner* [1900] 2 QB 267 (lease).
[14] *Hendry v Chartsearch Ltd* [1998] EWCA Civ 1276, per Millett and Henry LJJ; Evans LJ leaving the point open.

exception of certain licences with security of tenure,[15] however, there are no specific statutory qualifications on the licensor's right to withhold consent or to impose conditions when granting it.[16]

10.9 Contractual qualifications on such right may be express or implied.[17] The right may be absolute[18] but that is rare. Such contractual discretions are usually restricted by the implication of a term, which may take a variety of forms (eg that it should not be exercised unreasonably/for an improper purpose/capriciously/arbitrarily/in bad faith etc[19]). It may also expressly/impliedly limit the factors the licensor may take into account when considering an application for consent (eg the assignee's identity,[20] his financial strength, the proposed use of the land, general estate management considerations[21] etc).

10.10 The typical form of express qualification, which requires the licensor's consent '... such consent not to be unreasonably withheld', takes effect as a limitation on his power to refuse/impose terms on the grant of consent rather than a covenant by him not exercise it unreasonably.[22] Accordingly an unjustified refusal or the imposition of an unreasonable condition is merely invalid and does not render him liable in damages;[23] the licensee's remedy is to seek a declaration that consent was unreasonably withheld or to assign on the basis that the refusal/condition was unlawful. In determining whether the licensor acted reasonably, some guidance may be derived from authorities on the equivalent proviso in leases.[24]

10.11 If the licensee assigns without consent, an application for *retrospective* consent will not engage any contractual limitation on the licensor's powers[25] since what is sought is not consent within the contract. If given, however, it may operate as a waiver of the breach, variation or estoppel. As, however, the purported assignment is ineffective to vest the rights in the assignee (see below)

---

[15] See eg Mobile Homes Act 1983, Sch 1, Pt I, para 8(1), (1B).

[16] Landlord and Tenant Act 1927, s 19 is inapplicable to contractual licences: *Lymington Marina Ltd v Macnamara* [2007] EWCA Civ 151, at [27]. Query as to the application of the Unfair Terms in Consumer Contracts Regulations 1999, SI 1999/2083.

[17] See eg *Lymington Marina Ltd v Macnamara* [2007] EWCA Civ 151, at [39]–[44]; *Rickman v Brudenell-Bruce* [2005] EWHC 3400 (Ch); *Sims v Mahon* [2005] All ER (D) 169 (Jun); *Price v Bouch* (1986) 53 P & CR 257.

[18] See eg *Lombard Tricity Finance Ltd v Paton* [1989] 1 All ER 918, at 923f.

[19] *Lymington Marina v Macnamara* [2007] EWCA Civ 151, at [44] (berth licence). See the review of authorities in *Horkulak v Cantor Fitzgerald International* [2004] EWCA Civ 1287.

[20] *Lymington Marina v Macnamara* [2007] EWCA Civ 151, at [44].

[21] Ibid, at [28], [37]–[45].

[22] *Treloar v Bigge* (1874) 9 Exch 151.

[23] *Lee v Berkeley Leisure Group Ltd* (1995) 73 P & CR 493 (Mobile Homes Act 1983 licence). See now, however, in relation to such licences n 15 above.

[24] See eg *International Drilling Fluids Ltd v Louisville Investments (Uxbridge) Ltd* [1986] Ch 513, at 519H–521D (assignment); *Straudley Investments Ltd v Mount Eden Land Ltd* (1997) 74 P & CR 306 (sub-lease).

[25] *Hendry v Chartsearch Ltd* [1998] EWCA Civ 1276, at [31], point (2), per Evans LJ.

the licensee should, rather than applying for retrospective consent, seek consent under the contract to a fresh assignment, thereby engaging the limitations (if any) in it on the licensor's powers.[26]

Implied prohibitions on assignment

10.12 The licence may impliedly prohibit the licensee from assigning his rights. The question is whether 'on the true construction of the contract, when interpreted in relation to the surrounding circumstances and its own subject matter, it was the intention of the parties that the contract should be assignable'.[27]

10.13 That may be so where the licensee's identity is not material to the licensor, eg tickets to watch sporting events, parking or storage licences[28] (although they are often made expressly non-transferable). Conversely a prohibition is likely to be implied if the licensee's personal characteristics/skills are relevant[29] or the licence is part of an arrangement under which he undertakes personal services (eg as domestic staff) or the licensor reposes personal confidence in him. For example:

- Licences granted to employees – even where the requirements of a service occupancy are not met (see **6.29**) – are usually personal and therefore non assignable, although the employee will in most cases be able to allow others to live with him (eg family members) unless the licence terms or the nature of the accommodation dictate otherwise.[30]

- A licence is likely to be impliedly personal if granted because of the licensee's personal characteristics (eg seamen's missions, almshouses– objects of charity) or relationship to the licensor (eg licences granted to office-holders or members of a company or unincorporated association etc).

- It also is likely to be personal where the burden on the licensor's land may vary depending on the licensee's personal attributes/requirements (eg a right to extract such quantity of minerals as the licensee needs).[31]

- That is to be contrasted with licences where the degree of user is fixed (eg a right to a certain quantity of materials) or limited by other objective criteria. For example, a licence granted for the benefit of the licensee's other land may be impliedly limited to the needs of that land so that

---

[26] *Barbados Trust Co Ltd v Bank of Zambia* [2007] EWCA Civ 148, at [62].
[27] *Shayler v Woolf* [1946] Ch 320, at 322.
[28] *J Miller Ltd v Laurence & Bardsley* [1966] 1 Lloyd's Rep 90 (mooring licence).
[29] *Tolhurst v Associated Portland Cement Manufacturers (1900) Ltd* [1903] AC 414, at 417.
[30] For a possible example in the context of building contracts, see *Linden Gardens Trust Ltd v Lenesta Sludge Disposals Ltd* [1994] 1 AC 85, at 105.
[31] *Tolhurst v Associated Portland Cement Manufacturers (1900) Ltd* [1903] AC 414. Query whether an implied limitation of reasonable user could warrant a finding that the licence was assignable.

changes in its ownership will not result in a material alteration in the burden on the licensor's land.[32] That may also be so where the frequency/extent of the licensee's user is impliedly limited to what is reasonable, taking account of the licensor's/other licensee's concurrent right to use the land.

10.14 In addition, the licence terms and the circumstances in which it was created may justify an implied limitation:

- If (eg) the licence is part of a wider transaction under which the licensee acquires some proprietary right/interest, its terms must be considered to determine if the licence is assignable at all or independently of such right/interest.

- A long-term licence which the parties contemplate is unlikely to be enjoyed by the licensee personally throughout its duration is more likely to be impliedly assignable than a transient right.[33]

- References in the licence to the licensee's successors/assigns strongly favour assignability.[34] The absence of such reference does not even raise a presumption to the contrary.[35]

- An express right to sub-licence the whole of the land for the whole of the term favours the implication of a right to assign.[36]

- Where the licence is granted for the benefit of the licensee's other land, it is likely to be assignable together with that land,[37] but not otherwise.

- The rights may only be assignable in their entirety rather than piecemeal[38] or only outright and not (eg) by way of charge.

Manner of assignment

10.15 General contractual rules determine how contractual rights 'in gross'[39] to use/occupy land may be assigned; they are therefore taken shortly. Two methods are possible: equitable assignments; and statutory assignments under

---

[32] See eg *Shayler v Woolf* [1946] Ch 320.
[33] *Tolhurst v Associated Portland Cement Manufacturers (1900) Ltd* [1903] AC 414, at 419.
[34] See eg *Clore v Theatrical Properties Ltd* [1936] 3 All ER 483. Cf *IDC Group Ltd v Clark* [1992] 1 EGLR 187, at 189M, aff'd [1992] 2 EGLR 184 (reference to successors in title insufficient to imply that the *burden* would pass to successors and, thus, that the rights were easements rather than licences).
[35] *Tolhurst v Associated Portland Cement Manufacturers (1900) Ltd* [1903] AC 414, at 423; *Shayler v Woolf* [1946] Ch 320.
[36] See eg *J Miller Ltd v Laurence & Bardsley* [1966] 1 Lloyd's Rep 90, at 95.
[37] *Tolhurst v Associated Portland Cement Manufacturers (1900) Ltd* [1903] AC 414, at 420, 423; *Shayler v Woolf* [1946] Ch 320.
[38] *Donington Park Leisure Ltd v Wheatcroft & Sons Ltd* [2006] All ER (D) 94.
[39] Ie which are not terms of some other interest (eg lease) or appurtenant to land.

the Law of Property Act 1925, s 136.[40] An assignment which purports to use one method but does not meet the relevant requirements is nevertheless valid if it satisfies the requirements for the other.[41]

10.16 An equitable assignment can take one of two forms: by the licensee informing the assignee that he transfers the right to use the land to him or by instructing the licensor, with the assignee's knowledge, to discharge his obligations by allowing the assignee to use the land. In the former case the licensor need not be given notice, although it is good practice to do so if only to avoid him subsequently obtaining a discharge of his obligations from the licensee. An equitable assignment requires a sufficient manifestation of the licensee's intention to assign, clear identification of the right being assigned and some act by the licensee by which the benefit is passed to the assignee; it is enough if he, by words/act, conveys to the assignee his intention to transfer the benefit of the right.[42] It need not be in writing or take any particular form.[43]

10.17 A statutory assignment must be absolute, in writing signed by the licensee and written notice of it must be given to the licensor. No consideration is required.[44] The requirement that the assignment be absolute prohibits the licensee from assigning his rights in this way by way of charge or for only part of the licence term.[45] A statutory assignment is effective from the time the licensor receives notice[46] and entitles the assignee to enforce his rights by action without having also to join the licensee.[47]

Effect of prohibited assignment

Between the licensee/assignee and licensor

10.18 A purported assignment of the licensee's right in breach of a condition or covenant or which the licence declares to be incapable of assignment is ineffective as against the licensor.[48] In such case the licensor will have no

---

[40] NB none of the circumstances in which choses in action can be assigned at common law apply to licences.
[41] *William Brandt's Sons & Co v Dunlop Rubber Co* [1905] AC 454, at 461.
[42] *Phelps v Spon-Smith & Co* [2001] BPIR 326, at 337–338. See as to the need for consideration for agreements to assign *Chitty on Contracts*, n 7 above, at para 19-027 et seq.
[43] Although an equitable assignment of an equitable chose in action must be in writing if caught by Law of Property Act 1925, s 53(1)(c), that is inapplicable in this context as a contractual licence is not an equitable 'interest or trust' – see Chapter 9. Contrast the position where the 'interest' component of a licence coupled with an interest is in land – below.
[44] *Holt v Heatherfield Trust Ltd* [1942] 2 KB 1, at 5.
[45] See by analogy *Forster v Baker* [1910] 2 KB 636.
[46] *Holt v Heatherfield Trust Ltd* [1942] 2 KB 1.
[47] Compare *Chitty on Contracts*, n 7 above, at paras 19-038–19-041 as to the need to join in the licensee to an action on the licence in cases of equitable assignments.
[48] *Linden Gardens Trust Ltd v Lenesta Sludge Disposals Ltd* [1994] 1 AC 85, at 108F (covenant against assignment 'very unlikely' to be construed as removing only the right, not the power, to make a valid assignment); *Helstan Securities Ltd v Hertfordshire CC* [1978] 3 All ER 262. Contrast the position regarding assignments of leases: *Old Groverbury Manor Farm Ltd v W Seymour Plant Sales & Hire Ltd (No 2)* [1979] 1 WLR 1397.

contractual liability to the 'assignee'[49] and may prevent him entering the land or claim damages for trespass should he do so. If the purported assignment is a breach of condition or a breach of covenant (see **10.6**) which entitles the licensor to terminate, he may do so. He may instead elect to affirm, in which case he must (of course) continue to allow the licensee to use the land. If, however, the licensor waives the breach or is estopped from relying on it[50] or subsequently acknowledges the 'assignee' as his licensee so as to give rise to a novation (below) the assignee becomes entitled to use the land.

Between the licensee and assignee

10.19 An ineffective assignment prima facie will not invalidate the agreement as between the licensee and the assignee and may take effect between them as a contract to assign[51] or possibly a declaration of trust by the licensee.[52] Such a contract may be absolute (in which case the licensee will be contractually liable to his assignee for failing to make title to the rights purportedly assigned[53]) or conditional, eg on securing the licensor's consent. In the latter case, the condition may be a 'pure' condition or – more likely – a promissory one. In the former case neither party has an obligation to ensure it is met and, if it is not, both are discharged from their obligations under the contract of assignment. In the latter case, the licensee prima facie does not absolutely promise to bring that about (although he may expressly do so[54]) but is likely to be under a duty of mere reasonable diligence (eg to use reasonable endeavours) to secure the licensor's consent.[55] What that requires varies according to its terms and the circumstances. At a bare minimum it will require him actually to apply for consent and, possibly, to respond to such reasonable requests for information as the licensor may make.[56]

10.20 An invalid assignment that takes effect as a declaration of trust may entitle the 'assignee' to enforce the contract direct against the licensor using the procedure in *Vandepitte v Preferred Accident Insurance Corp*[57] unless prohibited by the licence.[58] Such a trust would not, however, entitle the 'assignee' to enjoy the right to use the land in breach of the licence terms.

---

[49] *Barbados Trust Co Ltd v Bank of Zambia* [2007] EWCA Civ 148, at [87].
[50] See by analogy *Woodfall's Landlord & Tenant* (Sweet & Maxwell, looseleaf), at para 16.081; *Orion Finance Ltd v Crown Financial Management Ltd* [1994] BCLC 607.
[51] *Linden Gardens Trust Ltd v Lenesta Sludge Disposals Ltd* [1994] 1 AC 85, at 108; *Devefi Pty Ltd v Mateffy Pearl Nagy Pty Ltd* [1993] FCA 152, at [36], point (3)(a).
[52] *Re Turcan* (1880) 40 Ch D 5, at 10–11.
[53] *Helstan Securities Ltd v Hertfordshire CC* [1978] 3 All ER 262, at 264.
[54] See eg *The Rolimpex* [1979] AC 351, at 371.
[55] See eg *Gamerco SA v ICM/Fair Warning (Agency) Ltd* [1995] 1 WLR 1226, at 1231B–1231C.
[56] See by analogy *Jolley v Carmel* [2000] 2 EGLR 153, aff'd [2000] 3 EGLR 68.
[57] [1933] AC 70, at 79. See also *Devefi Pty Ltd v Mateffy Pearl Nagy Pty Ltd* [1993] FCA 152, at [36], point (3).
[58] *Barbados Trust Co Ltd v Bank of Zambia* [2007] EWCA Civ 148, at [47], [119]; contrast ibid, at [139].

Effect of valid assignment

Between licensee/assignee and licensor

10.21 The result of a valid assignment is that the assignee steps into the licensee's shoes[59] and therefore takes subject to any defect in the licensee's title (eg if vitiated by mistake, misrepresentation etc), to any condition/qualification in the licence agreement on the exercise of the right and to any defence to an action by the assignee to enforce his right that would have available against the licensee.

10.22 A valid assignment of the benefits does not, of course, *pass* the burdens of the licence (eg the obligation to pay the licence fee); the licensor may continue to look to the licensee. The licensor may also look to the assignee if he was required to covenant directly to observe the licence terms, eg as a condition of granting consent to the assignment. He may also do so under the conditional benefits rule, but only if the right assigned (here, to use the land) is expressly or impliedly conditional on the performance of some corresponding obligation (eg to pay the licence fee).[60] The question whether a benefit is conditional is one of construction. Hence:[61]

> 'An instrument may be framed so that it confers only a conditional or qualified right, the condition or qualification being that certain restrictions shall be observed or certain burdens assumed, such as an obligation to make certain payments. Such restrictions or qualifications are an intrinsic part of the right: you take the right as it stands, and you cannot pick out the good and reject the bad. In such cases it is not only the original grantee who is bound by the burden: his successors in title are unable to take the right without also assuming the burden. The benefit and the burden have been annexed to each other ab initio, and so the benefit is only a conditional benefit.'

For example, in *Tolhurst v Associated Portland Cement Manufacturers (1900) Ltd*[62] an assignee of a contractual right to a supply of chalk for use on a piece of land was not required to take chalk from the supplier, but having done so was bound by a solus agreement in the licence to satisfy all his requirements for that land from the supplier. The assignee, however, will not be liable direct to the licensor under this principle if the obligation and the right are, properly construed, independent.[63] Even so, his rights are precarious in that if the licensee fails to perform the obligation the licensor may be able to terminate. If the licensee does so, the assignee may be liable to indemnify him. The mutual benefit and burden principle may also operate so as to bind the assignee (see Chapter 9).

---

[59] *Muskett v Hill* (1839) 5 Bing NC 694, at 710.
[60] *Aspden v Seddon (No 2)* (1876) 1 Ex D 496; *Westhoughton UDC v Wigan Coal & Iron Co Ltd* [1919] 159, at 171–172.
[61] *Tito v Waddell (No 2)* [1977] Ch 106, at 270A–270C.
[62] [1903] AC 414.
[63] *Radstock Co-Op v Norton Radstock* [1967] Ch 1094.

Novation

10.23 The effect of a novation is not to assign the benefit of the original rights but to extinguish the original contractual licence and replace it with a new one between the licensor and the new licensee. The necessary consideration is provided by the mutual release of the rights/obligations of the original parties and the assumption of the new ones by the new parties. The consent of all three is required to a novation. In contrast to an assignment:

(1) A novation necessarily effects a discharge of the future rights and obligations of the parties under the original licence[64] but not accrued ones, unless the arrangement also amounts to a release.

(2) The new licensee's liability to the licensor is not, unlike the assignee's, limited to those which pass under the conditional benefits rule (and possibly the mutual benefit and burden principle).[65]

(3) The new and old licensees are not concurrently liable to the licensor, unlike the licensee and assignee (where the conditional benefits principle applies or the assignee covenanted directly with the licensor). Accordingly the licensor will not be able to terminate the new licence if the old licensee fails to perform his outstanding duties, if any. Nor will the new and old licensees generally owe each other duties in relation to the discharge of their obligations under their respective licences.

(4) The terms of the new licence may, of course, be different from the original licence terms.

10.24 The distinction between a novation and assignment is sometimes difficult to draw in practice, particularly if the licence is (only) assignable with the licensor's consent. In such case the issue is: to what is the licensor consenting – the substitution of the original contract or merely a change in the identity of the person entitled to use the land under the original licence? For example, the fact that under the arrangement the new licensee is liable to pay may be ambiguous since that may be a condition of the licensor's consent and/or because he is liable under the conditional benefits rule. He may also tender payment on the licensee's behalf. Even if the terms on which he occupies are different, that may be by virtue of some contemporaneous agreement to vary the original licence terms. The answer depends on the parties' intentions and in particular whether the new arrangement was to have the attributes listed in **10.23(1)–(3)**.

---

[64] See by analogy *QFS Scaffolding Ltd v Sable* [2010] EWCA Civ 682 (surrender).
[65] See eg *Cornish v Stubbs* (1870) LR 5 CP 334, at 338, 340, although that can be explained on the basis the licence was a term of the licensee's tenancy (over other land) and, as such, bound licensor's successor. See for an example *Baybut v Eccle Riggs Country Park Ltd* [2006] All ER (D) 161 (Nov). Of course the position is different if the assignee contracts directly with the licensor as part of the consent to assign.

Licences and the mutual benefit and burden principle

10.25 The mutual benefit and burden principle concerns the running of the burden (rather than the benefit) of obligations, where the successor enjoys the benefit of some related right. The circumstances in which it applies are briefly considered in Chapter 9.

10.26 Where such a right concerns land, it may be a licence (or akin to one). In most if not all cases where the principle applies the original arrangement creating the right and obligation has contractual force, the one providing consideration for the other. Both must have been intended to pass (or be capable of passing) to the parties' respective successors in title, in the sense that they were not meant to be purely personal to the original parties. Such intention, if not express, may be implied taking into account the factors listed at **10.13** and **10.14**. If (eg) as is often the case, the rights are agreed between adjoining landowners and intended to benefit their respective properties, both the benefit and the burden will usually have been intended to run to their respective successors.

10.27 It is as yet uncertain, where the principle applies, whether and in what circumstances the assignee may disclaim the benefit (or merely desist from enjoying it) in order to avoid the corresponding burden.[66]

Licences coupled with an interest

10.28 A licence coupled with an interest will be assignable if the interest itself is assignable; if not, then not. As most interests in land are prima facie assignable[67] so too are the relevant licences. As, however, the licence is essentially ancillary to the interest, it cannot be assigned independently of it. An assignment of an interest that is in its nature *capable* of assignment but which amounts to a breach of covenant is effective to vest title to it (and the ancillary licence) in the assignee, subject to the covenantee's remedies for the breach; the owner of the interest has the power, if not the right, to assign.[68]

10.29 An assignment of the interest component must comply with the formalities and registration requirements for interests of that type in order to vest legal title in the assignee. In contrast to where the licence is a mere term of the interest (eg lease), it is uncertain whether the benefit of a licence coupled with an interest passes automatically on an assignment of the interest or whether it must be expressly assigned.[69]

---

[66] Compare *Halsall v Brizell* [1957] 1 Ch 169, at 182; *IDC Group Ltd v Clark* [1992] 1 EGLR 187, at 190G–190H; and *Davies v Jones* [2010] 1 P & CR 423, at [32]–[34].
[67] *Muskett v Hill* (1839) 5 Bing NC 694, at 707, 710.
[68] See *William Brandt's Sons & Co v Dunlop Rubber Co* [1905] AC 454, at 461; *Old Groverbury Manor Farm Ltd v W Seymour Plant Sales & Hire Ltd (No 2)* [1979] 1 WLR 1397.
[69] *Kumar v Dunning* [1989] QB 193, at 198; [1987] 2 All ER 801; [1987] 3 WLR 1167.

Estoppel licences

10.30 An 'estoppel licence', as the term is used here, is to be distinguished from an orthodox (e g contractual) licence created independently of the equity whose revocation is protected by estoppel. A consideration of the transmissibility of the latter types of estoppel is beyond the scope of this book.[70] What follows concerns the former.

Inchoate equity

Assignment of the equity

10.31 Although it is possible to find indications in authorities that the equity is personal to the representee and therefore cannot be shared by – or passed to – others,[71] the weight of authority favoured the view that such estoppels are proprietary interests,[72] which are prima facie transmissible. It is thought to follow that the benefit of the equity is prima facie assignable.[73]

10.32 However, the particular expectation which the representor created or the representee held can be critical. If it is of a purely personal right – e g based on a particular attribute of the representee (such as the employee's widow in *Binions v Evans*,[74] the common-law wife in *Pascoe v Turner*[75] and the daughter-in-law in *Hardwick v Johnson*[76]) or the particular personal relationship between the parties (e g as partners) – there will usually be no expectation that its benefit could be assigned to someone else. In such cases, whether or not the equity is assignable, it would not be unfair for the owner to assert his rights against an assignee. Even so, those representees will usually expect to be able to share the land (e g with friends/family) unless the context otherwise indicates. In contrast, if the expectation arises in a purely commercial context or is of a right/interest that is freely alienable (e g a freehold interest[77]) or which benefits the representee's other land (as in *Crabb v Arun DC*[78]), the equity is prima facie assignable (but not, in the latter case, separately from the land).

---

[70] See e g *Brikom Investments Ltd v Carr* [1979] QB 467.
[71] See e g *Jones v Jones* [1977] 1 WLR 438, at 443 (representee's spouse); *Matharu v Matharu* (1994) 68 P & CR 93, at 98 (representee's widow). The point was raised but not decided in *Fryer v Brook* [1998] BPIR 687, at 693A–693B.
[72] See Chapter 9. See now Land Registration Act 2002, s 116 (burden).
[73] *Plimmer v Wellington Corp* (1884) 9 App Cas 699 (lessee of representee's purchaser, although arguably a case of promissory – rather than proprietary – estoppel); *ER Ives Investments Ltd v High* [1967] 2 QB 379, at 395A. See Ruoff and Roper *Registered Conveyancing* (Sweet & Maxwell, looseleaf), at para 15.031. Spencer Bower and Turner *Estoppel by Representation* (LexisNexis Butterworths, 4th edn, 2004), at para VI.2.11; Gray and Gray *Elements of Land Law* (Oxford University Press, 5th edn, 2009), at para 9.2.20.
[74] [1972] 1 Ch 359.
[75] [1979] 1 WLR 431.
[76] [1978] 1 WLR 683, at 688G–688H.
[77] Eg the promise of land on which to build a house, as in *Dilwyn v Llewelyn* (1862) 4 De GF & J 517.
[78] [1976] Ch 179.

Independent equity of stranger

10.33 Rather than relying on an assignment of someone else's equity, a person may be able to assert his own, independent equity if he is one of the class of persons to whom the representation is directed or could have been expected to rely on it and he did so. So too if his expectation arises without any direct promise to him but the circumstances are such as to amount to standing-by by the owner. See generally Chapter 4.

Post judgment

10.34 The nature of the right/interest that is granted by the court to satisfy the equity (ie personal or proprietary) and its terms will determine whether its benefit is capable of passing to successors in title, whether it requires to be registered to do so and the formalities for a valid assignment.

SUB-LICENCES

10.35 The licensee's grant of a sub-licence is to be distinguished from his exercise of the licensor's authority to permit others onto the land, which depends on the application of ordinary agency principles. In the former case (which is dealt with here) the licensee exercises a right, independent of the licensor's agreement, to allow others to use the land.

Bare licences

10.36 A bare licence cannot justify entry onto the land by someone to whom it does not extend because it creates no 'right'[79] which he can allow others to enjoy and/or because the permission is personal to him. However, he may have the licensor's actual or ostensible authority to invite others onto the land. Ostensible authority may be conferred where the licensee is put in a position by the licensor to manage the land or control access to it. For example, a party guest[80] may have apparent authority to allow a stranger into to a house.[81] An employee may also have apparent authority to direct a customer to ancillary areas of his employer's premises to which the public do not usually have access, unless the customer ought to have realised he was acting outside his authority.[82] Factual possession by the licensee is thought to be sufficient itself to confer a power to grant sublicences or may, at least in most cases, clothe him with the licensor's ostensible authority.

---

[79] See **8.1**.
[80] *Jones and Jones v Lloyd* [1981] Crim LR 340.
[81] *Robson v Hallett* [1967] 2 QB 939, at 954B ('When, having knocked at the front door of the dwelling-house, someone who is inside the dwelling-house invites the person who has knocked to come in, there is an implied authority in that person which can be rebutted on behalf of the occupier of the dwelling-house to invite him to come in, and so licence him to come into the dwelling-house itself').
[82] *Mountney v Smith* [1904] HCA 7; (1904) 1 CLR 146.

10.37 That authority may be expressly/impliedly restricted or excluded by the licensor or by virtue of circumstances from which the stranger ought to have been aware of the limitations on it. Conversely a bare licensee who exceeds his actual authority may still bind the licensor if he acts within the apparent scope of his authority.[83]

10.38 The licensor may at any time countermand a licence granted by the licensee with his actual/ostensible authority, subject to the invitee having reasonable time to leave. If the licence is granted without his authority, the invitee is a trespasser from the outset and may be treated as such by the licensor, subject to the limitations on self-help referred to in Chapter 13.

Contractual licences

Right to create sub-licences

10.39 A well-drafted licence will expressly say whether the licensee may grant sub-licences. In the absence of such term, that is a question of construction in the broader sense of ascertaining the parties' objective common intentions, in light of the express terms of the licence (in particular the nature of the licensee's right), the nature of the premises and the context in which the licence was created.[84] Although many of the principles considered above in relation to assignment are likely to be relevant here, a non-assignable licence may in theory give the licensee the right to grant sub-licences and an assignable licence may prohibit the creation of sub-licences. A licence whose benefits can only be assigned in toto may entitle the licensee to grant multiple (concurrent or consecutive) sub-licences.[85]

10.40 The same principles will also determine the limitations if any on the licensee's right to grant sub-licences. For example, a licence that prohibits assignment may permit some sub-licences but would impliedly prevent a purported sub-licence of the whole of the land for the whole of the licence term. And whereas a business licence, which the licensee is intended to commercially exploit, may permit him to grant sub-licences for reward, a service occupier/licensee (eg) may only be able to grant bare sub-licences. The licence terms and the surrounding matrix of facts will also determine what, if any, limitation there is on the scope of such right, eg as to the creation of multiple, concurrent sub-licences.[86]

---

[83] Ibid.
[84] *Staffordshire AHA v South Staffordshire Waterworks Co* [1978] 1 WLR 1387, at 1399H. The suggested distinction in *Frank Warr & Co v London CC* [1904] 1 KB 713, at 722–723 between recreational and user licences – the first being construed strictly – is considered unsound.
[85] See eg *Donington Park Leisure Ltd v Wheatcroft & Sons Ltd* [2006] All ER (D) 94.
[86] See eg *Lymington Marina Ltd v Macnamara* [2007] EWCA Civ 151.

10.41 Whilst therefore each case is sensitive to the licence terms and facts:

- The right to grant sub-licences is likely to be implied where the licensee has a right to exclusive occupation (a fortiori possession) of the land. For example, residential licences to occupy self-contained accommodation (eg houses or caravans).

- Even so, an individual who does not occupy the premises as his residence (eg a hotel guest) is unlikely to be able to allow others to occupy, as distinct from casual visitors.

- That may be true also of licensees who exclusively occupy as their residence part of a larger area retained by the licensor (eg hostel residents, lodgers with exclusive use of a room) where the licensor has a legitimate interest in controlling who has access to the premises.

- The right may be more difficult to imply in (particularly non-exclusive) user licences.

- An exception is a user licence granted for the benefit of the licensee's other land (eg a contractual right of access) which may be enjoyed by the licensee's invitees.

- A licence may permit sub-licences if it is of such length that the objective observer would have contemplated that licensee was unlikely to be able to enjoy its benefit throughout the whole of the contract term.[87]

The factual situation must sometimes also be considered to determine whether strangers are the licensor's or licensee's invitees. For instance, where a licence is given to operate a concession within a larger area, customers will be the licensor's visitors rather than the licensee's until they enter an area within the latter's exclusive control.

Sub-licences created in compliance with licence

10.42 A contractual sub-licence must, of course, satisfy the relevant requirements for its creation set out in Chapter 3. A sub-licence granted in compliance with the licence terms entitles the sub-licensee to use the land as against the licensor. However, the licensor cannot directly enforce the licence terms against him nor of course may he enforce the sub-licence terms against the licensor, for lack of privity of contract.[88] The licensor may treat him as a trespasser if the sub-licensee exceeds the licence terms. If a contractual (as distinct from gratuitous) sub-licensee merely exceeds the terms of his own sub-licence then unless the licensee terminates it is thought the licensor's rights against the sub-licensee depend on whether his use is nevertheless within that

---

[87] Ibid, at [24].
[88] Ibid, at [21].

permitted by the licence. A sub-licence of the whole of the licensee's rights for the whole of the licence term may take effect as an assignment, unless prohibited by the licence terms.[89]

10.43 The sub-licence will end automatically on the determination of the licence. In that case the sub-licensee may have the usual packing-up period (see Chapter 12) but in assessing what is reasonable as against the licensor, the court is likely to have regard (at least predominantly) to the terms surrounding the creation of the head licence.

Sub-licences created in breach of term

10.44 A sub-licence granted in breach of the licence terms is nevertheless effective in estoppel as between the licensee and the sub-licensee (see **8.25–8.28**). The estoppel does not bind the licensor, who can treat the sub-licensee as a trespasser, unless the licensee has a right to exclusive possession of the land[90] or the licensor is prevented from relying on the breach by waiver/estoppel or treats the sub-licensee as his own licensee.

Licences and the mutual benefit and burden principle

10.45 The position is analogous to that appertaining when the licensee seeks to assign the benefit of the licence – specifically whether the rights are intended to be personal to the original parties – and the reader is referred to **10.25–10.27**.

Licences coupled with an interest

10.46 The position is similar to that considered at **10.28–10.29**. Prima facie the owner of a proprietary right/interest in land has the power (if not the right, as against someone with a superior title) to create derivative rights or interests, whether of a proprietary nature or not. Whereas an assignment of such interest will need to comply with the relevant formalities and registration requirements, a mere sub-licence need not – see Chapter 3.

Estoppel licences

10.47 The analysis set out at **10.30–10.33** applies by analogy in relation to the representee's ability to allow someone else to use the land to which his equity applies. That is likely to depend on the nature of the expectation that gave rise to it, which may in turn depend in part on the nature of the land and the representee's use/occupation. Even where the equity is incapable of transmission the representee in most cases may allow others onto the land insofar as that was contemplated by the representor/representee.

---

[89] See by analogy *Milmo v Carreras* [1946] KB 306.
[90] Although the licensor may have a claim if the sub-licensee's acts cause damage to his interest. See by analogy **9.52**.

BRUTON TENANCIES

10.48 *Bruton v London & Quadrant Housing Trust*[91] establishes that a lease may be granted by someone who has no proprietary interest in the land; whilst a landlord must have capacity to grant a lease, lack of title is not a question of capacity. Accordingly a licensee may create a tenancy, albeit not a 'proprietary' one and therefore not one that binds persons with a superior interest.[92] As against the licensor therefore it determines automatically on the determination of the licence. Nevertheless the tenancy is binding in estoppel between the licensee and his tenant and therefore imports into their relationship (eg) the statutory rights and obligations of parties to a lease[93] and the general common-law exemption of liability of the landlord in relation to the repair, condition and fitness for purpose of the land.[94]

10.49 The requisite characteristics of a *Bruton* tenancy are those for an ordinary lease (see Chapter 3): it must confer a right of exclusive possession for a defined or ascertainable term and be supported by consideration and the parties must intend to enter into legal relations. The requirement that it grant a *right* to exclusive possession (not necessarily exclusive possession in fact) effectively means that in practice such tenancies can – or at least will – only be granted by licensees who have a right to possession or factual possession (eg management and control) of the land.

---

[91] [2000] 1 AC 406.
[92] *Kay v Lambeth LBC* [2006] 2 AC 465.
[93] See eg Chapter 3 n 6.
[94] See eg *Cavalier v Pope* [1906] AC 428; *Duke of Westminster v Guild* [1985] QB 688, now partially removed by statute in relation to certain residential tenancies (eg Landlord and Tenant Act 1985, s 8) and by Defective Premises Act 1972.

Chapter 11

THE PARTIES' NON-CONTRACTUAL RIGHTS AND OBLIGATIONS

Liability arising from the condition or use of the premises	11.2
Occupiers' Liability Act 1957	11.3
Occupiers' Liability Act 1984	11.18
Defective Premises Act 1972	11.21
Negligence	11.26
Liability for escape of dangerous things	11.27
Private nuisance	11.30
Causation	11.30
Authorisation	11.32
Adoption	11.34
Continuation	11.35
Non-domestic rates	11.38
Council tax	11.39
Tax implications of granting the licence	11.41
Value added tax	11.42
Stamp duty land tax	11.48
Statutory compensation on compulsory acquisition	11.51
General	11.51
Disturbance payments	11.52
Home loss payments	11.53
Planning and environmental liabilities	11.54
Planning control	11.54
Environmental Protection Act 1990	11.58

11.1 The creation of the licence may give rise to common-law or statutory obligations that one party owes to the other and/or to strangers. The potential implications can be classified as follows:

- responsibility for the condition and use of the premises;

- liability to third parties under the rule in *Rylands v Fletcher*[1]/in nuisance arising from the state of the land or activities conducted on it;

- liability for non-domestic rates (business premises) and council tax (residential premises);

---

[1] (1868) LR 3 HL 330.

- the tax consequences of granting a licence;
- compulsory purchase and the licensee; and
- liability for breaches of planning control and environmental legislation.

What follows considers on whom the relevant responsibilities fall and in what circumstances a licensee can claim compensation for the compulsory acquisition of the land. For a full treatment of the implications, reference should be made to the appropriate specialist works. Of course where liability is owed to a stranger the parties to the licence are generally free to agree between themselves which of them bears ultimate responsibility.

LIABILITY ARISING FROM THE CONDITION OR USE OF THE PREMISES

11.2 One party to the licence may owe to the other and/or to strangers duties in relation to the condition and use of the premises:

- as occupier, under the Occupiers' Liability Acts 1957 and 1984;
- under the Defective Premises Act 1972; and/or
- in negligence, eg by creating or authorising the danger that causes damage or injury.

These are neither mutually exclusive nor exhaustive. Additional duties may be owed by virtue of some other relationship or circumstances (eg under workplace legislation). Liability in nuisance and under the rule in *Rylands v Fletcher*[2] are dealt with separately.

Occupiers' Liability Act 1957

The scope of the duty

11.3 Section 2(2) of the Occupiers' Liability Act 1957 imposes on an occupier a 'common duty of care ... to take such care as in all the circumstances of the case is reasonable to see that his visitor will be reasonably safe in using the premises ...'. The duty extends to dangers arising from the physical state of the land and/or fixed or moveable structures on it, but not operational activities[3] (unless they in turn create a dangerous condition on the land) as to which ordinary principles of negligence, breach of statutory duty etc apply. Thus where the premises are – or include features that are – moveable (eg cranes,

---

[2] (1868) LR 3 HL 330.
[3] *Tomlinson v Congleton BC* [2004] 1 AC 46.

scaffolding, lifts etc) occupancy liability only arises from the dangerous condition of these features and not the manner in which they are used.

11.4 The duty is to avoid personal injury or damage to persons or property lawfully present on the land.[4] Liability extends to consequential financial loss,[5] but not pure economic loss. The duty does not extend to the security of the visitor's goods against theft[6] or damage caused by a third party, as to which, however, liability may occasionally arise in negligence[7] at common law or by virtue of some implied contractual term (see **8.43–8.44**).

The nature of the duty

11.5 The duty is to take such care as is reasonable in all the circumstances to see that the occupier's visitors are 'reasonably safe'. What that entails in any particular case is fact-sensitive;[8] although a mere warning will not suffice 'unless in all the circumstances it was enough to enable the visitor to be reasonably safe'.[9] The occupier is not liable 'without more' for dangers caused by an independent contractor's faulty works of construction, maintenance or repair if he acted reasonably in entrusting the work to such person and had taken such steps (if any) as he reasonably ought in order to satisfy himself that the contractor was competent and the works were done properly.[10] The duty does not apply to risks willingly accepted by the visitor.[11] His knowledge of the danger, although not to be equated with willing acceptance, is relevant both to what the occupier must do to discharge his duty and whether the damage was sustained in whole or part by the visitor's own fault.

11.6 The duty may arise whether the dangerous condition is the result of natural causes or the natural state of the land or some positive action (or inaction) by the occupier or others, including the other party to the licence. However, different considerations apply in each case to determine the existence and scope of the duty, eg whether the occupier ought to have appreciated the particular danger and what he could and should have done to abate the risk of injury or damage.

11.7 The purpose of the visitor's presence defines the extent of the duty: it is to see that he is reasonably safe 'in using the premises for the purposes for which he is invited or permitted ... to be there'.[12] If, then, the visitor is injured when acting outside the temporal, physical or purposive limits of his licence, he

---

[4] Eg pursuant to a storage licence. Note the goods need not be owned by the person who brings them on to the land: Occupiers' Liability Act 1957, s 1(3)(b).
[5] *AMF International v Magnet Bowling* [1968] 1 WLR 1028.
[6] Ibid, at 1050E–1050F.
[7] *Clerk & Lindsell on Torts* (Sweet & Maxwell, 19th edn, 2006), at paras 8-51–8-56, 12-41, 21-24–21-27.
[8] See Occupiers' Liability Act 1957, s 2(3), (4).
[9] Ibid, s 2(4)(a).
[10] Ibid, s 2(4)(b).
[11] Ibid, s 2(5).
[12] Ibid, s 2(2).

will not be owed this duty of care but the more limited one under the Occupiers' Liability Act 1984. The licensor's obligation:[13]

> '... only extends so long as and so far as the invitee is making what can reasonably be contemplated as an ordinary and reasonable use of the premises ... for the purposes for which he is invited ... So far as he sets foot on so much of the premises as lie outside the invitation or uses them for purposes which are alien to the invitation he is not an invitee but a trespasser.'

A licensee, however, may not be a trespasser if he exceeds the scope of his licence involuntarily[14] and its scope may be construed generously if he reasonably believes he is entitled to go into a particular area and the contrary was not made clear.[15] Furthermore it is also possible, according to a recent tentative suggestion in *Harvey v Plymouth CC*,[16] that there is a category of licensees who, having used the land for purposes other than those contemplated, are not owed a duty of care under the 1957 Act but nevertheless remain the licensor's 'visitors'. Subject to that possible qualification, if a licensee is permitted to enter for one purpose but does so for another, he is a trespasser from the outset; if, however, he enters for various purposes, not all of which are impermissible, he is not a trespasser, at least until he starts to put the unauthorised purposes into effect.[17] Of course if the licence is terminable by notice and the licensee's activities do not automatically make him a trespasser, the common duty of care will only cease once it expires.[18]

11.8 In determining whether the occupier has discharged his duty regard should be had to all the circumstances, including (eg) the purpose of the visitor's presence, the conduct to be expected of him, the nature and cause of the danger and whether it was or ought to have been apprehended by the occupier and/or visitor, the nature of the occupier's interest in the land and the extent of his control, what if any warnings or guards could have prevented the injury, the cost/time the various possible means of abating the danger would have taken and (at least where the danger is the result of natural causes/features) the occupier's resources.

---

[13] *Hillen and Pettigrew v ICI (Alkali) Ltd* [1936] AC 65, at 69; *The Carlgarth* [1927] P 93, at 110 ('When you invite a person into your house to use the staircase, you do not invite him to slide down the banisters, you invite him to use the staircase in the ordinary way in which it is used').
[14] Eg by accidentally stepping outside the permitted area: *Braithwaite v South Durham Steel Co* [1958] 1 WLR 986, at 990–991.
[15] See eg *Gould v McAuliffe* [1941] 2 All ER 527; *Pearson v Coleman Bros* [1948] 2 KB 359.
[16] [2010] EWCA Civ 860, at [22] ('a person may remain a "visitor" within the meaning of the Act even when he is using the premises for a purpose going beyond the scope of his licence').
[17] See *Byrne v Kinematograph Renters Society Ltd* [1958] 1 WLR 762, at 776.
[18] Query the position during any grace period, as to which see Chapter 12.

The person who owes the duty

11.9 The common duty of care is owed by the 'occupier'.[19] Although imposed 'in consequence of [his] occupation or control of premises',[20] it is not limited to dangers *created* by it. Who is the occupier in any particular case is to be determined by applying common-law principles.[21] The foundation of liability is occupational control; that is 'control associated with and arising from presence in and use of or activity in the premises'.[22] An occupier, therefore, is someone with:[23]

> '... a sufficient degree of control over premises that he ought to realise that any failure on his part to use care may result in injury to a person coming lawfully there ... [I]t is not necessary for a person to have entire control over the premises. He need not have exclusive occupation. Suffice it that he has some degree of control. He may share the control with others. Two or more may be "occupiers." And whenever this happens, each is under a duty to use care towards persons coming lawfully on to the premises, dependent on his degree of control. If each fails in his duty, each is liable to a visitor who is injured in consequence of his failure, but each may have a claim to contribution from the other.'

The answer in each case 'depends on the particular facts ... and especially upon the nature and extent of the occupation or control in fact enjoyed or exercised ... over the premises'.[24] An occupier need not have the power to permit or prohibit entry; eg a contractor-licensee may occupy the area of land where he is working, as well as (or to the exclusion of) the licensor.

11.10 The task then is to identify the particular hazard causing the injury and ask who, by virtue of his control of that part of the premises, could have taken reasonable steps to prevent its occurrence. Occupation may arise as a result of legal or factual control of land and depends in part on the scope and duration of the user and the extent to which that person was able – and could reasonably have been expected – to take steps to mitigate the hazard. For example, a bare licensee with no right to remove/guard against the dangerous condition may nevertheless, by virtue of his occupation, be under a duty (only) to warn.

One/both parties in occupation

11.11 A person may occupy personally or through his agent(s). If the licensor was not originally occupying the land, he will not assume occupation merely by virtue of having granted a user licence, even if the licensee is his agent. Conversely if the licensor was originally in occupation he will not necessarily

---

[19] Occupiers' Liability Act 1957, s 2(1).
[20] Ibid, s 1(2).
[21] Ibid.
[22] *Wheat v E Lacon & Co Ltd* [1966] AC 552, at 589.
[23] Ibid, at 578.
[24] *Creed v McGeoch & Sons Ltd* [1955] 1 WLR 1005, at 1009.

cease to be so merely by granting the licence.[25] During its subsistence he may occupy, as against strangers, through a licensee who is his agent, even if the licensee has factual occupation of the whole of the land.[26] Even where that is not the case, the licensor may be in occupation: (a) by virtue of his contemporaneous personal use of the land; (b) by having reserved sufficiently extensive rights of access/control in the licence agreement; or (c) by having granted a series of licences (whether or not the licensees are his agents), none of which individually confer a right of occupation but which collectively amount to occupation by the licensor.

11.12 Occasionally both the licensor and licensee may be in contemporaneous occupation of separate – or even the same – areas.[27] For example, a licensee may be in occupation of his own unit (eg a self-contained market stall and possibly the adjacent area) while the licensor occupies the common parts/access. Where both are in occupation of the same area, the nature and extent of their respective duties may differ, depending on the nature, extent and duration of their rights and the degree of control each exercises.[28] Hence in *Wheat v E Lacon & Co Ltd*[29] the licensor remained in occupation, having reserved the right to enter to undertake repairs, and was responsible for the structural condition of the land, but not dangers arising from day-to-day matters (eg whether a room was illuminated and floor coverings safely laid), for which the residential licensees, whose occupation rights gave them control over those matters, were liable. Where there are different causes for which one or the other is responsible as occupier (or where one party is in occupation and the other creates the danger), each may be liable, with a right to contribution from the other, although the amount will vary according to their respective culpability.

11.13 The identity of the occupier(s) and the duty he/they owe(s) has to be judged in each case by reference to all the circumstances, including the licence terms, the condition of the land, the parties' actual use of it, the cause of the particular injury/damage and what steps one or the other could reasonably have been expected to take, in light of their respective powers, to prevent it.[30] Accordingly only the broadest guidance is possible:

---

[25] See eg *Maddocks v Clifton* [2001] EWCA Civ 1837 (farmer-licensor liable notwithstanding licensee ran equestrian centre). Contrast the position of the lessor, who necessarily lacks occupational control.

[26] See eg *Stone v Taffe* [1975] 1 WLR 1575 (brewery in control of a public house through its manager). Compare the concession in *Stone v Taffe* that the manager was not himself in occupation with *Wheat v E Lacon & Co Ltd* [1966] AC 552.

[27] See eg *Fisher v CHT Ltd* [1966] 2 QB 475 (club proprietor and restaurant manager held to occupy restaurant). In *AMF International v Magnet Bowling* [1968] 1 WLR 1028 the owner was liable for damage to a contractor's materials for failing to exercise greater care in supervising building operations; the main contractor was liable on the basis his duties included taking precautions against flooding.

[28] *Wheat v E Lacon & Co Ltd* [1966] AC 552, at 578, 586, 587.

[29] [1966] AC 552.

[30] See also Occupiers' Liability Act 1957, s 2(3).

- A licensor who was originally in occupation will remain so if the licensee has a mere right of (particularly non-exclusive) user.

- A licensee who has primary control of a particular area of land, such as a contractor working on part of a site (eg installing lifts), may be in occupation of it (the lift shaft). Even then, the licensor may also be in occupation if he retains supervisory control over the works.

- A temporary lodger (eg hotel guest), particularly one who shares the land with the licensor or others, is unlikely to be in occupation but even if he is, will owe only a very modest duty, eg to warn.

- A residential licensee with sole use of a self-contained area of the land will usually be in occupation although the extent of his duty will depend in large part on the licence terms, eg his ability to mitigate the danger.

- Even then, however, the licensor may also be in occupation (eg if he retains a right of entry to undertake maintenance or repairs)[31] but not in relation to transient dangers, as distinct from permanent conditions, that he either could not reasonably have been expected to know of or had insufficient time to abate.

- It is a question of construction whether a licence to occupy a structure (eg a caravan or houseboat) gives the licensee occupational control of the land where it stands or its curtilege.

- A licensee in occupational control (eg a main contractor on a building site) may be responsible for a danger created by his sub-licensees or even another licensee if he was or ought to have been aware of it and had the legal ability, under the licence terms, and sufficient time to abate it.

- The length of the licence term is a relevant factor in determining whether the licensee is in occupation (eg a short-term right, eg to occupy holiday accommodation, may not confer control) and if so what could have been expected of him in relation to the danger. As is the extent to which the licensee was entitled – and could be expected – to alter the state/condition of the land.

- A licensor in occupational control is liable to visitors to satisfy himself as to the competence of licensees he authorised to undertake works to the land.[32]

Note, however, that even where a party to the licence is not in occupational control or the person injured is not his visitor, he may be liable for having created the relevant danger (see below).

---

[31] *Wheat v E Lacon & Co Ltd* [1966] AC 552.
[32] See eg *Gwilliam v West Hertfordshire Hospitals NHS Trust* [2003] QB 443 (licensee supplying amusements for fair).

The persons to whom the duty is owed

11.14 The duty is owed to 'his [ie the occupier's] visitors'.[33] Consent to their presence may be express or implied. Hitherto courts in this context have been prepared to infer consent from the owner's mere failure to prevent the use of his land.[34] Of itself, however, that is unlikely to be sufficient now to give rise to an implied licence (see Chapter 4). Inaction in the face of a trespass may, however, give rise to an estoppel (proprietary/by acquiescence) although the fact (if true) that the trespass was originally deliberate is relevant to whether the trespasser detrimentally relied on the owner's failure to act and whether it would be unconscionable for the latter subsequently to assert his title to the land.[35] Whether the estoppel licensee is a 'visitor' in cases of mere standing by – as distinct from positive encouragement – is undecided. So too where the estoppel results from the promise of – or the defective grant of – a proprietary right (eg an easement) it is uncertain whether the licensee is a 'visitor', first, since the owner's 'consent' is not to do the thing which the right would have permitted but to right itself and, second, given that a dominant owner is not owed the common duty of care by the servient owner[36] it is hard to see why the situation should be different where the promise is of such an easement.

11.15 Leaving that aside, it follows that an occupying licensor owes the common duty of care to his licensees[37] and to their lawful sub-licensees. Section 2(1) of the Occupiers' Liability Act 1957 might at first sight suggest that no duty is owed to the latter since they are not 'his' visitors. Section 3(1), however, provides in relation to contractual licences that:[38]

> '... where an occupier ... is bound by contract to permit persons who are strangers to the contract to enter or use the premises, the duty of care which he owes to them as his visitors cannot be restricted or excluded by that contract but (subject to any provision in the contract to the contrary) shall include the duty to perform his obligations under the contract, whether undertaken for their protection or not, in so far as those obligations go beyond the obligations otherwise involved in that duty.'

That obligation is, when read in conjunction with the Occupiers' Liability Act 1957, s 5, the common duty of care, unless the licence terms impose a greater duty on him. If, however, the sub-licences were granted in breach of the licence terms his duty is only the lesser one under the Occupiers' Liability

---

[33] Occupiers' Liability Act 1957, s 2(1).
[34] See eg *Lowery v Walker* [1911] AC 10, at 12, 14. See, however, *Edwards v Railway Executive* [1952] AC 737, at 746 ('repeated trespass of itself confers no licence').
[35] *Lester v Woodgate* [2010] EWCA Civ 199, at [39].
[36] *Greenhalgh v BRB* [1969] 2 QB 286.
[37] See also Occupiers' Liability Act 1957, s 5 (discussed in Chapter 8) regarding contractual duties of care.
[38] Occupiers' Liability Act 1957, s 3(4) extends this right to persons who have a right of entry as tenants – presumably including *Bruton* tenants (see **10.48–10.49**).

Act 1984[39] unless the licensee had his ostensible authority to permit the others to enter or he waives – or is estopped from relying on – the breach.

11.16 An occupying licensee owes the common duty of care (and, where applicable, a concurrent contractual duty[40]) to his sub-licensees. Despite the apparent width of s 3(1) above such duty is not owed to the licensor who enters by virtue of rights reserved in the licence agreement, nor to other licensees or their sub-licensees since they are not the licensee's 'visitors'[41] nor does he 'permit' them to enter. That connotes some act of dominion or derivation from his rights, whereas the reservation pursuant to which they enter defines/limits their scope. Nevertheless he will owe them the lesser duty of care under the 1984 Act.[42] If, of course, they enter not by virtue of rights reserved by the licence agreement but at the licensee's invitation, his duty is the higher one under the 1957 Act.

Exclusion or restriction of the duty

11.17 The common duty is owed 'except in so far as [the occupier] is free to and does extend, restrict, modify or exclude his duty ... by agreement or otherwise'.[43] He may do so by notice or by a licence term, subject to the provisions of the Unfair Contract Terms Act 1977 and Unfair Terms in Consumer Contracts Regulations 1999.[44] Their impact is beyond the scope of this book.

Occupiers' Liability Act 1984

11.18 An occupying licensor/licensee owes to someone on the land who is *not* his visitor a duty to take 'such care as is reasonable in all the circumstances ... to see that he does not suffer injury'[45] caused by a danger arising from the state of the premises or things done or omitted to be done on them.[46] The duty is owed if:

---

[39] A person may be a lawful visitor vis-à-vis one person and a trespasser vis-à-vis another: *Ferguson v Welsh* [1987] 1 WLR 1553, at 1563.
[40] Occupiers' Liability Act 1957, s 5.
[41] *McGeown v Northern Ireland Housing Executive* [1995] 1 AC 233, at 246A ('The concept of licensee or visitor involves that the person in question has at least the permission of the relevant occupier to be in a particular place') (public rights of way); *McKinley v Montgomery* [1993] NI 93, at 97–98 ('[the claimant] was entitled to be on the club premises by virtue of being a lady member and was not a "visitor" to whom a duty was owed by the other members under s 2(1) of the 1957 Act').
[42] See the discussion regarding public rights of way and user encouraged by the occupier in *McGeown v Northern Ireland Housing Executive* [1995] 1 AC 233, at 246–248.
[43] Occupiers' Liability Act 1984, ss 1(1)(a), 2(1).
[44] SI 1999/2083.
[45] Liability under the 1984 Act (unlike the 1957 Act) is only for personal injury, not loss or damage to property: Occupiers' Liability Act 1984, s 1(8).
[46] Occupiers' Liability Act 1984, s 1(4). Ie not operational activities, for which any liability lies in negligence.

- the occupier knows, or has reasonable grounds to know of, the danger and that the other person is (or may be) in its vicinity, whether or not that person is entitled to be there; and

- the risk is one he may reasonably be expected to offer the other some protection against in all the circumstances.[47]

The duty may 'in an appropriate case' be discharged by taking reasonable steps to warn of the danger or discouraging that person from incurring the risk.[48] No duty is owed in respect of risks willingly accepted.[49] Whether it is broken in each case is a question of fact to be determined by reference to the circumstances as they existed at the time of the injury.

11.19 The tests for 'occupier' under the Occupiers' Liability Acts 1957 and 1984 are the same. So too, liability under the 1984 Act is limited to dangers arising from the state/condition of the land and not pure operational activities, as to which common-law principles apply.[50]

11.20 The duty is owed to persons who are not the occupier's visitors, namely:

- to 'pure' trespassers;

- by an occupying licensor to unlawful sub-licensees. Their licensee (if in occupation) however will owe them the common duty of care under the 1957 Act as they are, as against him, lawful visitors;[51]

- by an occupying licensor to a licensee who as a result of exceeding the terms of his licence becomes a trespasser or who remains on the land after it has ended. It may also be owed to a licensee who, although still his 'visitor', is using the land for purposes other than those intended (if such category of persons exists);[52] and

- by an occupying licensee to his licensor and to other licensees (and their sub-licensees) who enter not at his invitation but by virtue of rights reserved in the licence agreement.[53]

---

[47] Ibid, s 1(3).
[48] Ibid, s 1(5).
[49] Ibid, s 1(6).
[50] *Keown v Coventry NHS Trust* [2006] 1 WLR 953.
[51] *Ferguson v Welsh* [1987] 1 WLR 1553.
[52] See **11.7**.
[53] See the discussion at **11.15** et seq.

Defective Premises Act 1972

Works in connection with provision of dwelling

11.21 Section 1 of the Defective Premises Act 1972 is of marginal relevance here. It imposes a duty in relation to works undertaken in connection with the provision of a dwelling to ensure such works render the dwelling habitable. It is owed to persons on whose behalf the works are done or who later acquire an interest in the dwelling. As (at least most) licences are not 'interests' for these purposes,[54] the duty will rarely be owed between the parties to the licence, except where the licensee undertakes such works (eg as contractor) for the licensor.

Licensor's obligation to repair/maintain (s 4(1))

11.22 Section 4(1) of the Defective Premises Act 1972 provides that where premises are let by way of a 'tenancy' under which the landlord owes a duty in respect of maintenance and repair, such duty extends to all who might reasonably be expected to be affected by defects in the state of the premises (eg the tenant's licensees). The duty cannot be excluded or restricted by a contract term.[55]

11.23 By virtue of s 4(6) 'tenancy' in s 4(1) includes 'a right of occupation given by contract or any enactment and not amounting to a tenancy'. Thus a contractual licensor who owes an occupying licensee a duty in relation to maintenance and repair owes a similar duty to sub-licensees whose presence could reasonably be foreseen. So too licences with security of tenure into which statutory duties regarding maintenance/repair may be implied come within s 4(6).[56] It applies even though the licensor is not in occupation and even if the sub-licensees are not his visitors for the purposes of the Occupiers' Liability Act 1957.

11.24 The duty applies where he knows or ought to know of such defect.[57] It is to take such care as is reasonable in the circumstances to see that they are reasonably safe from personal injury or property damage caused by a 'relevant defect'.[58] A 'relevant defect' is one in the state of the premises occurring on or after the 'material time' (ie the earlier of the date of the licence, any agreement to grant it or the licensee commencing occupation[59]) and which is caused or continued as a result of an act or omission on the licensor's part which

---

[54] See Chapter 9.
[55] Defective Premises Act 1972, s 6(3).
[56] See Chapter 6. This, of course, does not include licences with limited security under the Caravan Sites Act 1968 unless their terms expressly/impliedly require the licensor to undertake works.
[57] Defective Premises Act 1972, s 4(2).
[58] Ibid, s 4(1).
[59] Ibid, s 4(3)(b).

amounts to a breach of his contractual duty to the licensee or – where the duty is to repair on notice – would have amounted to a breach, had he had such notice.[60]

Licensor's right to repair/maintain (s 4(4))

11.25 Liability under the Defective Premises Act 1972, s 4(1) is extended by s 4(4) to a licensor who has an express or implied right (not obligation) to enter premises to carry out any description of maintenance or repair. In such case the duty arises when he is or by notice or otherwise could put himself in a position to exercise it. A right to enter to carry out works that do not amount to 'maintenance' or 'repair' does not qualify.[61] Nor is a duty owed to the licensee if the particular defect is caused or continued by his own breach of contract (as to which see Chapter 8).

Negligence

11.26 In many cases the licensor's and licensee's liability towards each other and others lies in negligence, as to which ordinary common-law principles apply. For example:

- One or other party (whether or not in occupation) may be liable for undertaking an activity he knows or ought to know carries a risk of injury/damage. His duty to those who may foreseeably suffer injury/damage is to take reasonable care to prevent that occurring.[62] For instance, one licensee who leaves land in an unsafe condition overnight may be responsible for injury suffered by another licensee as a result.[63] The duty varies according to the circumstances and may in some cases be greater than that of an occupier – eg to neutralise the danger, not merely warn of its presence.[64] He may avoid liability, however, if he reasonably believed the danger would be removed or guarded against by someone else (eg a contractor-licensee who leaves open a newly painted window reasonably expecting the licensor to close it when dry) or if the works in question were approved (eg a subcontractor-licensee working under the supervision of a main contractor), at least if the condition creating the danger was discoverable by inspection.

- Where the danger is caused by a licensee or sub-licensee who is an independent contractor, the licensor/licensee who engaged him may be liable for failing to exercise reasonable care in his selection and (where appropriate) supervision.[65]

---

[60] Ibid, s 4(3).
[61] *Lee v Leeds CC* [2002] 1 WLR 1488, at [80]–[81].
[62] *Glasgow Corp v Muir* [1943] AC 448, at 454. See also *Excelsior Wire Rope Co v Callan* [1930] AC 404; *AC Billings & Sons Ltd v Riden* [1958] AC 240 (both licensees).
[63] See eg *Corby v Hill* (1858) 4 CB(NS) 556.
[64] See eg *Johnson v Rea* [1962] 1 QB 373, at 381, 383.
[65] See eg *Bottomley v Todmorden Cricket Club* [2004] PIQR 277.

- An occupying licensor/licensee owes a common-law duty of care for the safety of his visitors, separate from the statutory duty under the Occupiers' Liability Act 1957, to see that they are reasonably safe from activities by a third person which he permits to be carried out on the land,[66] at least to the extent they involve an unusual danger of which he knew or ought to have known.[67] Thus an occupying licensor may be liable for injury caused by one licensee to another or possibly to a sub-licensee and an occupying licensee may be liable to one of his sub-licensees for the activities of another sub-licensee.

- A person (whether or not in occupation) who invites others onto land owes them a duty 'to take reasonable care that the place does not contain or to give warning of hidden dangers, no matter whether the place belongs to the invitor or is in his exclusive occupation'.[68] The duty applies to dangers of which he knows, or ought to know, whether or not he created them.[69] Thus the duty may be owed by a (non-occupying) licensor to his licensees and by a (non-occupying) licensee to his sub-licensee. For example, a head contractor may owe this duty to its sub-contractor, at least until the latter takes exclusive control of the land.[70] It may also apply to dangers created by another licensee acting within the limits of his licence that the invitor should have foreseen created a risk of injury.[71]

- Where a stranger suffers injury due to the acts of one party to the licence, the other may be concurrently liable if (eg) they were undertaken at his direction or under his supervision or he owed the stranger duties as occupier under the Occupiers' Liability Acts 1957 and 1984. Apart from that, if he does not retain such control nor direct the activities that cause the injury or damage, he is unlikely to owe a duty of care in relation to them.[72] The mere fact he could have foreseen the injury and prevented it is not enough to make him liable.

- The proprietor of lodgings or a boarding house owes a duty to take reasonable care for the safety and security of his lodgers' or guests' possessions.[73] This is in addition to any other duty owed at common law, custom (eg innkeepers), contract or bailment (see **8.43**). No such duty is owed as occupier generally at common law[74] or under the Occupiers' Liability Act 1957.

---

[66] *Glasgow Corp v Muir* [1943] AC 448, at 462. *Fairchild v Glenhaven Funeral Services Ltd* [2002] 1 WLR 1052, at [131] (rev'd on other grounds [2003] 1 AC 32); *Glaister v Appleby-in-Westmorland Town Council* [2009] EWCA Civ 1325, at [47].
[67] *Fairchild v Glenhaven Funeral Services Ltd* [2002] 1 WLR 1052, at [116]–[120].
[68] *Hartwell v Grayson Rollo & Clover Docks Ltd* [1947] KB 901, at 913.
[69] Ibid.
[70] See eg *Canter v Gardner & Co* [1940] 1 All ER 325, at 329.
[71] *Glasgow Corp v Muir* [1943] AC 448.
[72] *Glaister v Appleby-in-Westmoreland Town Council* [2009] EWCA Civ 1325, at [40].
[73] *Scarborough v Cosgrove* [1905] 2 KB 805, at 811, 813; *Appah v Parncliffe Investments Ltd* [1964] 1 WLR 1064.
[74] *Tinsley v Dudley* [1951] 2 KB 18.

LIABILITY FOR ESCAPE OF DANGEROUS THINGS

11.27 Under the rule in *Rylands v Fletcher*[75] a person who in the course of a non-natural (or, in modern parlance, non-ordinary[76]) use of land for his own purposes stores, accumulates[77] or creates on land something that has a special propensity to cause damage if it escapes[78] is liable for such escape[79] without proof of negligence, if it causes damage of the type that was foreseeable.[80] Thus a licensee may be liable,[81] eg where water escapes from pipes laid with permission through the licensor's land.[82]

11.28 The occupier of the land from which the thing escapes may be concurrently liable if it was brought or collected there for his purposes.[83] His occupation need not be exclusive. Nor is personal presence required: constructive occupation through agents or independent contractors suffices.[84] Indeed mere consent to the user may be sufficient[85] and may be inferred if it was contemplated the licensee would bring the thing onto the land for the purpose of exercising the rights granted by the licence.[86]

11.29 Therefore a licensee may be liable if he undertakes the relevant activities on his own behalf. The licensor will be liable if the licensee conducted the relevant activities on his behalf or he retains occupation, at least if the licensee acted subject to his supervision and direction; he may also be liable merely by virtue of having consented to the user, unless by doing so he ceded occupation to the licensee.

---

[75] (1868) LR 3 HL 330.
[76] *Arscott v Coal Authority* [2004] EWCA Civ 892, at [29].
[77] Eg things naturally occurring on land and accumulated there, such as percolating spring water collected in ponds.
[78] *Transco v Stockport MBC* [2004] 2 AC 1, at [10]. See *Clerk & Lindsell on Torts*, n 7 above, at paras 21-06–21-13.
[79] The escape must be from the land: *Read v J Lyons & Co Ltd* [1947] AC 156.
[80] *Cambridge Water Co v Eastern Counties Leather plc* [1994] 2 AC 264, at 302.
[81] *Rainham Chemical Works v Belvedere Fish Guano Co* [1921] 2 AC 465, at 479.
[82] *Charing Cross Electricity Supply Co v Hydraulic Power Co* [1914] 3 KB 772, at 779. The suggestion at (ibid) 785 that the licensee must occupy at least the area of the escape puts the requirement too highly; it is enough that the licensee has some control, which the fact of having brought or accumulated the thing on the land establishes.
[83] *Whitmores Ltd v Stanford* [1909] 1 Ch 427, at 437–438.
[84] *Rainham Chemical Works v Belvedere Fish Guano Co* [1921] 2 AC 465.
[85] Ibid, at 480A–480B, 483 ('As occupiers they would be under a personal obligation to their neighbours not to let this non-natural user of the land, which they occupied, become a source of damage to them … Even if they actually employed nobody, but simply suffered others to manufacture upon the site which they nevertheless continued to occupy, I think they are still under liability to third parties, if what is thus allowed by them, upon the land which they occupy, causes damage').
[86] Compare *Hale v Jennings Bros* [1938] 1 All ER 579, at 585.

PRIVATE NUISANCE

Causation

11.30 A person may be liable for having caused, authorised, adopted or continued a nuisance. Where the nuisance arises from positive acts, the person responsible for its creation (either personally or through his servants/agents) is liable, whether or not he occupies or has any interest in the land from which it emanates. It is no defence for him to assert those acts were done with the authority (or on behalf) of another. Where the nuisance is a continuing one resulting from a state/condition of the land (not (eg) purely operational activities), the creator's liability continues even though he may no longer be able to abate it.

11.31 Thus a licensee may be liable as the actual wrongdoer even if the acts were authorised by the licensor or undertaken on his behalf and such liability (eg in respect of a condition he created) may continue after the licence ends. The licensor may be concurrently liable if the licensee acts on his behalf or subject to his supervision[87] although if the licensee is an independent contractor, the licensor is only liable if the acts of their very nature involved a risk of damage to a third party[88] or consisted of the withdrawal of support from neighbouring land or works to a party/dividing wall which cause damage or resulted in the escape of fire. If conversely the licensor created the nuisance which results from the condition of the land before granting the licence he remains liable for its continuation notwithstanding the licence terms prevent him from abating it; in such case the licensee may be concurrently liable if he adopts or continues it. A licensor may also be liable as creator if the nuisance consists of the very presence of the licensee(s) on his land, ie quite apart from authorisation of their activities.[89]

Authorisation

11.32 A licensor may also be liable if he allows his licensee to commit/continue an activity that he knows (or ought to know) amounts to a nuisance.[90] A licensor may therefore be liable for a licensee's nuisance if it results from the very acts that the licence authorises. Apart from that, however, the licensor does not authorise such nuisance if he lacks the power to prevent the licensee causing it.[91] By comparison a landlord is generally not liable for his

---

[87] See eg *A-G v Tod-Heatley* [1897] 1 Ch 560 (public nuisance created by trespassers).
[88] *Bower v Peate* [1876] 1 QBD 321, at 326.
[89] *A-G v Corke* [1933] Ch 89; *Lippiat v South Gloucestershire Council* [2000] QB 51, at 61D–61F; *Winch v Mid Bedfordshire DC* [2002] All ER (D) 380 (Jul). Compare *Page Motors Ltd v Epsom & Ewell BC* (1981) 80 LGR 337, at 346, where an initially unauthorised travellers' camp was held to have been adopted by the local authority owner, which had contained its travellers problem by not moving them on. See generally Bright 'Liability for the Bad Behaviour of Others' (2001) 21 OJLS 311.
[90] *White v Jameson* (1874) LR 18 Eq 303.
[91] See eg *Hall v Beckenham Corpn* [1949] 1 All ER 423 (no power for park authority to prohibit noisy activity that was not contrary to its by-laws).

tenant's nuisance unless he specifically authorises it or the nuisance is certain (or virtually certain) to result from the purpose for which the premises are let[92] rather than the manner in which the tenant uses the land.[93]

11.33 Actual occupation (or a right of occupation) by the licensor, whilst material, is not essential to establish liability on this basis. It is sufficient that the licensor has a legal interest in land that gives a right to possession, which in turn confers an ability to exercise control over it.[94] It is uncertain, however, whether mere (actual/constructive) knowledge of the acts constituting the nuisance and the legal and practical means to abate it, shorn of any right to possession or supervisory control of the licensee, is sufficient; in such case the licensor's position may be thought analogous to the landlord's. However, *Jones (Insurance Brokers) Ltd v Portsmouth CC*[95] indicates that the key to responsibility in nuisance is the degree of control over the thing or activity that causes the nuisance and held that the defendant's mere contractual right/duty to maintain the particular features that caused the nuisance itself conferred sufficient control to fix it with liability.

Adoption

11.34 A licensee may be liable for a nuisance that predates the licence or is created (either naturally or as a result of someone else's acts) during it without any positive act on his part if he makes use of the particular feature causing the nuisance (eg leaking pipework) for his own purposes and knows or ought to know of its propensity to cause harm.[96] Similarly a licensor may be liable for adopting a nuisance created by his licensee or which arises naturally during the licence term if he subsequently uses the particular feature for his own purposes.

Continuation

11.35 An occupier may be liable for continuing a nuisance, regardless of its origin, 'if with knowledge or presumed knowledge of its existence he fails to take any reasonable means to bring it to an end though with ample time to do so'.[97] To be liable on this basis, it is thought the party to the licence must be in actual possession or control of the land from which the nuisance emanates.[98]

11.36 If therefore a nuisance arises naturally on the land or is created by someone else (eg the licensor, other licensees or trespassers), an occupying licensee may be liable if he knew or ought to have known of its existence, was

---

[92] *Rich v Basterfield* (1847) 4 CB 783; *Smith v Scott* [1973] Ch 314, at 321C–321E. But compare *Tetley v Chitty* [1986] 1 All ER 663, at 671.
[93] *Smith v Scott* [1973] Ch 314.
[94] Compare *Winch v Mid Bedfordshire DC* [2002] All ER (D) 380 (Jul), at [35], [45].
[95] [2003] 1 WLR 427, at [10].
[96] *Sedleigh-Denfield v O'Callaghan* [1940] AC 880, at 905.
[97] Ibid, at 894.
[98] *Jones (Insurance Brokers) Ltd v Portsmouth CC* [2003] 1 WLR 427.

able under the licence terms to abate it[99] and failed, after a reasonable time, to do so. An occupying licensor may also be liable during the licence term for continuing a nuisance if, with actual/constructive knowledge of it, he failed to exercise a right reserved by the licence agreement to abate it. Where the condition arises after a licence is granted, the licensor is thought to be liable – depending on the extent of the rights granted by the licence – only if the damage caused was reasonably foreseeable, as to which knowledge of it (or the means of knowledge) may be essential.[100] A licensor who is not in occupation during the licence term may be liable for a nuisance created by his licensee if after subsequently resuming occupation he fails to abate it. Such liability does not cease merely by later granting another licence of the land, even if its terms preclude him from abating the nuisance.[101]

11.37 The parties' liability on this basis is not absolute but depends on the application of the 'measured duty of care'.[102] What that requires in each case is fact-specific, taking into account the difficulty/cost of abating the nuisance, the nature and duration of the parties' respective rights over the land, the extent of their control and ability to alter its condition, their resources and the nature and extent of other people's interest in the land.[103] It follows that whilst both the licensor and licensee may be concurrently liable, their duties may differ. Accordingly whilst each may have a right of contribution against the other under the Civil Liability (Contribution) Act 1978, their liability between themselves is not necessarily equal.

NON-DOMESTIC RATES

11.38 The parties' liability for non-domestic rates depends on who (if either) is in occupation of all/part of the land.[104] The case-law on the meaning of 'occupation' is voluminous;[105] only a cursory treatment is possible. In broad terms the requisite elements of 'occupation'[106] are as follows:

(1) First, there must actual occupation. A mere user licensee is not chargeable. A licensor may be in occupation either directly (whether by himself or via agents) or through his licensees' collective use, even if none of them is individually in occupation.

---

[99] *Smeaton v Ilford Corpn* [1954] Ch 450, at 462 ('In order to establish liability for continuing a nuisance by failing to prevent it, one must necessarily prove that the person so failing must be in a position to take effective steps to that end').
[100] Contrast *Wringe v Cohen* [1939] 4 All ER 241; *Sedleigh-Denfield v O'Callaghan* [1940] AC 880.
[101] *Brew Bros v Snax (Ross)* [1970] 1 QB 612 (lease).
[102] *Sedleigh-Denfield v O'Callaghan* [1940] AC 880; *Leakey v National Trust* [1980] QB 485; *Holbeck Hall Hotel Ltd v Scarborough BC* [2000] 2 All ER 705; *Anthony v Coal Authority* [2005] EWHC 1654, at [129]–[133].
[103] *Clerk & Lindsell on Torts*, n 7 above, at paras 20-20–20-23.
[104] Local Government Finance Act 1988, s 43(1).
[105] See e g *Ryde on Rating and the Council Tax* (LexisNexis Butterworths, looseleaf), at Ch 2.
[106] *John Laing & Sons Ltd v Kingswood Area Assessors* [1949] 1 KB 344, at 350; see also *LCC v Wilkins (Valuation Officer)* [1957] AC 362.

(2) Second, the occupation must be exclusive for the particular purpose in issue:[107]

> 'Occupation is exclusive if the occupier can exclude all other persons from using the land in the same way as he does; occupation does not cease to be exclusive because other persons use the land in some other way, for their different uses may make them separately rateable. Exclusive occupation can arise if land is used pursuant to an exclusive right or title, or if the use of the land, albeit not in pursuance of an exclusive right or title, is such that it in fact excludes others from using the land for the same purposes. Occupation is not exclusive if it is subject to the overriding control and direction of another.'

Thus an exclusive licence that implicitly confers a right of occupation renders the licensee rateable, eg a licence to dig and remove minerals involving open-cast mining and reinstatement.[108] As, however, exclusive occupation is not synonymous with exclusive possession, both parties may be in sole occupation for different purposes at the same time. Where there are two potentially competing occupations, the paramount one is rateable.[109] Thus a service occupier (eg pub manager) is not rateable as his occupation is constructively that of his employer/licensor.[110] As is a bare licensee's.[111] A lodger's occupation will usually be subservient to his licensor's.

(3) The occupation must be of some value or benefit to the occupier; occupation at least in part for one's own purposes suffices.

(4) The occupation must not be too transient. A weekly periodic licence may qualify[112] but fleeting or intermittent occupation will not.[113]

COUNCIL TAX

11.39 Council tax is payable on all dwellings[114] except those classed as exempt.[115] The kernel of liability is residence. What constitutes residence for these purposes is a question of fact and degree.[116] Where two or more people

---

[107] *Ryde on Rating and the Council Tax*, n 105 above, at Div B, Ch 2, para A[52].
[108] *Roads v Trumpington Overseers* (1870) LR 6 QB 56.
[109] *Westminster CC and Kent Valuation Committee v Southern Rly Co Ltd* [1936] AC 511.
[110] *Glasgow Corp v Johnstone* [1965] AC 609; *Valuation Commissioner (Northern Ireland) v Fermanagh Protestant Board of Education* [1969] 1 WLR 1708.
[111] See the authorities in *Ryde on Rating and the Council Tax*, n 105 above, at Div B, Ch 2, section F3.
[112] See eg *R v Green* (1829) 9 B&C 203 (almshouse occupants).
[113] See eg *Roberts v Aylesbury Overseers* (1853) 1 El &Bl 423, at 433 (market stall holders). See generally *Ryde on Rating and the Council Tax*, n 105 above, at Div B, Ch 2, section E.
[114] As defined by Local Government Finance Act 1992, s 3.
[115] As defined by ibid, s 4 and Council Tax (Exempt Dwellings) Order 1992, SI 1992/558.
[116] See the authorities in 39(1B) *Halsbury's Laws* (4th edn reissue, 2008), at para 237, n 4.

qualify[117] liability falls on the person who has the principal legal interest in the land, specifically the person who first satisfies one of the following descriptions:

- a resident with a freehold interest in all/part of the dwelling;
- a resident leaseholder whose lease is of all/part of the dwelling and is not inferior to the interest of another;
- a resident with a statutory or secure tenancy of all/part of the dwelling;
- a resident who has a contractual licence to occupy all/part of the dwelling;
- a bare resident; or
- the owner.[118]

11.40 If therefore the licensor is a resident freeholder[119]/lessee, he rather than the licensee is liable. That is so even where they occupy separate parts, if they together comprise a single chargeable unit. If the licensor is not resident, liability falls on the resident (contractual or bare) licensee.[120] Where two persons qualify in the same category (eg if a resident contractual licensee grants a contractual residential sub-licence), they are jointly and severally liable.[121]

TAX IMPLICATIONS OF GRANTING THE LICENCE

11.41 Detailed guidance on this notoriously complex area is outside the scope of this book. For this, reference should be made to the relevant statutory provisions and specialist texts. Only the most curtailed treatment is possible.

Value added tax

11.42 Value added tax is chargeable on any supply of goods or services in the UK made by a taxable person in the course or furtherance of a business carried on by him[122] for a consideration.[123]

---

[117] As defined by Local Government Finance Act 1992, s 6(5); Local Government Act 1992, s 69(1).
[118] Local Government Finance Act 1992, s 6. See, however, the special rules as to (inter alia) caravans: ibid, s 7.
[119] Query whether a resident licensor in adverse possession is to be treated as having such an interest. See eg Gray and Gray *Elements of Land Law* (Oxford University Press, 5th edn, 2009), at para 2.1.29. If not, his occupying contractual licensee is liable to tax.
[120] Local Government Finance Act 1992, s 6(2)(d), (e).
[121] Ibid, s 6(3).
[122] Value Added Tax Act 1994, s 4(1).
[123] Ibid, s 5(2).

11.43 The grant of a licence to use/occupy land is capable of amounting to a taxable supply. However, the Value Added Tax Act 1994, Sch 9, Group 1, item 1 contains exemptions for land and buildings provided by Council Directive 2006/112/EC. Paragraph 1 exempts supplies consisting of 'the grant of ... any licence to occupy land' except as specified in sub-paras (a)–(n). The exceptions to the exemption – which are therefore potentially chargeable supplies – include, so far as relevant:

- supplies made pursuant to a developmental licence;[124]

- the grant of a licence consisting of a right to take fish, unless made in conjunction with a grant of the fee simple of the relevant land;[125]

- the provision in a hotel, inn, boarding house or similar establishment of sleeping accommodation or accommodation in rooms provided in conjunction with sleeping accommodation or for the purpose of a supply of catering;[126]

- a licence to occupy holiday accommodation;[127]

- the provision of seasonal pitches for caravans and the grant of facilities at caravan parks to persons for whom such pitches are provided;[128]

- the provision of pitches for tents or camping facilities;[129]

- the grant of facilities for parking a vehicle;[130]

- the grant of any right to fell and remove standing timber;[131]

- the grant of facilities to house/store aircraft or to moor/store a ship, boat or other vessel;[132]

---

[124] Ibid, Sch 9, Group 1, item 1(b). See the definition in note (7) ibid.
[125] Ibid, item (c). See generally as to sporting rights HMRC's VAT Notice 742 'Land and Property', at para 6.
[126] Ibid, item (d).
[127] Ibid, item (e). See also notes (11), (12). Note (13) contains a non-exhaustive definition of 'holiday accommodation'.
[128] Ibid, item (f). Note (14) defines seasonal pitches. This does not include pitches at permanent residential caravan parks and travellers' sites.
[129] Ibid, item (g).
[130] Ibid, item (h). This includes a licence to use a garage or parking bay/space, a right to park vehicles in (eg) a car park, a licence of land to construct a garage, a licence of a purpose-built car park and the provision of storage for bicycles and touring caravans. See generally HMRC's VAT Notice 742 'Land and Property', at para 4.
[131] Value Added Tax Act 1994, Sch 9, Group 1, item (j).
[132] Ibid, item (k).

- the grant of any right to occupy a box, seat or other accommodation at a sports ground, theatre, concert hall or other place of entertainment;[133] and

- the grant of facilities for playing any sport or participating in any physical recreation.[134]

11.44 HMRC's VAT Notice 742 'Land and Property' sets out detailed guidance on some of these exceptions.[135] It also sets out the Commissioners' views that a licence falls within the Group 1 exemption if:

- it is granted in return for a consideration paid by the licensee;

- it is to occupy a specified area of land, even if the precise area can be changed from time to time by the licensor;

- it is for the occupation of the land by the licensee;

- any other person's right to enter the land does not impinge on the licensee's occupational rights; and

- it allows the licensee either physically to enjoy the land for the purpose of the grant or to exploit it economically for the purposes of his business.[136]

11.45 As the exemption from VAT relates only to occupation licences, mere user licences are potentially chargeable supplies. The distinction, however, is sometimes difficult to draw in practice. Each case turns on its particular facts. The Commissioners give the following examples of licences which, in their view, are to occupy land:

- the provision of office accommodation, such as a specified bay, room or floor, together with the right to use shared areas such as reception, lifts, restaurant, rest rooms, leisure facilities etc;

- the provision of a serviced office that includes use of telephones, computer system, fax machine, photocopiers etc;

- granting a concession to operate a shop within a shop, where the concessionaire is granted an area from which to sell its goods or services;

- granting space to erect advertising hoardings;

---

[133] Ibid, item (l).
[134] Ibid, item (m). See VAT Notice 742, at para 5 for more guidance.
[135] See also VAT Notice 709/3 for the treatment of hotels and holiday accommodation and VAT Notice 701/20 for accommodation provided by – and the provision of services to – caravans and houseboats.
[136] VAT Notice 742, para 2.5.

- granting space to place a fixed kiosk on a specified site, such as a newspaper kiosk or flower stand at a railway station;

- hiring out a hall or other accommodation for meetings, parties etc, which may include the use of a kitchen area, lighting and furniture;

- granting a catering concession, where the caterer is granted a licence to occupy a specific kitchen and restaurant area, even if the grant includes use of kitchen or catering equipment; and

- granting traders a pitch in a market or at a car boot sale.[137]

11.46 Examples of licences the Commissioners regard as not ones to occupy land, and thus potentially chargeable to VAT, are:

- sharing business premises where more than one business has use of the same parts of the premises without having their own specified areas;

- providing another person with access to office premises to make use of facilities, such as remote sales staff away from home having access to photocopiers etc at another office;

- allowing the public to tip rubbish on the land;

- storing goods in a warehouse without allocating any specific area for them;

- granting an ambulatory concession, such as an ice cream van on the seafront or a hamburger van at a football match;

- allowing public admission to premises or events, such as theatres, historic houses, swimming pools and spectator sports events, which can include admission to a series of events, such as a season ticket; and

- any grant of land clearly incidental to the use of the facilities on it, such as hiring out safes to store valuables or the right to use facilities in a hairdressing salon or granting someone the right to place a wall-mounted or free-standing gaming machine.[138]

11.47 If an occupation licence is combined with other services (which of themselves would be taxable), the precise nature of the supply must be determined. It may consist of: a composite supply comprising an exempt licence to occupy land to which the rights are incidental; a composite supply

---

[137] VAT Notice 742, para 2.6. See also as to what constitutes 'occupation': *Commissioners of Customs & Excise v Sinclair Collis Ltd* [2001] STC 989; *Newnham College Cambridge v HM Revenue & Customs* [2008] UKHL 23.

[138] VAT Notice 742, para 2.7. See as to the latter Case C-275/01 *Sinclair Collis Ltd v Commissioners of Customs & Excise* [2003] STC 898.

where the licence is incidental to the other rights, which are VAT-able; or a multiple supply, requiring the consideration to be apportioned between the two.[139]

Stamp duty land tax

11.48 Stamp duty land tax (SDLT) is imposed on land transactions[140] that involve the acquisition for consideration of a 'chargeable interest' in or over land or over UK land, other than an 'exempt interest'.[141]

11.49 A 'chargeable interest' is defined as including an estate, right or power in or over land.[142] 'Exempt interests' include 'a licence to use or occupy land'.[143] The grant, assignment, variation or termination of a licence 'in gross' is therefore not liable to SDLT[144] or notifiable.[145] This obviously includes contractual licences and bare licences (which in any event are not chargeable for lack of consideration). In the case of licences coupled with an interest the grant or transfer of the interest, unless exempt, may be subject to tax.

11.50 The grant of a licence 'in gross', however, may accelerate an obligation to file a return and pay SDLT in relation to a related, notifiable transaction. Normally that must be done within 30 days of the effective date, which for a contract to grant, transfer etc a chargeable interest which contemplates completion is usually the date of completion.[146] Where, however, a contract is substantially performed otherwise than by (and prior to) formal completion, the effective date is the date of substantial performance.[147] A contract is 'substantially performed' for these purposes if (inter alia) the purchaser or a connected person takes possession of the whole, or substantially the whole, of the subject matter of the contract.[148] It is immaterial whether he does so under the contract or by virtue of a temporary licence (or, for that matter, lease).[149] If such a contract is later formally completed, both the contract and the transaction effecting completion are notifiable transactions and SDLT is payable on the later only to the extent (if any) that the amount of tax chargeable on it is greater than that chargeable on the earlier.[150] On the other hand, if the purchaser is already in occupation at the time of exchange under an existing licence (or other interest) then so long as it remains enforceable pending completion, mere continuance in possession in the interim is not substantial performance for these purposes.

---

[139] *De Voil Indirect Tax Service* (LexisNexis online), at para V4.112(iii).
[140] Finance Act 2003, s 42(1).
[141] Defined ibid, s 48(2).
[142] Ibid, s 48(1).
[143] Ibid, s 48(2)(b).
[144] Ibid.
[145] Ibid, s 77.
[146] Ibid, s 44(2).
[147] Ibid, s 44(4).
[148] Ibid, s 44(5)(a).
[149] Ibid, s 44(6).
[150] Ibid, s 44(8).

STATUTORY COMPENSATION ON COMPULSORY ACQUISITION

General

11.51 Land and interests in land may be compulsorily acquired, subject to payment of compensation. Neither the Acquisition of Land Act 1981 nor the Compulsory Purchase Act 1965 defines land for these purposes. Subject then to any definition in the enabling Act, the right to acquire 'land', for which compensation is payable, includes 'any estate, interest easement servitude or right in or over land'.[151] A licence to use or occupy land is not, however, an interest in land (see Chapter 9) and thus cannot be acquired compulsorily unless the enabling Act makes express provision.[152] Nor is compensation payable in respect of it under the 1965 Act. To this general rule are three exceptions:

(1) First, if the licence is coupled with an interest in land, the acquiring authority may compulsorily acquire (and be liable to pay compensation for) that interest and in valuing it account will be taken of any ancillary rights, such as the licence.

(2) Second, as estoppel licences are generally thought to be interests in land, it is considered the representee's inchoate equity may be compulsorily acquired subject to compensation being paid.[153] After relief is granted by the court to give effect to that equity, the form it takes will determine whether it may be acquired in this manner.

(3) Third, the licensee may be entitled to a disturbance payment or home loss payment (see **11.52–11.53** below).

The acquiring authority will, however, normally take free of the licensee's interest (Chapter 9). A licensor who is liable in damages to his licensee by virtue of the compulsory acquisition of his interest may claim compensation for disturbance in respect of that liability.[154]

Disturbance payments

11.52 The Land Compensation Act 1973, s 37(1) entitles a person who has no compensatable interest (which includes most licensees) to a disturbance

---

[151] Interpretation Act 1978, Sch 1.
[152] *Bird v Great Eastern Rly Co* (1865) 19 CBNS 268; *Frank Warr & Co v London CC* [1904] 1 KB 713.
[153] See by analogy *DHN Food Distributors Ltd v Tower Hamlets LBC* [1976] 1 WLR 852. Although the reasoning in that case – namely that the contractual licence was binding on the successor as it gave rise to a constructive trust – is no longer good, the result may be justifiable on the basis set out in the text. Whether a licence that binds successors only by virtue of some supervening constructive trust qualifies as a compensatable interest is doubtful – see Chapter 9.
[154] *Walton Harvey Ltd v Walker and Homfrays Ltd* [1931] 1 Ch 274.

payment if he is in 'lawful possession'[155] of the land from which he is displaced as a result of its compulsory acquisition. 'Lawful possession' includes physical occupation with the permission of the person who has the right to possession in law with the intention of excluding unauthorised persons. A licensee in exclusive occupation thus qualifies.[156] A licensee who is not in 'lawful possession' may apply for a discretionary payment under s 37(5).

Home loss payments

11.53 A licensee of a dwelling displaced as a result of its compulsory acquisition is entitled to a home loss payment if he occupied it (or a substantial part of it), as his only or main residence by virtue of (inter alia) a contract of employment, restricted contract, protected occupancy or assured agricultural occupancy or introductory tenancy (as to which see Chapter 6) and did so during the whole of the year prior to acquisition.[157] A licensee who meets the criteria at the date of acquisition but not for the whole of the previous year may apply for a discretionary home loss payment.[158] The Land Compensation Act 1973, s 33 extends the right to the displaced former residents of caravans on a caravan site if no suitable alternative site is available on reasonable terms.

PLANNING AND ENVIRONMENTAL LIABILITIES

Planning control

11.54 A local planning authority that considers a breach of planning control may have occurred can serve a temporary stop notice[159] on anyone who is the owner or occupier or has an interest in the land or who is carrying out operations on it. In addition it may serve a planning contravention notice requiring information[160] on such persons and on someone who is 'using [the land] for any purpose'.[161] Failure to comply with the notices is an offence.[162] Accordingly a licensor or licensee in occupation or carrying out relevant operations and a licensor who has an interest in the land may be served with either type of notice; other licensees may (only) be served with the latter.

11.55 In addition the authority may serve an enforcement notice requiring the recipient to take steps to remedy a breach of planning control and/or any consequential injury to amenity.[163] Such notice may be served on the owner[164]

---

[155] Land Compensation Act 1973, s 37(2)(a), (3).
[156] *Wrexham Maelor BC v MacDougall* (1993) 69 P & CR 109, at 120–121. That the licence is terminable merely affects the level of compensation – ibid.
[157] Land Compensation Act 1973, s 29(4).
[158] Ibid, s 29(2).
[159] Town and Country Planning Act 1990, s 171E(4).
[160] Ibid, s 171C(2).
[161] Ibid, s 171C(1). See the definition of 'use' in s 336(1).
[162] Ibid, s 171G (temporary stop notice); ibid, s 171D (planning contravention notice).
[163] Ibid, s 173(4), (5).
[164] Defined in ibid, s 336(1) as the person entitled to receive the rack rent.

and occupier of the land and any other person having an 'interest' that is materially affected by it.[165] An occupying licensee[166] therefore may be served with notice but will not usually be liable for failing to take any step required by it,[167] although he may be liable, if he has control of the land, for continuing any activity specified in it or causing or permitting its continuation.[168] A licensor may be liable in those circumstances as well as under the Town and Country Planning Act 1990, s 179(1) if he owns or has an interest in the land.

11.56 Pending an enforcement notice taking effect, the local planning authority may serve a stop notice prohibiting the carrying out of an activity on the land on any person who appears to have an interest in it or to be carrying on the stipulated activities.[169] A licensee may thus only be served if he carries on such activities, personally or through others, whether he does so on his own behalf or for the licensor. The licensor may be served if he has an interest in the land or the licensee is carrying on those activities on his behalf.

11.57 A breach of condition notice may be served in the event of a breach of condition of planning permission on any person who carries/carried out 'the development' and any person who has 'control' of the land.[170] As between the licensor and licensee the question of control depends on the licence terms and is one of fact and degree.

Environmental Protection Act 1990

11.58 A local authority has power under the Environmental Protection Act 1990, s 80 to serve an abatement notice to prevent a 'statutory nuisance'[171] arising or continuing. Such notice may require the recipient to cease the activities causing the nuisance or take steps to abate it; failure to comply without reasonable excuse is an offence.[172]

11.59 Except as set out at **11.60**, the notice may be served on the 'person responsible' for the nuisance,[173] ie whose act default or sufferance caused or threatens to cause it.[174] That includes both the actual creator of the nuisance and the person on whose behalf he acted;[175] the mere fact he may also be a licensor/licensee is entirely incidental. The licensor may be liable (concurrently with the licensee) by permitting the acts that constitute the nuisance or failing

---

[165] Ibid, s 172(2).
[166] See eg *Stevens v Bromley LBC* [1972] Ch 400; see also *Scarborough BC v Adams* [1983] JPL 673 as to occupation.
[167] Town and Country Planning Act 1990, s 179(1) – see, however, the definition ibid, s 336(1).
[168] Ibid, s 179(4).
[169] Ibid, s 183.
[170] Ibid, s 187A(1), (2).
[171] As defined in Environmental Protection Act 1990, s 79.
[172] Ibid, s 80(4).
[173] Ibid, s 80(2)(a). If the person responsible cannot be found or the nuisance has not yet occurred, the notice must be served on the 'owner': s 80(2)(c).
[174] Ibid, s 79(7).
[175] Ibid, s 81(2).

to exercise control over them reserved to him by the licence agreement.[176] The licensee may be liable for causing the nuisance or by permitting or suffering his sub-licensee to do so, but not if the acts were caused by the licensor or another licensee exercising rights reserved by the licence agreement. If the licensee caused the nuisance but is not entitled under his licence terms to undertake the works required by the notice to abate it, he may have 'reasonable excuse' for failing to comply.

11.60 Where the nuisance arises from a defect of a structural character only the 'owner' may be served.[177] That may be the licensor, even if he has no duties under the licence agreement in relation to repair.[178] If the person responsible cannot be found or the nuisance is merely anticipated, both the owner and 'occupier'[179] may be served which, in the latter case, may be either the licensor or licensee, depending on the licence terms and circumstances.[180]

---

[176] See eg *Clayton v Sale UDC* [1926] 1 KB 415.
[177] Environmental Protection Act 1990, s 80(2)(b).
[178] See by analogy *Birmingham DC v Kelly* (1985) 17 HLR 572.
[179] Environmental Protection Act 1990, s 80(2)(c).
[180] For an example of an abatement notice served on a licensee see *Cambridge CC v Douglas* [2000] All ER (D) 2424.

Chapter 12

TERMINATION OF LICENCES

Bare licences	12.2
Effluxion of time	12.2
Automatic determination	12.3
Notice/demand	12.5
Contractual licences	12.11
Effluxion of time	12.12
Automatic determination	12.13
Exercise of option	12.15
Termination on notice	12.16
Termination for breach	12.28
Repudiation	12.31
Agreement, abandonment	12.32
Frustration	12.33
Disclaimer	12.35
Miscellaneous non-contractual limitations on termination	12.38
Wrongful purported termination	12.40
Licences coupled with an interest	12.47
Estoppel licences	12.48
The inchoate equity	12.48
The relief	12.50
The grace period	12.51
When the period applies	12.51
The length and purpose of the period	12.53

12.1 Once it is determined that a licence is expressly or impliedly terminable (as to which see Chapter 8) the question then arises: how may it be brought to an end? That depends initially on its proper classification (ie bare, contractual, estoppel or coupled with an interest), as different methods of termination apply to each. Once classified, consideration must then be given to its terms. The termination of a licence that attracts security of tenure must comply with the relevant statutory regime, as to which see Chapter 6.

BARE LICENCES

Effluxion of time

12.2 A bare licence granted for a specified period or until a particular date terminates by effluxion of time at the end of that period or on the stipulated date,[1] unless extended in the meantime by the licensor. A licence that is expressly/impliedly granted for a reasonable period of time expires at the end of that period. Where an implied licence arises from circumstances (eg the presence of facilities on the land or the personal relationship between the parties), it is a question of intention whether it constitutes a standing invitation that ceases when those circumstances no longer exist or was for a single entry or to last merely for a reasonable period of time. In each case, notice to terminate is unnecessary.

Automatic determination

12.3 A bare licence also automatically terminates:

- upon the fulfilment of the purpose for which it was granted (eg permission to collect a stray ball);

- if granted until a particular event (eg 'until I return from abroad'), on its occurrence;

- upon the death of either party or the licensor assigning the land;[2]

- by the licensor otherwise divesting himself of the right to possession (eg by letting the land or declaring himself trustee for another);

- by the licensor doing some other act incompatible with its continuation[3] (eg by demolishing or radically altering its subject matter) although such act may instead be regarded as an implied election to terminate, taking effect once the licensee becomes aware of it;

- by the licensee unilaterally quitting the land,[4] unless the licence constitutes a standing invitation or was granted for an (in)definite period rather than for a single occasion/event; or

- if granted in contemplation of the parties entering into some other agreement (eg lease, sale of the land) when they are no longer intending to proceed to exchange.[5] That intention may be inferred from words/acts or circumstances from which the objective observer would deduce that the

---

[1] *Sandhu v Farooqui* [2004] 1 P & CR 19, at [20].
[2] *Terunnanse v Terunnanse* [1968] 1 All ER 651, at 656; *Wallis v Harrison* (1834) 4 M&W 538. In contrast the contractual licensee may be unable to exercise his rights against the licensor's successor but the licence is not thereby brought to an end – see Chapter 9.
[3] *Webb v Paternoster* (1619) 2 Roll Rep 143.
[4] See by analogy *Australian Blue Metal Ltd v Hughes* [1963] AC 74, at 97–98 (contractual licence).
[5] *Colin Dawson Windows Ltd v King's Lynn BC* [2005] 2 P & CR 19.

transaction is not to proceed,[6] although more often it will require some communication between the parties.[7]

A licensee who fails to adhere to the terms of his licence may thereby automatically end it, at least if by doing so he evinces an intention to disclaim – see **4.9–4.13**.[8] Not every unauthorised user has that effect. Nevertheless a licensee who exceeds the scope of his licence will be a trespasser at least *to the extent that* he does so.[9] And if his conduct does not amount to a disclaimer and the licence is a standing invitation or granted for an (in)definite period, as distinct from a one-off permission, the licensee may be able to resume lawful use/occupation pursuant to it, unless the licensor brings it to an end in the meantime.

12.4 The peremptory determination of the licence as a result of acts/circumstances outside the licensee's control has the potential to cause hardship, particularly if he has no forewarning/knowledge. He is protected by the fact that he may not be treated immediately as a trespasser, notwithstanding the licence's termination, but must be given a reasonable time (the grace period) to vacate – see **12.51–12.54**. In contrast it is considered that a licensee who is not present at that time may be peremptorily barred from re-entering, although the licensor must make available to him any possessions left on the land – see **9.25**.

Notice/demand

12.5 A bare licence is revoked by any words or acts that evince an intention to treat it at an end. Whether they do so is determined objectively[10] and is a question of fact.[11] No form is necessary;[12] the licensor's oral demand to quit will do,[13] as may conduct, such as physically taking possession or preventing entry. Acts/words that are objectively insufficient to amount to revocation but which are subjectively intended and understood as such by the parties may, even if not effective to terminate the licence, amount to an estoppel by convention preventing them from asserting that it continues.

---

[6] *Sandhu v Farooqui* [2004] 1 P & CR 19, at [25].
[7] *BANES v Nicholson* [2002] All ER (D) 327 (Feb); *Sandhu v Farooqui* [2004] 1 P & CR 19, at [23]–[25]; *Totton and Eling Town Council v Caunter* [2008] All ER (D) 133 (Jun).
[8] But see *Harvey v Plymouth CC* [2010] EWCA Civ. 860, at [22] for the suggestion that a licensee who uses the land for purposes other than those contemplated may remain the licensor's 'visitor' within the meaning of the Occupiers' Liability Act 1957, albeit not one to whom the common duty of care is owed.
[9] See e g *Trustees of Grantham Christian Fellowship v Scouts Association* [2005] EWHC 209 (Ch).
[10] *R (Fullard) v Woking Magistrates Court* [2005] EWHC 2922 (Admin), at [22]
[11] See e g *Lambert v Roberts* [1981] 2 All ER 15, at 19; *Gilham v Breidenbach* [1982] RTR 328; *Snook v Mannion* [1982] Crim LR 601; *R (Fullard) v Woking Magistrates Court* [2005] EWHC 2922 (Admin), at [27].
[12] A bare licence is excluded from Protection from Eviction Act 1977, s 5: s 3A(7)(b).
[13] *Crane v Morris* [1965] 1 WLR 1104, at 1108.

Notice by licensor

12.6 A bare licence is revocable by the licensor at any time, even if the licensee has not yet finished what he was initially authorised to do,[14] unless the circumstances are such as to raise an estoppel. However, it appears that the licence may not always be *peremptorily* revoked with the licensee merely having a grace period in which to quit the land. The parties may have intended at the outset that any revocation would only be effective after a reasonable period of time.[15] And there is authority that in exceptional cases the licensee may also be entitled to notice stating a particular date, a reasonable period of time after service, on which it takes effect (the dated notice) – see *Canadian Pacific Railway Co v The King*[16] and *Governing Body of Henrietta Barnett School v Hampstead Garden Suburb Institute*,[17] both of which were treated in *Parker v Parker*[18] as cases of gratuitous licences. The reconciliation of this rule with the principle that such licences, being gratuitous, are dependent on the licensor's will is thought to lie in the concept of the executed licence (see Chapter 13): the original permission implicitly entitled the licensee to a reasonable period of notice; the licensee having acted on it by entering the land, the licensor cannot retrospectively revoke what he has granted.[19] A similar result may be reached by applying estoppel principles.

12.7 What notice is, in any particular case, required 'depends on the nature of the licence and particularly on how and for what reason it came into existence',[20] to which may be added the parties' expectations, the contemplated use of the land and its actual use at the date of revocation. For example, if the licensee is physically absent from the land, it is thought the licence may be peremptorily revoked. A casual visitor's licence may be terminable forthwith, subject to him having a grace period in which to leave,[21] or after a reasonable time, also measured by how long he needs to quit the land. An occupier may be entitled to a longer period to vacate.[22] And a licensee who relied on the licence's continuation, eg by taking steps (such as planting crops) or entering into

---

[14] *Canadian Pacific Railway Co v The King* [1931] AC 414, at 430–431; *Winter Garden Theatre (London) Ltd v Millennium Productions Ltd* [1948] AC 173, at 188–189, 193–195, 198; *Lambert v Roberts* [1981] 2 All ER 15, at 19 ('a licence which is revocable without prior notice'); *Davis v Lisle* [1936] 2 KB 434, at 439, 441; *Robson v Hallett* [1967] QB 939.

[15] *Governing Body of Henrietta Barnett School v Hampstead Garden Suburb Institute* (1995) 93 LGR 470, at 511.

[16] [1931] AC 414. The case is widely regarded as a special one on its facts: *Minister of Health v Bellotti* [1944] KB 298, at 308.

[17] (1995) 93 LGR 470.

[18] [2003] EWHC 1846 (Ch), at [273] and [278] respectively.

[19] Compare the grace period – **12.51–12.54**.

[20] *Parker v Parker* [2003] EWHC 1846 (Ch), at [276].

[21] *Winter Garden Theatre (London) Ltd v Millennium Productions Ltd* [1948] AC 173, at 188, 200–201; *Robson v Hallett* [1967] 2 QB 939, at 953 ('a very short time').

[22] *Canadian Pacific Railway Co v The King* [1931] AC 414, at 432; *Winter Garden Theatre (London) Ltd v Millennium Productions Ltd* [1948] AC 173, at 205; *Robson v Hallett* [1967] 2 QB 939, at 954, [1967] 2 All ER 407, at 413; *Lambert v Roberts* [1981] 2 All ER 15.

commitments on that assumption, may be entitled to a period of time to (literally or figuratively) reap what he has sown[23] or unwind those commitments.

12.8 If the licence is only terminable on giving reasonable notice the licensee does not become a trespasser until such time has passed[24] or (possibly) he manifests an intention to stay notwithstanding the fact he has been given notice.[25] A licensor who forcibly evicts the licensee before then commits a trespass to his person or goods[26] even though only reasonable force is used and even though no injunction to require the licensor to allow him to continue to use the land in the interim would have been granted.

Notice by occupier

12.9 A person in occupation – or at least control – of land may have the licensor's actual or apparent authority to terminate the bare licence of a mere visitor. Hence in *Lambert v Roberts*[27] it was assumed such a person could require police officers attending a house to leave, failing which they became trespassers. Whether he has such authority is to be determined by applying ordinary principles of agency.

Notice by licensee

12.10 Since a gratuitous licensee is (by definition) under no obligation to use the land he need not terminate the licence but may simply desist from entering the land and allow it to expire automatically or by effluxion of time. It is thought to follow that if he chooses to terminate the licence, he may do so peremptorily[28] and he may of course disclaim[29] by words/acts evincing his intention not to rely on it.

---

[23] *Winter Garden Theatre (London) Ltd v Millennium Productions Ltd* [1948] AC 173, at 199.
[24] See e g *Robson v Hallett* [1967] 2 QB 939, [1967] 2 All ER 407.
[25] *Davis v Lisle* [1936] 2 KB 434, at 438 (refusal to vacate during grace period); but see *R (Fullard) v Woking Magistrates Court* [2005] EWHC 2922 (Admin), at [28] (grace period).
[26] *Aldin v Latimer Clarke Muirheas & Co* [1894] 2 Ch 437, at 448.
[27] [1981] 2 All ER 15.
[28] See e g *Winter Garden Theatre (London) Ltd v Millennium Productions Ltd* [1948] AC 173, at 196: 'the licensees are entitled to a reasonable time after notice to put an end to their commitments whereas the licensors would have no protection against the licensees walking out at any moment ...'; *Australian Blue Metal Ltd v Hughes* [1963] AC 74, at 98: 'the [licensees] could at any time bring the agreement effectively to an end simply by ceasing work without even having to send a peremptory notice to that effect'. Although both cases concern contractual licences (as to which sed quaere now) the dicta is considered good as regards bare licenses.
[29] See Chapter 4; *BP Properties Ltd v Buckler* (1987) 55 P & CR 337; *Odey v Barber* [2007] 3 All ER 543.

CONTRACTUAL LICENCES

12.11 A contractual licence may be brought to an end in any way in which a contract may be terminated. The principal methods of doing so are therefore taken shortly. As discussed in more detail below[30] a contractual licence may (only) be determined according to its terms; where therefore the licence terms impose conditions on the exercise of that right, a party who wishes to terminate must comply with them.[31]

Effluxion of time

12.12 Contractual licences for a fixed term automatically terminate at the end of the stipulated period; no notice is necessary. A licence for a fixed term or which contains an express right to terminate in specific circumstances or at certain times is unlikely to be also impliedly terminable generally on notice.[32] Of course the parties may agree to extend the contract term and any agreement to do so will usually provide its own consideration. Whereas such an agreement, in the case of a lease, necessarily takes effect as a surrender and regrant,[33] the extension of the licence term can take effect as a mere variation. If after a fixed-term licence ends the licensee continues to use the land, it is a question of intention whether a new contractual licence arises by implication or the licensee's presence is merely at the licensor's sufferance.[34] If the latter, that arrangement will usually be terminable peremptorily.[35]

Automatic determination

12.13 A licence that is granted until a certain event (e g 'until I secure planning permission for redevelopment') automatically expires on its occurrence unless, on its true construction, notice must be given or it merely gives one or both parties the right to terminate in those circumstances. A licence that is expressly/impliedly conditional on the continuation of certain circumstances automatically expires on their cessation.[36] For example, a non-owning partner's right to use land for partnership purposes automatically expires on its dissolution or winding up or him ceasing to be a partner.[37] A service occupier's licence to occupy his employer's accommodation is also implicitly conditional on the continuation of his employment and thus automatically terminates

---

[30] See **12.17** et seq, **12.40** et seq.
[31] *Wallshire v Advertising Sites* [1988] 2 EGLR 167.
[32] *Winter Garden Theatre (London) Ltd v Millennium Productions Ltd* [1948] AC 173; *Jani-King (GB) Ltd v Pula Enterprises Ltd* [2007] EWHC 2433, at [60] et seq; *ServicePower Asia Pacific Pty Ltd v ServicePower Business Solutions Ltd* [2009] EWHC 179 (Ch), at [25]–[27]. See e g *Colcheseter & East Essex Co-op Ltd v Kelvedon Labour Club & Institute Ltd* [2003] EWCA Civ 1671.
[33] *Well Barn Farming v Backhouse* [2005] 3 EGLR 109.
[34] See **13.3**.
[35] *Isaac v Hotel de Paris* [1960] 1 WLR 239, [1960] 1 All ER 348. See, however, Chapter 13 for limitations on the licensor's right to exercise self-help.
[36] *Sandhu v Farooqui* [2004] 1 P & CR 19, at [20].
[37] See **6.8–6.9**.

Termination of Licences 211

when it ends, even if he is unfairly or unlawfully dismissed.[38] He is not entitled to reasonable notice[39] or one that complies with the Protection from Eviction Act 1977, s 5.[40]

12.14 The stipulated event or circumstances must be conceptually certain[41] but need not be defined with the same clarity as is required for leases. For example, a licence for the duration of the war is valid,[42] as is one permitting the land to be used until required for road widening.[43] So too is a licence that is terminable (only) on the happening of such events. If, however, the event itself is too vague, applying general contractual principles, the licence may be construed as being terminable generally on reasonable notice.

Exercise of option

12.15 A fixed-term licence may contain a break clause entitling the parties to elect to terminate early. Such a right is very unlikely to be implied.[44] An express right may be exercisable unconditionally or – more usually – on the satisfaction of certain conditions, eg as to when it is exercisable or the manner of its exercise. In either case they must be strictly complied with for the exercise to be effective.[45] Where the right is granted to two or more persons (eg joint licensors or licensees) prima facie they must all join in – see **12.26(5)**. Where the right is granted to the licensee who has assigned the right to use the land, it is a question of construction of the licence and assignment whether it can be (and, if so, has been) assigned to his successor and, if not, whether the licensee may exercise it notwithstanding the assignment, eg in order to avoid his continuing obligations to the licensor (see Chapter 10).

Termination on notice

12.16 A licence may be terminable generally by notice if:

- its terms expressly so provide;

- it is granted for an indefinite period but is, properly construed, impliedly terminable at one/other party's election; or

- it is a periodic licence.

---

[38] *Ivory v Palmer* [1975] ICR 340; *Whitbread West Pennines Ltd v Reedy* (1988) 20 HLR 642.
[39] *Crane v Morris* [1965] 1 WLR 1104, at 1108.
[40] *Norris v Checksfield* [1991] 4 All ER 327, at 332–333.
[41] *Sifton v Sifton* [1938] AC 656.
[42] *Lace v Chantler* [1944] KB 368, at 372.
[43] *Prudential Assurance Co Ltd v London Residuary Body* [1992] AC 386.
[44] See eg *Kirklees MBC v Yorkshire Woolen District Transport Ltd* (1978) 77 LGR 448.
[45] See by analogy *Finch v Underwood* (1876) 2 ChD 310 (lease).

An effective notice, once given, cannot be withdrawn without the other party's consent unless the licence provides otherwise.[46] However, it has been tentatively suggested that where notice is given by non-instantaneous means (eg post) the server may be able to countermand it effectively so long as his decision to do so is communicated before the original notice is served or deemed to be served on the recipient.[47]

Manner of exercise – express term

12.17 Where the validity of a notice is challenged, the contract term under which it is served must be construed to determine precisely what it requires. For example:

(1) An express term as to the form/contents of the notice may be mandatory or directory. If the former, the serving party's notice must strictly comply in order to be effective.[48]

(2) Whether such a term is a condition or not is a question of construction. It will usually be if it is determinative of the parties' rights,[49] eg as to the date on which the notice must be expressed to take effect.

(3) The required length of notice is also a question of construction. For example:

- A licence may provide that it terminates forthwith on notice – see eg *R (First Real Estates (UK) Ltd) v Birmingham CC*[50] ('on receipt of written notice at any time').
- It may provide that the licence will terminate a certain time after notice is given; if so, the notice need only manifest an immediate intention to terminate without stating when it takes effect.[51] That date is then ascertainable from the licence terms.
- If the licence requires the serving party to give (say) 'one month's notice', the notice need not specify the precise date when it takes effect.[52]
- However, in certain circumstances the licence may require the server not merely to give a certain *period* of notice but to give a *dated* notice, ie that states when it takes effect – see below.

(4) Whether a term that permits notice only to be *given* before/after a certain date or within a certain period of time must be strictly complied with

---

[46] *May v Borup* [1915] 1 KB 830, at 832 (lease).
[47] *Kinch v Bullard* [1998] 4 All ER 650, at 656.
[48] *Wallshire v Advertising Sites* [1988] 2 EGLR 167.
[49] See by analogy *Warborough Investments Ltd v Central Midland Estates Ltd* [2006] EWHC 2622 (Ch), at [63].
[50] [2009] EWHC 817 (Admin), at [39]–[41].
[51] *Australian Blue Metal Ltd v Hughes* [1963] AC 74, at 100.
[52] *W Davies (Spitalfields) Ltd v Huntley* [1947] 1 KB 246 (lease).

depends on whether time is/is not of the essence.[53] If it is, a notice that is served too early/late or outside the stipulated period is ineffective.

Manner of exercise – implied term

12.18 If the contract is silent about how it may be brought to an end but is, properly construed, impliedly terminable on notice, the length and form of notice must also be determined by implication. That depends on the parties' objective intentions[54] which are to be determined in light of the purpose of the licence, its express terms and the circumstances existing when it was created.[55] The implied term is likely to take one of the following forms:

- The licence may be terminable forthwith,[56] subject to the licensee having a period of grace to vacate.

- The licence may be terminable on giving reasonable notice.[57] In such case the serving party need only manifest an immediate intention to bring the licence to an end without stating when his notice is to take effect. Most indefinite licences are terminable in this manner.

- Where a licence is terminable on reasonable notice it may be an implied requirement that the serving party specify in his notice the particular date on which it will expire, which is reasonable in the circumstances (the dated notice), as in *Parker v Parker*.[58] However, not all licences require a dated notice;[59] in practice few do.

- A periodic licence[60] may be impliedly terminable on a period's notice.[61] If so, it is a question of construction whether the period of notice given may

---

[53] See *Chitty on Contracts* (Sweet & Maxwell, 30th edn, 2008), at para 21-013 for when time is impliedly of the essence.
[54] *Winter Garden Theatre (London) Ltd v Millennium Productions Ltd* [1948] AC 173; *Tungsten Electric Co Ltd v Tool Metal Manufacturing Co Ltd (No 3)* [1954] 2 All ER 28.
[55] *Australian Blue Metal Ltd v Hughes* [1963] AC 74, at 99; *Winter Garden Theatre (London) Ltd v Millennium Productions Ltd* [1948] AC 173, at 204–205.
[56] See eg *Winter Garden Theatre (London) Ltd v Millennium Productions Ltd* [1948] AC 173, at 196.
[57] *Australian Blue Metal Ltd v Hughes* [1963] AC 74, at 98 ('it does not require very much to induce a court to read into an agreement of a commercial character, either by construction or by implication, a provision that the arrangements between the parties, whatever they may be, shall be terminable only upon reasonable notice'). Eg in *Winter Garden Theatre (London) Ltd v Millennium Productions Ltd* [1948] AC 173, at 205 the terms requiring advance payment, the continuation of the licence after the end of the fixed term and the grant of sub-licences were held to justify a finding that the licence was not terminable peremptorily but on reasonable notice.
[58] [2003] EWHC 1846 (Ch).
[59] *Australian Blue Metal Ltd v Hughes* [1963] AC 74, at 100–101.
[60] Ie a licence that is expressed to be periodic or continues automatically from one period to another unless determined. That may be inferred from the reservation of a periodic licence fee.
[61] *Winter Garden Theatre (London) Ltd v Millennium Productions Ltd* [1948] AC 173, at 195.

expire at any time or only at the end of a period of the licence.[62] That, however, is only one possible inference: periodic licences may be terminable merely on giving reasonable notice.[63] If a periodic licence grants the right to occupy a dwelling as a residence and is not an excluded licence,[64] s 5 of the Protection from Eviction Act 1977 requires that the notice is in writing, expires at least 4 weeks after service and contains certain statutorily-prescribed information.[65] This requirement does not apply to fixed-term licences or indefinite licences that are impliedly terminable on reasonable notice.[66]

(Non-)compliant notices

12.19 Once the requirements of a valid notice are ascertained from the licence terms, the particular notice must then be interpreted in order to establish whether it complies:

(1) Where the relevant term is mandatory rather than directory, a notice that fails to comply is ineffective. As stated above, stipulations as to the minimum period of notice are probably mandatory. Where then (eg) a licence requires the server to give 'not less than' one month's notice, a short notice is invalid. A notice that gives sufficient time may, however, request/propose that it take effect early without affecting its validity.

(2) A notice can specify in the alternative two or more dates on which it will expire, where the serving party is uncertain of conforming with the requirements of the licence. For instance, it may specify a particular date and, in the alternative, a formula from which the correct date can be ascertained (eg 'on [*date*] or a reasonable period of time after service of this notice on you' or 'on [*date*] or at the end of the next full period of your licence which will expire next after service of this notice on you, whichever is the later'). So long as it is clear which is intended to govern if the two dates produce different results, and that date is compliant with the licence term, the notice will be valid.

(3) A notice that is expressed merely to take effect on the earliest date on which a notice served on that date could validly terminate the licence is effective[67] unless either:

---

[62] Eg monthly periodic licence starting on the 1st; whether notice served on the 15th expires on the 15th day of the following month or on the 1st day of the subsequent month.
[63] See eg *Smith v Northside Developments* [1987] 2 EGLR 151, at 152L; *Mehta v Royal Bank of Scotland* [1999] 3 EGLR 153, at 156E–156F, 158M.
[64] See Protection from Eviction Act 1977, s 3A.
[65] See Notices to Quit (Prescribed Information) Regulations 1988, SI 1988/2201. The Act's requirements cannot be waived: *Polarpark Enterprises Inc v Allason* [2007] EWHC 1088 (Ch), at [27].
[66] *Parker v Parker* [2003] EWHC 1846 (Ch), at [289].
[67] *May v Borup* [1915] 1 KB 830, at 832; *Allam & Co v Europa Poster Services* [1968] 1 All ER 826.

(a) the licence requires a dated notice to be given; or
(b) it is terminable by notice expiring on a particular day when some event occurs, of which the recipient may be ignorant. Where therefore an agreement provided that it was terminable on 'any one of the days appointed as special transfer sessions by the justices' a notice that stated it was to take effect on the earliest date on which it could validly do so was ineffective; the court would not impute knowledge by the recipient of the date of the next relevant sessions.[68]

(4) Where the notice contains a defect that relates to its contents or intended meaning (as distinct from its formal requirements or the manner of its service) it may nevertheless be valid if either:

(a) the relevant term in the licence/notice, properly construed, is merely precatory; or
(b) the notice can be construed in a compliant manner, ie if the objective recipient would be left in no reasonable doubt that the notice contains a mistake and what it was intended to say and if the notice would, as corrected, comply.[69] For example, if the notice purports to take effect on an impossible day (eg prior to the date of service) or there is an inconsistency between the day/date but one of them complies with the requirements of the licence.

Of course a party who receives a non-compliant notice may waive the defect by agreeing to treat it as valid[70] or may be estopped from asserting it is invalid if he has led the server to believe otherwise and as a result it would be unconscionable for him now to do so.[71] However, mere silence by the recipient in the face of a defective notice is unlikely to be regarded as an implicit representation that it is valid unless the circumstances are such that he could have been expected to speak.

12.20 Where a licence is terminable on reasonable notice, what is the effect of a notice that gives no – or an unreasonably short – period of time? In *Minister of Health v Bellotti*[72] such a notice was held to be effective, albeit the licensor could not in fact recover possession until a reasonable time after service. Other authorities – eg *Dorling v Honnor Marine Ltd*[73] – have held a mere repudiation of the agreement or demand for possession to be an effective exercise of a contractual right to terminate. These at first sight are doubtful, first, in

---

[68] *Phipps & Co Ltd v Rogers* [1925] 1 KB 14.
[69] See eg *Mannai Investment Co Ltd v Eagle Star Life Assurance Co* [1997] AC 749. The most obvious instances are notices that contain obvious typographical errors or are expressed to take effect on an impossible day.
[70] See by analogy *Elsden v Pick* [1980] 1 WLR 898, at 906A–906B, 907H–908A, 909B.
[71] See by analogy *In re Swanson's Agreement* [1946] 2 All ER 628; *Fifield v W&R Jack Ltd* [2001] L&TR 4.
[72] [1944] KB 298.
[73] [1963] 2 All ER 495, at 502; *Sharneyford Supplies Ltd v Edge* [1985] 1 All ER 976, at 978. But see the doubts expressed in *Decco Wall International v Practitioners in Marketing Ltd* [1971] 2 All ER 216, at 231, 234.

appearing to conflate anticipatory/repudiatory breaches (which require acceptance in order to bring the licence to an end) and the exercise of a unilateral contractual *right* to terminate[74] and, secondly, in appearing to resurrect the rule, disapproved in *Hurst v Picture Theatres Ltd*,[75] that a wrongful purported revocation of a licence was nevertheless effective to terminate the licensee's right to use the land – see **12.42** et seq.

12.21 The *Bellotti* rule, moreover, at first blush appears difficult to reconcile with *Canadian Pacific Railway Co v The King*,[76] in which an unreasonably short notice to terminate an implied licence arising from negotiations for the grant of an interest in land was held to be invalid. That was followed in *Governing Body of Henrietta Barnett School v Hampstead Garden Suburb Institute*,[77] which held that the school licensee was also entitled to a dated notice and sought to distinguish *Bellotti* on the – unconvincing[78] – basis that those cases, unlike *Bellotti*, involved a public law element.[79] Albeit both authorities were regarded in *Parker v Parker* as instances of gratuitous licences, in that case the court considered there was no 'bright line' distinction with contractual licences[80] and held that a dated notice may be required to terminate a licence that involved no public law element.[81]

12.22 These authorities can be reconciled on the basis that the results turn on the different rights to terminate implied in the various licence agreements (see **12.18**). Thus:

(1) Where the licence contains an express term as to the length of notice, a short notice is invalid;[82] in these circumstances *Bellotti* has no application.

(2) Where there is none, the question then is what term ought to be implied. *Dorling v Honnor Marine Ltd* and similar authorities can be explained as examples of licences that were, properly construed, terminable peremptorily. In such cases, which are likely to be rare, a simple demand for possession or assertion that the licensee has no rights may be an effective election to terminate and not a mere repudiatory breach.

(3) Where a licence is terminable merely on giving reasonable notice, the notice itself need not specify when it takes effect. If – unwisely – it does, it is valid only if: (a) the date given is reasonable; (b) it makes clear that in the event the stipulated date does not give reasonable notice, the recipient

---

[74] *Tungsten Electric Co Ltd v Tool Metal Manufacturing Co Ltd (No 3)* [1954] 2 All ER 28, at 45, overruled on a different point [1955] 2 All ER 657.
[75] [1915] 1 KB 1.
[76] [1931] AC 414 (licence to maintain telegraph poles along railway tracks).
[77] (1995) 93 LGR 470, at 511–512 (licence to share occupation of school premises).
[78] Kerbel 'Unreasonable Revocation of a Licence' [1996] Conv 63, at pp 67–68.
[79] In *Governing Body of Henrietta Barnett School v Hampstead Garden Suburb Institute* (1995) 93 LGR 470 the shared occupation of school premises.
[80] [2003] EWHC 1846 (Ch), at [276].
[81] Ibid, at [279].
[82] *Wallshire v Advertising Sites* [1988] 2 EGLR 167.

is entitled to the latter; (c) the date is not an essential term of the notice, ie it is a mere indication as to what period of notice the server considers is reasonable; or (d) the notice can be read so that decision to terminate is severable from the date when it is expressed to take effect. *Bellotti* is thought to be explicable on one/other of the latter two bases. A notice that gives a referential date (eg 'upon completion of the phase 1 works') is valid (only) if the date is capable of reasonable ascertainment and in practice allows a reasonable time.[83]

(4) The converse situation is where the licence *does* require a dated notice, as a matter of implication, but the actual notice fails to give a date or gives one that is unreasonably short, as in *Canadian Pacific Railway*, *Henrietta Barnett* and *Parker v Parker*. Such a notice is invalid. Although these were, according to *Parker*, cases of gratuitous licences, the process of implication as to the manner of termination is analogous to that for contractual licences. The implication of a dated notice was warranted in *Canadian Pacific Railway* because of the public interest in the continuation of a telegraph service and/or because the parties expressly contemplated the owner would set a date for the telegraph company to leave if negotiations for a lease were unsuccessful[84] and in *Henrietta Barnett* because of the parties' expectations, derived from the public interest in the orderly operation of the school licensee and the background context, ie the statutory procedure/time frame required to be observed for its relocation/closure.[85] In *Parker v Parker*[86] the term was apparently justified because the parties contemplated when the licence of substantial premises was granted that the licensee would need to know the specific date when he was to leave in order to be able to vacate in an orderly manner. Where, however, a dated notice is required the serving party's position is invidious: he may be unaware of (all of) the circumstances relevant in determining the appropriate length of notice (see **12.23**) and even if he has a contractual right to require the other party to provide information in order to assess what is reasonable[87] that is often a difficult judgment. The safest (although commercially unattractive) course in such cases is to err on the side of caution by allowing a generous period.

What constitutes reasonable notice?

12.23 The 'reasonable notice period' is conceptually distinct from the 'grace period': the former postpones the date when the licence terminates; the latter is

---

[83] *Henry Boot & Sons (London) Ltd v Uttoxeter UDC* (1924) 88 JP 118.
[84] *Tungsten Electric Co Ltd v Tool Metal Manufacturing Co Ltd (No 3)* [1955] 2 All ER 657, at 676, 684.
[85] *Governing Body of Henrietta Barnett School v Hampstead Garden Suburb Institute* (1995) 93 LGR 470, at 512.
[86] [2003] EWHC 1846 (Ch), at [286].
[87] As suggested in *Winter Garden Theatre (London) Ltd v Millennium Productions Ltd* [1948] AC 173, at 200, but doubted in *Australian Blue Metal Ltd v Hughes* [1963] AC 74, at 101.

a period of time to which the licensee may be entitled thereafter[88] before he can be treated as a trespasser. Their purpose, as well as their effect, often differs; whereas the grace period merely entitles the licensee to remove himself and his belongings ('packing up time') the reasonable notice period may, depending on the circumstances:

- give the licensee who has incurred substantial expenditure or entered into commitments time to realise the fruits of his work or to unwind his position. For example, an agricultural licensee may be entitled to sufficient time in order to harvest his crop. And in *Winter Garden Theatre (London) Ltd v Millennium Productions Ltd*[89] a theatre licensee was entitled to a sufficient run in order to recoup his expenditure and work out his contracts. That, however, is not always the case: in *Australian Blue Metal Ltd v Hughes*[90] the licensee was not allowed sufficient time to realise a reasonable return on his investment but merely sufficient time to remove the minerals already severed from the land;

- allow the licensee time to make alternative arrangements, eg in *Canadian Pacific Railway Co v The King*[91] to relocate his telegraph system; in *Bellotti*[92] to find alternative accommodation; and in *Henrietta Barnett* to allow statutory procedures for relocating or disbanding the school to be completed.[93] Where conversely the licensee gives notice to terminate a licence under which he renders services to the licensor, the period of notice may be what is reasonable to allow the licensor to engage someone else; or

- in simpler cases (eg tickets for sporting events) the reasonable notice period may fulfil the same function as the 'grace period' by allowing the licensee sufficient time merely to quit the land.

However, the distinction between the reasonable notice period and the grace period is rarely acknowledged in practice, the licensee often being said merely to have a 'reasonable' time to leave before he becomes a trespasser.

12.24 What is reasonable is in each case sensitive to the parties' intentions and circumstances, including the purpose(s) for which the licence was granted and

---

[88] *Australian Blue Metal Ltd v Hughes* [1963] AC 74, at 101–102. See also *Winter Garden Theatre (London) Ltd v Millennium Productions Ltd* [1948] AC 173, at 199, 204–205.
[89] *Governing Body of Henrietta Barnett School v Hampstead Garden Suburb Institute* (1995) 93 LGR 470, at 511.
[90] [1963] AC 74, at 99–100.
[91] [1931] AC 414. See also the dictum in *Winter Garden Theatre (London) Ltd v Millennium Productions Ltd* [1948] AC 173, at 684 ('removing [his goods] does not merely mean removing them into the street, but removing them to some reasonable place for their accommodation'); *Australian Blue Metal Ltd v Hughes* [1963] AC 74, at 99 ('time on the one hand for the [licensee] to deploy their labour and equipment profitably elsewhere and, on the other hand, for the [licensor] to find another licensee').
[92] [1944] KB 298.
[93] [1931] AC 414, at 508, 511.

its terms (eg the period by reference to which the licence fee is payable,[94] although not always decisive[95]). The relevant circumstances are those existing when the notice is given[96] so far as they were in the parties' contemplation when the licence was entered into. Circumstances affecting the licensor are also potentially relevant.[97] Principles of proprietary estoppel – or at least the factors relevant to whether an equity has arisen, ie reliance, detriment – may also affect the length of notice in a particular case.[98] Each case turns on its facts.[99] Compare *Parker v Parker*[100] (2 years to vacate castle); *Chandler v Kerley*[101] (one year – mistress's occupation of house); *Minister of Health v Bellotti* (3 months – flats); *Winter Garden Theatre v Millennium Productions* (one month – theatre licence); *Iveagh (Earl) v Martin*[102] (one week's notice for licence to use a quay held sufficient in absence of evidence it would create difficulties for the licensee, eg in fulfilling current contracts).

Form and contents of notice

12.25 The licence may contain other (express or implied) terms as to the form or contents of the notice. Those must be interpreted to determine whether the requirements are precatory or mandatory. In summary:

(1) An express term requiring the serving party to give written notice is likely to be mandatory; if so, an oral notice will be ineffective[103] (although the recipient may waive the requirement and, if acted on, the notice may give rise to an estoppel). Such a term may be implied if (eg) the licence terms require notice to be 'served' in order to bring it to an end.[104] Periodic (non-excluded) licences of residential accommodation[105] require written notice, as may licences with statutory security of tenure.

(2) A notice may be served 'without prejudice' to the server's contention that an earlier notice is effective.[106]

(3) A notice must be clear and certain in its terms in order to bring home to the reasonable recipient the server's intention to terminate the licence. The

---

[94] *Wilson v Tavener* [1901] 1 Ch 578 (reasonable notice terminable at end of period).
[95] *Mehta v Royal Bank of Scotland* [1993] 3 EGLR 153, at 156E–156F, 158M.
[96] *Australian Blue Metal Ltd v Hughes* [1963] AC 74, at 99; *Mehta v Royal Bank of Scotland* [1993] 3 EGLR 153, at 156G–156H.
[97] *Winter Garden Theatre (London) Ltd v Millennium Productions Ltd* [1948] AC 173, at 210: 'the assessment of what is reasonable may depend on a great variety of factors ...'; *Australian Blue Metal Ltd v Hughes* [1963] AC 74, at 102: what is 'fair and reasonable between the parties'.
[98] *Parker v Parker* [2003] EWHC 1846 (Ch), at [253]–[255].
[99] *Canadian Pacific Railway Co v The King* [1931] AC 414, at 432.
[100] [2003] EWHC 1846 (Ch), at [286].
[101] [1978] 2 All ER 942, [1978] 1 WLR 693.
[102] [1960] 2 All ER 668, at 687C.
[103] *Tennero Ltd v Majorarch Ltd* [2003] All ER (D) 115 (Nov), at [32].
[104] *Andrews v Cunningham* [2007] EWCA Civ 762, at [51]. A term that 'a notice' (as distinct from 'notice') must be given may have the same effect – ibid.
[105] Protection from Eviction Act 1977, s 5.
[106] See by analogy *Royal Bank of Canada v Secretary of State for Defence* [2004] 1 P & CR 448.

question is whether it is clear to a reasonable person reading it. A notice that is expressed to be contingent or conditional (eg 'Please accept this as notice to terminate the licence in the event I am able to secure alternative facilities by the 19th') is ineffective. However, a notice that manifests an immediate election to terminate the licence whilst expressing the intention to cancel it in future should circumstances change ('I may wish to withdraw this notice if I have not secured somewhere else by the 19th') is effective[107] but the purported reservation of a right to withdraw it is not (see **12.16**).

(4) It must extend to all of the land and all of the purposes for which the land is used, unless the licence permits partial termination.

(5) (Subject to what follows) the notice must be given by (or on behalf of) the person in whom the rights of the licensor or licensee are vested at the time. Where the licensee has assigned the right to use the land, it is thought the right to terminate prima facie follows, even if the licensee retains certain rights for himself.

(6) Unless the licence expressly requires, a written notice need not be signed by the party giving it.

(7) However, the notice must be sufficiently clear that the reasonable recipient would know that it was given by/on behalf of the person entitled to give it under the licence terms (eg 'I, your licensee, hereby give notice …'). It need not, however, identify him by name unless the licence requires.

(8) A notice given by an agent with general authority need not specify the fact of his agency if the circumstances are such that the reasonable recipient would know that he could act upon it in the knowledge that the other party to the licence is bound by it.[108]

(9) In contrast an agent with special authority merely to give notice must state or otherwise clearly identify the name of the principal on whose behalf he acts.[109]

(10) However, a notice may be *delivered* (rather than *given*) by an agent; personal service by the party giving notice is unnecessary, unless the contract requires it.

---

[107] *May v Borup* [1915] 2 KB 830, at 832–833.
[108] See by analogy *Lemmerbell Ltd v Britannia LAS Direct Ltd* [1998] 3 EGLR 67, at 70; *Prudential Assurance Co Ltd v Excel UK Ltd* [2010] L&TR 7.
[109] *Allam & Co v Europa Poster Services* [1968] 1 WLR 638.

(11) In both cases the agent must have (actual or ostensible) authority when the notice is served. If he does not, the notice is invalid even if the person on whose behalf it was apparently served subsequently purports to ratify it.[110]

12.26 If the licence is granted to two or more joint licensees or by two or more joint licensors, the question arises whether all of them must give notice to the other party in order to terminate the licence. The relevant rules are as follows:

(1) A periodic licence may be terminated by notice given by any one of the joint licensors (or licensees) unless the licence terms expressly require them all to join in. The person giving notice need not have the others' authority to do so.[111]

(2) The same is thought to be true, by analogy, in relation to an indefinite licence that is terminable on reasonable notice. Although such a licence is for a single term (unlike a periodic licence, which continues for successive terms unless/until determined) no party has bound himself contractually to allow the licence to continue beyond a reasonable period of time.[112] The licence therefore continues only so long as it is the will of each of the parties that it does so.

(3) The giving of such notice will rarely amount to a breach of trust by the serving party which his co-licensors/licensees can restrain in advance.[113]

(4) However, a non-compliant notice by one of the joint licensors/licensees (eg which gives insufficient notice or is served out of time)[114] will not bind the others unless it is given with their authority. That is so even if the recipient purports to waive the defect.

(5) So too a notice that purports to exercise a break clause in a fixed-term licence will only be effective if consented to by all of the joint licensors (or licensees, as the case may be), unless the licence terms allows any one of them to terminate.[115]

(6) Where all of the co-licensors/licensees must give notice, a notice that appears to be given by only one of them may be valid if it is clear from the context in which it was given that it was also being served on behalf of the others.[116]

---

[110] See by analogy *Thompson v McCullough* [1947] 1 KB 447; *Divall v Harrison* [1992] 2 EGLR 64.
[111] See by analogy *Hammersmith LBC v Monk* [1992] 1 AC 478 (joint tenants); *Parsons v Parsons* [1983] 1 WLR 1390 (joint landlords); *Harrow LBC v Qazi* [2004] 1 AC 983, at [113]; [2003] 4 All ER 461; *Fletcher v Brent LBC* [2006] EWCA Civ 960, at [34].
[112] *Hammersmith LBC v Monk* [1992] 1 AC 478, at 483–484.
[113] *Crawley BC v Ure* [1996] QB 13.
[114] *Hounslow LBC v Pilling* (1993) 25 HLR 305 (lease).
[115] *Hammersmith LBC v Monk* [1992] 1 AC 478.
[116] *Hackney LBC v Hackney African Organisation* (1997) 77 P & CR D18.

(7) A notice given by one co-licensor/licensee that is ineffective applying the above rules cannot subsequently be made effective by being ratified by the others.[117]

Service on recipient

12.27 At common law, a notice may be served by causing it to be received by – or to come to the attention of – the recipient(s). Specifically:

(1) A notice may be delivered by ordinary, registered or recorded delivery post, fax or e-mail. Nevertheless at common law a notice was not served if it was sent to – but not in fact received by – the recipient. The Interpretation Act 1978, s 7 now provides a rebuttable statutory presumption of delivery in the ordinary course of post. It remains open to the recipient to prove that the notice, although sent, was not in fact delivered to him. If, however, it was delivered, but for whatever reason did not come to his attention, then service is effective. The risk of delivery lies with the serving party but thereafter the recipient bears the risk that it does not come to his knowledge.

(2) A notice is also good if it is left in the recipient's presence, provided it is identified as such by the server.[118]

(3) The notice need not be served directly on the party; it may be served on someone who has his (actual or ostensible) authority to accept it. If he lacks authority or his authority does not extend to receiving notice, then service is ineffective.[119]

(4) If he does have authority, then the notice is valid even if he did not in fact forward/communicate it to his principal.[120]

(5) Where there are joint licensors/licensees, notice must be served *on* all of them unless the contract provides otherwise or the actual recipient has authority to accept service on behalf of the other(s).[121]

The licence terms may of course restrict or expand the available methods of service, eg by incorporating the Law of Property Act 1925, s 196 or permitting service to be effected at the party's last known address. Where specified methods of service are set out in the licence agreement it is a question of construction whether they are mandatory (so that a failure to use them renders the notice ineffective, even if the recipient in fact receives it) or merely provide additional means by which service may be validly effected.

---

[117] *Right v Cuthell* (1804) East 491, at 500.
[118] See eg *New Hart Builders Ltd v Brindley* [1975] 1 Ch 342.
[119] Query if in such case the principal can subsequently ratify.
[120] *Tanham v Nicholson* (1871) LR 5 HL 561.
[121] See by analogy *Blewett v Blewett* [1936] 2 All ER 188 (service of s 146 notice).

Termination for breach

12.28 The relevant rules as to termination for breach of the licence terms are those applicable to contracts, not leases.[122] The term broken must be either a condition or an intermediate term, of which the breach was sufficiently serious, or the licence must contain an express right to terminate in those circumstances.[123] Automatic termination for breach will rarely be implied.[124] Accordingly the innocent party may generally elect whether to terminate or affirm; if the latter, the licence continues.[125] In at least two cases, however, a breach may have the effect of unilaterally terminating the licence: first, where it can be considered an effective election to terminate by the wrongdoer (see **12.22(2)**); second, where it consists of the unlawful/unfair dismissal from employment of a service occupier (see **12.13**).

12.29 It is generally thought that a licensee may not apply for relief from forfeiture where the licensor terminates for breach.[126] None of the statutory powers to grant relief apply.[127] Nor is there an inherent equitable jurisdiction to grant relief in relation to contractual licences generally.[128] However, the jurisdiction may extend to contracts that create possessory rights,[129] including (e g) equipment leases[130] where the primary object of the bargain is to achieve a specific, attainable result or the right to terminate is security for the payment of money.[131] Accordingly it is arguable, but probably only in exceptional cases where the licence confers a right to possession (see **2.36**), that the equitable jurisdiction applies.[132]

12.30 Where the licence is ancillary to some proprietary interest, the licensee may, in his capacity as owner of that interest, be able to apply for relief from

---

[122] See e g *Verrall v Great Yarmouth BC* [1980] 1 All ER 839. The concept of forfeiture and relief from forfeiture in relation to licences was described as 'novel' in *Donington Park Leisure Ltd v Wheatcroft & Sons Ltd* [2006] All ER (D) 94, at [51].
[123] See e g *Cyma Petroleum Ltd v CAS Business Services* [2000] All ER (D) 1214, at [175]–[178].
[124] *Trustees of Grantham Christian Fellowship v Scouts Association* [2005] EWHC 209 (Ch), at [33].
[125] See e g *Dudley Port Warehousing Co Ltd v Gardner Transport & Distribution Ltd* [1995] EGCS 5.
[126] Gray and Gray *Elements of Land Law* (Oxford University Press, 5th edn, 2009), at paras 4.1.69, 10.3.11. The position may be different in Australia – see e g *Devefi Pty Ltd v Mateffy Pearl Nagy Pty Ltd* [1993] FCA 152, at [36], point (3)(B)(ii).
[127] Law of Property Act 1925, s 146; Supreme Court Act 1981, s 38; and County Courts Act 1984, s 138.
[128] *Sports International Bussum BV v Inter-Footwear Ltd* [1984] 1 WLR 776, at 794 ('The recognised boundaries [of the equitable doctrine] do not include mere contractual licences'); see also the obiter comments in the CA: [1984] 1 All ER 376, at 385.
[129] *Sports International Bussum BV v Inter-Footwear Ltd* [1984] 1 WLR 776, at 786; *The Scaptrade* [1983] 2 AC 694, at 704.
[130] *On Demand Information plc v Michael Gerson (Finance) plc* [2001] 1 WLR 155, at 171.
[131] *Shiloh Spinners Ltd v Harding* [1973] AC 691, at 723, [1973] 1 All ER 90, at 101.
[132] The issue was recently left open in *Berrisford v Mexfield Housing Co-Operative Ltd* [2010] EWCA Civ 811, at [12].

forfeiture if it is terminated for breach. If relief is granted, the licence to which it is ancillary will automatically revive.[133]

Repudiation

12.31 One party to the licence may commit an anticipatory or repudiatory breach if he either renounces the contract or disables himself from performing it before performance is due. A repudiation requires a clear (express or implied) refusal to perform. It is a question of fact whether the acts/words in question amount to such a refusal. A party may disable himself by action (eg by the licensor selling the land to someone who is not bound by the licence) or inaction (eg by failing to provide facilities essential for the exercise of the licensee's rights). The innocent party may either accept the anticipatory breach and treat the licence at an end or affirm. In the latter case, he may subsequently terminate if the wrongdoer persists in refusing to perform his obligations when due.

Agreement, abandonment

12.32 The contractual doctrine of rescission by agreement/abandonment, rather than the leasehold doctrine of surrender, applies to contractual licences.[134] The parties may of course expressly agree to bring the licence to an end early, in which case the mutual discharge of their future rights/obligations under it provides the required consideration. That, however, will not discharge any accrued rights/obligations (eg licence fee arrears) unless the agreement also amounts to a release. An abandonment may be implied where one party so conducts himself by (in)action as to entitle the other to assume – and the other does assume – that they have agreed to abandon the licence sub silentio.[135] That may be inferred from a long period of delay or inactivity on both sides. Whilst the relevant conduct by one party must have come to the knowledge of the other, his acts in reliance need not be known by the first. For example, if the licensee disappears owing licence fee arrears, an abandonment may be inferred if the licensor resumes possession, thereby treating the licence as at an end, whether or not the licensee is aware of that fact. Abandonment may also be implied from a radical change in user from that permitted by the licence to which the licensor acquiesces.[136] But abandonment can only be inferred from unequivocal acts; eg mere non-use of the land by the licensee (in the absence of a positive obligation) of itself will rarely be enough.

Frustration

12.33 A licence is frustrated where:[137]

---

[133] See eg *Starside Properties Ltd v Mustapha* [1974] 1 WLR 816; *Underground (Civil Engineering) Ltd v Croydon LBC* [1990] EGCS 48.
[134] *Bone v Bone* [1992] EGCS 81.
[135] *The Hannah Blumenthal* [1983] AC 854, at 924D–924G.
[136] *Healey v Hawkins* [1968] 1 WLR 1967, at 1974–1975 (bare licence).
[137] *National Carriers v Panalpina (Northern) Ltd* [1981] AC 675, at 700F–700G.

'... there supervenes an event (without default of either party and for which the contract makes no sufficient provision [eg by allocating the risk of its occurrence]) which so significantly changes the nature (not merely the expense or onerousness) of the outstanding contractual rights and/or obligations from what the parties could reasonably have contemplated at the time of its execution that it would be unjust to hold them to the literal sense of its stipulations in the new circumstances; in such case the law declares both parties to be discharged from further performance.'

The doctrine applies to contractual licences to use/occupy land. For example:

- A licence to hold concerts on certain days in a music hall is frustrated if the hall is destroyed by fire without fault by either party and for which neither assumed responsibility under the contract.[138]

- A licence to use rooms for a certain day to watch a particular event that is subsequently cancelled or postponed.[139] Whilst on one view the benefits conferred by the licence are still enjoyable (the use of the room on the day), the substance and purpose of the licence (to watch the event) is not.

- The death or incapacity of one of the parties to a contract by which one provides personal services to the other will frustrate any ancillary licence to use the land for those purposes.

- The involuntary unavailability of one party may also frustrate the licence if under it acts/services were to be performed within a certain period, of which time is of the essence. If the unavailability is only temporary or no specific time for performance is stipulated or time is not made of the essence, the question is one of degree.

- A requisition of the land may frustrate the licence, again, depending on the length of the (likely) interruption relative to the length of the licence term.

- If the sole act(s) permitted by the licence are rendered illegal after the contract is created but before the period of enjoyment commences or is complete (although in the latter case the question is also one of degree).[140]

12.34 Such licences are automatically discharged on the occurrence of the frustrating event without the need for election by either party.[141] The financial consequences of frustration are determined by the Law Reform (Frustrated Contracts) Act 1943, s 1(2)–(3).

---

[138] *Taylor v Caldwell* (1863) 3 B&S 826.
[139] *Krell v Henry* [1903] 2 KB 740 (the *Coronation* case).
[140] *National Carriers v Panalpina (Northern) Ltd* [1981] AC 675, at 702–703.
[141] Ibid, at 712G; *Hirji Mulji v Cheong Yue SS Co Ltd* [1926] AC 497, at 505.

Disclaimer

12.35 The liquidator of a company licensee/licensor in the course of winding up has the power to disclaim a contractual licence if it is an unprofitable contract under the Insolvency Act 1986, s 178(3)(a) and thus onerous property within s 178(2). A similar power is given to a trustee appointed to administer the estate of a bankrupt individual who was party to a licence.[142] A licence that contains unperformed obligations by that party amounts to onerous property for these purposes.[143]

12.36 The effect of disclaimer is to determine the party's future rights and liabilities under the licence but will not (except so far as is necessary to release it/him) affect the liability of any other person,[144] eg a guarantor[145] or the original licensee whose assignee is insolvent/bankrupt.[146] They remain liable under the licence, eg for past and future licence fees. In the case of an insolvent individual, the disclaimer also releases the trustee from personal liability from the commencement of his trusteeship.[147]

12.37 The liquidator or trustee can also disclaim an interest to which the licence is ancillary if it is not (or not readily) saleable or may give rise to a liability to pay money or perform any other onerous act[148] and, by doing so, disclaim the licence itself. However, it is thought the licence cannot be disclaimed independently of the interest.[149]

Miscellaneous non-contractual limitations on termination

12.38 A party's right to terminate is subject to the application of general contractual principles, such as waiver or election between remedies. Its exercise may be suspended entirely (or for a period of time) by virtue of a supervening equity.[150] For example, a licensor who induces the licensee to believe the licence will not be terminated at all/in accordance with the licence terms and thereby to act or refrain from acting in a way he otherwise would (not) have done may be estopped from subsequently doing so.[151]

---

[142] Insolvency Act 1986, s 315(1).
[143] *Eyre v Hall* [1986] 2 EGLR 95.
[144] Insolvency Act 1986, s 178(4) (company), s 315(3) (individual). See *Capital Prime Properties Ltd v Worthgate Ltd* [2000] BCC 525 in relation to the application of this section to already-vested rights and benefits.
[145] *Hindcastle Ltd v Barbara Attenborough Associates Ltd* [1996] 1 All ER 737 (guarantor of lessee).
[146] *Warnford Investments Ltd v Duckworth* [1978] 2 All ER 517 (company tenant by assignment).
[147] Insolvency Act 1986, s 315(3)(b).
[148] Ibid, ss 178(3), 315(2)(b).
[149] Compare *Environment Agency v Hillridge Ltd* [2003] EWHC 3023 (Ch), at [43] (site licence could not be disclaimed whilst retaining the benefit of the trust deed which was an integral part of the terms on which the waste management licence was held; disclaimer was of both).
[150] *Plimmer v Wellington Corp* (1883-84) 9 App Cas 699, at 714.
[151] *Ramsden v Dyson* (1866) LR 1 HL 129. See for a more recent case that failed on the facts *Yarmouth Harbour Commissioners v Harold Hayles Ltd* [2004] EWHC 3375 (Ch).

12.39 The licensor's termination of the licence may be unlawful because it violates the licensee's right to protection from discrimination[152] or because the licensor is a public body whose decision is challengeable on judicial review grounds[153] or on the basis it interferes with the licensee's Art 1 (peaceful enjoyment of possessions), Art 8 (respect for home) or Art 14 (discrimination) rights under the European Convention on Human Rights and Fundamental Freedoms 1950. Statutory fetters may also restrict the licensor's right to bring proceedings, eg if the licensee is a company in liquidation or administration[154] or subject to a moratorium[155] or an individual who is bankrupt or the subject of a voluntary arrangement.[156] A consideration of these topics is beyond the scope of this book.

Wrongful purported termination

12.40 A licensor who purports unlawfully to terminate the licence and prevents the licensee exercising his rights may be liable in damages.[157] Such damages are assessed according to general contractual principles[158] and may include aggravated damages (if the manner of his treatment is such as to warrant them) and/or exemplary damages (if the licensor's conduct is also a tort and was calculated to secure a benefit greater than the normal level of compensatory damages). Residential licensees who are wrongfully evicted may also claim statutory damages under the Housing Act 1988, ss 27–28.[159]

12.41 The issue whether the licensee may continue to use the land notwithstanding the unlawful purported termination of the licence and/or claim damages for the manner of his removal from the land (as distinct from the loss of its use) requires greater consideration. The question then is whether the licensor's wrongful act is nevertheless effective to terminate the licensee's right to use the land.

Specifically performable licences

12.42 Early cases lent support to the proposition that the licence could be terminated independently of the contract. In *Wood v Leadbitter*[160] a claim for

---

[152] See eg Sex Discrimination Act 1975, s 20; Race Relations Act 1976, s 29; Disability Discrimination Act 1995, ss 19, 22, 23; Equality Act 2006, s 46.
[153] See eg *Wandsworth LBC v A* [1999] All ER (D) 1498; *R v Wear Valley DC ex parte Birks* [1985] 2 All ER 699.
[154] See generally Insolvency Act 1986, Sch B1.
[155] Under Insolvency Act 1986, Pt I.
[156] Ibid, ss 252, 285.
[157] See eg *Mehta v Royal Bank of Scotland* [1993] 3 EGLR 153. A licensor may be liable in damages for failing to give adequate notice to revoke even a bare licence if the licensee suffers personal injury or property damage or nuisance to other premises. See eg *Aldin v Latimer Clark Muirhead & Co* [1894] 2 Ch 437 (obstruction of ventilators without notice, injuriously affecting licensee's neighbouring premises); *Vaughan v Vaughan* [1953] 1 QB 762.
[158] See eg *C&P Haulage v Middleton* [1983] 1 WLR 1461, [1983] 3 All ER 94.
[159] Eg *Mehta v Royal Bank of Scotland* [1993] 3 EGLR 153.
[160] (1845) 13 M&W 838. *Hurst v Picture Theatres Ltd* [1915] 1 KB 1 explained *Wood v Leadbitter* on the grounds that the claim was not in contract but for assault, on the basis the licence

assault arising from the licensee's early forcible eviction failed, the reasoning being that the licence's attributes were in part a matter of law and not merely the parties' intentions. The licence was regarded as inherently revocable at the licensor's will, even if such revocation was a breach of contract; he had the power, if not the right, to terminate at any time.[161] It followed the licensee was a trespasser thereafter. Accordingly it was thought that the licensor may be liable in damages for the wrongful revocation of the licence and the loss of use of the land, but not for the way in which he removed the licensee so long as only reasonable force was used.

12.43 The correctness of this rule was always doubtful.[162] In any event it has not survived the fusion of law and equity, at least in relation to specifically performable licences. It is now settled that such licences cannot be terminated independently of the contract: their terms govern how the licensees' rights may be brought to an end.[163] The right to use the land is not distinct from the contract but is merely one of its terms. The licensor impliedly promises not to revoke the licence[164] or not to prevent the use of the land unless/until the contract has been validly terminated.[165] Those promises may be enforced by injunction or specific performance, to which it is no defence that the licence is of short duration, although it may be a relevant factor in the exercise of the court's discretion.[166]

12.44 Accordingly the licensee whose contract is specifically enforceable has the right to continue to use the land notwithstanding the licensor's wrongful purported termination; it is not necessary that the licensee actually *has* obtained equitable relief against the licensor; it is enough that he *could* have done so (even, it is thought, if it would have been refused as a matter of discretion[167]). In such cases then the licensee is not a trespasser. If he confines himself to a claim in damages, he may claim both for the loss of use of the land and the manner of his removal, even if the licensor uses no more force than is reasonable.

---

conferred permission to be on the land, to which proof that it had been withdrawn – rightly or not – was a defence. See, however, the doubts as to this explanation in *Winter Garden Theatre (London) Ltd v Millennium Productions Ltd* [1948] AC 173, at 193–194.

[161] *Hounslow LBC v Twickenham Garden Developments Ltd* [1971] Ch 233, at 249C.

[162] See the criticism of *Thompson v Park* [1944] KB 408 in *Hounslow LBC v Twickenham Garden Developments Ltd* [1971] Ch 233, at 249.

[163] *Winter Garden Theatre (London) Ltd v Millennium Productions Ltd* [1946] 1 All ER 678, at 680 (CA); *Hounslow LBC v Twickenham Garden Developments Ltd* [1971] Ch 233, at 254D–254E.

[164] *Hurst v Picture Theatres Ltd* [1915] 1 KB 1.

[165] *Winter Garden Theatre (London) Ltd v Millennium Productions Ltd* [1948] AC 173, at 189 ('The licence in such a case is granted under general conditions, one of which is that a well-behaved licensee shall not be treated as a trespasser until the event which he has paid to see is over and until he has had reasonable time thereafter to depart').

[166] *Verrall v Great Yarmouth BC* [1981] QB 202 (2-day licence for annual conference).

[167] Eg balance of hardship. Query the position if the licensor has an equitable defence.

Licences that are not specifically performable

12.45 If equity will not assist the licensee, it is less certain whether he can continue rightfully to use the land notwithstanding the unlawful purported termination or claim damages for the manner of his eviction (in addition to the loss of the use of the land). In *Thompson v Park*[168] a licensee to whom equitable remedies were unavailable was held to be a trespasser notwithstanding the licensor's revocation may have been unlawful.[169] Since then, however, the *Winter Gardens* case[170] and *Verrall v Great Yarmouth BC*[171] disapproved of this limited resurrection of *Wood v Leadbitter*, albeit in circumstances where the issue did not directly arise.[172] Further, in *Hounslow LBC v Twickenham Garden Developments Ltd*[173] an application for an injunction by a licensor who was assumed to have unlawfully revoked the licence was refused; although the licence was held to be specifically performable, it was made clear that the decision was not based on that fact. Accordingly, whilst academic opinion on point is not unanimous,[174] the weight and trend of authority appears to favour the view that a licensor who has wrongly purported to revoke may not treat the licensee as a trespasser, even if the licence is not specifically enforceable.

12.46 In the converse situation – where the wrongdoing licensor seeks equitable relief to restrain his licensee from using the land rather than relying on self-help – an injunction is likely to be refused even if the licence is not specifically performable, as the *Hounslow* case illustrates.

LICENCES COUPLED WITH AN INTEREST

12.47 Licences that are coupled with an interest are incapable of termination independently of the interest to which they attach (unless the licence permits that) but end automatically on the determination – by whatever means – of that interest. The rules as to termination therefore depend on the type of interest to which the licence is ancillary and the terms on which it is held. For example, a mining licence that grants a right to mine a certain quantity of materials or for

---

[168] [1944] KB 408 (see, however, the criticisms of this decision in *Hounslow LBC v Twickenham Garden Developments Ltd* [1971] Ch 233, at 249).
[169] [1944] KB 408, at 409 ('the court cannot specifically enforce an agreement for two people to live peacefully under the same roof') and 410 ('That licence has been withdrawn. Whether it as been rightly withdrawn or wrongly withdrawn matters nothing for this purpose'). Relief could also have been refused on the basis of lack of clean hands.
[170] *Winter Garden Theatre (London) Ltd v Millennium Productions Ltd* [1948] AC 173.
[171] [1981] QB 202.
[172] In *Winter Garden Theatre (London) Ltd v Millennium Productions Ltd* [1948] AC 173, the licence was held to be impliedly terminable; in *Verrall*, specific performance of the licence was granted.
[173] *Hounslow LBC v Twickenham Garden Developments Ltd* [1971] Ch 233, at 240–250.
[174] Compare *Megarry & Wade: The Law of Real Property* (Sweet & Maxwell, 7th edn, 2008), at para 34-010; *Clerk & Lindsell on Torts* (Sweet & Maxwell, 19th edn, 2006), at para 19-49; contrast *Hill & Redman's Law of Landlord and Tenant* (LexisNexis Butterworths, looseleaf), at paras A[384]–A[387].

a certain period of time is irrevocable until the interest has been determined, that is, until the permitted quantity has been mined or the stipulated period of time has elapsed.[175]

ESTOPPEL LICENCES

The inchoate equity

12.48 The concept of 'termination' is apt to mislead when used in relation to the inchoate equity, although similar considerations apply. For example, if the expectation was of a right to use the land until a certain date/occurrence, the representee has no expectation of being entitled to use the land thereafter. The equity therefore does not survive beyond then. Similarly where his expectation is dependent on certain circumstances continuing to exist (eg the parties being in partnership[176]) he will not expect to be able to use the land if they do not. Also, where the expectation is contingent (eg a right to use the land so long as he pays outgoings) those conditions, whilst not strictly 'terms' entitling the representor to terminate, must be complied for the representee to be able to assert that in the circumstances existing he expected to be able to continue to use the land. However, the assignment of the representor's interest in circumstances where his successor takes free of the equity (eg because it is not substantively registered or protected by actual occupation) does not have the effect of terminating the equity but merely restricts the representee to a personal claim against the representor.

12.49 Other factors, whilst not strictly terminating events, may warrant the court refusing relief in the exercise of its discretion, eg because the representee has already had sufficient satisfaction for his equity[177] or lacks clean hands.[178] Misbehaviour on his part, if sufficiently serious, may also warrant refusing relief[179] or affect the form of relief granted.

The relief

12.50 The equity does not survive the court order that gives effect to it.[180] The form of relief and its terms therefore determine whether and if so how it may be terminated. Subsequent misconduct by the representee will rarely,[181] if

---

[175] *Australian Blue Metal Ltd v Hughes* [1963] AC 74, at 94.
[176] Eg *Uglow v Uglow* [2004] EWCA Civ 987 (continuation of partnership).
[177] See eg *Watts & Ready v Storey* (1983) 134 NLJ 631.
[178] Eg *Willis v Willis* [1986] 1 EGLR 62; *Gonthier v Orange Contract Scaffolding Ltd* [2003] EWCA Civ 873; *Williams v Staite* [1979] Ch 291, at 299D.
[179] *Brynowen Estates Ltd v Bourne* (1981) 131 NLJ 1212; *Hardwick v Johnson* [1978] 1 WLR 683, at 689.
[180] But see *Jones v Jones* [1977] 1 WLR 438, at 442, as to which sed quaere.
[181] *Williams v Staite* [1979] Ch 291, at 298B ('Their conduct would have to be bad in the extreme before they could be turned out of their home').

THE GRACE PERIOD

When the period applies

12.51 The grace period is generally ascribed to a rule of law rather than an implied term of the licence.[183] It potentially applies at least to both gratuitous and contractual licences.[184] It supervenes after the licence has come to an end and provides a measure of protection to a licensee who might otherwise suffer undue hardship as a result by preventing the licensor from treating him as a trespasser until he has had a reasonable time to quit the land – such as the police officers in *Robson v Hallett*[185] who were assaulted before being given chance to leave after being asked to do so.

12.52 In what circumstances it applies, however, is not wholly free from doubt:

- A licensee present on the land when his licence is peremptorily terminated (eg for breach or, in the case of bare licences, on the licensor's death) will be entitled to a grace period.[186]

- The position regarding licences terminable on reasonable notice is less clear. The court in *Australian Blue Metal Ltd v Hughes*[187] inclined to the view that the reasonable notice period included sufficient time for the licensee to quit the land. The *Winter Garden* case also contains some indication that the reasonable notice period and the grace period are alternatives.[188] However, in that case the grace period was added to the period of reasonable notice.[189] So too in *Cornish v Stubbs*[190] it appears the licensee was allowed a grace period after notice to terminate his tenancy of other land had expired. Nevertheless the logic of *Australian Blue Metal Ltd v Hughes* is considered sounder; what is a reasonable notice period in any particular case takes into account the circumstances in so far as they affect the licensee when notice is served and whilst factors

---

[182] *Williams v Staite* [1979] Ch 291, at 297H–298B (terminable), 300B (not terminable).
[183] *Winter Garden Theatre (London) Ltd v Millennium Productions Ltd* [1948] AC 173, at 204.
[184] Ibid.
[185] [1967] 2 QB 939, [1967] 2 All ER 407.
[186] *Australian Blue Metal Ltd v Hughes* [1963] AC 74, at 101–102 ('the period of grace is imposed for the protection of a party who might otherwise suffer undue hardship from sudden termination').
[187] Ibid, at 102.
[188] *Winter Garden Theatre (London) Ltd v Millennium Productions Ltd* [1948] AC 173, at 199.
[189] *Winter Garden Theatre (London) Ltd v Millennium Productions Ltd* [1948] AC 173, at 199, 205 – see *Australian Blue Metal Ltd v Hughes* [1963] AC 74, at 102.
[190] (1870) LR 5 CP 334, at 337.

affecting the licensor may restrict the length of the period, at a bare minimum it should be what is sufficient to allow the licensee to remove himself and his possessions.

- So too if the licence sets out expressly the required period of notice to terminate, the parties may be taken to have implicitly agreed that it is sufficient to enable the licensee to vacate. Nevertheless he may be entitled to a grace period if he can show the agreed period was in fact inadequate for those purposes, if at least that could have been foreseen when the licence was entered into.

- Where the licensee serves notice to terminate, the justification for granting him a grace period is not obvious since generally he may choose when to give it and therefore ought to be in a position to have vacated completely by the time it expires. That may not be so, however, if the licence is not terminable generally on notice but only at certain times or on the occurrence of certain events.

- Similarly, the imposition of a grace period in relation to fixed-term licences is also difficult to justify because the licensee knows from the outset when he must quit the land and can plan accordingly.

The present state of authorities, however, precludes any concluded view about the availability of the grace period in cases other than peremptory termination. It is thought that prima facie (at least) it is unavailable, although the court may be guided in each instance by the reasonable needs of the licensee at the time of termination insofar as they were contemplated by the parties when the licence was granted.

The length and purpose of the period

12.53 The purpose of the grace period is to give the licensee a reasonable time after the licence expires in order to quit the land in an orderly fashion, ie 'packing up' time.[191] It is not 'to prolong the user sanctioned by the licence merely for the benefit and convenience of the licensee'.[192] Where the licensee is a casual visitor it is merely the time he needs to leave with reasonable expedition by the most appropriate route.[193] Where he is in occupation, it is the time needed to remove himself and his possessions from the land, not to secure

---

[191] *Winter Garden Theatre (London) Ltd v Millennium Productions Ltd* [1948] AC 173, at 204: 'Its purpose is to enable the former licensee to adjust himself to the new situation by vacating the premises'; *Cornish v Stubbs* (1870) LR 5 CP 334, at 339: 'The only question is whether the tenant has a right to a reasonable time after the revocation of his licence to take away his goods; and I am clear that he has'; *Australian Blue Metal Ltd v Hughes* [1963] AC 74, at 102: 'so that the [licensee] could remove his equipment and the fruits of his labours without becoming a trespasser'; *Parker v Parker* [2003] EWHC 1846 (Ch), at [286]: a 'period of grace within which to remove himself and his belongings from the [premises]'.
[192] *Winter Garden Theatre (London) Ltd v Millennium Productions Ltd* [1948] AC 173, at 205. Compare the purpose of the reasonable notice period – **12.23**.
[193] *Robson v Hallett* [1967] 2 QB 939, at 954, [1967] 2 All ER 407, at 413.

alternative accommodation. Where the licensee has allowed others to use the land, it may include the time reasonably required to secure their removal. The grace period will not come to an end if the licensee subjectively decides not to leave, although it may once he manifests that intention, eg by making no effort to do so.[194]

12.54 It is uncertain whether the period is to be judged only by factors affecting the licensee or whether the licensor's interests are also taken into account.[195] Where the licensee is unaware of the terminating event (eg in the case of a bare licence, the licensor's death) it is thought the period will be calculated from the time he becomes aware of it or at least takes into account the time reasonably taken for him to do so. Although, as stated, the grace period has been ascribed to a rule of law there seems no reason in principle why the parties may not expressly agree either that the licensee is/is not entitled to a grace period or how long it will be.[196]

---

[194] *R (Fullard) v Woking Magistrates Court* [2005] EWHC 2922 (Admin), at [28].
[195] *Winter Garden Theatre (London) Ltd v Millennium Productions Ltd* [1948] AC 173, at 204 ('the assessment of what is reasonable may depend on a great variety of factors and cause considerable difficulty in particular instances'). Compare **12.24** in relation to the reasonable notice period.
[196] Ibid ('The period of grace can, of course, be the subject of agreement').

Chapter 13

POST TERMINATION

The licensee's obligations on termination	13.4
Obligation to quit	13.4
Removal of chattels	13.6
Things incorporated into the land	13.10
Enforcing the licensee's obligations	13.15
Self-help	13.15
Injunction	13.18
Possession	13.19
Damages for continued use of land after expiry of licence	13.23

13.1 This chapter concerns the parties' rights and obligations after the licence (and any grace period) has come to an end. Licences with statutory security of tenure are subject to the provisions in the relevant statutory scheme and are mentioned separately.[1]

13.2 The termination of the licence brings to an end the parties' primary rights and obligations under it and may alter the common-law/statutory duties one party owes to the other.[2] If the former licensee continues to use/occupy the land it also marks the beginning of his liability for damages in trespass as well as the start of the running of the relevant prescription/limitation period (if any) in his favour, unless the parties enter into some new arrangement.

13.3 Of course if the licensor expressly/impliedly consents to the licensee's continued presence, a new licence (or possibly lease) arises between them. If he accepts payment or other consideration in return, a contractual licence may arise by implication/conduct. The question is: what is the appropriate inference as to the parties' intentions[3] from their dealings and the circumstances; in particular, with what intention was payment (if any) received?[4] For instance:

---

[1] See Chapter 6.
[2] Eg under the Occupiers' Liability Act 1957 regarding the state and condition of the land. See Chapter 11.
[3] Whether determined subjectively or objectively is uncertain – compare *Longrigg, Borough & Trounson v Smith* [1979] 2 EGLR 42, at 43 (subjective); *Land v Sykes* (1992) 1 EGLR 1, at 4 (objective).
[4] See by analogy *Clarke v Grant* [1950] 1 KB 104, at 106; *Longrigg, Borough & Trounson v Smith* [1979] 2 EGLR 42 (leases).

- No new licence arises if payment is accepted under protest or as mesne profits/damages for the former licensee's continued unlawful use of the land[5] or if the licensor was about to issue possession/injunction proceedings at that time, unless it represents a decision to sanction that use.[6]

- So too if payment is made under some colourable assertion by the licensee of an existing right to continue to use the land the court will be slow to attribute to the parties an intention to create a new licence that neither in fact had.[7]

- On the other hand, if the licence fee continues to be tendered/accepted without qualification and the licensee continues to make use of the land, the appropriate inference – in the absence of some alternative explanation – will often be that a new licence (prima facie on the same terms as the old) was impliedly agreed.

- However, in such case it may remain open to the licensor to prove that he demanded or accepted payment by mistake[8] or inadvertently.[9]

- If payment is merely made towards shared expenses arising from the parties' continued use of the land (eg a flat-sharing arrangement), that is not in return for the right to use the land but consistent with the licensee remaining at the licensor's will or sufferance.

- If payment is accepted whilst the parties are in negotiations for a new licence which terminate without agreement, the licensee's payment in respect of his use of the land during that time may occasionally give rise to a new implied contractual licence (which is periodic or terminable on reasonable notice) or possibly periodic tenancy but more often to a mere licence – or, if he is in possession, tenancy – at will.[10]

The following applies where no such new arrangement has arisen between the parties.

---

[5] See by analogy *Westminster CC v Basson* (1990) 62 P & CR 57; *Vaughan-Armatrading v Sarsah* (1995) 27 HLR 631.
[6] *Land v Sykes* [1992] 1 EGLR 1, at 4–5.
[7] See by analogy *Marcroft Wagons Ltd v Smith* [1951] 2 KB 496.
[8] See by analogy *Clarke v Grant* [1950] 1 KB 104, at 106.
[9] See by analogy *Legal & General Assurance Society Ltd v General Metal Agencies Ltd* (1969) 20 P & CR 953, at 963–964.
[10] Compare *Bretherton v Paton* [1986] 1 EGLR 172; *Cardiothoracic Institute v Shrewdcrest Ltd* 1986] 1 WLR 368.

THE LICENSEE'S OBLIGATIONS ON TERMINATION

Obligation to quit

13.4 A licensee who continues to use/occupy or re-enters the land after his licence (and any relevant grace period) has expired is, of course, a trespasser.[11] A contractual licensee will also be in breach of his express or implied obligation to quit the land or deliver up possession at the end of the licence term.[12] As set out at **8.25** et seq, he is obliged to do so even if his licensor has no legal title or right to the land.

Sub-licences and Bruton tenants

13.5 That obligation also requires the licensee to ensure that his sub-licensees also cease to use the land and any *Bruton* tenants deliver up possession by the time the licence/grace period expires. It is not enough for him merely to terminate their rights without also securing their removal.[13] As against the licensor the termination of the licence automatically brings to an end derivative rights/interests, such as sub-licences[14] and *Bruton* tenancies.[15] Thus if by then the licensee has failed to secure their removal they are, as against the licensor, trespassers.

Removal of chattels

13.6 Unless they have become part of the land or fixtures (see below) or the licence terms provide otherwise, the licensee's obligation to quit/deliver up possession requires him to remove his possessions from the land on the expiration of the licence.[16]

13.7 The licensee has a correlative right to do so. The grace period (see **12.51** et seq) if applicable may extend that right for a reasonable time beyond the termination of the licence, if needed – eg if the licence is terminated peremptorily (eg for breach) or possibly by notice that gives insufficient time to remove them before it expires.[17] If he fails to remove his chattels within time it was formerly thought the licensor was not required to give him a further chance to do so,[18] although (subject to what is said below) unless the licensee has abandoned them the licensor will be liable in conversion if he deals with or uses

---

[11] *Wood v Leadbitter* (1845) 13 M&W 838; *Thompson v Park* [1944] KB 408.
[12] See by analogy *Henderson v Squire* (1869) LR 4 QB 170 (leases).
[13] *Henderson v Squire* (1869) LR 4 QB 170; *Clevedon Trust Ltd v Davis* [1990] Ch 940.
[14] *Shepherd's Bush Housing Association v HATS Co-Operative* (1992) 24 HLR 176.
[15] *Bruton v London & Quadrant Housing Trust* [2000] 1 AC 406. See *Kay v Lambeth LBC* [2006] 2 AC 465.
[16] See eg *Penarth Dock Engineering Co Ltd v Pounds* [1963] 1 Lloyd's Rep 359; *Strand Electric v Brisford* [1952] 2 QB 246; *Swordheath Properties Ltd v Tabet* [1979] 1 All ER 240.
[17] See eg *Cal Brown Ltd v Van Wagner UK Ltd* [2005] EWHC 1901 (Ch), at [42] (obiter). Compare a tenant's right in certain circumstances to remove his fixtures after the end of his tenancy (*Woodfall's Landlord & Tenant* (Sweet & Maxwell, looseleaf), at paras 13.157–13.158).
[18] See eg *Clerk & Lindsell on Torts* (Sweet & Maxwell, 19th edn, 2006), at para 17-13.

them,[19] such as by removing them to a distant site[20] or authorising someone else to take them.[21] And a mere refusal to make them available for collection after demand is thought now to amount to a conversion.[22] The licensor, however, is not liable to deliver them to the licensee or to allow him to re-enter to remove them once the licence (and any grace period) has passed. In the interim the licensor will usually owe the licensee the duties of an involuntary bailee in relation to the goods.[23]

13.8 Subject to future statutory intervention[24] in the case of storage licences (eg parking rights) a licensee who overstays his welcome may have his goods lawfully detained by the licensor, provided sufficient warning is given that they may be taken and released upon payment, the fee is reasonable, the goods are released without delay upon tender and there are means by which the licensee might communicate his offer of payment to the licensor.[25] The circumstances must be such that the licensee consented to (or is to be taken to have consented to) or willingly assumed the risk of the chattels being seized, ie was aware of the consequences of the trespass, such as by evidence that he saw and understood the significance of the licensor's warning. The presence of warnings of a type the licensee should have read in places where they should have been seen raises a rebuttable presumption of knowledge.[26]

13.9 It is doubtful whether a licensor whose licensee refuses to remove his chattels after the licence expires or give directions for their delivery or who cannot be found despite reasonable efforts has a statutory power to sell them, remitting the balance of the sale proceeds (after costs) to the licensee.[27] That power may not extend to an involuntary bailee.[28] If the goods are causing damage to the land or anything on it[29] a licensor who is entitled to possession may, under the remedy of distress damage feasant, seize and impound the goods until the licensee claims them and tenders appropriate compensation for the damage. That does not apply to livestock, for which the Animals Act 1971, s 7(1) provides a procedure for their detention and, in some cases, sale.

---

[19] *Hanson (W) (Harrow) Ltd v Rapid Civil Engineering Ltd* (1987) 38 BLR 106.
[20] *Cal Brown Ltd v Van Wagner UK Ltd* [2005] EWHC 1901 (Ch), at [43].
[21] *Smith v Bridgend CC* [2002] 1 AC 336, at [69]–[70].
[22] *Clerk & Lindsell on Torts*, n 18 above, at para 17-22; *Thorgood v Robinson* (1845) 6 QB 769, at 772. See eg *Howard E Perry & Co Ltd v British Railways Board* [1980] 1 WLR 1375.
[23] As to which see 45(2) *Halsbury's Laws* (4th edn reissue), at para 606.
[24] On 17 August 2010 the Government announced its intention to introduce into Parliament a Freedom Bill that will (inter alia) make clamping of vehicles on private land in England and Wales without specific legal authority subject to civil or criminal sanction. At the time of writing no draft legislation is available.
[25] *Arthur v Anker* [1997] QB 564, [1996] 3 All ER 783.
[26] *Vine v Waltham Forest LBC* [2000] 4 All ER 169.
[27] Torts (Interference with Goods) Act 1977, ss 12, 13 and Sch 1.
[28] *Clerk & Lindsell on Torts*, n 18 above, at para 17-17, text at n 83.
[29] This may include an inability to use part of the land as a result of the presence of the trespassing chattels: *Arthur v Anker* [1997] QB 564, [1996] 3 All ER 783.

Things incorporated into the land

Obligation to remove/reinstate

13.10 Licences, even bare licences, are irrevocable in the sense that the licensee cannot be compelled to undo (or pay compensation for) what he has lawfully done pursuant to it, once it is brought to an end,[30] unless he expressly or impliedly agreed to do so. The concept of the 'executed licence', although bearing certain similarities to estoppel, is distinct: it requires actual (express or implied) consent, not a mere belief/expectation; the defence arises from the fact the relevant acts were authorised, not reliance and detriment; and whereas estoppels may be prospective and suspensory in effect the executed licence is permanent but only in respect of things done during its continuance – after the licence comes to an end, the licensee may not continue to enjoy the rights and the licensor may remove or undo what the licensee has done; he merely cannot require the licensee to do so.

13.11 Under the principle *quicquid plantatur solo, solo cedit* a licensee who is permitted to alter the land (eg dumping spoil, adjusting levels, blocking windows etc), erect something on it (eg a building), incorporate something in it (eg pipes, cables) or attach fixtures to it cannot be required to remove them or restore the land to its former condition at the end of the licence term, unless he undertook to do so.[31] Such an undertaking will only occasionally be implied: eg a licence permitting the laying of a pipe and its use for an (in)definite period is unlikely to give rise to such any implication; a licence merely to 'keep' a pipe in the land for a period may do so.

Right to remove

13.12 Conversely the licensee has no right to remove his fixtures or things that have become part of the land or to claim compensation for improvements at the end of the licence term unless its terms expressly allow him to do so.[32] In this respect a licensee's position is worse than a tenant's.[33]

Land, fixtures and chattels

13.13 The rules in **13.10-13.12** concern things that have become part of the land or fixtures, as distinct from mere chattels (to which those at **13.6–13.9** apply). The licence terms cannot affect the character of the licensee's chattels

---

[30] *Armstrong v Sheppard & Short Ltd* [1959] 2 QB 384, at 399. See more generally *Liggins v Inge* (1831) 7 Bing 682, at 691; *Feltham v Cartwright* (1839) 5 Bing NC 579, at 572–573; *Wood v Manley* (1839) 11 Ad & E 34, at 37–38.

[31] Eg *Never-Stop Railway (Wembley) Ltd v British Empire Exhibition (1924) Inc* [1926] Ch 877.

[32] Ibid, at 886; *C&P Haulage v Middleton* [1983] 1 WLR 1461, at 1468, [1983] 3 All ER 94, at 98–99.

[33] Although the right to remove chattels is not limited to tenants it is confined to persons with successive or derivative interests. See the lists in *Woodfall's Landlord & Tenant*, n 17 above, at para 13.132 and *Megarry & Wade: The Law of Real Property* (Sweet & Maxwell, 7th edn, 2008), at paras 23-010–23-020.

but merely whether he is entitled to remove them as against the licensor.[34] The traditional tripartite classification (land, fixtures, chattels) applies in this context, albeit there is no concept equivalent to tenant's fixtures; only chattels are removable, unless the licence provides otherwise. Accordingly the distinction between fixtures and something that is part of the land is generally unimportant in this context.

13.14 Whether a chattel has become a fixture/part of the land depends on both the degree and purpose of its annexation to the land,[35] although modern law now attaches greater significance to the latter than the former.[36] An article is prima facie a fixture if it has some substantial connection with the land or buildings on it. An article resting on the land by its own weight will usually remain a chattel unless installed in order to improve the land permanently.[37] In considering the degree of annexation, the question is whether the thing can be removed without substantial damage to the land and the chattel and without destroying its essential identity and utility.[38] A building (eg) will be regarded as part of the land unless constructed in such a way as to be removable as a whole or in sections (as distinct from removable only by destroying its character as a building, eg by reducing it to its constituent parts).[39] As regards the purpose of annexation, the licensee's intention, as the annexor, is material only insofar as it can be objectively ascertained from the circumstances.[40] If the chattel is attached to the land merely for a temporary purpose and its better enjoyment as such (eg tapestries, ornaments, paintings) rather than permanently to improve the land, it remains a chattel.[41] For example, a houseboat connected to services and attached to the land by ropes and anchors.[42]

ENFORCING THE LICENSEE'S OBLIGATIONS

Self-help

13.15 A licensor with factual possession or the right to possession (or occupation which confers control[43]) of the land may exercise self-help once the licence (and any grace period) has expired, eg by physically ejecting the former licensee who remains on the land,[44] using no more force than is reasonable in the circumstances.[45] The right to self-help, however, ceases if/when the former

---

[34] *Melluish v BMI (No 3) Ltd* [1996] AC 454; [1997] 2 All ER 513, [1997] 1 WLR 687.
[35] *Elitestone v Morris* [1997] 2 All ER 513, [1997] 1 WLR 687, at 692A–693D, 696D–698G.
[36] *Berkley v Poulett* [1977] 1 EGLR 86, at 89A–89B.
[37] *Holland v Hodgson* (1872) LR 7 CP 328, at 335.
[38] See the dictum in *Hellawell v Eastwood* (1851) 6 Ex 295, at 312.
[39] *Elitestone v Morris* [1997] 1 WLR 687, at 692H, 696H; *Wessex Reserve Forces & Cadets Association v White* [2006] 1 P & CR 405.
[40] *Re De Falbe* [1901] 1 Ch 523, at 535.
[41] *Hellawell v Eastwood* (1851) 6 Ex 295, at 312.
[42] *Chelsea Yacht & Boat Co Ltd v Pope* [2000] 1 WLR 1941.
[43] *Manchester Airport plc v Dutton* [2000] 1 QB 133. See by analogy *Thomas v DPP* (2009) The Times, November 25.
[44] *Wood v Leadbitter* (1845) 13 M&W 838.
[45] *Revill v Newbury* [1996] QB 567.

licensee's presence on the land itself matures into factual possession.[46] Nor can it be exercised if a court has refused to grant injunctive relief/possession to prevent the licensee's continuing trespass.[47] Where the former licensee's use is discontinuous, the licensor need not exercise self-help but can simply prevent him from re-entering the land.

13.16 The right to self-help is generally discouraged.[48] First, a licensor who uses excessive force against the licensee's person commits an assault or battery,[49] although that does not of itself render the fact (as distinct from the manner) of taking possession unlawful. Second, the right is excluded or modified by statute as follows:

(1) The re-entry must be peaceable: a licensor who, without lawful authority, uses or threatens violence against the licensee or property for the purpose of securing entry onto certain types of property[50] commits an offence if the licensee is, to the licensor's knowledge, present at the time and opposes the entry.[51] That the licensor may be entitled to possession as against the licensee does not amount to 'lawful authority' for these purposes.[52] It is, however, a defence to show that the licensor is (or is acting on behalf of) a 'displaced residential occupier'.[53] A breach gives rise to criminal liability only, not civil remedies.[54]

(2) The Protection from Eviction Act 1977 substantially modifies a licensor's right physically to exclude certain categories of residential licensees. The Act imposes criminal sanctions but does not give the licensee a civil remedy in damages for breach of statutory duty,[55] although where the Act renders the taking of possession unlawful[56] (not merely a criminal offence) the licensee may sue for the fact – as well as, where appropriate, the manner – of his removal. The restrictions are as follows:

  (a) Section 3 of the Act applies (inter alia) to premises occupied 'as a dwelling'[57] under a licence (other than an 'excluded licence' as

---

[46] *Powell v McFarlane* (1977) 38 P & CR 452, at 476.
[47] *Burton v Winters* [1993] 1 WLR 1077.
[48] *McPhail v Persons Unknown* [1973] Ch 447, at 456E; *Secretary of State v Meier* [2010] 1 All ER 855, at [27].
[49] *Hemmings v Stoke Poges Golf Club* [1920] 1 KB 720 (forcible eviction of service occupier following termination of employment); the result in this case would now be different as a result of Protection from Eviction Act 1977.
[50] See the definition of 'premises' (s 12(1)(a)) and 'building' (s 12(2)) in Criminal Law Act 1977.
[51] Criminal Law Act 1977, s 6.
[52] Ibid, s 6(2).
[53] Ibid, s 6(1A), eg where the licensee lived with the licensor as his lodger. The exception for 'protected intending occupiers' in s 12A is inapplicable as the licensee's occupation was, by definition, originally consensual – compare s 12A(2)(c), (4)(c), (6)(c).
[54] *Jones v Foley* [1891] 1 QB 730; *Hemmings v Stoke Poges Golf Club* [1920] 1 KB 720.
[55] *McCall v Abelesz* [1976] QB 585; [1976] 1 All ER 727.
[56] See eg Protection from Eviction Act 1977, ss 2 and 3 – see points (2)(a) and (b) below.
[57] This may include mixed residential/commercial premises: *Pirabakaran v Patel* [2006] 4 All ER 506.

defined in s 3A[58]) and makes it unlawful for the licensor to recover possession otherwise than by court proceedings where the licence has come to an end but the 'occupier'[59] continues to reside in them.[60] Section 3(2A) extends the prohibition to licences that are restricted contracts entered into after the commencement of the Housing Act 1980, s 69. Section 8(2) also extends it to any type of premises of which the licensee had exclusive possession under the terms of his employment. The requirement that the premises be occupied 'as a dwelling' excludes hotel guests[61] and holidaymakers, who are in any event excluded under s 3A together with bare licensees. Caravans stationed on protected sites are separately protected.[62] A possession order, once obtained, must be enforced by a writ/warrant of possession; the licensor may not personally execute it.[63]

(b) The prohibition in s 2 against exercising a right of a re-entry otherwise than by court proceedings whilst any person is lawfully residing in premises that are *let* as a dwelling is extended to where a service occupier has exclusive possession of the premises under the terms of his employment,[64] but not other licensees.

(c) A licensor who unlawfully deprives, or attempts to deprive, a 'residential occupier'[65] (who may be a licensee) of his occupation of premises or any part of them commits an offence unless he believed, and had reasonable cause to believe, that the occupier had ceased to reside there.[66] A bare licensee, including one whose payments are not in return for the right to occupy (eg a contribution towards outgoings), is not a 'residential occupier' for these purposes.[67]

---

[58] Broadly, if (a) under its terms the licensee shares occupation with the licensor (or a member of his family) and immediately before the licence was granted and at the time it comes to an end the licensor (or the family member) occupied as his only or principal home premises of which the whole or part of the shared accommodation formed part (in the case of sharing arrangements with family members the licensor must also occupy as his only or principal home premises in the same building, which is not a block of flats); (b) the licence was granted as a temporary expedient to someone who was a trespasser; (c) the licence is granted for holiday accommodation only; (d) it was gratuitous; (e) the licensee is one of the persons specified in Protection from Eviction Act 1977,s 3A(7A)–(7C); or (f) the accommodation is a hostel within s 3A(8). See eg *Desnousse v Newham LBC* [2006] QB 831, [2007] 2 All ER 218.

[59] As defined in Protection from Eviction Act 1977, s 3(2), ie 'any person lawfully residing in the premises or part of them at the termination of the [licence]'.

[60] Protection from Eviction Act 1977, s 3(1), (2B).

[61] *Brillouet v Landless* (1995) 28 HLR 836.

[62] Caravan Sites Act 1968, s 5(5). See **6.62–6.63**.

[63] *Haniff v Robinson* [1993] QB 419.

[64] Protection from Eviction Act 1977, s 8(2).

[65] Ie a 'person occupying the premises as a residence, whether under a contract or by virtue of any enactment or rule of law giving him the right to remain in occupation or restricting the right of any other person to recover possession of the premises': Protection from Eviction Act 1977, s 1(1).

[66] Protection from Eviction Act 1977, s 1(2).

[67] *West Wiltshire DC v Snelgrove* (1998) 30 HLR 57, at 60, 62. An obligation to insure and maintain the property may be consideration for these purposes: *Polarpark Enterprises Inc v Allason* [2007] 2 EGLR 85, [2008] 1 P & CR 64, at [31].

(d) A licensor (or his agent) who, with the intent of causing a residential occupier to give up occupation of the whole or part of the premises or to refrain from exercising any right or pursuing any remedy in respect of them, does acts likely to interfere with the peace or comfort of the occupier or members of his household, or persistently withdraws or withholds services reasonably required for the occupation of the premises as a residence, commits an offence.[68] 'Acts' for these purposes do not include pure omissions,[69] although a failure to act may amount to a withholding/withdrawal of services. The conduct in question need not be independently unlawful.[70] A single act that has a continuing effect (eg disconnecting the electricity supply) can amount to a 'persistent' withdrawal of services for these purposes.[71]

(e) A licensor who, but for the residential occupier's right to remain or the above restrictions on his right to recover possession, would be entitled to occupy the premises[72] also commits an offence if he does acts likely to interfere with the peace or comfort of the residential occupier or members of his household or persistently withdraws or withholds services reasonably required for the occupation of the premises as a residence and (in either case) knows or has reasonable cause to believe that the conduct is likely to cause the residential occupier to give up occupation of the whole/part of the premises or to refrain from exercising any right or pursuing any remedy in respect of the whole or part of the premises (whether or not he intends that result),[73] unless he proves he had reasonable grounds for doing the acts or withdrawing or withholding the services in question.[74] Unlike in (d), therefore, no specific intent is required here.

(3) The limitations on the right physically to recover possession from a licensee entitled to station and occupy (or merely occupy) as his residence a caravan on a 'protected site' under the Caravan Sites Act 1968 are set out at **6.62–6.63**.

Also, the licensor may, in the process of exercising self-help, commit an offence under various criminal statutes not specifically related to the recovery of possession, eg the Protection from Harassment Act 1997. In practical terms, the totality of these restrictions means that self-help may only be safely exercised in relation to licences other than for residential occupation, when the licensor's right to possession is clear and the licensee (and his sub-licensees, if any) are not physically present on the land at the time.

---

[68] Protection from Eviction Act 1977, s 1(3).
[69] *R v Ahmad* (1986) 18 HLR 416, (1986) 52 P & CR 346.
[70] *R v Burke* [1991] 1 AC 135.
[71] *Hooper v Eaglestone* (1977) 34 P & CR 311 (decided under Caravan Sites Act 1968, s 3(1)(c)).
[72] See the expanded definition of 'landlord' in Protection from Eviction Act 1977, s 1(3C).
[73] Protection from Eviction Act 1977, s 1(3A).
[74] Ibid, s 1(3B).

13.17 Conversely the manner in which the licensee continues to use/occupy the land after the expiry of the licence/grace period may itself give rise to various criminal offences,[75] but these are not specific to licences and are beyond the scope of this book.

Injunction

13.18 It is inappropriate for a licensor to seek an order for possession against a former licensee if: (a) the licensor does not have the right to possession or occupation and control[76] of the land; (b) the former licensee is merely using the land in some limited (eg intermittent) manner which does not amount to factual possession or occupation and control; (c) the licensor himself remains in factual possession notwithstanding the former licensee's continued presence and thus has no need to 'recover' it;[77] or (d) third parties (eg other licensees[78]) are lawfully occupying the land concurrently with the former licensee – although possession orders act in personam rather than in rem,[79] in practice the bailiff will, when executing a writ of possession, remove all those present on the land, whether or not they were parties to the action.[80] In all such cases the licensor's appropriate remedy is rather an injunction to restrain the former licensee's continued trespass.

Possession

Remedy

13.19 In contrast a licensor who has the right to (or was in fact in) possession or occupation and control of the land before being ousted by his former licensee may seek an order for possession against him if there are no other persons concurrently in lawful occupation of the land. The licensor may within those proceedings also apply for an injunction to restrain him from using the land until trial and/or from returning to the land after a possession order is executed.[81] An interlocutory injunction may be granted if the criteria in *American Cyanamid v Ethicon*[82] are met, although in reality that will only be so

---

[75] See eg Criminal Justice and Public Order Act 1994, ss 61, 68.
[76] *Manchester Airport plc v Dutton* [2000] 1 QB 133.
[77] *Secretary of State v Meier* [2010] 1 All ER 855, at [9], [11].
[78] Unless they occupy discrete areas, in which case the licensor may of course seek possession only of that part occupied by the former licensee. The question is one of degree – possession may be sought against the former licensee if the others' use is intermittent or insubstantial: ibid, at [7].
[79] Ibid, at [6].
[80] *R v Wandsworth County Court ex parte Wandsworth LBC* [1975] 1 WLR 1314. Any person present who has a better right to possession may apply for leave to defend and, if successful, will be put into possession in preference to the licensor. But the original order for possession continues to bind the former licensee: *In re Wykeham Terrace* [1971] Ch 204, at 209–210, [1970] 3 WLR 649. Contrast the judgments in *Secretary of State v Meier* [2010] 1 All ER 855, at [36] and [68] as to whether a limited possession order may be made in relation to land that is lawfully occupied by third parties in common with the former licensee.
[81] *Secretary of State v Meier* [2010] 1 All ER 855.
[82] [1975] AC 396.

if the former licensee has no arguable defence to the claim or the balance of convenience clearly favours the licensor and either the action is not disposed of (for whatever reason) at the first hearing or the case is one of urgency.[83] An interim possession order may not be made in the licensor's favour against his former licensee.[84]

Procedure

13.20 Possession actions against former licensees must normally be issued in the county court for the area where the land is situated.[85] Although the High Court has concurrent jurisdiction the licensor should only issue there if there are exceptional circumstances,[86] which he must certify.[87]

13.21 The action is to be started using claim form N.5.[88] CPR Part 55 applies.[89] The licensor may rely on the summary procedure for possession.[90] The particulars of claim must be filed and served with the claim form[91] and set out the prescribed information.[92] Any financial claim (eg licence fee arrears, mesne profits) should be included.[93] Service may be effected by one of the usual methods,[94] at least 2 days (5 days for residential property) before the first hearing.[95] The former licensee need not acknowledge service[96] or file a defence in advance,[97] although not to do so risks an adverse order in relation to the costs of that hearing. At the hearing, the court will either decide the claim (if able to) or, if it is genuinely disputed on grounds that appear to be substantial, give case management directions.[98] The licensor may apply for summary judgment under CPR Part 24.[99]

---

[83] *Patel v WH Smith (Eziot) Ltd* [1987] 2 All ER 569, at 573.
[84] Civil Procedure Rules 1998 (CPR), SI 1998/3132, r 55.21(2).
[85] CPR, r 55.3(1). See for the jurisdiction County Courts Act 1984, ss 15, 21(1).
[86] CPR PD 55, para 2.1. Eg where there are complicated disputes of fact, points of law of general importance or a claim against trespassers involving a substantial risk of public disturbance or serious harm to persons or property that requires immediate determination. The value of the property and the amount of the financial claim are relevant factors but of themselves rarely justify a High Court action.
[87] CPR, r 55.3(2).
[88] CPR PD 55, para 2.6.
[89] CPR, r 55.2(1)(a)(iii), (b). The definition in CPR, r 55.1(b) includes a former licensee whose licence has expired and who remains in occupation.
[90] See eg *Whitbread West Pennines Ltd v Reedy* (1988) 20 HLR 642 (former service occupier).
[91] CPR, r 55.4.
[92] CPR PD 55, para 2.1 and CPR Part 16 set out the required information. If the licence was in writing, a copy should be included – CPR PD 16, para 7.3(1).
[93] CPR, r 16.3(2).
[94] See CPR, r 6.3.
[95] CPR, r 55.5(2).
[96] CPR, r 55.7(1).
[97] CPR, r 55.7(2).
[98] CPR, r 55.8.
[99] See for an example *Cal Brown Ltd v Van Wagner UK Ltd* [2005] EWHC 1901 (Ch).

13.22 The possession order must not take effect more than 14 days (6 weeks in cases of exceptional hardship) after the date it is made.[100] This limitation applies in both the High Court and county courts but the appellate court also has inherent jurisdiction to stay the order until any appeal is determined.[101] Execution of a possession order in relation to a dwelling occupied by a former agricultural employee under his terms of employment as licensee may also be stayed or suspended on terms.[102] The order is enforced by a writ of possession[103] (High Court) or warrant of possession (county court).[104] If the former licensee returns after it is executed, the licensor may apply for a writ (or warrant) of restitution[105] and/or seek to commit for contempt if an injunction was granted in support of the possession order.

DAMAGES FOR CONTINUED USE OF LAND AFTER EXPIRY OF LICENCE

13.23 A licensee who continues to use or occupy the land notwithstanding the termination of his licence is liable in damages to his licensor if either: (a) the licensor owns the land/has a right to (or was in fact in) possession or occupation and control; or (b) the licensee's continued presence renders the licensor liable in damages to a third party, such as a superior owner (eg for failing to deliver up possession at the end of his term) or another contractual licensee who is prevented from using the land as a result of the former licensee's continued presence.[106] In the latter case the licensor may be entitled to an indemnity if such liability was foreseeable; in the former case (dealt with below) he may claim damages.

13.24 A licensor who claims damages may seek either recovery of the loss he has suffered or restitution of the benefit which the former licensee has received as a result of his unlawful continued use/occupation of the land. The licensor may elect between them at any time up to judgment.[107]

13.25 The conventional measure of damages entitles the licensor to be put in the position he would have been had the trespass not occurred or (in cases of contractual licences) had the licensee complied with his obligation to quit the land at the end of the contract term. Conventional compensatory damages may include out-of-pocket expenses (eg the cost of removing any sub-licensees

---

[100] Housing Act 1980, s 89.
[101] *Admiral Taverns (Cygnet) Ltd v Daniel* [2009] 4 All ER 71, [2009] 1 EGLR 35.
[102] Protection from Eviction Act 1977, s 4(2A), (3)–(5), (7)–(10).
[103] Rules of the Supreme Court 1965 (RSC), SI 1965/1776, Ord 54, r 3(1)(a). RSC Ord 113, r 7 applies, rather than RSC Ord 45, r 3(2), as the former licensee is a 'trespasser' within CPR, r 55.1(b).
[104] County Court Rules 1981 (CCR), SI 1981/1687, Ord 26, r 17(1).
[105] *Wiltshire CC v Frazer (No 2)* [1986] 1 WLR 109.
[106] See by analogy *Bramley v Chesterton* (1857) 2 CBNS 592.
[107] *Ministry of Defence v Ashman* [1993] 66 P & CR 195, at 200–201.

whom the licensee failed to remove[108]) and loss of profits (eg by virtue of the licensor's inability to exploit the land commercially during the period of the trespass), provided they satisfy the normal rules as to remoteness, causation, mitigation etc.

13.26 The licensor may instead claim damages assessed by reference to the former licensee's 'gain'. Although in theory that may in an appropriate case require him to disgorge all the profits arising from his unlawful use,[109] that is only likely to be so where they are directly attributable to the land rather than the manner in which he used it or the licensee stands in a fiduciary relationship to the licensor. More likely the former licensee's 'gain' is the sum he would have had to pay to secure the right to continue to use/occupy the land after the licence expired.[110] This alternative measure of damages is claimable even though the licensor has suffered no loss, assessed on the traditional compensatory basis, because he would not have used or allowed others to use the land during the relevant period.[111] It is, however, claimable in addition to any damages which the licensor is required to pay to a third party by virtue of the trespass.

13.27 Such damages have been assessed using two approaches: first, what hypothetical parties at arm's length in the parties' positions and with their knowledge of the material facts would have agreed at the outset for the continued use of the land;[112] second, merely a reasonable fee for the use of the land, without reference to hypothetical negotiations.[113] These approaches yield the same results in this context. In both, the measure of damages is the proper value to the former licensee of his continued use of the land.[114]

13.28 Prima facie that is to be measured by the open market value of the land (where the licensee is in sole occupation/possession) or 'price' for the right (where he merely uses it). If the former licensee's presence prevented the licensor using other land as well, damages may be calculated on the basis of the market value of the whole.[115] The former licence fee may be good evidence of the market rate, unless there is positive evidence to the contrary.[116] In other cases evidence of the former licensee's profits from the use of the land may be a useful reference point when assessing a fair price for the notional licence, unless

---

[108] *Henderson v Squire* (1869) LR 4 QB 170.
[109] *A-G v Blake* [2001] 1 AC 268; see also *Forsyth-Grant v Allen* [2008] 2 EGLR 18.
[110] See eg *Penarth Dock Engineering Co Ltd v Pounds* [1963] 1 Lloyd's Rep 359.
[111] *Swordheath Properties Ltd v Tabet* [1979] 1 All ER 240, at 242.
[112] See eg *Phillips v Homfray* (1871) LR 6 Ch App 770, at 780–781 (wayleave to carry coal unlawfully mined). For detailed consideration as to the calculation of damages in trespass relating to the removal of minerals or other things from the land see *McGregor on Damages* (Sweet & Maxwell, 18th edn, 2009), at paras 33-028–33-039, 34-045.
[113] See eg *Bracewell v Appleby* [1975] Ch 408 (damages in lieu of injunction to restrain continued use of right of way).
[114] *Penarth Dock Engineering Co Ltd v Pounds* [1963] 1 Lloyd's Rep 359, at 362; *Field Common Ltd v Elmbridge BC* [2008] EWHC 2079 (Ch), at [59], [77]–[79].
[115] *Henderson v Squire* (1869) LR 4 QB 170.
[116] It is thought the licensor need not in every case adduce positive evidence of the market value of the land: see eg *Dean and Chapter of Canterbury Cathedral v Whitbread plc* [1995] 1 EGLR 82.

they are negligible/artificially low or impossible to assess.[117] However, as such damages seek to value the benefit of the use of the land to the former licensee, it is open to him to show that the value to him was less than the market value and thus what he would have paid.[118] For example, if the former licence fee was a concessionary rate, he may show that he would not have stayed on at the true market rate.[119] In such case the value of the land to him will usually be the higher of that rate and what he would have paid for alternative premises.[120]

---

[117] *Severn Trent Water Ltd v Barnes* [2004] 2 EGLR 95, at 100A.
[118] *Field Common Ltd v Elmbridge BC* [2008] EWHC 2079 (Ch).
[119] See e g *Ministry of Defence v Ashman* (1993) 66 P & CR 195, (1993) 25 HLR 513. See, however, the doubts expressed in *Inverugie Investments v Hackett* [1995] 1 WLR 713. But see also *Forsyth-Grant v Allen* [2008] 2 EGLR 18; *Field Common Ltd v Elmbridge BC* [2008] EWHC 2079 (Ch).
[120] *Ministry of Defence v Thompson* [1993] 2 EGLR 107.

Appendix 1

SAMPLE LICENCES

Informal gratuitous licence	A1.1
Contractual licence to share house	A1.2
Licence to use structure on licensor's land	A1.3
Contractual licence to use serviced office accommodation	A1.4
Licence of part of commercial premises including provision of services by licensee	A1.5
Novation agreement regarding shared occupation by licensees	A1.6

A1.1

INFORMAL GRATUITOUS LICENCE

To:

Of:

I, [*name*] of [*address*] hereby permit you to use my land at [ ] for the following purposes, namely [ ] on the following terms and conditions:

1. You may only use the land for those purposes.
2. You may only use the land between [ ] and [ ] on [each Saturday].
3. This licence is personal to you. You may not pass its benefits to anyone else or permit anyone else to enjoy its benefits.
4. Your use the land at your own risk. I am not to be responsible for any loss or damage or for death or personal injury or for damage or destruction of property, howsoever and to whomsoever caused.
5. You shall comply with such directions as I may give as to the use of the land.
6. This licence is not exclusive.
7. It shall continue until terminated in accordance with clause 8 below.
8. Either of us may bring this licence to an end at any time [immediately/by giving [ ] days' notice, which we agree is a reasonable period of time in the circumstances].

To confirm your agreement to these terms, please sign and date a copy of this letter and return it to me at the above address.

Signed:

Dated:

I agree to the above terms:

Signed:

Dated:

A1.2

CONTRACTUAL LICENCE TO SHARE HOUSE

THIS AGREEMENT is made the [ ] day of [ ] 20

BETWEEN:

(1) [*name*] of [*address*] ('the Owner'); and
(2) [*name*] of [*address*] ('the Licensee').

Definitions

In this Agreement:

1.1 'the Common Parts' means the parts of the House (other than the bedrooms) and the entrance ways to the House.

1.2 'the Deposit' means £[ ] paid as security for the due observance and performance by the Licensee of the terms of this Agreement.

1.3 'the Furniture and Furnishings' means the Owner's furniture and furnishings in the House set out in the attached inventory which the Owner may from time to time replace.

1.4 'the House' means the Owner's property at [*address*] in which the Room is situated.

1.5 'the Licence Fee' means £[ ] per [ ] [payable by equal instalments in advance on the [ ] day of each [ ]].

1.6 'the Licence Term' means the period [of [ ] *or* from [ ] until [ ] *or* until the Licence is determined in accordance with clauses 6.1 and 6.2 below [whichever occurs first].

1.7 'the Rights' means:

    1.7.1 the right to occupy the Room as a residence for the Licence Term;

    1.7.2 for the aforesaid purposes, the right (in common with the other residents of the House) to use the kitchen for the storage preparation and cooking of food and the [ ] as a common room and (in common with the other residents, the Owner, and his employees, agents and contractors) the remainder of the Common Parts as a means of access;

    1.7.3 the right to use the Furniture and Furnishings; and

    1.7.4 the right to park a single private motor vehicle in the parking area at the front of the House in common with all others with a like right.

1.8   'the Room' means bedroom number [   ].

Grant

2.   The Owner grants the Licensee the Rights.

Payment

3.1   The Licensee shall pay to the Owner:

    3.1.1   the Deposit on entering into this Agreement;

    3.1.2   the Licence Fee; and

    3.1.3   on demand a proportionate part of the [council tax,] water, sewage, electricity and gas charges payable in respect of the House according to the number of occupants in the House during the relevant period.

Use of House

3.2   The Licensee must not use the Room other than as his private residence.

3.3   The Licensee shall not make any copy of keys referred to in clause 4.1 below.

3.4   The Licensee must not permit anyone else to use the Room as his or her residence but this shall not prevent him allowing someone to temporarily stay with him.

3.5   The Licensee may not permit, for reward, anyone else to exercise the Rights.

3.6   The Licensee must not use the House or cause, suffer or permit his licensees and invitees to use the House in such way as to cause nuisance, annoyance, damage, disturbance, inconvenience or interference to the Owner, his employees, agents and contractors, the other residents of the House and their invitees and licensees [and to the owners occupiers or users of any adjoining or neighbouring land].

3.7   The Licensee must not interfere with or obstruct the other residents' occupation and use of the House.

3.8   The Licensee must not keep any pet in the House.

State and Condition

3.9   The Licensee must keep the interior of the Room, the Common Parts of the House and the Furniture and Furnishings in a clean and tidy condition and must not remove any of the Furniture and Furnishings.

3.10   The Licensee shall make good all deterioration or damage to the House and decorations and Furniture and Furnishings wilfully negligently or accidentally caused by himself and his invitees and licensees.

3.11   The Licensee shall at his own cost replace with articles of a similar kind and value any Furniture and Furnishings broken or damaged beyond repair as reasonably requested by the Owner.

3.12   The Licensee shall occupy the House in a licensee-like manner.

Access

3.13 The Licensee shall permit the Owner access to the Room as often as may be required for the purpose of [cleaning the Room, observing its state and condition and exercising the rights referred to in clause 4.4 below].

3.14 The Licensee must not in any way impede the Owner or his agents in the exercise of his right of possession and control of the House and every part of it.

Vehicles

3.15 The Licensee shall ensure that any motor vehicle used when exercising the Rights is in a roadworthy condition and insured with an insurance office of repute and displays a valid vehicle excise licence and (if appropriate) has a valid MOT certificate.

Other Persons

3.16 The Licensee must indemnify the Owner and keep the Owner indemnified against all claims, demands, actions, proceedings, losses, damages, costs and expenses or other liabilities arising in any way from the exercise or purported exercise of the Rights or his or his invitees' and visitors' use of or presence on the Land and/or the breach of any of the terms of this Licence.

Deliver Up

3.17 Upon the determination of this Licence howsoever caused the Licensee must vacate the House, leaving the Room clean and tidy and return the keys to the Owner immediately.

Owner's Obligations

4.1 The Owner will provide the Licensee keys for the Room and the front and rear doors of the House on signing this Agreement. If the Licensee loses his keys, the Owner will provide a replacement set at the Licensee's cost.

4.2 The Owner will discharge the [council tax,] water, sewage, electricity and gas charges payable in respect of the House.

4.3 The Owner will supply a written statement to the Licensee of the sums paid in respect of such costs and the Licensee's share under clause 3.1.3 above.

4.4 The Owner will:

    4.4.1 repair and keep in repair the structure and exterior of the House and will keep in good decorative order and condition the interior of the House, fair wear and tear excepted; and

    4.4.2 keep in repair and proper working order the installations in the House for the supply of water, gas and electricity and for sanitation and for space heating and heating water,

4.5 provided that the Owner [has notice of the relevant condition and] shall not be responsible for repairs, defects or conditions attributable to any breach of these Licence terms by the Licensee or to rebuild or reinstate the House as a result of fire, tempest, flood or other inevitable accident.

4.5 The Owner will ensure that the Furniture and Furnishings comply and will comply during the Licence Period with the Furniture and Furnishings (Fire) (Safety) Regulations 1988[1] (as amended) and any substitute regulations in force for the time being.

4.6 The Owner will insure the House with an insurance office of repute against [ ] hazards.

4.7 The Owner may not prevent the Licensee from exercising the Rights but shall not be liable for the acts or omissions of any other resident in the House and his invitees or licensees.

4.8 The Owner shall repay the Deposit within a reasonable period of time after the determination of this Agreement, subject to deduction of a reasonable amount to compensate the Owner for any damage, liability or loss caused by any breach of the terms of this Agreement.

Other

5.1 It is hereby agreed that the Owner retains full right of possession of the House during the Licence Term, subject to the Rights.

5.2 This Licence is personal to the Licensee only. It does not entitle the Licensee to exclusive possession or control of the Room or the exclusive possession control or use of any other part of the House nor amount to a lease or tenancy nor to an agreement to grant a lease or tenancy.

5.3 Nothing in this Licence is intended to confer any benefit on any person who is not a party to it.

5.4 The Owner may at any time and from time to time require the Licensee to transfer his occupation to another bedroom within the House on giving not less than [ ] advanced notice, in which case this Agreement shall continue with that room being substituted for the current definition of the Room.

5.5 The Rights may not be assigned.

Termination

6.1 This Agreement [will determine automatically at the end of the Licence Term *or* may be determined at any time by either party upon not less than four (4) weeks' written notice to the other].

6.2 The Owner may terminate this Agreement on not less than twenty-eight (28) days' notice if the Licensee:

    6.2.1 fails to pay any sum due hereunder more than fourteen (14) days after it is due; or

    6.2.2 fails to observe any of the obligations contained in clauses 3.2 to 3.16 above,

---

[1] SI 1998/1324.

without prejudice to any other right or remedy the Owner may have in respect of such breach. In that event the Licensee will not be entitled to any refund of any part of the Licence Fee paid in respect of the period after the notice takes effect.

I AGREE to the above terms:

Signed:

        Owner

Signed:

        Licensee

A1.3

LICENCE TO USE STRUCTURE ON LICENSOR'S LAND

THIS LICENCE is made on the [ ] day of [ ] 20

BETWEEN:

(1) [*name*] of [*address*] ('the Owner'); and
(2) [*name*] (Co. reg. no. [ ]) whose registered office is at [*address*].

1. *Definitions*

In this Licence:

1.1 'the Deposit' means the sum of £[ ].
1.2 'the Hoarding' means the illuminated advertising hoarding on the [ ] flank wall of the House.
1.3 'the House' means the dwelling house that forms part of the Land.
1.4 'the Land' means the Owner's land at [*address*], title to which is registered at HM Land Registry under title no [ ].
1.5 'the Licence Fee' means the sum of £[ ] plus VAT (or any other tax of a similar nature) per [ ].
1.6 'the Licence Term' means [ ].

2. *Grant*

In consideration of the Licence Fee the Owner grants the Licensee:

2.1 The right to display posters and advertisements on the Hoarding during the Licence Term.
2.2 For the aforesaid purposes, the right:

  2.2.1 to enter the Land and place temporary scaffolding and ladders against the [ ] wall of the House;

  2.2.2 to run electric cables down the [ ] wall of the House and attach it to that wall, making good any damage caused thereby; and

2.2.3 to make and maintain an electrical connection between the Hoarding and the electricity supply for the House.

3. *The Licensee's Obligations*

The Licensee agrees with the Owner:

3.1 To pay the Deposit on entering into this Licence as security for the due performance of its obligations under it.
3.2 To pay the Licence Fee throughout the Licence Term on the [ ] day of each [ ] commencing on [*date*].
3.3 To pay all rates and other local taxes payable in respect of the Hoarding and to supply proof of such payment to the Owner on demand. If the Licensee fails to make such payment, the Owner shall be entitled to be indemnified by the Licensee on demand in respect of any payment he makes of such rates and taxes.
3.4 To pay on demand the cost of electricity consumed by the Hoarding during the last bill period together with a reasonable proportion according to user of the standing charge for the common electricity supply to the House and Hoarding.
3.5 Not to display any poster or advertisement that is or may be offensive, a nuisance or annoyance or which fails to comply with all applicable legislation, statutory instruments and regulations or which fails to comply with the British Code of Advertising Practice in force from time to time.
3.6 To remove as soon as possible any poster or advertisement that is prohibited by any lawful body with power to prohibit its display.
3.7 To maintain and repair and keep in good repair and condition and if necessary to renew or replace the Hoarding and cabling during the Licence Period. If the Licensee fails to do so the Owner may undertake such works as are required under this clause and recover his costs of doing so from the Licensee as a debt.
3.8 For the aforesaid purposes to periodically inspect the Hoarding and the cabling serving it not less often than [ ].
3.9 To comply with all requirements of statute and regulation and of the electricity supplier in respect of the state and condition of the Hoarding and cabling.
3.10 To effect and throughout the Licence Term keep in force a policy of insurance with a reputable insurance office incorporating the standard conditions and exemptions of the insurance company to cover death, personal injury and damage to the Land and personal property arising from the presence of the Hoarding and cabling and the exercise of the rights granted in the amount of not less than £[ ] in respect of any one claim.
3.11 To make available to the Owner on request a copy of the policy and its terms of cover and provide proof of payment of the premium.

3.12　To pay out the sums received from the insurance company on the occurrence of an insurable event in rebuilding, replacing, renewing or repairing the Hoarding and cabling and make good any loss and any damage to the House.

3.13　To fully indemnify and keep the Owner fully indemnified against all actions, claims, penalties, liabilities, demands and losses arising directly or indirectly out of any act or omission by the Licensee or his employees, the exercise or purported exercise of the rights and the presence of the Hoarding and cabling.

3.14　To provide the Owner with a copy of any correspondence or notice from the local planning authority and any other statutory body in respect of the Hoarding or the posters and advertisements displayed on it.

3.15　To comply at its own cost with any direction made by the local planning authority or any other statutory body with powers in respect of the Hoarding or the said posters and advertisements.

3.16　To pay on demand the reasonable costs and expenses (including professional fees) incurred by the Owner in repairing all and any damage to or defects or deterioration in the state and condition of the House caused by any breach of clause 3.7 above.

3.17　To remove the poster or advertisement on the Hoarding on the determination of this Licence and to make good any damage to the House caused by doing so to the reasonable satisfaction of the Owner.

4. *The Owner's Obligations*

The Owner agrees with the Licensee:

4.1　Not to interfere with the exercise of the rights granted hereby.

4.2　To maintain and repair and keep in proper repair and condition the [ ] flank wall of the House but this shall not require the Owner to keep it in any better condition than it is at the date hereof or to remedy any defect or condition caused by the exercise of the rights hereby granted or any breach by the Licensee of these terms.

4.3　Not to obstruct and not to permit anyone else to place or erect on the Land anything that may obstruct the Hoarding.

4.4　To do all such things as are necessary to maintain the electricity supply to the Hoarding including payment of the electricity consumed by the House and the Hoarding and any standing charges.

4.5　To permit the Licensee to connect with the electricity supply to the House for the purpose of providing an electrical supply to the Hoarding, the Licensee complying with the requirements of the electricity supplier and all relevant regulations and making good any damage to the House caused thereby.

5. *Miscellaneous*

5.1　The Owner gives no warranty that the Land is or will remain during the Licence Term lawfully or physically capable of being used for the purposes specified.

Sample Licences 257

5.2 This rights granted by this Licence may not be assigned without the Owner's prior consent (such consent not to be unreasonably withheld) nor may the Licensee permit anyone else to exercise or enjoy them.

5.3 Any notice under this Licence must be in writing and shall be sufficiently and effectually given if sent by registered post or recorded delivery to the Owner at the House and to the Licensee at its registered office.

6. *Termination*

6.1 This Licence will automatically determine at the end of the Licence Term.

6.2 This Licence may be determined by the Owner before then [immediately *or* at the end of [ ]] following service of written notice on the Licensee in the event it fails to comply with the terms of this Licence and (if capable of remedy) fails to remedy such breach within [ ] days after written demand.

6.3 This Licence will determine automatically in the event the Licensee goes into liquidation (whether compulsory or voluntary) except for the purpose of amalgamation or reconstruction or has an administration order made against it.

AS WITNESS the hands of the parties the day and year first before written

Signed:

       Owner

Signed:

       For and on behalf of the Licensee

A1.4

CONTRACTUAL LICENCE TO USE SERVICED OFFICE ACCOMMODATION

PARTICULARS

Date:

Licensor:	[ ] (Co. reg. no. [ ]) whose registered office is at [*address*].
Licensee	[ ] (Co. reg. no. [ ]) whose registered office is at [*address*].
Building:	the Licensor's building at [*address*].
Deposit:	£[ ].
Licence Period:	the period from [ ] to [ ] and thereafter from month to month until determined as set out in clause 5 below.
Licence Fee:	£[ ] per [ ].

Office:	the [office/rooms/suite of rooms] in the Building numbered [ ] and outlined in red on the annexed plan.
Office Hours:	from [ ] am to [ ] pm Monday to Friday, subject to alteration by the Licensor.
Permitted Uses:	the use of the Office for [ ].
Rights:	(i) the right to use the Office for the Permitted Uses;
	(ii) the right to use the common parts of the Building for the purpose of access to and from the Office in common with the Licensor, the other occupiers of the Building and their invitees and licensees,
	subject to the Regulations.
Regulations:	the rules and regulations regarding operation and use of the Building and Office as the Licensor may from time to time in its absolute discretion make and notify the Licensee.
Services:	the Services set out in Part II of Schedule 3.
Service Charge:	[ ]% of the cost of providing the Services determined in accordance with Part III of Schedule 3.

THIS AGREEMENT is made on the date set out in the Particulars BETWEEN:

(1) the Licensor named in the Particulars; and
(2) the Licensee named in the Particulars.

1. *Rights*

1.1 The Licensor grants the Licensee the Rights for the Licence Period on the terms set out in this Agreement.

2. *Terms*

2.1 The terms in Schedule 1 shall have effect.

3. *Licensee's Obligations*

3.1 The Licensee agrees to observe and perform the obligations set out in Schedule 2.

4. *Licensor's Obligations*

4.1 The Licensor agrees to observe and perform the obligations set out in Part I of Schedule 3.

5. *Termination*

5.1 Either party may determine this Agreement upon not less than [ ] written notice to the other party.

5.2 The Licensor may terminate this Agreement on not less than seven (7) days' notice if the Licensee:

5.2.1 fails to pay any of the sums payable hereunder more than fourteen (14) days after it is due;

5.2.2 fails to observe any of the other obligations set out in Schedule 2; or

5.2.3 enters into liquidation or administration or becomes incapable of paying its debts as they fall due,

without prejudice to any other right or remedy the Licensor may have in respect of such breach. In that event the Licensee will not be entitled to any refund of any part of the Licence Fee paid in respect of the period after the notice takes effect.

5.3 On the termination of the Licence:

5.3.1 unless the Licensor otherwise directs the Licensee may not remove any fixture it has installed but such fixtures shall remain in the Office and become part of the Licensor's property without payment of compensation;

5.3.2 if the Licensor so directs, the Licensee shall remove any such fixture and make good the walls ceilings and floors to which it was attached and the decorative surfaces; and

5.3.3 if the Licensee has not removed his chattels from the Office by the date of termination, he irrevocably authorises the Licensor (should the Licensor so choose) to remove them and, in the event he does not reclaim them within a further period of seven (7) days, to use, destroy or dispose of them as the Licensor shall in its absolute discretion think fit without any liability or compensation.

SCHEDULE 1

1. The Licensor gives no warranty that the Office may lawfully be used or is physically suitable for the Permitted Uses.
2. The Licensor may at any time and from time to time change the Office to another office comprising a single area of [not less than [ ] square metres or similar size to that set out on the plan] within the Building on giving not less than [ ] advance written notice to the Licensee, in which case the provisions of this Agreement shall apply to the Licensee's use of that office as if it were the Office.
3. The Licensor may in its absolute discretion:

    3.1 alter the Office Hours on giving not less than [ ] days' notice to the Licensee, except in cases of emergency; and

    3.2 close and keep closed the Building or any part of it for operational reasons and/or in the interests of safety and security. If the Building is closed for a consecutive period of more than

[ ] the Licensor shall reimburse a proportionate part of the instalments of Licence Fee paid during the period of closure.

4. It is agreed the Licensor retains full rights of possession of the Building and Office and that this Licence does not entitle the Licensee to exclusive possession, control or use of any part of it nor amount to a lease or tenancy nor to an agreement to grant a lease or tenancy.

5. It is agreed that the Licensor requires unrestricted access to the Office at all times in order to provide the Services.

6. Nothing in this Licence is intended to confer any benefit on any person who is not a party to it.

7. This Licence is only capable of being assigned with the Licensor's prior consent, which shall not be unreasonably withheld or granted subject to unreasonable conditions.

SCHEDULE 2

Payment

1. The Licensee shall pay to the Licensee:

    1.1 the Deposit upon entering into this Agreement as security for the due performance and observance of his obligations under it;

    1.2 the Licence Fee in advance on the [ ] day of each month, the first such payment (or a due proportion of it from the date of this agreement until the [ ] day of the next calendar month) to be made on the date hereof, without deduction or set off; and

    1.3 on demand the Service Charge without deduction or set off.

2. If VAT or any other tax of a similar nature is due upon any such sum the Licensee shall pay that as well as such sum.

Use

3. The Licensee may only use the Office for the Permitted Uses.

4. The Licensee shall at all times observe and ensure that his employees and invitees and licensees observe the Regulations.

5. The Licensee must not display any sign or notice in the Office windows or on the exterior walls of the Office [that has not been approved in advance by the Licensor].

State and Condition

6. The Licensee must keep the Office [in a clean and tidy condition, clear of rubbish and] free from obstruction.

7. The Licensee must not store anything in or block or place any obstruction in the common parts and passageways of the Building.

8. The Licensee must not alter, cut or add to the cables, pipes, wiring and other conducting media within the Office.

9. The Licensee must not cut, maim or damage the walls, floors or ceilings of the Office or alter its structure nor decorate the Office in colours

other than those approved in advance by the Licensor, using not less than one base coat and two top coats.

Nuisance, etc

10. The Licensee must not use the Office or suffer or permit its employees to use the Office in such way as to cause nuisance, annoyance, damage or disturbance, inconvenience, interference or damage to the Licensor, the other occupiers of the Building and their licensees and the owners, occupiers or users of any adjoining or neighbouring land.
11. The Licensee may not bring into the Building or cause, permit or allow any of its employees or licensees to bring anything that is or may be or become dangerous, hazardous, noxious or harmful to health or a nuisance or annoyance.
12. The Licensee must not impede in any way the Licensor and its servants or agents in relation to the operation of the Building or interfere with or obstruct the other occupiers' use of it or their respective offices.

Insurance

13. The Licensee shall effect and throughout the Licence Term keep in force a policy of insurance with a reputable insurance office incorporating the standard conditions and exemptions of the insurance company to cover all claims arising from the exercise of the Rights and the Licensee's use and occupation of the Office and the activities undertaken there in the amount of not less than £[ ] in respect of any one claim for death, bodily injury or damage to or destruction of property.
14. The Licensee shall make available to the Licensor on request a copy of the policy and its terms of cover and provide proof of payment of the premium.

Requirements

15. The Licensee shall obtain from the appropriate authorities and maintain throughout the Licence Term all necessary permits, licences and consents in relation to his occupation and use of the Office for the Permitted Uses.
16. The Licensee shall throughout the Licence Term comply with all statutes, rules and regulations as may apply from time to time in respect of its occupation and use of the Office for the Permitted Uses.
17. The Licensee shall fully indemnify and keep the Licensor fully indemnified against all actions, claims, penalties, liabilities, demands and losses arising directly or indirectly out of any act or omission by the Licensee or his employees, the exercise or purported exercise of the Rights and in respect of any non-observance of the Regulations or the terms of this Licence by the Licensee or any person whom he has permitted to exercise the Rights.

Access

18. The Licensee will at all times permit the Licensor to enter the Office for the purpose of providing the Services or inspecting its state and condition.

Assignment, etc

19. The Licensee may not assign or attempt or purport to assign the benefit of this Licence.
20. The Licensee may not permit anyone to occupy the Office or any part of it but this clause shall not prevent its use by the Licensee's employees.

Vacation

21. On the termination of this Agreement (howsoever caused) the Licensee will vacate the Office leaving it in a clean and tidy condition and free of all chattels.

SCHEDULE 3
Part I

1. The Licensor shall not interfere with the Licensee in its exercise of the Rights.
2. Subject to payment of the Service Charge, the Licensor shall provide the Services unless prevented from doing so by circumstances beyond its control.
3. Within [ ] after the termination of this Agreement (howsoever caused) the Licensor shall return the Deposit, subject to deduction of a reasonable amount to compensate it for any damages or loss caused or liability incurred by any breach by the Licensee of this Agreement.

Part II

'the Services' means [ ].

Part III

The Service Charge shall be calculated in the following manner [ ].

AS WITNESS the hands of the parties the day and year first before written

Signed:

       Licensor

Signed:

       Licensee

A1.5

LICENCE OF PART OF COMMERCIAL PREMISES INCLUDING PROVISION OF SERVICES BY LICENSEE

PARTICULARS

THIS LICENCE is made the [ ] day of [ ] 20

BETWEEN:

1. *Parties*

1.1 [*name*] of [*address*] ('the Licensor'); and
1.2 [*name*] of [*address*] ('the Licensee').

2. *Recitals*

2.1 The Licensor owns [ ] ('the premises') which is a licensed entertainment centre for events, functions and theatrical productions.
2.2 The Licensee has applied to be given a licence to provide catering services at the premises and the Licensor has agreed to grant it a licence to do so on the terms set out below.

3. *Defined terms*

3.1 'catering services' shall mean the provision of hot and cold food, meals, snacks and non-alcoholic drinks for daily catering and event catering.
3.2 'daily catering' means the operation of provision of catering services in the café/restaurant area of the premises edged red on the attached plan during the hours of operation.
3.3 'events' shall mean the events, functions and theatrical productions taking place in the function rooms and auditorium at the premises.
3.4 'event catering' means the provision of catering services for events.
3.5 the 'hours of operation' shall mean [ ] to [ ] each day between [1st April] and [31st October] and from [ ] to [ ] each day between [1st November] and [31st March], excluding [Christmas Day, Boxing Day and New Year's Day].
3.6 the 'licence fee' shall mean:

   3.6.1 £[ ] for the first two (2) years of the term, £[ ] for the third and fourth years of the term and £[ ] for the final year of the term; plus

   3.6.2 [ ]% of the gross income from event catering.

3.7 the 'licence term' shall be a fixed term of five (5) years commencing on [ ].

4. *Rights*

4.1 The Licensor grants to the Licensee:

4.1.1 the exclusive right to provide daily catering during the hours of operation to visitors to the premises and the [exclusive] right to provide event catering at the premises for the licence term;

4.1.2 the right, in common with the Licensor, to use the kitchen and food preparation area hatched [ ] and the washrooms hatched [ ] on the plan; and

4.1.3 the right to use such equipment, utensils, cutlery and crockery as the Licensor may provide from time to time during the licence term.

5. *The Licensee's Obligations*

5.1 The Licensee shall pay the licence fee in clause 3.6.1 plus VAT thereon by equal monthly instalments in advance on the first day of each month without deduction or set off.

5.2 The Licensee shall provide daily catering during the hours of operation.

5.3 The Licensee shall provide event catering to the events booked by the Licensor for which catering services are required.

5.4 The Licensee shall not interfere with the Licensor's possession of the premises during the licence term.

5.5 The Licensee will provide all necessary labour, ingredients, stock in trade and consumables and sufficient equipment, utensils, cutlery, crockery, table linen, napkins and table decorations required for the provision of the catering services.

5.6 The Licensee shall at his own cost ensure that all such equipment may be used in a safe manner and is regularly and sufficiently inspected, maintained, repaired and where necessary replaced.

5.7 The food and drink provided by the Licensee shall be good and wholesome and shall be stored, handled and prepared in compliance with all relevant food, health and hygiene standards in force from time to time.

5.8 The Licensee will ensure that all members of staff have basic food handling and hygiene qualifications.

5.9 The Licensee shall ensure that the food preparation areas are kept in a clean, tidy and hygienic condition at all times and in such condition as to satisfy all relevant environmental health standards in force from time to time.

5.10 The Licensee shall provide the catering services throughout the licence term according to the prices set out in the menu from time to time.

5.11 The Licensee shall consult with the Licensor at least once every quarter about the menu and the prices charged for food and drinks in providing the catering services.

5.12 The Licensee shall ensure that the presentation of all catering and serving staff, table settings, equipment, crockery and cutlery is at all times to such standard as the Licensor may reasonably require.

5.13 The Licensee must personally perform the catering services. He may employ such staff as he shall require to do so provided that such persons are at all times under his direct and personal supervision and control.

5.14 The Licensee shall obey such rules and regulations in relation to the use of the premises and the provision of the catering services as the Licensor shall from time to time in its absolute discretion impose.

5.15 The Licensee shall publicly promote the catering services and in doing so expend no less than £[ ] per annum.

5.16 The Licensee shall ensure that his staff show due respect and treat with courtesy the Licensor's members of staff and all visitors to the premises.

5.17 The Licensee shall indemnify and keep indemnified the Licensor against all and any claims, costs, penalties and damages as may be owed by the Licensor to any third party as a result of the breach of the terms of this Agreement or the provision of the catering services.

5.18 The Licensee shall take out public liability insurance in an insurance office of good repute in the sum of no less than £[ ] for any one claim and shall, upon request, provide a copy of such policy and proof of payment of the premium to the Licensor.

5.19 The Licensee must comply in all respects with the requirements of all statutes applicable to the premises or the exercise of the rights in clause 4 above.

6. *The Licensor's Obligations*

6.1 The Licensor shall permit the Licensee to enter and use the premises to provide catering services during the licence term on the terms set out in this Licence.

6.2 Subject to clauses 7.6 and 7.7 below the Licensor shall open and keep open the premises during the hours of operation and for the duration of any event.

6.3 The Licensor shall be responsible for the maintenance repair and upkeep of the premises and cleaning of the common parts, including the auditorium and restaurant seating area (but not the removal of the Licensee's utensils, cutlery, crockery, table linen, napkins and table decorations from the restaurant seating area, which shall be the responsibility of the Licensee).

6.4 The Licensor shall make reasonable efforts to ensure that the premises are at all times adequately lit and heated and receive a supply of water, gas and electricity and sewage and waste disposal services.

6.5 The Licensor shall not less than seven (7) days in advance inform the Licensee of an event for which the Licensee is to provide event catering and what catering is required.

6.6 The Licensor shall charge the person booking an event the cost of any event catering and shall remit payment to the Licensee, less the licence fee set out in clause 3.6.2 not more than [ ] days after receipt of payment.

6.7 The Licensor shall insure and keep the premises insured against all usual risks including any loss or damage, personal injury death or property damage caused to any visitor to the premises as a result of their state and condition and the Licensor's operations conducted in it in an insurance office of repute in the amount of not less than £[ ] in respect of any one claim.

7. *Terms*

7.1 For the avoidance of doubt the Licensor retains the full right of occupation and possession of the premises during the licence term subject only to the rights granted hereby.

7.2 The rights are not capable of assignment and are personal to the Licensee and may only be exercised by himself and his employees, customers and persons making deliveries to him.

7.3 The Licensor has an absolute discretion as to the booking or cancellation of any event and the terms of any such booking (including the provision or otherwise of event catering).

7.4 The Licensor is under no obligation to cause, encourage or require any person booking such event to order event catering.

7.5 The Licensor may use or allow others to use the areas edged [ ] and hatched [ ] and [ ] on the plan in common with the Licensee.

7.6 The Licensor may in its absolute discretion alter the hours of operation for operational reasons on giving not less than [ ] hours' advance notice save in case of emergency.

7.7 The Licensor may close and keep closed the premises or any part of it on any one or more of the days specified in clause 3.5 above in the interests of the safety and security provided that he shall give the Licensee at least twenty-four (24) hours' advance notice of such closure save in cases of emergency.

7.8 The parties hereto recognise that they have a mutual interest in the presentation of all services provided at the premises in the best possible way and in seeking to improve such services and shall from time to time as is appropriate liaise and discuss such matters.

8. *Termination*

8.1 This agreement will determine automatically at the end of the licence term.

8.2 This agreement may be terminated forthwith before then by the Licensor (without prejudice to any other right or remedy he may have against the Licensee) in the event:

8.2.1 the Licensee fails to pay the licence fee (or any part of it) more than fourteen (14) days after it is due;

8.2.2 the Licensee becomes bankrupt or enters into a composition with his creditors or individual voluntary arrangement;

8.2.3 the Licensee becomes incapable for any reason of performing his obligations under this agreement;

8.2.4 the Licensee fails to remedy any breach of the terms of this agreement within seven (7) days of being given notice to do so by the Licensor; or

8.2.5 the Licensor reasonably determines that the standard of catering provided by the Licensee has fallen below the level reasonably to be expected under the terms of this Agreement.

8.3 This Agreement may be determined by either party at any time forthwith on notice in the event the premises are destroyed or substantially damaged or become unusable for a continuous period in excess of [ ] provided that in such case the Licensor shall repay to the Licensee a proportionate part of the licence fee payable in advance for the month in which the said event shall occur unless it occurs as a result of any breach by the Licensee of the terms of this Agreement.

AS WITNESS the hands of the parties the day and year first before written

Signed:
                        Licensor

Signed:
                        Licensee

A1.6

NOVATION AGREEMENT REGARDING SHARED OCCUPATION BY LICENSEES

NOVATION AGREEMENT made the [ ] day of [ ] 20

BETWEEN:

(1) [*name*] ('the Licensor');
(2) [*name*] ('the Outgoing Licensee');
(3) [*name*] ('the Continuing Licensees'); and
(4) [*name*] ('the New Licensee').

Recitals

1. This novation agreement is supplemental to:

    1.1 a licence agreement dated [*date*] ('the Licence') between the Licensor and the Outgoing Licensee and the Continuing Licensees in relation to their occupation of part of the Licensor's premises known as [ ] ('the Premises') a copy of which is attached hereto as Schedule 1; and

    1.2 an agreement [of the same date] between the Outgoing Licensee and the Continuing Licensees in relation to their shared occupation of the Premises ('the Occupation Agreement') a copy of which is attached hereto as Schedule 2.

2. The Outgoing Licensee wishes to vacate the Premises and to be discharged from his obligations under the Licence and the Occupation Agreement.

3. The Licensor is willing to accept the New Licensee in place of the Outgoing Licensee under the Licence and the Continuing Licensees are willing to accept the New Licensee in place of the Outgoing Licensee

under the Occupation Agreement and the New Licensee is willing to accept the rights and obligations under those agreements in the place of the Outgoing Licensee.

Release

4. In consideration clause 6 below and the premises, the Licensor and Outgoing Licensee as from this date mutually release and discharge each other from all and every future right, obligation and liability under the Licence.

5. In consideration clause 7 below and the premises, the Outgoing Licensee and the Continuing Licensees as from this date mutually release and discharge each other from all and every future right, obligations and liability under the Occupation Agreement.

Licence

6. In consideration of clauses 4 and 5 and the premises the Licensor grants to the New Licensee and the Continuing Licensees the right to occupy the Premises on the same terms and conditions set out in the Licence and [for the remaining balance of the Licence term] as if the name of the New Licensee were substituted for that of the Outgoing Licensee.

Sharing Agreement

7. In consideration of clause 5 and the premises the New Licensee and the Continuing Licensees hereby enter into an occupation agreement in respect of their shared occupation of the Premises on the same terms and conditions set out in the Occupation Agreement as if the name of the New Licensee were substituted for that of the Outgoing Licensee.

Miscellaneous

8. Nothing herein is intended to release or waive any accrued right, claim cause of action, obligation or liability:

    8.1 of the Licensor and Outgoing Licensee under the Licence; and

    8.2 of the Outgoing Licensee and Continuing Licensees under the Occupation Agreement.

9. It is agreed between the Continuing Licensees that nothing herein is intended to affect their mutual rights and obligations under the Occupation Agreement and that it shall continue and remain in full force and effect except for the substitution of the New Licensee for the Outgoing Licensee.

AS WITNESS the hands of the parties the day and year first before written

Signed:

Licensor

Signed:

Licensee

Signed:

New Licensee

Signed:

Continuing Licensees

Appendix 2

NOTICES

Licensor's consent to assignment	A2.1
Notice of assignment of benefit of licence	A2.2
Notice to terminate bare licence (non-dated)	A2.3
Notice to terminate licence (terminable forthwith)	A2.4
Notice to terminate periodic licence terminable at end of period (non-dwelling)	A2.5
Notice to terminate periodic licence at end of period (dwelling)	A2.6
Notice to terminate periodic licence terminable on reasonable notice (non-dwelling) or indefinite licence	A2.7
Notice to terminate periodic licence terminable on reasonable notice (dwelling)	A2.8
Agent's notice to terminate licence requiring dated notice	A2.9
Licensee's notice to terminate indefinite or periodic licence terminable on reasonable notice (non-dwelling)	A2.10
Letter in response agreeing to accept short service	A2.11
Acknowledgement of title preventing running of limitation period	A2.12
Acknowledgement of title preventing acquisition of prescriptive rights	A2.13

A2.1

LICENSOR'S CONSENT TO ASSIGNMENT

To:

Of:

I [*name*] of [address], your licensor, hereby give consent in accordance with clause [ ] of your licence dated [*date*] ('the Licence') to your proposed assignment to [*name*] of [*address*] ('the Assignee') of the [rights of the licensee contained in the Licence].

[This consent is conditional upon:

(i)   you and the Assignee entering into the assignment by no later than [*date*];

(ii)   the Assignee giving me notice of the assignment within [ ] days of its occurrence;

(iii)   the Assignee no later than [*date*] entering into a direct covenant with me to pay the licence fee and to observe and perform the obligations of the licensee contained in the Licence whilst it remains vested in him.]

For the avoidance of doubt, this consent is not intended to amount to a novation of the Licence and you shall remain liable to perform the obligations of the licensee for the duration of the licence term notwithstanding the said assignment, without prejudice to any right or remedy I may have against the Assignee.

Signed:

Dated:

A2.2

NOTICE OF ASSIGNMENT OF BENEFIT OF LICENCE

To:

Of:

I [*name*] of [*address*] hereby give you notice that [*name*] of [*address*] assigned to me on [*date*] the benefit of the rights contained in the licence agreement made between you and him dated [*date*] and that I am and have been from the date first mentioned the person entitled to the benefit of the licensee's rights contained in the said agreement.

Signed:

Dated:

A2.3

NOTICE TO TERMINATE BARE LICENCE (NON-DATED)

To:

Of:

I [*name*] of [*address*] hereby give you notice to terminate your licence of the [rooms at [*address*]] which you [use/occupy] as my licensee and to vacate that property.

Signed:

Dated:

A2.4

NOTICE TO TERMINATE LICENCE (TERMINABLE FORTHWITH)

To:

Of:

I [*name*] of [*address*] hereby give you notice to terminate your licence of the property known as [ ] ('the Land') which you use as my licensee. You are required to quit and cease to use the Land forthwith on receipt of this notice.

Signed:

Dated:

A2.5

NOTICE TO TERMINATE PERIODIC LICENCE TERMINABLE AT END OF PERIOD (NON-DWELLING)

To:

Of:

I [*name*] of [*address*] hereby give you notice to terminate your licence to [use/occupy] the property known as [ ] ('the Land') and to [vacate/cease to use] the Land on [ ]day the [ ] day of [ ] or at the expiry of the next full [week/month/quarter/year] of your licence which will expire next after service of this notice on you, whichever is the later.

Signed:

Dated:

A2.6

NOTICE TO TERMINATE PERIODIC LICENCE AT END OF PERIOD (DWELLING)

To:

Of:

I [*name*] of [*address*] hereby give you notice to terminate your licence to occupy the premises at [*address*] ('the Land') and to quit and deliver up the Land which you occupy as licensee on [ ]day the [ ] day of [ ] or at the end of the next full period of your licence which will expire more than four (4) weeks after the service of this notice on you, whichever is the later.

Your attention is drawn to the information contained in the Schedule to this notice.

Signed:

Dated:

SCHEDULE
Prescribed Information

1. If the tenant or licensee does not leave the dwelling, the landlord or licensor must get an order for possession from the court before the tenant or licensee can lawfully be evicted. The landlord or licensor cannot apply for such an order before the notice to quit or notice to determine has run out.
2. A tenant or licensee who does not know if he has any right to remain in possession after a notice to quit or a notice to determine runs out can obtain advice from a solicitor. Help with all or part of the cost of legal advice and assistance may be available under the Legal Aid Scheme. He should also be able to obtain information from a Citizens' Advice Bureau, a Housing Aid Centre or a rent officer.

A2.7

NOTICE TO TERMINATE PERIODIC LICENCE TERMINABLE ON REASONABLE NOTICE (NON-DWELLING) OR INDEFINITE LICENCE

To:

Of:

I [name] of [address] hereby give you notice to terminate your licence to [use/occupy] the property known as [ ] ('the Land'). [I require you to [vacate/cease to use] the Land [on [ ]day the [ ] day of [ ] or] at the expiry of a reasonable period of time after service of this notice on you whichever is the later.]

Signed:

Dated:

A2.8

NOTICE TO TERMINATE PERIODIC LICENCE TERMINABLE ON REASONABLE NOTICE (DWELLING)

To:

Of:

I [*name*] of [*address*] hereby give you notice to terminate your licence to occupy the property known as [*address*] ('the Land'). I require you to vacate the Land [on [ ]day the [ ] day of [ ] or] at the expiration of a reasonable period of time after service of this notice on you, being not less than four (4) weeks after service whichever is the later.

Your attention is drawn to the information contained in the Schedule to this notice.

Signed:

Dated:

SCHEDULE
Prescribed Information

1. If the tenant or licensee does not leave the dwelling, the landlord or licensor must get an order for possession from the court before the tenant or licensee can lawfully be evicted. The landlord or licensor cannot apply for such an order before the notice to quit or notice to determine has run out.
2. A tenant or licensee who does not know if he has any right to remain in possession after a notice to quit or a notice to determine runs out can obtain advice from a solicitor. Help with all or part of the cost of legal advice and assistance may be available under the Legal Aid Scheme. He should also be able to obtain information from a Citizens' Advice Bureau, a Housing Aid Centre or a rent officer.

A2.9

AGENT'S NOTICE TO TERMINATE LICENCE REQUIRING DATED NOTICE

To:

Of:

I [*name*] of [*address*] on behalf of [*name*] of [*address*], your licensor, hereby give you notice to terminate your licence to [use/occupy] the property known as [ ] ('the Land'). I require you to [vacate/cease to use] the Land on [ ]day the [ ] day of [ ], which is a reasonable period of time following service of this notice on you.

Signed:

On behalf of:

Dated:

A2.10

LICENSEE'S NOTICE TO TERMINATE INDEFINITE OR PERIODIC LICENCE TERMINABLE ON REASONABLE NOTICE (NON-DWELLING)

To:

Of:

I [name] of [address], your licensee, hereby give you notice to terminate my licence to [use/occupy] the land at [ ] ('the Land') dated [date] and that I shall [cease to use/quit and deliver up possession of] the Land on the Land [on [ ]day the [ ] day of [ ] or] at the expiration of a reasonable period of time after service of this notice on you [whichever is the later].

Signed:

Dated:

A2.11

LETTER IN RESPONSE AGREEING TO ACCEPT SHORT SERVICE

To:

Of:

I [name] of [address] hereby acknowledge receipt of your notice to terminate my licence to [use/occupy] the property known as [ ] ('the Land') on [date].

I hereby agree to accept such notice as valid, notwithstanding any defect in it and that it may not be in accordance with the licence terms and I agree to [vacate/cease to use] the Land on that date.

Signed:

Dated:

A2.12

ACKNOWLEDGEMENT OF TITLE PREVENTING RUNNING OF LIMITATION PERIOD

To:

Of:

I [name] of [address] hereby acknowledge that I am in possession of [ ], of which you are the [owner/tenant/licensee] with your consent and as your licensee and I acknowledge your title to the land.

I hereby acknowledge that this licence will continue until it is expressly withdrawn or terminated.

Signed:

Dated:

A2.13

ACKNOWLEDGEMENT OF TITLE PREVENTING ACQUISITION OF PRESCRIPTIVE RIGHTS

To:

Of:

I [*name*] as owner of [ ] hereby acknowledge that I have not and do not claim any [right of way] across the land known as [ ], of which you are the [owner/tenant/licensee] and that such use as I and my predecessors have had of that land has been with your consent and the consent of your predecessors in title.

I further acknowledge that such use as I may make of your land in future is with your consent and as your licensee. I hereby acknowledge that this licence will continue until it is expressly withdrawn or terminated.

Signed:

Dated:

Appendix 3

STATEMENTS OF CASE

Claim Form – injunction/possession	A3.1
Particulars of Claim – licence fee arrears	A3.2
Particulars of Claim for injunction/damages to restrain trespass after termination of contractual licence	A3.3
Particulars of Claim for possession (adapting Form N.121)	A3.4
Defence – licence not expired	A3.5
Defence – estoppel	A3.6

A3.1

CLAIM FORM – INJUNCTION/POSSESSION[1]

The Claimant's claim is for:

(1) A Declaration that the Defendant's licence to use serviced office accommodation within the Claimant's building located at [*address*] [automatically determined by effluxion of time on [*date*] *or* was validly terminated by the Claimant on [*date*]];

(2) Possession of the said premises;

or

An injunction to restrain the Defendant from entering or remaining or being on or occupying the said premises or using it without the Claimant's prior permission;

(3) Damages for trespass [expected to exceed £5,000 but not £15,000];[2] and

(4) Interest pursuant to section 69 of the County Courts Act 1984 on any sum found to be due at such rate and for such period as this Honourable Court shall think fit.

---

[1] Form N.5 should be used.
[2] Civil Procedure Rules 1998, SI 1998/3132, r 16.3(2).

A3.2

PARTICULARS OF CLAIM – LICENCE FEE ARREARS

1. The Claimant is and has been since [*date*] the [registered owner/lessee/licensee] of land and premises known as and located at [*address*] title to which is registered at HM Land Registry under title number [ ] ('the Land').
2. By an oral agreement made on or about [*date*] the Claimant granted the Defendant the right to use the Land as licensee for a period of [ ] [days/weeks/months] starting on [*date*] for the purposes of [ ] ('the Licence').

    or

    By an agreement in writing made on [*date*] between the Claimant and the Defendant ('the Licence') the Claimant granted the Defendant a licence to use the Land for a period of [ ] [days/weeks/months] from [*date*]. A copy of the Licence is exhibited hereto marked 'POC1'.
3. It was a term of the Licence that the Defendant pay the Claimant a licence fee of £[ ] per [day/week/month] exclusive of VAT from [*date*] payable in [advance/arrear] on the [ ] day of each [week/month].
4. In breach of the said term the Defendant has failed to pay the Claimant the licence fees due under the Licence and there is now due and owing to the Claimant the sum of £[ ], plus VAT.
5. A schedule setting out the sums due under the Licence, the amounts paid by the Defendant and the sums outstanding is exhibited hereto marked 'POC2'.
6. The Claimant claims interest on the aforesaid sums due pursuant to section 69 of the County Courts Act 1984 at the rate of 8%, alternatively at such rate and for such period as this Honourable Court shall think fit. A calculation of the interest due and the daily rate is set out in the said schedule.

AND the Claimant claims:

(1) The aforesaid sum of £[ ]; and
(2) The aforesaid interest.

A3.3

PARTICULARS OF CLAIM FOR INJUNCTION/DAMAGES TO RESTRAIN TRESPASS AFTER TERMINATION OF CONTRACTUAL LICENCE

1. The Claimant is and has been since [*date*] the [registered owner/lessee/licensee] of land and premises known as [ ] and located at [*address*] title to which is registered at HM Land Registry under title number [ ] ('the Land'). The Land does [not] consist of or include residential premises.

2. By an oral agreement made on or about [*date*] the Claimant granted the Defendant the right to [cross/park on/station an ice-cream van on the Land and trade from it] as licensee ('the Licence').

or

By an agreement in writing made on [date] between the Claimant and the Defendant ('the Licence') the Claimant granted the Defendant a licence to use the Land for [ ] purposes. A copy of the Licence is exhibited hereto marked 'POC1'.

3. The Licence was granted for a fixed period of [ ].

or

The Licence was granted until [date].

or

It was an express term of the Licence that it should be terminable by either party on [one] [week's] written notice to the other.

or

The Licence was granted for an indefinite period of time. In the premises it was an implied term that it may be determined by either party on reasonable notice. The Claimant avers [one] [week/month] constitutes such reasonable notice.

4. The Licence automatically expired by effluxion of time on [*date*].

or

By letter to the Defendant dated [date] the Claimant gave notice to terminate the Licence on [*date*]. A copy of the said letter is attached hereto marked 'POC2'.

or

On [*date*] the Claimant orally gave the Defendant notice to terminate the Licence. Such notice took effect a reasonable time thereafter, [namely on [ ] *or* which time expired before the issue of these proceedings].

or

By letter dated [*date*] the Defendant gave the Claimant notice to terminate the Licence on [*date*]. Notwithstanding any deficiency in that letter (which is not admitted) the Claimant responded on [*date*] accepting the Defendant's said notice as good and sufficient to determine the Licence on that date.

5. Notwithstanding the termination of the Licence on [*date*] the Licensee has wrongfully continued to use the Land thereafter without the Claimant's consent. Such use amounts to a trespass, which continues.

6. By reason of the matters aforesaid the Claimant has been deprived of the use of the Land or the opportunity to charge the Defendant a

reasonable fee therefor and/or his occupation of it has been interfered with or the Defendant has been benefited by reason of his said wrongful use. A reasonable sum for the Defendant's use of the Land since [*date*] is £[ ] per [ ] [*or if the Claimant has suffered actual loss, eg loss of other licence income, set out as particulars of special damage*].

7. The Claimant is entitled to and clams interest pursuant to section 69 of the County Courts Act 1984 at such rate and for such period as this Honourable Court shall think fit.

AND the Claimant claims:

(1) An Order that the Defendant be restrained whether by himself or by instructing or encouraging any other person from entering the Land, being on it or bringing anything onto it or using it without the Claimant's prior permission;

or

An Order that the Defendant do forthwith or within such time as this Honourable Court shall think fit quit and cease using the Land and do cause any person authorised by him to use to Land to quit and cease using it and do remove or cause to be removed all and any of his and their possessions therefrom;

(2) Damages, to be assessed; and
(3) The aforesaid interest to be assessed.

A3.4

PARTICULARS OF CLAIM FOR POSSESSION (ADAPTING FORM N.121)

1. The Claimant has a right to possession of [ ] ('the Land') which is occupied by the Defendant, who has remained on the Land without the Claimant's consent or licence.
2. The Defendant has never been a tenant or subtenant of the Land.
3. The land mentioned in paragraph 1 does [not] include residential property.
4. The Claimant's interest in the Land (or the basis of the Claimant's right to possession) namely the circumstances in which it was and is occupied without his licence or consent is as follows:
4.1 The Claimant is and has been since [*date*] the registered owner of the Land, title to which is registered at HM Land Registry under title number [ ].
4.2 By an agreement in writing made on [*date*] between the Claimant and the Defendant the Claimant granted the Defendant a licence to occupy the Land for the storage of [ ] for a period of [ ]. A copy of the Licence is exhibited hereto marked 'POC1'.
4.3 The following were express terms of the Licence namely that the Defendant should:

4.3.1 effect and throughout the licence term keep in force a policy of insurance with a reputable insurance office incorporating the standard conditions and exemptions of the insurance company to cover all claims arising from the exercise of the rights conferred by the Licence and the Defendant's occupation of the Land in the amount of £[ ] in respect of any one claim for bodily injury or damage to property;

4.3.2 make available to the Claimant or its agent upon request a copy of the policy and its terms of cover and provide proof of payment of the premium;

4.3.3 vacate the Land on the determination of the Licence.

4.4 It was a further term that in the event the Defendant was in breach of the Licence terms, the Claimant may terminate it by notice expiring seven (7) days after service.

4.5 On [date] the Claimant requested that the Defendant produce a copy of the policy of insurance effected by the Defendant pursuant to the Licence and provide proof of payment of the premium.

4.6 In breach of the Licence the Defendant failed within a reasonable time or at all to produce a copy of the said policy or proof of payment of the premium. In further breach it is averred the Defendant in fact allowed the insurance policy in force for the Land to lapse on or about [date].

4.7 On [date] the Claimant served on the Defendant notice to terminate the Licence, as it was entitled to. A copy of that notice is exhibited hereto marked 'POC2'.

4.8 Such notice took effect and the Licence terminated on [date].

4.9 Notwithstanding that, the Defendant has failed to quit and deliver up possession or occupation of the Land to the Claimant and has wrongfully continued and continues to occupy it without the Claimant's consent. Such occupation amounts to a trespass.

5. The circumstances in which the Land has been occupied are as follows:

5.1 The Defendant has occupied the Land since the commencement of the Licence initially as licensee but as trespasser following the expiration of the notice referred to in paragraph 4.7 above on the date referred to in paragraph 4.8 above.

5.2 Such occupation continues. Paragraph 4.9 above is repeated.

6. By reason of the matters aforesaid the Claimant has been deprived of the use and occupation of the Land. A reasonable charge for the use and occupation of the Land by the Defendant since [date] is £[ ] per [ ], totalling £[ ] to date and continuing hereafter at the said rate until possession is delivered up [or if the Claimant has suffered actual loss, eg loss of other licence income, set out as particulars of special damage].

7. The following persons are to the Claimant's knowledge in possession of the land: the Defendant [and [name]].

8. The Claimant claims interest on all sums due at such rate and for such period as this Honourable Court shall think fit pursuant to section 69 County Courts Act 1984.

AND the Claimant claims:

(1) Possession of the Land;
(2) Damages in respect of the Defendant's said trespass from [*date*] until possession be delivered up at the rate of £[ ] per [ ] or such other rate and/or for such other period as this Honourable Court shall think fit;
(3) The aforesaid interest, to be assessed; and
(4) Costs.

A3.5

DEFENCE – LICENCE NOT EXPIRED

1. Paragraph 1 of the Particulars of Claim is admitted.
2. By an [oral/written] agreement made on or about [*date*] the Claimant granted the Defendant the right to place an advertising hoarding on the western flank wall of the Claimant's house known as and located at [*address*] ('the Licence') at a [weekly/monthly/annual] licence fee of £[ ]. [A copy of the Licence is exhibited hereto marked 'Def 1'.]
3. The Licence was granted for a fixed period of [ ].

or

The Licence was granted until [*date*].

or

It was an express term of the Licence that it should be terminable by either party on [one] [month's] written notice to the other.

or

The Licence was for an indefinite period and accordingly is impliedly terminable on reasonable notice.

or

The Licence is on its true construction a [weekly/monthly/annual] periodic licence. In the premises it was an implied term of the Licence that it may be determined by either party on giving the other at least one full period of notice expiring at the end of that period.

or

The Licence impliedly requires the party terminating it to give notice which states a date, a reasonable period of time after service, on which it takes effect.

4. The Defendant has paid the licence fee due under the Licence, the last such payment being made on [*date*] in respect of the period until [*date*]. The Defendant has subsequently tendered the licence fee due for the period thereafter, but the Claimant has wrongly refused to accept it.
5. On or about [*date*] the Claimant purported to terminate the Licence by a notice to served on the Defendant on [*date*]. A copy of that letter is exhibited hereto marked 'Def [2]'.

6. It is denied that notice was effective to terminate the Licence in that

   the Licence makes no provision for its termination at any time during the fixed term.

   or

   it fails to give the Defendant one month's notice, as expressly required by the Licence terms, but is expressed to take effect forthwith.

   or

   it does not terminate on the last (or first) day of a period of the licence and/or did not give the Defendant at least one full period's notice following service.

   or

   the date on which it purports to take effect, namely [ ] is unreasonably short and does not give the Defendant reasonable notice to vacate the land. It is averred a reasonable period of notice is [ ].

   or

   the notice failed to state a date on which it takes effect.

   or

   the date on which the notice purports to take effect, namely [ ], was not a reasonable period of time after service of the notice, which it is averred was at least [ ].

7. Accordingly it is denied that the Defendant is a trespasser and that the Claimant is entitled to the relief sought.
8. It is admitted the Defendant has continued and continues to use the land. It is averred he was (and is) entitled to do so as licensee by reason of the aforesaid.

A3.6

DEFENCE – ESTOPPEL

1. The Defendant adopts the defined terms set out in the Particulars of Claim. As to paragraph 1 it is admitted the Claimant is the owner of the Land.
2. As to paragraph 2 of the Particulars of Claim, it is admitted and averred that the parties entered into the licence agreement dated [*date*] ('the Licence') whereby the Claimant granted the Defendant the right to extract chalk from the Land for a period of ten (10) years. It is admitted the document exhibited to the Particulars of Claim is a true copy of the Licence.
3. It is admitted the Licence contained the break clause set out in paragraph 3 of the Particulars of Claim.

4. The Defendant admits receipt of the notice referred to in paragraph 4 of the Particulars of Claim. It is denied that such notice was effective to terminate the Licence and that the Claimant is entitled to possession by reason of the matters set out below.

5. At all material times the Defendant has been in the business of mining and selling chalk.

6. On or about [*date*], after the grant of the Licence, the Defendant approached the Claimant and sought assurance that he would continue to enjoy the rights granted for the balance of the original Licence term. At the time the Defendant had identified other land which was for sale and contained substantial chalk deposits and to which he could relocate his said business. The Defendant informed the Claimant of those facts.

7. The Claimant indicated to the Defendant that as they were on good terms and the Claimant had no use for the Land in the foreseeable future he would not seek to exercise the break clause or recover possession of the Land from the Defendant during the Licence term.

8. The said agreement amounted to an implied variation of the licence agreement so as to remove the clause referred to in paragraph 3 above or waiver of the Claimant's right to exercise it, for which the Defendant gave consideration by agreeing also not to exercise it.

9. Alternatively the Claimant's said statement amounted to an express oral representation that he would not exercise the said break clause.

10. The statement was made with the intention and/or had the effect (which the Claimant knew or ought to have known) of inducing the Defendant to believe (and the Defendant did believe) that he would be able to enjoy the right to extract chalk from the Land for the remainder of the Licence term.

11. The Defendant relied on that representation and acted on that belief by desisting from exercising the break clause and purchasing the alternative land (which has since been sold to a third party), which he otherwise would have done. The Defendant further relied on it by undertaking substantial work at his own cost improving the access to (and drainage of) the Land, which he would not have done but for the said representation and belief nor was he required to do under the Licence terms. A schedule setting out the works and cost is exhibited hereto. The Claimant was or ought to have been aware of the Defendant's said acts and that they were done in the said belief.

12. By reason of the matters aforesaid it would be unconscionable for the Claimant to exercise the break clause or to rely on his said notice and seek possession of the land and he is estopped from doing so.

13. In the premises it is denied that the Licence has been terminated alternatively by reason of the aforesaid there has arisen an equity in the Defendant's favour by which he is entitled to continue to use the Land.

14. Accordingly it is denied that the Defendant is a trespasser and that the Claimant is entitled to possession of the Land.

INDEX

References are to paragraph numbers.

Access	7.11
Acknowledgment of title preventing	
acquisition of prescriptive rights	A2.13
Acknowledgment of title preventing	
running of limitation period	A2.12
Adverse rights	5.1
acquisition	5.1
consent, nature of	5.3
limited duration	5.6–5.8
limited scope	5.9–5.11
permission to limited persons	5.12
prescription	5.1, 5.2
quality of consent necessary to prevent acquisition	5.4
user in excess of licence	5.5
Advertising hoardings	6.12
Agent's notice to terminate licence	
requiring dated notice	A2.9
Agricultural licences	6.16
Agricultural Holdings Act 1986	6.20
conversion, subject to	6.18
exceptions	6.19
Agricultural workers	6.49
Assignment	10.2
bare licences	10.2, 10.3
benefits assignable, whether	10.5
contractual licences	10.4
express prohibitions	10.6, 10.7
implied prohibitions	10.12
limitations on	10.6, 10.7
manner of	10.15–10.17
prohibited, effect	10.18–10.20
qualified prohibitions	10.8
valid, effect	10.21, 10.22
Bailment	3.21, 3.22
Bare licences	2.11
creation	4.4
terms	8.1
terms, granted on	2.12
Benefit of licence	10.1
assignment	10.2
bare licences	10.36
contractual licences	10.39
estoppel licences	10.30
assignment of equity	10.31, 10.32
inchoate equity	10.31
independent equity of stranger	10.33
post judgment	10.34
licences coupled with interest	10.28, 10.29

Benefit of licence—*continued*	
mutual benefit and burden	
principle	10.25–10.27, 10.45
Bruton tenancies	10.48, 10.49
estoppel licences	10.47
licences coupled with interest	10.46
sub-licences	10.35
sub-licences created in breach of term	10.44
sub-licences created in compliance with licence	10.42, 10.43
sub-licences, right to create	10.39–10.41
Bruton tenancies	10.48, 10.49
obligation to quit	13.5
Building licences	6.15
Burden of licence	9.1
bare licences	9.7
contractual licences	9.8
constructive trust	9.12
current position	9.9, 9.10
exceptions to general rule	9.11
licence as proprietary interest	9.8
new licences	9.18, 9.19
statutory security of tenure	9.20
estoppel licenses	9.29
effect after judgment	9.33
inchoate equity – registered land	9.32
inchoate equity – unregistered land	9.29–9.31
licences converted by Law of Property Act 1925	9.34–9.36
licences coupled with interest	9.24, 9.25
licences together with other interests	9.38
licensee's interest	9.39, 9.40
licensor's interest	9.41, 9.42
licensor's successors in title	9.2
matrimonial home rights	9.37
mutual benefit and burden principle	9.26
need to register – registered land	9.4, 9.5
need to register – unregistered land	9.6
persons deriving title through licensor	9.48
persons with no right to use land	9.51
persons with superior interest to licensor	9.43

Burden of licence—*continued*	
tort	
successor	9.21, 9.22
successor's purchasers	9.23
Business licences	6.2
advertising hoardings	6.12
building licences	6.15
concession stands	6.11
distinguishing leases and licences	6.3, 6.4
front of house rights	6.13
holiday accommodation	6.23
market stalls	6.11
mineral rights	6.14
mobile structures	6.24, 6.25
nature of right	6.5–6.7
occupation in anticipation of performing duties	6.35
partnership	6.8, 6.9
post-employment occupation	6.36
service occupiers	6.27, 6.28
effect	6.37
test for	6.29, 6.34
shared or serviced office accommodation	6.10
shops	6.11
Caravan sites	6.60
Claim form – injunction/possession	A3.1
Compulsory acquisition	
disturbance payments	11.52
home loss payments	11.53
statutory compensation	11.51
Concession stands	6.11
Condition or use of premises	11.2
Constructive trust	9.12
Contractual licence	
agricultural workers	8.56
assured occupancies under Housing Act 1988	8.57
mobile homes occupiers	8.59
Rent (Agriculture) Act 1976	8.56
assignment	10.4
conduct, arising by	4.28
consideration	2.19, 2.20
contractual licence	2.13
contractual licence to share house, sample	A1.2
contractual licence to use served office accommodation, sample	A1.4
creation	4.24–4.26
exclusivity	8.15, 8.16
family arrangements	2.15
implied	4.27
imputation of contractual intent	2.16–2.18
licence fee, payment of	8.45
licensee's obligations	8.45
maintenance	8.41, 8.42
repair	8.41
security	8.43, 8.44
licensor's obligations	8.25
fitness for purpose	8.36

Contractual licence—*continued*	
licensor's obligations—*continued*	
non-derogation	8.33–8.35
quiet enjoyment	8.29
title	8.25
responsibility for condition of premises	8.47–8.49
right to terminate	8.18
scope	8.13, 8.14
security of tenure	8.54
Housing Act 1985	8.54
restricted contracts under Rent Act 1977	8.55
statutory control of terms	8.50
Contract Terms Act 1977	8.50
Supply of Goods and Services Act 1982	8.53
Unfair Terms in Consumer Contract Regulations 1999	8.50
termination	8.18
termination for breach	8.23
terms	8.4
ascertaining	8.5
construction	8.7, 8.8
express	8.9
implied	8.10–8.12
incorporation	8.6
Co-owners	4.3
Council tax	11.39, 11.40
Custom	5.38
Customary rights	3.31
Dangerous things, escape of	11.27–11.29
Defective Premises Act 1972	11.21
licensor's obligation to repair/maintain	11.22–11.24
licensor's right to repair/maintain	11.25
works in connection with provision of dwelling	11.21
Defence	
estoppel	A3.6
licence not expired	A3.5
Easements	3.23
Environmental Protection Act 1990	11.58–11.60
Estoppel licences	2.24, 4.31
basic equitable right	8.61, 8.62
commercial sphere	4.35
creation	4.32
detriment, nature of	4.38
domestic sphere	4.36
expectation	4.33
reliance, nature of	4.37
relief	8.63
relief granted	4.40
representation	4.34
terms	8.60
unconscionability	4.39
Exclusive possession	3.5
joint possession	3.8
nature of right	3.6

Index

Exclusive possession—*continued*
   sharing agreements 3.8
   terms indicating 3.13
   terms negativing 3.13
Express licence
   creation 4.5

Family arrangements
   contractual intent, and 2.15–2.18
Front-of-house rights 6.13

Highways 3.33, 3.34
Holiday accommodation 6.23

Implied licence 4.15
   consent 4.15, 4.16
     circumstances justifying inference 4.20
     encouragement as overt conduct 4.19
     overt conduct justifying 4.17, 4.18
Informal gratuitous licence
   sample A1.1

Letter in response agreeing to accept short service A2.11
Licence of part of commercial premises including provision of services by licensee
   sample A1.5
Licence terms 8.1
Licence to use facility on licensor's land
   sample A1.3
Licences
   bailment, and 3.21, 3.22
   bare 2.11
   certainty 3.4
     definition 3.3
     exclusive possession 3.5
     joint possession 3.8
     nature of 3.6, 3.7
     occupation pending negotiations 3.17
     sharing agreements 3.8
   terms
     parties' expressed intentions 3.16
     shams 3.15
   concept of 2.2
   contractual 2.13
   customary rights, and 3.31
   distinguishing from other private rights/interests 2.5, 2.6, 3.1
   easements, and 3.23
   estoppel 2.24
   flexibility 1.13
   future developments 1.11
   highways, and 3.33, 3.34
   history 1.3
   importance of 1.14
   leases, and 3.2
   matrimonial homes rights, and 3.37, 3.38

Licences—*continued*
   nature of 2.1
   non-proprietary lease, and 1.9
   profits, and 3.23
   public rights distinguished 2.7
   range of 1.4
   recent developments 1.8
   residential sphere 1.5
   town greens 3.32
   traditional analysis 1.2
   traditional function 1.7
   trusts, and 3.27
   types 2.8
   variety of function 1.6
   village greens 3.32
   wayleaves, and 3.35, 3.36
Licences coupled with an interest 2.21–2.23, 4.29, 4.30
   terms 8.64
Licensee's notice to terminate (non-dwelling) A2.10
Licensor
   status of 4.2
Licensor as squatter 5.1
   continued use 5.17
   limitation in favour of third parties 5.23
Licensor's consent to assignment A2.1
Limitation 5.15
   continued use after licence expires 5.17
   grant after expiry of period 5.18
   licensee against licensor 5.16
   owner, against 5.19
   possession during subsistence of licence 5.16
   renewal after expiry of period 5.18
   third parties, and 5.23, 5.24
Lodgers 6.21, 6.22

Market stalls 6.11
Matrimonial home rights 3.37, 3.38, 6.65
   bankruptcy, and 6.70
   termination 6.67
Mineral rights 6.14
Mobile Homes Act licensees 6.56
Mobile structures 6.24, 6.25

Negligence 11.26
Non-contractual rights and obligations 11.1
Non-domestic rates 11.38
Notice of assignment of benefit of licence A2.2
Notice to terminate bare licence (non-dated) A2.3
Notice to terminate licence (terminable forthwith) A2.4
Notice to terminate periodic licence on anniversary of licence (dwelling) A2.6
Notice to terminate periodic licence terminable on anniversary of licence (non-dwelling) A2.5

Notice to terminate periodic licence terminable on reasonable notice (dwelling)	A2.8
Notice to terminate periodic licence terminable on reasonable notice (non-dwelling)	A2.7
Novation	10.23, 10.24
Novation agreement regarding shared occupation by licensees	
sample	A1.6
Nuisance	9.54, 9.55
Occupation licences	6.1
Occupiers' Liability Act 1957	11.3
exclusion or restriction of duty	11.17
nature of duty	11.5
one/both parties in occupation	11.11–11.13
person who owes duty	11.9, 11.10
persons to whom duty owed	11.14
scope of duty	11.3, 11.4
Occupiers' Liability Act 1984	11.18–11.20
Ouster principle	
user licences, and	7.6
Parking rights	7.13
Particulars of claim	
injunction to restrain trespass after termination of contractual licence	A3.3
licence fee arrears	A3.2
Partnership	6.8, 6.9
Planning control	11.54
Possession	2.29
actual	2.33
factual	2.32
occupation, and	2.35
possession, for	A3.4
Post termination	13.1
damages for continued use of land after expiry of licence	13.23
enforcing licensee's obligations	
self-help	13.15–13.17
injunction	13.18
licensee's obligations	13.4
obligation to quit	13.4
Bruton tenants	13.5
sub-licences	13.5
possession	13.19
procedure	13.20–13.22
Post-employment occupation	6.36
Prescription	5.25
consent, form of	5.28
consent, meaning	5.26, 5.27
licensors, and	5.29
third parties, by	5.30
Private nuisance	11.30
adoption	11.34
authorisation	11.32, 11.33
causation	11.30, 11.31
continuation	11.35–11.37
Profits	3.23

Proprietary estoppel	4.31
detriment, nature of	4.38
expectation	4.33–4.36
nature of reliance	4.37
relief granted	4.40
unconscionability	4.39
Public authority accommodation	6.39
agricultural workers	6.49
Housing Act 1988	6.53–6.55
occupation under Rent (Agriculture) Act 1976	6.50–6.52
Housing Act 1985	6.39
licences treated as introductory tenancies	6.45, 6.46
licences treated as secure tenancies	6.39
restricted contracts	6.47, 6.48
Public rights of way	5.31
Relevance of	2.29–2.31
Remedy	13.19
removal of chattels	13.6
Residential licences	6.21
Residential licensees with security of tenure	6.38
Right to	2.36, 2.37
things incorporated into land	
chattels	13.13
fixtures	13.13, 13.14
land	13.13, 13.14
obligation to remove/reinstate	13.10, 13.11
right to remove	13.12
Rights of way	5.31
Rylands v Fletcher	11.27–11.29
Service occupiers	6.27, 6.28
test for	6.29, 6.34
Shops	6.11
Stamp Duty Land Tax	11.48–11.50
Storage rights	7.13
Tax implications	11.41
Termination of licences	12.1
bare licences	12.2
abandonment	12.32
agreement	12.32
automatic	12.3, 12.4, 12.13, 12.14
breach	12.28–12.30
contents of notice	12.25, 12.26
contractual licences	12.11
disclaimer	12.35–12.37
effluxion of time	12.2, 12.12
exercise of option	12.15
express term as to notice	12.17
form of notice	12.25, 12.26
frustration	12.33, 12.34
implied term as to notice	12.18
licences not specifically performable	12.45, 12.46
non-compliant notices	12.19
non-contractual limitations	12.38, 12.39

Termination of licences—*continued*
bare licences—*continued*
notice	12.16
notice by licensee	12.10
notice by licensor	12.6–12.8
notice by occupier	12.9
notice/demand	12.5
reasonable notice	12.23, 12.24
repudiation	12.31
service of notice on recipient	12.27
specifically performable licences	12.42–12.44
wrongful, purported	12.40
estoppel licences	12.48
inchoate equity	12.48, 12.49
relief	12.50
grace period	12.51
application	12.51, 12.52
length	12.53, 12.54
purpose	12.53, 12.54
licences coupled with interest	12.47

Town greens 3.32, 5.35–5.37

Trespass
claim by licensee	9.53
claim by licensor	9.52

Trusts 3.27

Unilateral licence
consent, manifestation of	4.7, 4.8
creation	4.6
express disclaimer	4.12
implied disclaimer	4.13
part-unauthorised user	4.14
unauthorised user	4.14
user, position of	4.9–4.11

User licences 7.1
access	7.11
easements, and	7.3–7.5
limited activities	7.12
occupation, and	7.2
ouster principle, and	7.6
placing structures on land	7.14
profits, and	7.3–7.5
removal of things from land	7.16–7.18
rights to place/erect something on land	7.13

Value added tax 11.42

Village greens 3.32, 5.35–5.37

Wayleaves 3.35, 3.36